On The Road Again

By: Adam DeRose

No part of this book may be reproduced without prior permission
from the author

To My Family,
The one I was born into and the one I married into.
And to fans of hockey and the Buffalo Sabres!

Contents

Prologue..7
August 2009..7
October 2009...8
November 2009..13
December 2009..19
January 2010..31
February 2010..31
March 2010..43
April 2010..54
2010 Playoffs...68
2010 Offseason..68
September 2010..69
October 2010..70
November 2010..86
December 2010..97
January 2011..108
February 2011..122
March 2011..123
April 2011..129
2011 Playoffs...137
2011 Offseason..139
October 2011..141
November 2011..159
December 2011..169
January 2012..196
February 2012..205
March 2012..243
April 2012..252
2012 Offseason..253
September 2012..254
October 2012..255
November 2012..271
December 2012..282
January 2013..302
February 2013..313
March 2013..315
April 2013..325

2013 Playoffs……………………………………………………...344
2013 Offseason……………………………………………………344
October 2013……………………………………………………....346
November 2013…………………………………………………….346
December 2013…………………………………………….…..….364
January 2014……………………………………………………….376
February 2014……………………………………………………...410
March 2014………………………………………………………....416
April 2014……………………………………………………….....454
Epilogue…………………………………………………………….455

"On the road again
Goin' places that I've never been
Seein' things that I may never see again,
And I can't wait to get on the road again.
On the road again
Like a band of gypsies we go down the highway
We're the best of friends
Insisting that the world keep turning our way
And our way
Is on the road again
Just can't wait to get on the road again"
--Willie Nelson

Prologue

I remember it vividly. I was standing on the edge of my toilet. I was trying to hang a clock, but the porcelain was wet. I slipped and hit my head on the edge of the sink. When I came to, I had a revelation! A vision! A picture in my head…that's when I experienced this prophetic idea of watching my Buffalo Sabres play in all 30 NHL cities! That's also how I got this huge bruise on my head.

August 2009

And it began…

I remembered my wife, Shannon, asking me if I wanted to go with her in October to Naples, Florida for an orthopedic seminar.

My initial response was, "Do I want to go to Nipples? Is this some kind of rhetorical question?"

"No, Naples, Florida," Shannon said correcting me.

"Nipples, Florida?" I persisted.

"No! Naples…God! You are helpless!!!" exclaimed an exasperated Shannon.

I said, "Huh, Naples? Are you sure?"

She said, "POSITIVE."

I thought Naples was only in Italy and New York State. I didn't know of any third Naples!

I said, "Yea, probably, but let me check my calendar." So, like any logical guy in Western New York would do, I went online to check the Buffalo Sabres season schedule to see if they would be playing in Florida while we'd be there. After I got the schedule uploaded, I asked Shannon for the exact dates of her conference. There must have been some kind of planetary alignment, because my Sabres were playing in Florida during the exact times we were going to be down there! Hell yeah; I'm going on this trip!

It turned out the Sabres were going to play on a Wednesday night, the same night we were scheduled to arrive in Florida. The Sabres had another game in the Sunshine State on Saturday. The Wednesday night game was against the Florida Panthers and the Saturday night game against Tampa Bay Lightning. Naturally, I Mapquested the town of Sunrise, Florida in relation to Naples and learned that the Panthers were just 90 short minutes away! Tampa, however, was almost two hours away.

I ran this by Shannon to find out if we could make it to *both* games. She had no problem with it; but a couple weeks later I learned that we couldn't make it to the second game in Tampa because we had to be back home in New York State on Sunday due to a baby shower Shannon was hosting for a coworker. We were going to be running low on funds if we got a hotel room and rental car for an additional day in Florida anyway, so it was settled: Shannon would do the booking of the hotel, flight, and rental car. I had the challenging job of finding hockey tickets.

I ended up going to StubHub where I located a pair of tickets in "the nose bleeds" for $10 bucks a pop. After searching longer and harder, I nailed a pair of 100 level seats that were a bargain at $18 each. I figured an extra $8 per seat was a sound investment to enabling us to be much closer to the action.

After I purchased the tickets, Shannon placed all of the reservations telling me she had a really big surprise for me, but that I could only receive it when we arrived in Florida. The first thing that popped into my pea brain was that Shannon had bought some beautiful ensembles from either Frederick's of Hollywood or Victoria's Secret, but it made no sense that I would have to wait until Florida for that! I asked, "Did you reserve a red Ford Mustang convertible for our rental car?" She stood in the doorway with her jaw dropped to the floor: "You ruin every surprise I try to give you!"

Back in the days when I was courting Shannon, she bought me a surprise. I asked if it was Buffalo Bills tickets; she got so pissed off because I guessed correctly! On our first wedding anniversary, I correctly guessed Buffalo Sabre tickets, absent any hints, validating how well we knew each other.

October 2009

October couldn't come quickly enough! But when it finally rolled around, Shannon was ecstatic that we were finally going for a vacation alone: just the two of us! Up until this point, virtually all our vacations involved family and/or friends. We finally had a getaway for ourselves. The hamster wheel began to turn in my little pea brain, creating enough juice to light up my dim witted light bulb…why be like the masses and vacation only once, or perhaps twice a year? Why don't we vacation every month? That's what we needed…just the two of us!

Next thing you know, I was looking at the Buffalo Sabres season schedule. I had seen my fair share of Sabres home games, and could still remember seeing them play in their former home, the Buffalo Memorial Auditorium, better known as "The Aud." Shannon and I have made several road trips with my buddies to see the Sabres play in Ottawa and North Carolina over the last few years. Because Buffalo is where I was born and raised, it didn't qualify as a destination vacation. I decided to plan a monthly secret mini vacation for Shannon and myself. Shannon would know we were going on a vacation, but she wouldn't know our destination!

Before we knew it, 4:00am Wednesday the 21st of October 2009 was upon us. We had to be up at that ungodly hour in order to make it to the Rochester International Airport by 5, with ample time to get through security, always the wild card. Security was uneventful and we soon boarded our plane, had a layover with a change of planes at LaGuardia, and then boarded the jet to Fort Myers. Shannon and I were probably the youngest passengers on that flight to Florida by a good 50 years.

Fort Myers Airport was small, reminiscent of a Fisher Price make believe airport. A few runways and a glorified shack housed the terminals. The airport had way too many old people with straw hats, and fluorescent colored tropical patterned button-down shirts.

Eventually, we made our way to the rental car check-in where I soon sported a huge stiffie just thinking about cruzin' around Florida in my red Ford Mustang convertible, giggity!

Once we were verified and cleared, the agent told us to go to the parking garage where another agent would show us to our car. Oh boy, oh boy, OH BOY!!! Ford Mustang, convertible here we come! Shwing!

Shannon and I turned the corner into the parking garage, and met an agent who showed us three convertibles telling us to pick the one we wanted. I looked around and grumbled under my breath, "Where the Hell is my Mustang!?" All I saw was a row of Chrysler Sebring convertibles. Man, talk about a huge buzz kill! Stiffie to softie instantly.

After putting the top down and throwing our luggage into the car, we were on our way to Naples in our…our…Sebring. Welcome to Florida, yawn.

You wanna know what upset me off the most? Sure you do. We drove past Alamo, Enterprise and Hertz and they **_ALL_** had Ford Mustang convertibles and to add insult to injury: the new Camaro!

Being a guy, I naturally did not bring a map. However I did print out directions from our hotel in Naples to the hockey arena in Sunrise. So with some great detective sleuthing skills, Shannon and I were able to find the highway to Naples fairly easily…we saw a highway sign that said "Naples 75 South, Tampa Bay 75 North."

We stayed at La Playa Beach Resort. Translated from Spanish to English: "The Beach Beach Resort"; seems a wee bit redundant if you ask me.

At check-in we were greeted and welcomed by $400 worth of "grab your ankles" fees: $100 per day just to stay there. Allegedly, it was a "room vandalism insurance" junk fee. Then, there was an extra $30 per day fee for a valet to park our boring Sebring. And on top of that, spread those legs…$17 per day to use the pool and the towels. Farewell to our remaining cash in our bank account: wiped out! Having fun yet?

I told myself, "Self, I've never heard of a hotel charging to use the pool; it's just one of the amenities. So, for $17 a day to use this pool, they better have some pretty sweet towels because those huge and fluffy plush puppies are coming home with us!"

Au contraire; they handed us a couple of crummy and frayed, nasty old towels with faded blue stripes that I wouldn't pawn off on Goodwill, let alone take home. But the pool had water in it (free of charge!) and was heated, too. Shannon and I hung out at the pool for a few hours and relaxed, which we needed desperately after being nickeled and dimed to death.

Before we knew it, it was time to leave the pool (and those lovely towels) and hit the road for our hockey game!

I have met too many people who bitch and complain about the North and how much it sucks (including some of my family members). Instead of ranting here, I'll tell you later why I love the North, especially Western New York. One of the cool things about living up North close to Canada is the ability to easily purchase great tasting Canadian beers! And it's dirt cheap! But down south in

Florida, we couldn't find a Canadian beer to save our lives! We ended up settling on Busch Light as the lesser of two evils, because although it's a shit beer, it tastes less like piss than Bud.

Finally, there we were, cruising from the Gulf Coast to the Atlantic Coast with the top down in our *smashingly sexy* (for a Floridian, maybe) silver Sebring convertible. The ride across the state of Florida to Sunrise was boring, all 101 miles of it. Initially, the drive was a bit southern, so to our left was swampy land, and to our right was the sun setting over some more marsh lands. Road signs occasionally told us that we could pull off into rest areas, which were a part of the Everglades National Park that offered hiking trails and boat launches. Hiking and boating were the last thing on our minds for fun in the Everglades. It baffled me that people would want to go into a habitat where pythons were taking over the alligator infested wetlands! With the convertible top still down, we locked the doors, and floored it to Sunrise.

After hour and a half of driving through hypnotizing marshland we finally reached civilization! We could distinctly see the BankAtlantic Center from a distance and before you could say the Buffalo Sabres are going to trample the Florida Panthers, we were parked and kicking back a couple of quasi-warm Busch Lights, which did not go down smoothly *at all*. We got over that fast and decided to head into the arena to grab some cold brewskis. The walk into the arena was bizarre because I was not used to humid 80 degree weather for a hockey game.

When I bought the tickets off of Stub Hub, I did not see exactly where our seats were located, so Shannon and I were thrilled to discover that our $18 seats were only 7 rows up from the ice! Our tickets were originally $95 a pop! And as if that weren't enough, we sat on the side where the Sabres shot at twice! Double score!

Being from Buffalo, I am used to hearing both the American and Canadian National Anthems being sung before every Sabres home game; not the case in Florida.

After the singing of the American National Anthem, it was almost time for puck drop. I took a quick glance around the arena and saw many empty seats; ¼ of the arena looked empty and almost ½ of those fans were Sabres fans!

Sabres owner Tommy Galisano (we were tight, that was why I call him "Tommy") is also the founder of PAYCHEX, with its headquarters in Rochester. A philanthropist, he hated the high taxes of New York State, so earlier in 2009, Tommy Boy jumped ship and relocated down to Naples. Well, I had my people try to get ahold of Tommy's people, to see if he would be at the game; I figured we could hang and chill out in a luxury box. Long story short, my people and Tommy's people couldn't hammer anything out so we just watched and enjoyed the game from our 7th row seats.

Within the first two minutes of the game, Mike Grier and Jason Pominville had scored to put the Sabres up 2-0. Topping that off, both goals were in our section! After the second goal, Florida goaltender Scott Clemmensen was yanked, and within four and a half minutes, Sabre forward Matt Ellis had made it 3-0. Buffalo's Tyler Myers fired a shot from the point to make it 4-0 around the half way mark of the 1st period.

Florida put some pressure on and Steven Reinprecht stuffed the puck in on the open side of Sabres goaltender Ryan Miller, after the Sabres had a crash collision mix-up in front of the net. With just over three minutes left in the 1st, Buffalo came back into Florida's zone, crashed the net, and Thomas Vanek squeaked one by backup goalie Tomas Vokoun to make it 5-1 Buffalo!

The 2nd Period started off intense with numerous great scoring opportunities on both sides of the puck, but by the end of the 2nd, there was no change in score.

In the dying minutes of the 3rd Period, Florida's Rostislav Olesz snuck the puck past Miller to make it 5-2 Buffalo.

It was a great game; our Sabres won and we didn't have to walk the "Walk of Shame" back to our car, as on previous Sabre road trips. There weren't any fights during the game, but, oh well.

Shannon and I experienced something in that arena that we never had experienced before. NEVER have we been so cold at a hockey game; it was bone chilling in there! We both wore T-shirts plus our jerseys yet we still rocked some serious THO (titty hard-on). I was at the Sabre's Winter Classic on New Year's Day 2008 at Ralph Wilson Stadium in Buffalo (Orchard Park) when it was near 0° Fahrenheit and snowy but I was still warmer there than in Florida. Who'da thunk it?

As we left BankAtlantic Center, I felt rain drops. *Rain drops keep falling on my head, but that doesn't mean my eyes will soon be turning red, crying's not for me, cause I'm never gonna stop the rain* *by complaining, because **MY SABRES WON**, nothing's worryin' me...*(That's my Weird Al version of B.J. Thomas' classic).

The ride back to the hotel was not fun. The weather changed from rain to a torrential downpour, Florida hurricane style. An hour and a half trip in the pouring rain with mesmerizing windshield wipers is worse than a WNY lake-effect snowstorm, if you ask me. We were awake since 4am so we were ready for our mattress after the game ended. Miraculously, we made it back to our "cheap towel store" in Naples; awake, alive, and in one piece by midnight.

The next few days were fun; I made snow angels in the sand, while some dude yelled at me. I told him, "I can't help myself; I'm from Buffalo!"

November 2009

Our next planned road trip was to Boston. Tickets, hotel reservations, and everything were perfectly planned for the Sabres/Bruins game on Saturday November 7, 2009 when on November 5th my Nana unexpectedly died. Hotel reservations were canceled for Boston and hockey game tickets sold to my coworker Dustin, whose parents live in the New England area.

Thankfully they were sent those tickets because Boston beat Buffalo 4-2.

***

Shannon and I were back on the road again headed to Philadelphia on November 14th to spend the weekend with her cousins; we happened to catch the Sabres/Flyers game while there, what a coincidence!

The last time I was in Philly was seven years prior, in 2002, during my senior year of high school at St. Joseph's Collegiate Institute when our track team competed in the Penn Relays. We competed in the 400 meter relay and I was the alternate runner, in case anyone was injured or became ill.

We arrived at Nichole and Vince's home in Levittown, Pennsylvania midday, then hung out for a while and enjoyed some drinks. When Nicole and Vince asked what we wanted to do before the game, I said that I was dying to try a true "Philly steak and cheese sub," made the authentic way. The closest place for a good steak and cheese according to Vince was at a joint called Steve's Prince of Steaks. So we tooled over to Steve's where I got a "real" steak and cheese sub. I had no clue that an authentic steak and cheese was made with...of all things...Cheese Whiz!

We took our carry out delicacies back to Nichole and Vince's where we enjoyed our lunch and *yes*, the sub was delicious! It tasted amazing. I often wondered how they ordered a Philly Steak and Cheese Sub in Philadelphia! When I was down in Philly for high school track, I felt like an idiot ordering a "Philly Steak and Cheese" in Philly...I was sure it'd scream "out of town-er."

When I asked Vince he was puzzled, so I explained that up in Buffalo and in Western New York, when we order chicken wings, we just call them "chicken wings" or "wings", not "Buffalo Wings" as they do elsewhere in the country. Vince caught my drift and clarified that they call them "Philly subs" or a "Steak and Cheese." Sounded simple enough!

And while we were at it, since we were in Pennsylvania, where the "State Beer" is YUENGLING, I didn't want to sound like a doofus at local bars when ordering beer, or have a repeat of an awkward negative experience we had up in Canada ordering beer.

To celebrate our engagement anniversary and at same time hit up our old haunts, I took Shannon up to Niagara Fall, Ontario for Valentine's Day. At Casino Niagara we went to the bar where I ordered a Molson and a Rickards. The Canadian bartender was a total beer snob and said, "Hey buddy, Molson is a huge beer company that makes many different brands such as Canadian, Canadian Light, Export, and so forth and it's pronounced Rickards, not Richards."

In the States, ordering a "Molson" means you get a Molson Canadian, incidentally. So to show Mr. Canadian Beer Snob that I know my Molson beers I said, "Yea, give me a Molson Brador!"

Mr. Beer Snob looked at me, stunned. "You know what a Brador is?!"

For many years, every time Grandpa Ziggy, Nana, and Uncle Michael took me up to the 1000 Islands in the north country of New York State to go fishing. Grandpa Ziggy preferred the Canadian waters, so we would get Canadian fishing licenses, which can be bought only in Canada, like at Canadian Tire. On the way home,

Uncle Michael would bring back Alexander Keith's, Kokanee, Molson Stock Ale, Molson XXX, and Molson Brador. So I grew up with Brador.

I asked, "So, do you have Brador?"

Mr. Beer Snob asked, "No! How do you know about Brador?!"

I said, "Don't worry about that. Do you have Molson XXX?"

Mr. Beer Snob asked, "No! How do you know about Triple X?!"

I said, "Don't worry about that. Do you have Molson Stock Ale?"

Mr. Beer Snob asked, "How do you know about Stock Ale!?"

I said, "Don't worry about it. Do you have Molson Ice?"

Mr. Beer Snob said, "No we don't…"

Since they had no Molson brews I wanted, I settled for a *Canadian*.

Mr. Beer Snob looked at Shannon, "Do you want a Red or a White?"

Shannon replied, "Red."

When the snob came back with Shannon's draft, he gloated, "So do you know what I meant when I asked Red or White?"

"A White is a Belgian style wheat beer and a Red is a lager, yes." Shannon snapped back.

"Oh, well *excuse me!* Looks like you guys know your beers!" he quipped, not merely a snob, but also a snot!

So after telling Vince that long story, Vince told me the proper way to order a Yuengling, which is done by asking for a "Lager."

We explained to Vince that Buffalo was heavily into Canadian beer, especially Labatt Blue. Buffalo was so obsessed with Labatt Blue that Labatt moved their USA headquarters from Norwalk, Connecticut to Buffalo a few years ago! We shared with Vince that Buffalonians refer to and request a Labatt as simply a "Blue."

After our little *linguistic of liquids* tangent, Shannon's other cousin Bobby and his wife Abi arrived. With Bobby "in the house" the talk becomes trash, quickly at that. Bobby started on us about wearing our Sabres colors at the game. He scared Shannon saying there was a good chance that beer would be dumped on us, or worse yet, that we might get into a fight! Shannon was quivering from Bobby's fear-mongering, so I told Bobby to knock it off after which he proceeds to warn us that in the old Philadelphia Eagles Stadium, they had a court house on location to handle the many fights that went on at the games.

I was able to convince Shannon to keep her colors on and wear her Sabres jersey to the game.

It was time to eat again after some breeze-shooting and they took us to Chickie's and Pete's Crab House and Sports Bar.

As soon as we entered, Vince and Bobby bragged that they never ever see any visitor team's jerseys there. Well, must be that Buffalo fans travel in packs, because there were Blue and Golds, Beauty and the Beast/Goats, and Donald Trump taupe/Slug jerseys everywhere in this local joint.

After we finally got a table, we ordered pizza and some World Famous Crabfries! The Crabfries were excellent, I must admit.

After that delicious dinner, we headed to Wachovia Center. It was brilliant how Philly had designed their sports Mecca: a 4-corner intersection with Citizens Bank Park (Phillies' baseball), Lincoln Financial Field (home of football's Eagles), Wachovia Center (home of the Flyers and 76ers) and the Spectrum (former home of the Flyers and 76ers)

For the record, the last event to go through the Spectrum was a Pearl Jam show. For the real record, Nirvana was ***The Best*** Seattle Grunge band and ***The Best*** band of the 1990s…Period!

While on the topic of music, I reminded Vince that Rick James and the Goo Goo Dolls were both from Buffalo and inquired about music groups from the Philly area.

Before Vince could answer, Bobby chimed in and said, "Hell yea! The Fresh Prince of Bel-Air is from West Philadelphia, where on the playground he spent most of his days, chillin' out maxin' relaxin' all cool and shooting some b-ball outside of the school…" Bobby continued to free style the rest of the walk into Wachovia Center.

We walked in through an entrance that had a restaurant and a live band playing, very cool. After going through the turnstiles, we headed to our seats in Section 220. Walking through the Center was fun; Shannon and I didn't get badly heckled. We saw a display of hats from past hat tricks that happened at the Flyers' home. While most places give the hats to charity, Philly puts them in a display case.

After getting our brews, Shannon and I navigated our way to our seats with Nichole, Vince, Abi, and Bobby, all festooned in their Orange and Whites.

Soon it was time for the National Anthem and then puck drop!

Philly showed a strong start with a few good chances on Sabre goalie Ryan Miller, but to no avail.

There has always been a deep animosity between these teams; Philly beat Buffalo back in 1974-75 for the Stanley Cup.

Every time these two teams play each other, it's always a grudge match and fights break out on a regular basis. Back in the mid to late 1990s, Buffalo's Rob Ray, Brad May, and Matt Barnaby were always mixing it up with Philly's top line and notorious goaltender, Garth Snow. Two games vividly stick out in my mind.

The first was a regular season game on February 4, 1997. Buffalo was in Philly and the game got out of control with an ice brawl, which even included the goaltenders fighting. In the midst of all the players on the ice fighting with their "dance partner", Buffalo's Dominick Hasek felt left out. Not wanting to be a wall flower, Hasek skated the length of the ice to get into the mix, where he found his dance partner Garth Snow! Rob Ray then left his date to cut in and steal Snow away from Hasek! The ref and linesmen were so outnumbered with their hands full that it took forever to control the chaos and divvy up the penalty minutes! It was awesome!

The two teams met again later that season in the 2nd round of the playoffs. Things picked up from where they left off in the regular season: only differences were the venue and the playbill. The boxing match was May 3, 1997 held at Marine Midland Arena (now known as First Niagara Center) in downtown Buffalo. The usual cast of characters included Rob Ray and Brad May. However, Buffalo had Steve Shields in net...well, that is until he skated the length of the ice to tee off on (none other than) Garth Snow. It was another great ice brawl; gloves, helmets, and sticks littered the ice as the MMA went wild!

Apparently Buffalo born and Sabre forward Patrick Kaleta and I shared the same déjà vu because he stormed into the Flyers zone dropping Philly's Ryan Parent. Next thing you know, Buffalo's Derek Roy set up Thomas Vanek on the power play to sneak one past Philly's goalie Ray Emery. Yes! That was correct Buffalo fans, you heard me right, I said the power play. Those words may seem foreign to us, a *power play goal*, but every now and then a blind squirrel finds a nut. Late in the 1st, Buffalo was on the power play again, and Pominville dinged one off the post that didn't go in...*just a bit outside. He tried the corner and missed.*

Philly didn't roll over and play possum. They were very much alive in the 2nd Period and came on strong until Buffalo's goalie Miller stepped up to the plate where he shut down the Flyers' top guns. With just over 5 minutes left in the 2nd, Buffalo was working hard, deep in the Flyers' zone, when Tyler Ennis (just called up that day from the AHL farm team, the Portland Pirates) had his hands on the puck, and eluded Flyer goaltender Ray Emery to make it a 2-0 Buffalo game.

About three minutes into the 3rd Period, Philly's Chris Pronger whipped the puck from the point, which flew by a startled Ryan Miller to make it a 2-1 Buffalo game.

Ray Emery had always given Buffalo some trouble in the past, especially when he played for Ottawa. But Sabre Paul "the Goose" Gaustad was able to tip in the rebound from the shot of Tyler Myers on the power play. Yes, once again, I said the POWER PLAY!!! The Goose's goal came at 6:25 in the 3rd to put Buffalo up 3-1.

Around the halfway point in the 3rd, Philly was short-handed when Flyers' Jeff Carter popped the puck past Buffalo's Ryan Miller making it a 3-2 Buffalo game. The struggle between both teams continued so Philly pulled their goalie, but couldn't turn it around: too late. Woo-hoo! Shannon and I didn't have to undertake the Walk of Shame, but we did have to deal with the crap spewing from Cousin Bobby's pie hole; Shannon and I welcomed him to join us up in Buffalo any time to attend a game.

When we got back to Nicole and Vince's house, they invited us to one of their favorite stomping grounds, Irish Rover Bar and Grill, which was a couple blocks away.

We liked the feel of the Irish Rover: an old two story house, similar to the type of dive that you find in Buffalo burbs of

Cheektowaga, West Seneca, or the Tonawandas! We met Nicole and Vince's friends, who we partied with until whenever, it's all a blur.

Sunday morning came too soon, so we watched a few episodes of FX's *It's Always Sunny in Philadelphia*. It was entertaining. The Buffalo Bills were playing in Tennessee, though, against the Titans, so Nichole, Vince, Bobby, and Abi took us to Miller's Ale House to watch the game. We liked Miller's, not only because it shared the name of my favorite current goaltender but because they had five different flat screen TVs playing five different games! It was fantastic! When one team was in-between plays or on commercial break, you could watch another game. It became confusing because they had one game on the PA with a play by play out of synch with the Bills' game. The Bills led the first 3 quarters, shit the bed, then handed the game over to their opponent, like every other Bills Sunday that 2009 season. We went back to Nichole and Vince's, gathered our stuff, and made the six hour trek back to the ROC.

December 2009

For a very long time, the idea of a special surprise mini vacation for just Shannon lingered in my mind. She loves New York City, and for a brief while, she even wanted to live there. The Macy's Thanksgiving Day Parade might be wonderful as would hanging out in the Big Apple, but I came up with something even better!

The Sabres were scheduled to play against the New York Rangers at Madison Square Garden (MSG) on a Saturday night in December. I thought, "Wait a minute...in December, Radio City Music Hall will be featuring their Christmas Spectacular with the Rockettes!" I was shocked to have been able to grab a pair of Sabre/Ranger tickets in the 400 level at MSG for a decent price on Stub Hub. Proving that this trip was meant to be, I miraculously found a pair of Rockettes tickets for the very next day! I went and booked both events like a true early bird in September and succeeded in keeping it a secret from Shannon.

The day after booking the tickets, I told everyone at work that I had already completed my Christmas shopping for Shannon. When coworkers asked what I got for Shannon I responded that we were attending a Sabres/Rangers game at MSG, after which they accused me of buying a present for myself that I was pawning off on Shannon! I explained that Shannon is also a huge Sabres fan and even named our black lab Teppo Numminen after Olympic Medalist and Sabres defenseman in the NHL.

I procrastinated booking a hotel until the last possible minute. So at the "one week in advance point," of all the discount hotel websites, HotWire had the best deal where they led us to the Hotel Reserve in SoHo. HotWire had some awesome hotels, but for $1000? I cannot justify a hotel room that costs more for one night than our mortgage payment! They had hostels half priced at $22 per night, but not wanting to be stabbed and mugged, Hotel Reserve at $199 per night sounded like a steal.

Shannon knew we were going on a mini getaway, but she was clueless as to where. In October, I told her to request the weekend of December 12th and 13th off work for our surprise excursion. As the weeks passed, she asked for hints, but I refused in order to spare us both of the hyper-analysis in her desperate attempt to find out where we were going.

As the departure time approached, and Shannon desperately wanted a hint. I told her to go and find her ice skates. That's when she went both crazy ballistic and happy, like a kid running down the stairs on Christmas morning; she was sure that she had deciphered the code and knew where we were escaping to.

Friday night arrived and we had to pack. Because she didn't know for sure where we were going, I told her to set out various outfits for different kinds of weather in order to throw her a curve ball. I asked her to prepare summer clothes, a swim suit, her Sunday best, cold winter weather clothes, and Frederick's of Hollywood negligees (I preferred Frederick's over Victoria's Secret: classier!). The plan was to awaken early and that I would pack for her.

At 4am on Saturday December 12th the alarm went off. Trying to be energetic, but still groggy, Shannon made her way to the shower to freshen and wake up. She was still unsure of the game plan because not only did I pack for her, but the night before, her dad asked if the flight itinerary had been printed out. Her parents enjoyed toying with her, too!

We were packed and on the road by 4:30am. When we passed by the ROC airport exit, Shannon realized we weren't flying anywhere she fell asleep in the car.

Shannon woke up in Scranton, PA 99.9% sure of where we were headed, increasingly excited and giddy.

By the time we hit Netcong/The Oranges area of New Jersey, I told Shannon that we were going to a Sabres game at MSG that night, the Rockettes Sunday morning, and skating at Rockefeller Center sometime in between. I also wanted to see the Ghostbusters and the Ninja Turtles, especially Michelangelo, and thank him for his good work. I didn't want to see Spiderman because I never got into him when I was a kid. Shannon dropped the bomb on me that they were fictitious and only make believe. Finding this out was like learning that Santa Claus, the Easter Bunny, the Tooth Fairy, or the Stay Puft Marshmallow Man weren't real! [I always thought it was odd how the Turtles, Ghostbusters, and Spidey never bumped into each other in New York City.]

We parked the car at the Port Imperial/Weehawken ferry station at around 10:30am and within minutes, we were aboard the ferry to the Big Apple!

Our ferry docked in Manhattan only a few slips away from the USS Intrepid. Years ago, for my 13th birthday, my old man, the Donald, took me to NYC; touring the USS Intrepid aircraft carrier and USS Growler submarine were two of the many amazing things we did.

We decided to carpe diem since we were right there, and in a "New York Minute," we were walking around the hanger deck of the USS Intrepid. The hanger deck was the level of the ship where the airplanes were stored. As we walked around, we saw one of the propellers from the Intrepid. Along with educational opportunities for the kiddies, they had a TBM- Avenger airplane, FJ-3 Fury jet aka-Sabre Jet (how fitting!), A-4 Skyhawk airplane, and a HUP-2 Retriever helicopter on display. Historical artifacts from crew members were displayed along with the history of the ship's service from WWII through the Cold War.

We then found our way to the flight deck, where an array of different aircraft were parked. The one aircraft that I immediately recognized was the F-14 Tomcat. I explained to Shannon that this was the jet flown by Maverick in the movie *Top Gun*. The canopy that Goose whacked his head on causing his brain injury which eventually killed him was there, too, and I animatedly and excitedly explained all this as if it were all new info. Shannon rolled her eyes saying, "I know. You've only made me watch that movie umpteen million times…"

An A-12 Blackbird, UH-1A Huey Helicopter, and an F-16 Fighter Jet from Syracuse, NY was also on display. The tail fin of the F-16 read "From the Boys of Syracuse."

We eventually made our way to the submarine USS Growler. Our tour guide explained that the sub was only in service for six years when its diesel engines caused it to become obsolete. We were also told that during her voyages, a crew of 88 men stayed at sea for three months. It was fascinating to walk through and see the old technology. It was even more amazing to see how Americans could build something without the aid of computers and that after the sub was commissioned, it only took 6 years for what was state of the art technology to become obsolete!

After touring the museum, we headed inland. Absolutely clueless as to where we were, we walked, and kept walking, next thing we knew we were in Times Square! Neon lights flickering and flashing everywhere, with a random chaotic mix of tourists and locals hustling and bustling. Did we stick out like a sore thumb and act like typical tourists and take photos? Duh, you betcha!

Our incessant wandering eventually found us at the neon lights for NBC and Radio City Music Hall. Walking by NBC, we remembered that Shannon's Uncle Steve worked for NBC, but we were unaware if he was working that day. Not having Uncle Steve's phone number, I contacted his son Jayson by text and within a matter of minutes we were with Uncle Steve underneath the Christmas tree at 30 Rockefeller Center!

Uncle Steve led the way up to his office where he gave us the five cent tour, including us seeing where he worked: watching TV! Uncle Steve's job was to program TV shows with commercial times so both local and nationally televised programs run smoothly. At TV central for NBC, I asked, "Hey Uncle Steve, did Howard Stern broadcast from here back in the day? You know, *W-NBC!*"

"Yes! Actually, you are standing in his former studio," Uncle Steve exclaimed. "His studio was remodeled into this office."

We then were shown where Conan O'Brien's old studio was located before taking Jay Leno's spot in LA (yes, Uncle Steve ran into Conan in the hallway a few times). We then stopped at Jimmy Fallon's Late Show studio. The set was beautifully decorated for Christmas. Uncle Steve shared the historical tidbit that the seats in Fallon's studio were once located in Radio City Music Hall.

Uncle Steve took us to the Saturday Night Live area and it was absolutely awesome! Walking down the hallway to the studio, we saw photos of past famous skits, everything from the Cone Heads to Justin Timberlake wearing a tutu with high heels! In the actual studio, the main stage where the monologue is performed looks much smaller than on TV. Being Saturday, a dress rehearsal was happening. Jacob from the *New Moon* series was the guest star. I wasn't sure what *New Moon* was, but I assumed it was about vampires, so figured that it must be dumb. We hung out in the back row of the balcony and watched the directors yelling at the maintenance set builders for making too much noise as the actors could not hear their own lines. We were soon kicked out of the studio; I didn't know if it was my Sabres jersey or what, but it wasn't as if I were recording the SNL bit on my cell to air before the show began! Bon Jovi was that night's music act and sound checks are done all day on Thursdays; I thanked my lucky stars that I didn't have to suffer through any Bon Jovi!

From SNL, Uncle Steve escorted us to MSNBC's studios. We saw all the cubicles and computers shown as the background of the newscast. We were even able to see and experience behind the scenes of a 30 second live news feed, right from the MSNBC.

Our tour ended at MSNBC. We hopped back onto the elevator to return to Uncle Steve's office and we were joined by news anchor Lester Holt! He resembled Clark Kent, wearing similar style glasses...*Lester Holt! News anchor by day, Superman by night!*

After we got off the elevator, I asked Uncle Steve if he ever ran into Natalie Morales. He said, "Not often, but yes Adam, she is cute!"

The dumb Pollock that I am, I blurted, "Natalie Morales is more than cute! She's HOT!" After which I was smacked by Shannon. I don't know what her problem was as I was simply stating a fact. Not to mention, just a few moments earlier, Shannon was drooling over *Jacob*...

Back at Uncle Steve's office, he asked if we needed directions to anywhere else in New York City. "YES! I *need* to find the Ghostbuster's Fire house!" Within a couple clicks of the mouse, I had directions to 14 N. Moore Street, home of Hook and Ladder #8!

Needing to return to work, he asked if we needed anything else. Shannon and I were starving, so he led us outside, across the street, past NBC's Today Show's studio (where I announced: "that's where Natalie Morales sits!") and around the corner to Pronto Pizza & Beer at 30 West 48th Street (Between Rockefeller Plaza and 6th Avenues), where according to their slogan, they "Delivered steamin' hot to you in our 'hot stack' thermal box". Those four slices of pizza and two Coronas were absolutely delicious!

Almost 4pm, we had yet to check into our hotel. Now in Midtown we needed to get to SoHo. Though I had a map of the city and the subway routes, we still got a little lost trying to find a subway entrance. I was Nervous about the time required to find our hotel, check in, and leave for Madison Square Garden. We hurried so we could be at the Garden before the game started.

We ran down a few blocks to the front of Grand Central Station where we figured we could catch the subway. Since we were lost, we asked a NYPD officer for directions and he pointed us in the right direction to our train. Phew!

We checked into our room at the wonderful Hotel Reserve on 51 Nassau Street in SoHo miraculously by 5:15pm… *"Old SoHo, where you drink champagne and it tastes just like cherry cola."*

The game started at 7pm, but we had no idea how long it would take to get to the Garden. After changing into our Sabre jerseys we descended to the lobby for directions where we were pointed toward the subway to MSG and both us and our team were wished "good luck!" by the front desk…*GO SABRES!*

As it turned out, we arrived at Madison Square Garden an hour early with time to spare. Unable to locate a nearby watering hole to kill some time, we ventured in, where we met a local couple who took the escalator up to the 400 level with us and explained how to get down to ice level to see the Sabres during the warm up session. Before descending to ice level, we grabbed a couple of cold ones.

As our Buffalo Sabres skated out the Zamboni entrance, we saw Buffalo natives Patrick Kaleta and Tim Kennedy skate past with

Syracuse native Tim Connelly. There was Shannon's favorite goalie, Ryan Miller! Other Sabres we saw skate included Tommy Vanek, Jason Pominville, Derek Roy, and local USA boys Tyler Meyers, Chris Butler, Drew Stafford, and Michael Grier. Toni Lydman skated over to where we were watching and flipped up two pucks for two little Sabre fans.

The warm up lasted for about 15-20 minutes but it felt like it flew by. After the warm up was over, we needed to get back to our seats. So we rode the escalator back up to the 400s. Before we made our way to our seats, we stopped at the same beer stand and beer guy to refuel. I told the guy I wanted one Coors Light and one Blue Moon. With my ¾ drunken beer still at hand, the beer guy asked me for my ID. I said, "Ok, hang on. Let me put down my beer so I can grab my ID," as I was saying so, I placed my beer down right in front of the beer guy.

Before we knew it, we were up in the 400s and singing the National Anthem. Our seats were right behind Sabres goaltender Ryan Miller. I'm not going to lie, it was cool being at the Garden where so many famous sporting events and concerts have taken place (such as Elvis) but our seats stunk. We could only see ¾ of the ice and if we wanted to see the offensive play in our end, we had to lean out of our seats or just stand up.

Right after puck drop, both teams were playing hard. There was a lot of energy and the play was back and forth…wide open and anybody's game. It was 6:25 into the 1st Period when Buffalo's Derek Roy opened the scoring by stuffing a rebound past the Rangers goalie Henrik Lundqvist. At first I couldn't tell how many Sabres fans were at the game, because the Rangers and Sabres both wear blue and white jerseys. But after that first goal, you could hear about 1/5 of the Garden cheering!

Midway through the 1st Period, Buffalo took a penalty. The offensive play was in Buffalo's end and they could not clear the puck. A one timer shot by Ryan Callahan tied the game at 10:22.

Soon both teams began playing a little sloppy, and the Rangers ended up with a 4-on-3 power play. New York's Marian Gaborik received a pass at the point and skated in towards the top left circle of Buffalo's Ryan Miller. Gaborik snapped a wrister past Miller to make it a 2-1 Rangers game.

With a little under six minutes left in the 1st Period, both teams were at even strength. The Sabres were in the offensive zone; moving the puck around. The puck changed hands a couple times at the point before Sabres defenseman Henrik Tallinder took a shot. Rangers' goaltender Lundqvist could not control the puck and Buffalo's own Patrick Kaleta tossed up the rebound into the wide open net at 14:28. The game was tied 2-2.

Play continued hard into the 2nd Period. Penalties were being handed out left and right to both teams. Four minutes into the second period, Buffalo found themselves shorthanded again, all the while New York was pressing and hitting hard in the offensive zone. There was also a lot of sloppy play on both sides of the puck, which left both teams open to many scoring opportunities.

Half way through the 2nd, Buffalo, yet again, found themselves on the penalty kill. New York had a bad dump into Buffalo's zone. The puck flew along the boards, behind Miller and back to the point where Patrick Kaleta picked up the puck. Kaleta danced around the lone Ranger at Buffalo's blue line and skated down the ice on a breakaway. As Kaleta entered the Rangers' zone, Lundqvist came out of the net to challenge Kaleta. The whole time I was thinking, "Don't hit the glass! Don't hit the glass!..." To my surprise and delight, Kaleta ripped the puck right past Lundqvist to score a shorthanded goal and make the game 3-2 Buffalo!

By the time the 3rd Period started, I began to get a little nervous. Consistently, whenever Buffalo had a lead, they would fall asleep, and slowly let the other team in. Well, the Sabres came on strong for about the first five minutes of the 3rd Period. Then they began to fall asleep and eventually laid back to protect their one goal lead.

In the dying minutes of the 3rd Period, the Rangers had a failed power play and the Sabres had a failed 4-on-2 rush. In a final attempt to tie the game, the Rangers pulled their goalie, but to no avail, they could not produce the tying goal. Buffalo had won the game 3-2 and Shannon and I did not have to walk the Walk of Shame!

After the game let out, it was close to 10pm and we wanted to see the Christmas tree lit up at Rockefeller Center. We migrated our way back up to Times Square again. I had to piss like a race horse, so we stopped into a Starbucks. Shannon got us some coffee while I piddled.

Once outside, I took a slug of my coffee. Man, that cup of coffee tasted like the cat's ass...right after the cat took a huge massive dump! I thought their coffee was horrible. With their poop coffee and high prices, I still couldn't figure out why people drank Shitbucks Coffee.

We eventually circumnavigated our way to 30 Rock again. 30 Rock was still a zoo that late at night, lots of people!

Shannon and I enjoyed seeing the Christmas tree all lit up and decorated.

Though the only things that were certain for us to do were the hockey game, Rockettes, and skating at Rockefeller, I also wanted to go to FAO Schwartz Toy Store. When my old man took me there when I was 13, I thought that it was one of the coolest places to go. So from the Rockefeller Center, Shannon and I walked a block down to Fifth Ave and saw the snow flake light display that was put on by Saks Fifth Ave before we ventured further down Fifth to FAO.

By the time we made it to FAO, it was 11pm and the store was closed. Oh well, at least we made it there.

By now, Shannon and I figured that we should start to venture back to the hotel. Shannon was hopeful that we would be able to catch Saturday Night Live and see the skit that they wouldn't let us see in the studio from earlier that day.

As we headed down 49th Street, we walked past the Plaza Hotel where Kevin McAllister stayed in *Home Alone 2*! Then I thought to myself that we should find out where Dunkin's Toy Chest was, but I figured that it fell in the category of Ghostbusters and Ninja Turtles and Spider Man, so I didn't say anything...

By the time we made it back to Hotel Reserve, it was midnight and we were dead tired...I guess going to bed at 11:30 at night, waking up at 4am, and then staying awake until midnight would make probably anyone tired.

We turned the TV on and put NBC on to watch SNL. I think we fell asleep before the monologue ended

7:15am came quick! We had left the TV on all night, so when we woke up, NBC's Sunday morning show was on. They were showing an empty ice skating rink at Rockefeller Center. It took us a little while to get our butts in gear and out of bed. Shannon and I wanted to squeeze in ice skating at Rockefeller Center before the Rockettes. We finally checked out of the hotel at 8:15am and made it to Rockefeller by 9:15ish. Our show time for the Rockettes down the street wasn't until 11:30am, so we were hopeful on squeezing everything in.

We finally hit the freshly Zamboni-ed ice at 10:20am. Shannon and I were at the front of the line, so we were able to skate on the fresh ice, but the ice quickly became full and beat up. We both had our pictures taken in front of Prometheus.

Time flew by and before we knew it, it was already 11am. We needed to get off the ice, take our skates off, and walk the block down the street to Radio City.

As we entered Radio City, we saw a beautiful grand and majestic chandelier that must have been two stories tall. We walked up the red carpeted stairs to the third level. Our seats were dead center in the balcony and the theater was magnificent.

Within minutes the house lights were dimmed and the orchestra began to play. The curtain opened and out came the orchestra. They were on a moving stage that came towards us, hit the edge of the stage, and then proceeded to slowly drop into the pit.

While the orchestra played, Santa showed up on stage and told everyone to put on their 3-D glasses. Once doing so, we watched 3-D Santa fly from the North Pole, to Niagara Falls, up the Falls, through the clouds, before flying through the streets of New York. On the ceiling of the center of the Hall, there was a huge disco ball that was lit up from a few different angles. It gave the effect of everyone being in a snow storm. Once in New York, Santa flew past the Statue of Liberty, and the magic pixy dust from the sleigh brought Lady Liberty to life. Santa then flew around the Empire State building before flying around Rockefeller Center and the Christmas tree. He finally parked the sleigh in front of Radio City and hoped out. All of a sudden, we all see Santa walking through the isle towards the stage, Ho Ho Ho-ing all the way.

Once on stage, Santa greeted us all and acted as the MC for the evening. He wasted no time in introducing the Rockettes to us, who performed a tap dance routine to "The Twelve Days of Christmas." The number they did was awesome, and coming from a guy who hates theater and dance; that was significant.

The next number that was performed was Little Clair's dream about her teddy bears coming to life and her dancing with them.

Once the bears were done, the Wooden Soldiers came on. These guys are awesome and amazing to see. I'm glad that Shannon and I had our seats in the balcony because we were able to see the marching lines of the Rockettes and Soldiers perfectly. The soldiers were choreographed to march in a plethora of spinning circles and pin wheels while walking through each other. It's tough to explain, so just see the show! The soldiers end their number by standing in a line, facing forward. The orchestra started to play a string instrument slowly, as if we were watching real time in slow motion. In synchronization with the music, the soldiers began to fall backwards in slow motion. It took a good minute or two for the 48 soldiers to fall down. It was entertaining.

The next act had the Rockettes singing as they came out on stage and they all piled into a double decker tour bus. The bus started to "pull away." The backdrop of the stage was the outside of Radio City Music Hall, and as the tour bus changed angles and rotated on the stage, the background of Radio City changed until the bus "turned the corner" and "drove" down 5th Avenue. Eventually the tour bus made its way to Central Park and actually drove off stage. Once the bus left the stage, an ice skating rink came up from underneath the stage and two figure skaters performed a couple of numbers including double axels and all the twirling stuff they do. It was interesting to watch the skaters perform their number on Teflon ice that was probably no bigger than 20 feet by 40 feet. Once they were done skating, the tour bus with the Rockettes came back on stage and they "drove" from Central Park down to Times Square where they hopped off the bus, did some more dance numbers and did the high kicks...the Rockettes had legs and they knew how to use them!

I won't give the rest of the show away, but there are some other scenes that were fun and spectacular, especially the final act, which included a live Nativity scene with real camels, sheep, and donkeys.

Sadly the show came to an end. I took Shannon a few years ago to see the Rockettes Christmas Spectacular up in Toronto at the

Humming Bird Center and it was awesome there, but after seeing it at Radio City, there's no other place to see it.

We waited for the crowd to die down a bit, so we sat in our seats, and took in the beauty of the Hall. Within minutes, an usher came up to kick us out because they needed to clean up before the next show, which was in an hour. I told the usher that I had a question about the show and she told me to shoot. I asked her, "Hey do the animals ever poop on stage?" The usher didn't know about that, but she did say that during one of the performances, one of the donkeys did not want to come on stage, and that the Shepard was fighting with the donkey.

After we left Radio City, there was one last place in New York that I needed to stop at before we headed back home…

We boarded the subway and traveled downtown to the Canal Street stop. Once on street level, we turned the corner and we found ourselves on N. Moore Street and from there I could see the Ghostbusters' Fire House. I could hear, faintly, in the background, the angels in heaven harking, the rain stopping, the clouds parting, and a ray of sun beaming down on me and the fire house.

As we walked to the fire house, we could see the Hook and Ladder #8's fire truck parked outside. After we turned the corner, I noticed that the side door was open. So naturally I had to walk in.

Inside, the fire hall looked different from what I remember it looking like. First of all, the fire fighters took out the Ghostbusters' old lockers and put in their own lockers. Secondly, I didn't see the desk where Jeanne sat or Dr. Peter Venkman's office. Most importantly, there was a mini bounce house in the middle of the hall with little kids bouncing around in it. I saw some dude and said, "Hello."

He said, "Hello" back to me.

I said, "I'm a huge Ghostbusters fan…and yea…just wanted to see the fire hall…" as I looked around like a space cadet little kid.

The dude said, "Man, I can't believe of all the people to walk in here, I let in some dude with a Buffalo Bills Santa hat on in here!"

Defensively, I said back to the dude, "Hey man! What? You don't like the Bills?!"

He said, "No man, I just love the Bills, but my odds…"

I asked him if he was from Buffalo and he said yea, East Aurora. I looked around the fire hall a little more and the dude said some little kid was having his birthday party there. Shannon and I still stood awkwardly looking around. I noticed that they had the Ghostbusters 2 sign inside the fire hall on display. I tried looking for the pole because Ray Stance of the Ghostbusters said that I really need to try the pole. Shannon did take my picture out in front of the Ghostbuster fire house.

After that, we hopped back on the subway to 42nd Street and headed west to our ferry terminal…

January 2010

January rolled around fast! Another month and another road trip?

My cousin Jordan moved to Phoenix a few years ago but was back in Buffalo for Christmas. He was in the process of opening a restaurant in Phoenix because he hated most of the food there and missed the good food of the northeast: chicken wings, chicken fingers, pizza; you know, the good stuff!

Jordan wound up talking to Uncle Michael and me about Las Vegas, saying that he was just four hours away, so he went to gamble at least once a month. Before long, the three of us were talking about craps and roulette and our favorite Vegas casinos. Jordan asked us to come down and visit. Uncle Michael asked his wife Aunt Kathy, "Hey Kathy, is it alright if Adam and I go down to visit Jordan in Las Vegas?"

Aunt Kathy stared at him with a puzzled look while she processed the request. I was pretty sure Aunt Kathy knew damn well nothing good was going to come out of a Vegas trip. "Um, ok Michael. Who's going to watch your restaurant while you are in Vegas? I'm sure not going to!"

"Hey, Buffalo is playing down in Arizona in January. Do you guys wanna come? Front row, ice level tickets?" asked Jordan.

I was ready to pounce on an opportunity to go to Phoenix, but unfortunately Shannon was working nights during January and unable to switch shifts with anyone, so needless to say, Arizona didn't happen this time around.

I wish it had, because Buffalo beat Phoenix 7-2!

February 2010

February began cold and snowy with the sun rising well past 7am and setting before 5pm. Miserable and depressed, I couldn't wait to see the sun and feel warm weather again!

Shannon and I had an extended mini vacation set up in front of us, traveling the east coast visiting family.

We planned to be leaving Rochester on Friday February 5th, but I had a little errand to run before our journey. I knew there wouldn't be time for shopping on Friday after work as I still had to pack up and load the van. I decided to go shopping a day early, smart fella that I am, to avoid leaving late Friday night.

Even though I'm married, I still feel weird walking into Victoria's Secret.

Why? Because of the manikins. Yes, the manikins! As a little kid, I was (and still am) petrified of manikins, which rank up there along with porcelain dolls (those creepy eyes open up and stare at me!). The creepiest, most scary manikins I ever saw were on the battleship and destroyer at the Buffalo Naval and Service Park. My father, the Donald, was a docent at the park who gave tours. The USS Little Rock had the scariest manikins, especially the dentist! Manikins scare the crap out of me because they look like dead people: just not in a casket. It gives me goose bumps just thinking about them!

This may sound a little kinky, but even though manikins scare me half to death, I'm slightly turned on by Victoria's manikins. Then I realize they are manikins, not humans. I get petrified, scurry for shelter from the scandalously clad manikins and find a different hot manikin tickling my fancy! "No! No! No!" I tell myself! "They are manikins! They scare you! Stop looking!" But I can't. I'm somehow drawn to them, and how kinky they look. "No! No! No! That's what they want you to think!" The battle goes on in my head until I find something for Shannon, buy it, and leave.

I also feel weird going in there because I feel the employees staring at me. I don't know if they think I am a creep, sex offender, or if I am just into women's clothing, like Tim Curry in *the Rocky Horror Picture Show*.

However, I do like the store because I feel like a kid in a candy shop, until I see those prices their outfits!

It is also *hard* walking around that store, emphasis on hard. It is difficult window shopping in that store without getting a boner. When I get one, it's even more difficult to stop it because everywhere I look something else turning me on even more! I've thought about "emptying the bullets out of the gun" or "getting all the sap out of the wood" before going to Victoria's Secret or Frederick's of Hollywood, but it's counterproductive, like going to Wegmans grocery store on a full stomach: nothing seems appealing!

But I wanted to surprise Shannon with a couple outfits for our mini vacation. Just one problem; I forgot Shannon's size and didn't want to make the mistake **AGAIN** of buy something that didn't fit. I ended up calling her and ruining the surprise to get the correct information. But at least Shannon did not know exactly which surprise I was getting her!

In the checkout line, the sales clerk gazed into my eyes and asked seductively, "Are these for your girlfriend?"

Looking at the dirty blonde, I said, "Nope. They're for my wife. One girl is plenty for me."

The sales clerk undoubtedly thought I was headed home to reenact *Rocky Horror* in front of the mirror.

I got home from work Friday evening at 4:45, needing to clean the house before we left. After cleaning I could pack. Shannon got home from work and joined my packing and the entire 2003 Dodge Caravan packed: Coke machine and all, by 6:30.

Yes, Coke machine! A few months prior, I came upon a 1960s vintage Coca-Cola pop machine that still worked. It chilled beer bottles to a frost brewed temperature. My Uncle Michael, in Raleigh, North Carolina, owns Ziggy's Restaurant and Sports Bar in Wake Forrest, so I gave him the Coke machine for his restaurant.

Before Uncle Michael's, we needed to stop in York, Pennsylvania for a DeRose family reunion. Unfortunately, the reunion was canceled Friday morning because the Mid-Atlantic was being slammed by a huge coastal snow storm that dumped well over a foot. Almost two feet of snow fell in Washington DC! Philadelphia was hit hard, also, along with Maryland. Most of the DeRose family lived in that snow-hit area, the family reunion was canceled. Shannon and I were still headed down because a little snow never hurt us Western New Yorkers. We also wanted to drop off that Coke machine and watch the Sabres take on the Carolina Hurricanes later that week!

My Aunt Joanne and her kids Matthew and Mark lived in York, where the reunion was to take place. Since they were going to be local anyway, I figured Shannon and I might as well stop in and visit.

Shannon and I left Rochester by 6:30pm on Friday night. We took I-390 South towards Pennsylvania. Ironically enough, that night, the Carolina Hurricanes were playing in Buffalo. On our drive down, I put the Sabres game on the radio. Unfortunately we drove out of radio reception by Corning, New York. Thankfully my mom was calling me with updates. Sadly, the Sabres lost the game and continued their losing streak to three games.

Anyway, after 390 South ended, we hopped onto Route 15 South. We were making great time and did not see any of the snow storm until we hit Williamsport, Pennsylvania.

In Williamsport, it was trying to snow, but nothing was sticking.

By the time we hit Harrisburg, Pennsylvania it was a total white out, and to make it worse, the roads had not been plowed. It was a little difficult driving south on I-83 due to the lack of snow removal. The snow was at least five inches. However, I did get great satisfaction in passing by 4x4 pickup trucks along the highway. It was always those fartknockers during the snow storm that thought they were "tough poop" because they had four wheel drive. Come to find out three miles up the road, they were backwards in the ditch...ah karma.

We did not pull into Heritage Hills Hotel in York, Pennsylvania until after 1am. The five hour trip took a little bit longer than we expected on account of the snow.

After we checked in, we decided to see if the Pub at the hotel was open, but to our dismay, it was already closed.

Considering our late arrival on Friday, that yielded us to waking up late on Saturday, noon to be exact.

The family reunion was to take place at the Heritage Hills resort, but since reunion plans were canceled, so were the day's festivities. Shannon and I decided that since we were only a stone's throw away from it, we might as well go and take a stroll down memory lane...Hershey Park, here we come!

We knew that it was the dead of winter and that the park was not open, but they did have Chocolate World, which was open.

Regardless, Shannon and I still went to Chocolate World. We took the "10 cent tour" as I called it. It was a ride where cows sang to us about how chocolate was made. Towards the end of the ride, the singing cows told us that Hershey's milk chocolate is enriched with vitamins and minerals because it has milk in it! Naturally the ride dumped us off into a huge gift shop that sold anything Hershey imaginable! Everything from candy, to clothes, to key chains, to food, to hot chocolate, to toys, and to, yes, more candy. There was also a special theater so one could view a candy movie or if one did not want to do that, then one could cough up some bucks and see one's picture on a customized candy bar.

After Hershey, Shannon and I traveled back to York. We were having dinner at Knickers, the restaurant at Heritage Hills. We dined with my Aunt Joanne, Cousin Mark and his girlfriend Dana, and Cousin Matt and his family. Towards the end of dinner, at 9 o'clock at night, my sister Sarah and her family showed up fashionably late.

After dinner ended, Shannon and I found ourselves bellied up to the bar in the Pub until 12:30am or so.

Sunday morning came way too quick. My sister Sarah had let her two little midgets loose on Uncle Adam and Aunt Shannon at the bright and early time of 8:30 am. We soon met our cousins back down at Knickers for breakfast, before we hit up the Avalanche Express snow tubing. Tubing was a lot of fun.

Before we knew it, it was already 2pm and Shannon and I needed to get back on the road again. We had a five hour ride ahead of us from York, Pennsylvania to Raleigh, North Carolina. My sister Sarah, on the other hand, had an even longer ride because she was going to her brother in law's house in Charlotte, North Carolina.

Our five hour ride to Raleigh turned into an eight hour ride. Apparently Washington DC did not have good snow removal. They had two days to take care of the snow, but the roads were still bad and snow covered. There were parts of Baltimore and D.C. where the snow removal was so bad that the four lane highway automatically and suddenly turned into a two lane highway; the lane reductions were unexpected. One second, you are driving in the hammer lane, the next second, the lane just ended because it had not been plowed. It did not help that the sun was glaring off the windshield either. There were other parts of the highway system where the far left and far right lanes were the only lanes plowed, and the center two lanes were pitted with inches of ice. Plus everybody and their mother were out on the roads. It literally took us three hours just to get through Washington.

Mom and Uncle Michael kept calling us and gave us Super Bowl updates along the way. Drew Brees and the New Orleans Saints beat Peyton Manning and the Indianapolis Colts 31-17.

It was a long day, but we finally reached Uncle Michael's by 11pm.

Monday morning was another morning that came way too quick. After I got my dupa (Polish for butt) in gear, Uncle Michael and I unloaded his Coke machine into his garage. After that, Uncle Michael, Grandpa Ziggy, Shannon, and I were off to Ziggy's Restaurant...and yes, my uncle named the restaurant after his father.

Tell you what, there's nothing like having a nice hot, fresh out of the oven pizza for breakfast!

Shannon and I couldn't stay too long at Uncle Michael's because we had to get back on the road again. We left Raleigh late afternoon for Myrtle Beach, South Carolina. Myrtle Beach was Uncle Michael's favorite destination to take his family to. He also said that it was only three and a half hours away from his house. Three and a half hours seemed like a walk in the park to all the traveling Shannon and I had just done.

Shannon and I stayed in North Myrtle Beach. We did not arrive there until around 8:30pm. We found our hotel easily, and before we knew it, we were standing on our balcony, freezing our dupas off in 30° F weather, looking at the moon lit beach and Atlantic Ocean. It was romantic for a few minutes, until we started getting numb, and not from the alcohol.

Even though I knew beforehand that it was only going to be in the 30s, I still packed shorts, because I was optimistic that during February, the Carolinas would get hit with a freak heat wave...but that didn't happen. I still had the mindset that I was going to be in the South and that the South was **GOING** to be warm! Well, that was not the case, especially since there was still some remnants of snow around Myrtle Beach. Also, the weathermen were calling for snow later that week! Boogie boarding was out of the question then.

Finally! Shannon and I had two and a half days of some actual alone time, time alone, for ourselves; some baby making practicing time! (Insert Beavis and Butt-head giggling, *Yeah! Yeah!*) And that other mushy romantic stuff like long walks on the beach and romantic candle light dinners...

The hell with Tuesday morning; Shannon and I slept until Tuesday afternoon! Both of us were quite tired from all the recent traveling. I felt a little bad that we slept in and wasted the whole morning, but oh well, we were on vacation!

Though it was early February, I was being optimistic and thoroughly convinced that the Carolinas were going to be nice and hot...oh contraire, it was in the high-20s to mid-30s when we were down there. Even though we were right on the water and it was beautiful, the wind coming right up off that water just sliced right through you.

The frigid temperatures did not keep us from checking out the scenery.

We soon found ourselves at the Gay Dolphin Arcade. There I was able to finally introduce Shannon to the baseball pinball game that I had been telling her about for years. When I was a kid, my family and I visited Myrtle Beach a lot. Besides the beach, the Gay Dolphin Arcade used to be our hot spot.

My favorite game to play at the arcade was Hitter's Rally by Seidel Amusement Machine Company (a game similar to Williams' Play Ball pinball game)!

The baseball pinball was simple. The machine pitches pinballs, i.e. "baseballs", and you had a bat, which was a flipper. There were strikes in the game. If you swung and missed, you got a strike. If you hit the baseball, it rolled over the baseball diamond playing field. In the outfield, there were designated holes that said, "single" "double" "triple" or "out." If you have enough skill, you could blast the baseball up a ramp, into the upper deck and score a home run. Just like baseball, 3 outs and the inning, and you're out; game over. It only cost a quarter to play and after two games, Shannon was hooked quicker than playing the penny slots in Vegas.

After I pealed Shannon away from baseball, we did some more sightseeing.

We drove up to Barefoot Landing. Barefoot Landing was a shopping center built on top of and around a swamp. There were a few walkways and bridges that spanned across the water to link you up to the other side of the Landing.

PS-there were alligators in the water too!

When we were there, Barefoot Landing was not a hopping place. It was dead and half of the shops were closed. However, Wee-R-Sweetz was open! Wee-R-Sweetz was a salt water taffy shoppe and they made the taffy on the premises. They had a taffy making machine that cut the taffy and wrapped it into the wax papers, but the machine was not running. We did buy a bag of taffy, but it only lasted until the parking lot.

The Barefoot Landing also had a House of Blues and one of my favorite 90s Grunge bands, Alice in Chains, was playing there...in another two weeks. Sadly we weren't spending that long in Carolina, so we did not get see Alice in Chains.

Eventually we were hungry and Shannon desperately wanted to go to Margaritaville, which was located at Broadway on the Beach. So we went, and it was very quiet, but we didn't mind. We had dinner, talked, and before we knew it, it was 9:45pm and they were calling "last call!" By 10pm, the house lights were turned on, Buffet TV was turned off and so was the music...total buzz kill.

Shannon and I decided to drive around for a little bit and try to find another local watering hole. We couldn't find anything open, even the adult shops were closed.

We finally found a bar that was open and they had a live band playing. I think there were 12 people in the bar, including the bartenders and band. I yelled for "Freebird" to be played, but like always, I was ignored...yes, I was "that guy!"

Wednesday rolled around and I was on a mission. I promised my buddies Kirk and Dave that I would buy them one of those creepy dead baby sharks in a jar. They were sold at the beach shops like Waves, Bargains, Giants, or Eagles Beachwear.

Every beach store we stopped in, we found the baby sharks, and they were creepy and disgusting. The sharks were located right next to the dead puffer fish that had the googly eyes. As I mentioned before, I had (and have) a fear of dead stuff, so I did not look at the jars when I picked them up to take them to the cashier's counter.

That night we attempted again to hit up the night life. We went back to Broadway at the Beach and stopped at Senor Frogs, which was a ghost town. From there, we walked over to the Hard

Rock Cafe, grabbed some brews and munchies, and then walked to a dueling piano bar. At the piano bar, the pianists (*hehe*) they played the Ghostbusters theme song and *Freebird* for me! And yes, that bar was pretty much dead too. The piano players were cool dudes, they also played Rob Zombie, Metallica, Nirvana, the Charlie Brown theme song, Back to the Future theme song, and they ended their night like Saturday Night Live did, with the soft piano playing in the background and the host thanking everyone...all for me! And yes, I know I was a dork.

Thursday was our last day at Myrtle Beach. We packed up early because we planned on touring the USS North Carolina in Wilmington, NC before getting back to Raleigh to see the Sabres take on the Hurricanes!

Before we left the hotel, Shannon and I had to make a stop at Apache Pier. It was only a few resorts down from us. We walked down the windy and freezing beach to the pier.

At Apache Pier, we walked the East Coast's longest wooden pier. There I bought a coconut monkey that looked like Popeye.

A few hours later, Shannon and I were wandering around inside the USS North Carolina's 16 inch 45 caliber turrets. It was defiantly a sight to see, climbing up and down four levels of the turret; seeing where the gun powder was stored and elevated up to the next level to where it met the shells, and from there to see the ammo finally hoisted up to the guns.

According to different plaques at the museum, USS North Carolina served in the Pacific during World War II and saw major combat. In August 1942, North Carolina served in the Battle of the Eastern Solomon Islands, where her anti-aircraft guns helped save and protect the aircraft carrier USS Enterprise. During the war, the Japanese had thought they sunk the North Carolina 6 times, but were unsuccessful. On September 15, 1942, a Japanese torpedo hit the hull of the North Carolina, but the fast actions of North Carolina's crew helped keep her afloat and in service with the fleet. By the end of World War II, North Carolina had lost 10 men in action and 67 were wounded. After the War, North Carolina was decommissioned on June 27, 1947 where she was placed in Inactive Reserve Fleet in Bayonne, New Jersey. She sat up there in New Jersey for 14 years, when in 1958, it was announced that USS North Carolina was going to be scrapped. This caused a huge uproar with Carolinians, which led to them creating the Save Our Ship Campaign. During the campaign, school children even brought in pennies and nickels to help contribute. Finally on October 2, 1961, USS North Carolina was finally brought home. To make a long story short, if you are ever in or around Wilmington, take the tour. It's well worth the time. Not only is it educational, but you get a great workout in too.

Shannon and I were on the ship for over two and a half hours and we still did not see everything! We were a little strapped for time because we still had a two hour ride back to Raleigh in front of us. So Shannon and I raced through the rest of the ship before getting back up to the poop deck. We did not have enough time to check out the bridge, so I promised Shannon that we would go back to Myrtle Beach and see the rest of the USS North Carolina and her alligator. Yes, that is correct, I said alligator. There was an alligator that lived in the murky water right next to USS North Carolina. When we were there in February, it was too cold for the gator to be out.

We made it back to Uncle Michael's house by 5:30pm. It didn't take us long to get ready for the hockey game. I think it took us longer to chug a beer than for us to put our Sabres jerseys on. Within seconds, Shannon and I were in our jerseys and ready to go. I brought along a few extra Sabre jerseys for Grandpa Ziggy, Uncle Michael, and his boys Alex and Nathan.

My sister Sarah was also in town and also going to the game with us. She was bringing her two munchkins Hannah and Jonah and her hubby Guitar Dude. Guitar Dude's real name was Eric, but I call him "Guitar Dude" because he played guitar in the metal band Earth Crisis, from Syracuse, New York.

We had very nice seats at the RBC Center; they were at the top of the 100 level section at center ice. I liked sitting in the middle because I got to see the plays develop. I was not a huge fan of sitting behind the net because the mesh netting obstructed my vision.

So, back to the story...National Anthem and then puck drop...

Within the first few minutes of the game, Buffalo was pressing in the offensive zone and it paid off because Buffalo's Derek Roy was able to slap the puck past Hurricane goaltender Manny Legace to make it 1-0 Buffalo. About ¼ of the RBC Center were Sabre fans and they let their presence be known! When I jumped up to cheer, I hit the ceiling and thought that I was going to blast my fist right through it!

Later on in the 1st Period, Sabre Jochen Hecht finally found the broad side of the barn and netted a goal to make it 2-0 Buffalo.

However, Carolina came back to rain on Buffalo's parade. With three minutes and 30 seconds left in the 1st, Carolina's Brandon Sutter was able to snag a power play goal to make it a 2-1 Buffalo lead.

Carolina was back on the power play again in the dying minutes of the 1st Period. With 2 seconds left in the opening period, Carolina's Ray Whitney scored on Buffalo's goalie Ryan Miller to tie the game, 2-2!

Once the 2nd Period rolled around, Buffalo just went to sleep. They let Carolina walk all over them. Midway through the 2nd Period, Buffalo had a crappy line change and Carolina skated in 3-on-0 into the Buffalo zone! Thankfully Miller shut down the Canes operation and prevented their go ahead goal! Continuing on that play, Buffalo recovered Miller's rebound and skated back into the Carolina end and fired a shot that Legace stopped. Then Canes got the puck back and skated back over into Buffalo's zone and Carolina's Stephane Yelle snapped the puck off the pipe and into the net to make it a 3-2 Carolina lead. Buffalo had some shining moments in the 2nd, but they were few and far between; Carolina dominated play and Buffalo in the 2nd and into the beginning of the 3rd Period.

During the 2nd Intermission, Uncle Michael and I were complaining about how horrible the Sabres play and effort was. I reminded Uncle Michael that Buffalo pulled that crap all the time. Uncle Michael told me that just because he has not lived in Buffalo for the past 25 years didn't make him a dummy to his Buffalo sports teams' performances. I reassured Uncle Michael that midway through the 3rd, that Buffalo would realize that they were playing a hockey game and they would get their shit together and score the equalizer...Well low and behold, I spoke the God's honest truth. Buffalo crapped out for the first half of the 3rd before they came around. It wasn't until the 12:53 mark of the 3rd Period when Derek Roy way able to get a horrible, sloppy goal to make it 3-3! And all the Yankee transplants went crazy! It felt like a Buffalo home game again!

The game went to Overtime. Buffalo defenseman Steve Montador had the puck behind the Buffalo net and tripped on the ice...*watch out for that ice, it's very slippery!* In doing so, Steve coughed up the puck to the pressing Carolina forward Sergei Samsonov, who rang the puck past Ryan Miller to win it for the Hurricanes 1 minute and 47 seconds into Overtime...Grandpa, Uncle Michael, Shannon, and I just stood there; shaking our heads in absolute disbelief!

After that, the whole party got into their respective cars to head back to Uncle Michaels. On the way back, Uncle Michael, Grandpa Ziggy, Shannon, and I stopped off at Kroger to get some donuts and hot chocolate.

Once we got back to Uncle Michael's house, we all commiserated about the Buffalo loss around a bottle of Mr. Tracy's Cherry Herrings...it's some really good cherry hooch!

Cherry Herring Ingredients:
1 gallon glass jar with lid
Cherries (the ones with pits)
Sugar

Whiskey...any whiskey will do, but Mr. Tracy used Barton Whiskey.

Fill jar to the top with cherries, then pour 1 cup of sugar, fill rest of the jar up with whiskey, cap the jar, and wait at least 1 year, if not two or more, then savor the wholesome warmness.

The next morning was rough, to say the least, for Uncle Michael and me. I think the two of us polished off a whole mason jar of cherries...we were a little foggy and hurting...until early afternoon.

Uncle Michael and the rest of us were slightly hungry, so he decided to take us to his restaurant Ziggy's Restaurant and Sports Bar, located at the Factory on 1839 South Main Street, Wake Forest, NC. There he spoiled us with delicious pizza, wonderful fried dough, wings that would give Buffalo a run for their hot sauce, and a good Philly steak and cheese. Though the sub was good, it was nothing like an authentic Philly or Jim's Steakout sub.

Eventually Saturday morning was upon us. That day, Shannon and I met up with Shannon's Uncle Bobby and Aunt Vicky, who also lived in Raleigh. Unfortunately Uncle Bobby was a Hurricanes fan...Jesus taught us to forgive those who trespass against us, so I suppose Uncle Bobby is forgiven.

Breakfast was fun with the two of them, but before we knew it, we were back on the road again.

Next on our travel plan was to head up north to Shannon's Aunt Betty and Uncle Warren's place outside Baltimore.

It had been a week since we were in the D.C. area and D.C. was hit with another snow storm. They were not even able to recover from the first storm the week prior. Driving conditions were very poor, but we made our way.

Aunt Betty and Uncle Warren had a special dinner made up for us...chicken wings with Franks Red Hot sauce! Angels from Heaven must have sent them a message! We ended up spending the night with Aunt Betty and Uncle Warren.

We had breakfast with them that Sunday morning. After breakfast, we were back on the road, headed home!

Round trip, 2004.0 miles!

March 2010

The last time I was in Detroit was in 2005. My father, the Donald, took me to Detroit during August for the Woodward Dream Cruise. The Cruise was one of the coolest things I have ever done with my dad. The Woodward Dream Cruise was the world's largest classic car event where muscle cars and hot rods converged for a week in Detroit and cruised up and down Woodward Ave.

However, this trip to Detroit was not for cars but to invade Hockeytown.

Back in January, I asked the Donald back if there was anything cool to do in Detroit or if there were any bars or restaurants native to the city that Shannon and I should go to.

"Why the hell would you want to go to Detroit?!" my old man said.

"Well, Shannon's brother Kyle is going to school at Bowling Green, Ohio, and he's only an hour away from Detroit. So I figured..." I said until my old man cut me off.

"Yeah to go see a hockey game or something?" my dad questioned.

"Of course," I said.

"Well, tell you what. If the stadium is downtown, just watch the game from Kyle's dorm room," said my old man.

I said, "Well, I just thought it would be a nice experience..."

My old man cut me off again and said, "What?! To die? Or to get shot? I wouldn't even go into downtown Detroit with the two guns I carry!"

Shannon piped up, "Yeah, I don't think we really need to go to the game. I don't really want to die…"

Me being me said, "Well, you gotta die sometime. And if you survive, well, you have a nice story to go along with it."

From as far back as I can remember, my old man had raised me on the philosophy "do as I say, not as I do." On the other hand, my mom would be the first one to say, "When the hell has Adam ever paid attention or listened to a word of what his father had said!?" And with that being said, Shannon and I were bound for Detroit Rock City!

It turned out that Shannon's brother Kyle was on spring break the week before the game. To be exact, the game was on a Saturday night, March 13, 2010, and Shannon and I were Kyle's ticket back to school.

Bowling Green, Ohio was about six hours away from Rochester, New York. Shannon, Kyle, and I left Rochester on Friday around 4pm. We hopped onto the 90 and drove the extremely boring and flat ride highway through New York, through Pennsylvania, and across the entire state of Ohio…emphasis on flat and boring.

One of the highlights of driving across the 90 was when we were in Ohio because we passed through Sandusky, home to Callahan Auto Parts! Callahan Auto Parts were best known for their brake pads.

By the time we arrived in Bowling Green, it was about 10pm. Kyle asked us if there was anything we wanted to do. He mentioned that there was a "downtown" Bowling Green with bars.

Before you could crack open a beer, we found ourselves walking down Main Street. Kyle took us into a cool bar called Cla-Zel. From the outside, it appeared to be an old movie theater, still with a ticket window and the huge neon billboard sign out front. The inside of the bar still had the movie screen, but they were showing music videos, and there was a dance floor in front of the screen. The actual bar was located in the center of the theater. That joint definitely had a cool atmosphere to it. They also had Labatt Blue, which helped the appeal.

After Cla-Zel, we continued bar hopping and soon found ourselves down the street at the Brathaus, a German style bar. It was cool in there too. They had church pews for seats. They also had a few autographs from Bowling Green alumni. They too had Labatt Blue. PS-Former Buffalo Sabre Brian Holzinger was a Bowling Green alumni and probably got drunk in the same bar that I was getting drunk in.

Before we knew it, it was 1:30 or 2am and Shannon and I had the midnight beer munchies. So Kyle walked us back down the street to the Corner Diner. After getting situated at the Corner Diner, the waitress told us that they only take cash and they did not have an ATM. However, the bar next door did have an ATM. So yours truly nominated himself to go next door to get some cash from the ATM.

I soon found myself at the ATM inside Howards Club H. After I got some cash, I was belly up to the bar to pop a shot of Jose Cuervo, before I wandered back next door to the Corner Diner.

As I approached my spiny stool at the diner, I noticed that my bacon cheeseburger and Coke that I had ordered had been up. That was the absolute best 2am bacon cheeseburger that I had ever had.

I think bed time was somewhere around 2:30am

Saturday morning, like every other morning, came around way too quick. My head was feelin' alright, but I was just a bit foggy. I did my usual morning routine: poop, shower, and brush teeth.

Since we were in Ohio, I really wanted to take Shannon and Kyle to the US Air Force Museum in Dayton, Ohio. A few years back in 2004, my old man, the Donald, took me there and I do have to say that it is one of the coolest places I had visited. The air force museum had three airplane hangars full of aviation history from a replica of the Wright Flier all the way up to the Stealth Bomber. And to top it off, the museum was free of charge! However, Bowling Green was two hours away from Dayton. I told Shannon and Kyle that the museum opened at 9am and I would like to get there when it opened because there was so much to see. Plus we were on a tight schedule. You see, we also had to go to the Buffalo Sabres @ Detroit Red Wings game that night. Detroit was an hour and a half north of Bowling Green. So, in usual fashion, we didn't even leave for the museum until 9:15am.

We finally arrived at the USA Air force Museum at 11:20 am. The first hanger at the museum documented the birth of aviation up through post WWI. There, they had a replica of the original Wright Flier along with pieces of the original propellers from the Flier.

There was also an exhibit on the Red Baron and how he was a WWI flying Ace. They did have a piece of cable from his plane that was shot down over France during the war...for the record, Snoopy shot down the Red Baron.

The three of us were not even done with half of the first hanger when I looked down at my phone to check out the time. It was already 12:20pm. I said, "Uh, hey guys, we've already spent an hour in the first hanger and we're not even done with it...there's still two more hangers to go, and we need to boogie by 2pm so we can get back to Bowling Green, pick up Kyle's friend, and then head up to Detroit for the game..."

There was just way too much to see at the museum to cram it into two and a half hours. There was a Holocaust exhibit with rare artifacts including a prisoner's uniform and firsthand accounts of what happened to those prisoners.

The museum also had the original, not replica, of Boeing B-29 *Bockscar,* which dropped the atomic bomb on Nagasaki on August 9th, 1945, during World War II. It felt a little weird walking around and underneath a piece of world history like that.

The museum had a small exhibit dedicated to Walt Disney and his efforts during World War II. Walt Disney Productions created 1200 cartoons for the military from patches, to movies, to aircraft nose art. There was one series named the "Snow White" Squadron, where each air craft was named and painted after Snow White or one of the Seven Dwarfs.

The museum was incredibly fun and full of great history and information. Unfortunately we were running low on time, so the three of us did not get to see everything or read every plaque. Two and a half hours was definitely not enough time to spend there. We needed more like a whole day.

We ended up booking out of the museum by 2pm because we still had a two hour car ride back up to Bowling Green, then drive north for about another hour to Detroit for the game.

Long story short, Shannon, Kyle, and I finally found ourselves drinking some of Rochester, New York's finest beer, Genesee Bock Beer, on top of the parking garage adjacent to Joe Louis Arena at 6:20pm. And yes, that was free advertisement for Genny considering we brought the Bock Beer across four state lines, just so we could enjoy its wonderful taste!

After downing a few of them beautiful frothy brews, we started to head in towards the arena.

We entered the arena from the Gordie Howe entrance; where we were greeted by a larger than life statue of Gordie Howe taking a slap shot.

We found our seats in short order; however, our seats were completely on the opposite side of where we entered the arena.

On our venture to our seats, we were not heckled too badly by the Red Wing fans. Honestly, they were nice and polite. I did not expect any jeering since there wasn't any real bad blood between the two teams.

Once we found our seats in section 212C, it was time for the starting lineup and National Anthem.

Sabres goaltender/Silver Medalist/Olympian MVP Ryan Miller was originally from East Lansing, Michigan. So when Miller was announced for Buffalo's starting goalie, he had a pretty big ovation; probably half the crowd cheered for him. Also, Ryan's brother Drew played for Detroit. There were quite a few fans that had homemade Miller t-shirts; ½ were in support of Buffalo and Ryan and the other ½ of the shirt was in support of Detroit and Drew.

Right before puck drop, local band Kiss was being blasted overhead as the two centers skated towards each other for the face off. Detroit came out hungry and the Sabres came out looking tired and slow. The night before, the Sabres had lost to the Minnesota Wild on home ice 2-3. In the meantime the Red Wings were in 9th Place and struggling to stay alive in the playoff hunt.

For the first few minutes, the Sabres were just chasing Detroit around as Detroit buzzed around all over the ice. It was just a matter of time before Detroit was going to score. Well, it only took two minutes and two seconds for Detroit's Pavel Datsyuk to score off of a rebound at an extremely difficult angle. Shannon and I had watched the whole play evolve behind Ryan Miller's right shoulder.

Within 3 minutes and 15 seconds into the 1st Period, Detroit's Patrick Eaves skated across Buffalo's blue line, fought off the Buffalo defenseman that was bugging him, and shoveled that puck in front of Ryan Miller, and scored.

I looked at Shannon and said, "Dah fudge!" Only I didn't say "fudge."

I then looked at Kyle and said, "You're driving home, but I'm going to get us to the casino first..."

Well, I had asked my old man a few months before about what to do in Detroit, but he wasn't too helpful. All he told me was that I was going to get shot. Well, I did some research anyway and found out that there were a few casinos in downtown Detroit. I figured that I would ask the guy next to me about Detroit, considering he was cheering for the Red Wings. I don't know, but I had a hunch that since he was cheering for Detroit, then he would know a little about the city.

The man was actually nice and he was probably in his 60s or so. He was not from Detroit originally, but rather Canada. I can't remember if he said he was from Nova Scotia or Newfoundland. Any who, his father moved the family down to Detroit while he was only 12. He said at the time, he had no idea what hockey was, which I thought was blasphemy for being Canadian. He said since living in Detroit, the Red Wings became his team. Considering that the Olympics had just ended two weeks before and that Canada had beat USA for the gold medal, I asked my new found buddy who he cheered for and if he had any difficulty picking sides. He said that he cheered for the Americans and that he did not have difficulty picking sides because he's American and has been one for quite some time. He told me some things about Detroit. He mentioned that there was a tram that my party could pick up right in front of the arena and it would take us around town. He did say that we should stop in Greektown and that there was a casino right there too. He also said that I would not get shot downtown.

The game went on and Buffalo still played like crap. Fortunately for us, Buffalo got a break on a goal by Jochen Hecht. Buffalo skated into Detroit's zone and Buffalo's Jason Pominville shot a bouncer towards the net. Detroit's goalie Jimmy Howard had difficulty with the bouncing puck and Buffalo's Hecht came skating by to pop in the rebound at seven minutes and two seconds into the 1st Period.

The game was definitely packed full of hard hits and Buffalo native Patrick Kaleta was not bashful when it came to dropping the hammer on a few Wings.

There was some sloppy play too that led to a couple of odd man rushes late in the 1st Period for both teams. At first glance, the pucks appeared to go in, but they did not and the score at the end of the first remained Detroit up 2-1.

Five minutes and 30 seconds into the 2nd Period, Buffalo got another break. Buffalo's Tim Connelly skated into the Red Wing's zone and hopped, skipped, and jumped around two Detroit defensemen before he took a shot on Howard. Howard made the save, but could not control the rebound, the puck bounced out right in front of him. Sabres forward Hecht slipped the puck past over an out of position and diving Howard and into the net to make it a tied 2-2 game.

After Buffalo tied it up, they went to sleep, as per usual. As a direct result, Detroit had several beautiful opportunities to go up by one or two or three goals, but Ryan Miller warded off the shot and kept Buffalo in the game.

Eventually all those beers caught up to me and I had to take a leak. It was quite the journey trying to find the latrine. It felt like there were only four sets of bathrooms for the entire Arena. Even during the play, there was still a line of 10 people deep waiting for the bathrooms.

The 3rd Period started and Buffalo looked good, laying the shots on heavy and skating quick, but Detroit was still awake, hungry, and playing with the energy of spring chickens. Both teams had great scoring chances throughout the 3rd Period, especially when Detroit was up on the power play.

Buffalo did have a great chance to go up by a goal with 4 and a half minutes left in the 3rd, but the Buffalo player cranked the puck off the post.

With less than two minutes left in the game, a Buffalo player took a delay of game penalty when he shot the puck over the boards. The Red Wings were dangerous enough to begin with, but when they were fighting for a playoff spot and on the power play, watch out because they can get red hot. The Red Wings had several opportunities in the dying seconds of the 3rd to win the game but Buffalo's goaltender and East Lansing's own Ryan Miller kept the Sabres in the game.

Since there was still time left over on Buffalo's penalty, it carried over into overtime, where they played 3-on-4 hockey. It didn't take long for Detroit to score. 30 seconds into overtime and Detroit's Brian Rafalski slapped a one timer past Ryan Miller to win 3-2 over Buffalo...Rafalski was Miller's team mate for Team USA hockey a few weeks before.

I liked the Joe Louis Arena. I liked how they had two levels and they were still able to cram in 20,000+ fans in there. I also liked how they sold Canadian beer, like Molson XXX.

What I didn't like: Buffalo not winning the game, but we still got a point because we made it to overtime.

After the game ended, we were going to take the tram around town. That plan was nixed because the tram was backed up. Also, our parking garage was going to close two hours after the game ended and I didn't want to risk being locked inside the parking garage. We figured that we would have been behind the 8 ball if we took the tram, so we decided to hop into the '03 Dodge Caravan and take the scenic route to the casino.

After a few red lights and a traffic circle, we drove past a Hard Rock Cafe, then found ourselves on Woodward Ave, driving past Comerica Park, which was home to the Detroit Tigers. We also drove past the sports bar Hockeytown, which we were advised to go to. I spun a U turn on Woodward to go back to Hockeytown to find parking. We couldn't find any parking in the immediate vicinity, but a few blocks down, we did stumble across Bookies Bar and Grill. It looked like a wonderful place to grab a quick drink and directions to the nearest casino.

I asked the two dudes outside, who were smoking, where the closest gas station was where I wouldn't get shot. The two dudes just looked at each other and laughed. They said, "Dude, you're in Detroit, you won't get shot! Just go back down Woodward and there are a few gas stations there. Or if you have enough to get back on the highway, just pull off at any exit..." Then they laughed and said jokingly, "Well, you might get shot wearing that!" referencing my Sabres blue and gold jersey.

I told them thanks and that my other question was where the closest casino was. They pointed over my shoulder and said that one. I turned around to look and said to them, "Hey, that's a parking garage!"

The two dudes said, "Yea, that's the parking garage *to* the casino."

I told them thank you, went inside, pounded my Labatt Blue and the three of us were on our way to the casino.

Before you could crack another one (which Shannon and I did) we were in the parking garage to the MGM Grand, and by the time Shannon and I were done guzzling our Genny Bock Beers, we were being ID-ed at the casino.

Shannon and Kyle eyed up the penny slots, but I really wanted to try my luck again at the roulette tables. After walking around the casino probably five times, I found a table. The minimum bid was $15...a little too much for me considering I didn't even make that much money an hour at work. I walked around a little more and found another packed roulette table. That one was $20 a round. Seeing how my Sabres lost in OT, I felt that luck was against me. Plus those table games were too much for me and I wasn't a high roller.

I walked around some more, got lost, found a bathroom, squirted, wandered around some more, found Shannon at a bar, and bought us both Corona's with lime. Kyle was being a party pooper and was upset that we were keeping him out so late. It was not even midnight. Apparently he had play rehearsal the next day at 6pm and he was whining that he was going to be screwed up and tired for rehearsal...Yes, that's correct, rehearsal was 6 at night...I had no comment. My mom always said, "If you don't have anything nice to say, then don't say it at all," hence my "no comment."

Kyle drove us back to Bowling Green. We didn't get back until 1:30 am. I stayed up late enough to nuke some Chef Boyardee. When I was done eating, we had to spring the clocks ahead due to daylight savings time, so it was technically 3am when we all passed out.

Considering that it was already Sunday morning, 10am came extra quick. Kyle was having some friends stop over for breakfast so they could meet Shannon and me. Apparently Kyle still needed some breakfast supplies so Shannon and Kyle ran out to Aldi real quick to pick some stuff up.

Shannon admitted to me that it was the little things in life in New York State that she liked and appreciated, like being able to buy alcohol on a Sunday morning. Apparently Aldi sold wine for $3 a bottle, but they didn't sell on Sundays. Gotta love New York, especially Erie County, where you can buy booze at 8am on a Sunday and the bars stay open 'til 4am!

One of Kyle's friends that stopped over was Sarah. Sarah was interesting. She made head cheese and she told us all about it...I was curious so I asked Sarah about it.

The head cheese that Sarah made came from a bore's head. As I mentioned earlier, I did not like dead stuff, but I knew that if I didn't ask Sarah about head cheese, then my mind would be wondering and pondering about it all day.

So I asked Sarah, "Where does one find a head of a bore?"

Sarah told me, "Craigslist."

Then I asked her, "So what do you do? Just type in pig's head under the search box?"

Sarah told me "no" and that she put out a wanted ad and within 24 hours, she had two responses; both were farmers who raised bores. Sarah ended up going to one of the farms because she wanted to see the process of killing a bore. Sarah said that it wasn't as bad as we would think...

Apparently the farmer shot the bore in the head with a gun to stun the pig and then slit its throat. The bore was then somehow clamped by its ass and lifted up so all the blood would drain out. Once the bore was raised up, the farmer began to clean the bore and take the hide off of it. Sarah said due to the bore being hung up and gravity, that the cleaning process was not as bloody and messy as one would think.

I asked Sarah, "Ok, then what happens? Does the farmer just chop off the head and toss it in a garbage bag?"

Sarah replied with, "Yeah, pretty much...I got the bag home and my husband Kent saw the snout sticking out through the bag and asked me what it was, and I told him...he didn't want any part in it..."

I asked Sarah how one goes about cooking a bore's head.

Sarah instructed me that one needed to let the bore's head sit in cold water for at least a few hours so the rest of the blood drains out of the skull.

I asked her if she did that step in her garage or outside.

She told me that she did it in her kitchen sink...sounds a little *Lord of the Flies* if you ask me.

After that, one had to clean the bore's ears and get all the shit out of there. Next, shave the head to get the hair off. Plus you have to clean the teeth to get all the shit off of that too. Additionally, before you throw the head into the pot, you need to pluck out the eye balls! Thanks, but, no thanks!

If you haven't thrown up yet, the next step was to toss the bore's head into a huge pot and garnish the boiling water with garlic, basil, bay leaves, and crap like that. Then the bore's head is cooked for however long it takes.

Eventually when it's done cooking, one needs to scalp the bore...peal back the skin off the bore's dome to get the meat and get rid of the gristle! Then the juice that the head had been cooking in was to be put into a pan. Next, dump the meat chunks into the pan of juices. At room temperature, the juice solidifies like Jell-O...kind of like fruit cake.

According to Sarah, head cheese went great as just chunks by themselves or on a sandwich...I hoped that I never wound up at her house for dinner, I just might end up on the menu!! Needless to say, I had a veggie sub at Subway for lunch that day.

After breakfast, Kyle took us back to Main Street, Bowling Green. Main Street, Bowling Green looked a lot different during the day time than at 2am. Any who, Kyle took us to some coffee joint named Grounds for Thought where I had some coffee to clear up the fog. The place was cool, it sold old vinyl and books. I ended up picking up a Jack Handy book. Jack Handy was the dude from Saturday Night Live that wrote the *Deep Thoughts*.

Kyle then took us over to the Cookie Jar, where they made, you guessed it...COOKIES! Surprisingly the cookies were really good, and according to Kyle, the Cookie Jar FedEx-ed cookies to anywhere.

Eventually we had to say our goodbyes and Shannon and I were back on the road again...traveling I-75 North up to Toledo, to the 90, eastbound through Cleveland, up through Erie and across Buffalo to Rochester.

Shannon and I got home by 9:30pm. Then it was bedtime.

April 2010

"I think it's time to put America back in North America!"--Canadian Bacon

I had a nice, secret, and romantic weekend planned for Shannon and me. Unfortunately, Shannon spoiled the surprise and found out where we were going. Originally Shannon knew that I was taking her somewhere on April 1st and 2nd, but she didn't know where. Plus she figured that it revolved around a hockey game. She tried her hardest to not look at the Sabres schedule, which she did a good enough job of. However, at the time, Shannon was on a really big vacation hunting kick. So when she logged onto Travelocity.com to research vacations, Travelocity listed the last vacation destinations that were recently researched, and she read "Toronto April 1st through 2nd."

"Crap!" Shannon said. Then she looked over her shoulder to the Sabres schedule, which was taped to the wall by the computer and saw that Buffalo was playing in Toronto on Thursday April 1st. "Crap! I spoiled the surprise!" Shannon shouted to herself before telling me that she spoiled her surprise. Oh well. No big deal.

Now Shannon and I were no strangers to Toronto. We had been up there for a Yankees/Blue Jays game, Nine inch Nails at the Molson Amphitheater, the Rockettes at the Hummingbird Center, and in the fall of 2009 Shannon ran the Toronto Marathon.

The Mountie tells Boomer that Honey has been taken to the capital. Boomer replies, "The capital Toronto." The Mountie says, "No, the capital of Canada is Ottawa." Boomer says, "Yeah, right. Do we look that stupid? Ottawa!" Roy Boy adds, "Nice try, Dudley."--Canadian Bacon

We left Rochester around noon on April 1st. On a good day, it takes about 3hours to get up to Toronto. Unfortunately it wasn't a good day. It took us closer to four and a half hours. There was no issue with the border crossing, but we hit typical stop and go traffic on the QEW.

If the Fast Ferry from the Port of Rochester to Toronto was still in service, then Shannon and I could have taken that, but nope, both cities fudged up that project. Though the ferry only ran for half a summer, the tax payers of Rochester were still paying for their half of the project.

Needless to say, QEW traffic was horrible, along with driving in downtown Toronto. But Shannon and I forged on through Chinatown and finally made our way to the Delta Chelsea Hotel.

After checking in, we got situated in our hotel room. After we put our Sabre jerseys on, we pounded a baby bottle of Sour Apple Pucker. Then Shannon and I headed out of the hotel and to the Hard Rock Cafe on Younge and Dundas.

We were not even a block away from the hotel when Shannon asked if I had the tickets for the game. As I searched my pockets, I said, "Yep, I left them back in the hotel room." So we walked back into the hotel, and rode the elevator back up to the 11th floor, got the tickets off the desk, and *then* we were on our way.

At the Hard Rock, I had my usual Mac and Cheese with chicken. Shannon decided to attempt being healthy and had a veggie burger. We both washed down our meals with Molson Canadians. I felt that Molson tasted so much better up in Canada than they did down in the States.

The manager came over to our table and told us that they don't serve our kind there. He was alluding to our Blue and Gold Sabre jerseys. He smiled and then told us that our waiter was also not "their kind" because our waiter was a Montreal Canadians fan.

On our walk to the Air Canada Center, we met up with two girls that asked us if we were going to the game. Shannon and I told them "yes" and they asked if they could follow us because they were going to the game too. They told us they were from Vancouver, and had no idea where they were going, so we told them we would help them out.

The two chicks were pretty cool. They were in Toronto on a business trip and decided last minute to find tickets to the game. Since they were from Vancouver, I asked them about the recent Olympic Winter Games. They said that they went to a couple Olympic hockey games.

I asked them how they were able to get their hands on Olympic hockey tickets and they told us that there was a lottery a few months earlier for the events and the one girl was able to get her hands on a Canada vs. Germany and Finland vs. Switzerland tickets. The girls said that it was just an awesome atmosphere to be up there and they loved the spotlight on Canada and how they felt a positive buzz and felt great to be Canadian.

Soon enough, the four of us found ourselves in front of the Air Canada Center. That was where we parted ways. We wished each other's team luck and told them, "Hope to see you soon."

Shannon and I had another baby bottle of Pucker that we needed to pound before heading into the ACC. Our plan was to do as much "pregaming" so we wouldn't drink as much beer at the game. Shannon and I proceeded onward to the parking lot directly across the street from the ACC. There, we parked our dupas on a curb between two cars, and killed the bottle in about three minutes; then it was game time! The reason why we had to stealth drink in secrecy was because in Toronto, by law, you are not allowed to tailgate!

"The Canadians are always dreaming up a lotta ways to ruin our lives. The metric system, for the love of God! Celsius! Neil Young!"--Gus, Canadian Bacon.

Inside the ACC, I had to take out a 2nd mortgage for the first round of beer. They had three different sizes; small, medium, and large. My philosophy had always been, "Go big or go home." So our two larger beers were just a few Loonies shy of $30! Man, $30 for two beers! To get a nice buzz on at the ACC would cost a crap ton of cash…glad we pregamed in the parking lot.

We were about 30 minutes early to the game, so we got to see the pregame warm ups, all the way up in the nose bleeds in section 324, row 17, and seats 9 and 10…translation, the furthest back seats in la chambre (that's French for "the house").

The ACC was pretty cool. It had special "oh shit!" grab bars in every row. Shannon liked them because she thought they were for the drunk people, for when they got up to pee or to cheer, so they wouldn't fall over. We had a great view of the ice in our tiny little corner. There was an upper deck (probably a press box or box suits) that hung out and over the seats in the section to the right of us, but it did not obstruct our vision.

After the American and Canadian National Anthems, it was time for puck drop!

Half way into the 1st Period, Toronto's Viktor Stalberg took a one timer shot from the slot and ripped it past Buffalo's goalie Ryan Miller to make it a 1-0 Toronto lead.

Moments later, Buffalo found themselves on the power play with Derek Roy finding the back of the net to tie it up 1 all.

Both goaltenders were hot. Buffalo's Ryan Miller and Toronto's Jean-Sebastien Giguere were stopping almost everything coming at them.

Five minutes into the 2nd Period, Toronto's Garnet Exelby was able to shoot the puck past Miller to make it a 2-1 Toronto game.

Not even three minutes later, Buffalo responded with a wrist shot off the stick of Steve Montador that clanked off the post and into the Toronto net to tie the game up at two apiece.

I had to admit that I liked the bathrooms at Air Canada Centre. They had TVs up in the bathroom, so even when I was taking a leak, I still didn't miss a moment of play.

Buffalo had a very bad give away half way through the 2nd Period. Toronto's Rickard Wallin intercepted the puck from Buffalo and just waltzed into the Buffalo zone on a break away, but Buffalo's goaltender Miller stood tall and shrugged the puck away to keep the game tied at 2-2.

It was midway in the 3rd Period when Toronto's Luke Schenn fired a slap shot from the Buffalo blue line, which made its way past the Buffalo goaltender and into the back of the net to make it a 3-2 Toronto lead.

With about a minute left in regulation, Buffalo pulled the goalie for the extra attacker. The Sabres had several great chances to tie the game up but just couldn't seal the deal. Toronto's Fredrik Sjostrom ended up netting the empty netter to make it a 4-2 Toronto victory.

Once the game ended, we had to walk the Walk of Shame, but it was not too bad. All the Leafs fans were nice, like all Canadians were, and there was not too much trash talking.

We eventually made our way down to Jack Astor's. Shannon ordered me a Canadian and she got some other local brew. While the bartender was getting our drinks, I had to go to the bathroom really badly. In Canada, they don't say "bathrooms" but rather they pronounce it "washrooms."

The Jack Astor's was a fun place. It had two floors, the first being the dining area, and the second floor being the bar. The upstairs was awesome because there were two bars, but they were separated by a catwalk that you could walk across.

On the catwalk, there were ledges for your drinks and a plethora of flat screen TVs that lined both sides of the cat walk so anyone on the first or second level could catch a game or two at the same time. There must have been at least 20 TVs. Shannon and I ended up catching the end of the Carolina Hurricanes vs. Ottawa Senators game. That night, if Buffalo won and Ottawa lost, then the Sabres would have won the North East Division. But instead, Buffalo screwed up and lost to Toronto and Ottawa beat Carolina in a shootout (fortunately, a few games later, Buffalo was able to clinch the division). After pounding down our tall boys, it was time to head out and find Wayne Gretzky's restaurant.

We eventually found the joint and quickly bellied up to the bar with two Leafs fans, who were also at the game. It was a lot of fun talking to those two dudes. I forgot their names because the beers were making my memory fuzzy, but if I had to wager a guess, I would have to say that their names were either Wayne or Gordie. They told us that they like to call American beer "light beer" and I told them that I didn't blame them. I then told them that my favorite beer of all time was Molson Brador. They looked at me all weird as if I had a third eye or was wearing a Sabres jersey or something. I told them that Brador was not as strong as a Molson XXX, but tastier. They still didn't believe me because they had never heard of it, nor did either bartender. I told the dudes that they could pick it up at the Beer Store or at Duty Free. We ended up trading off rounds with each other. Eventually we needed to part ways.

Shannon and I began the trek back to the Delta Chelsea. The walk back was a little fuzzy. I knew we stopped into some pizza shack that sold slices. Shannon and I had the midnight beer munchies, so we wolfed down our slices. The pizza joint was getting kind of scary because a few shady dudes came in and looked like they were going to cause trouble, so we booked it.

I think we made our way to Richmond Street, where all the night clubs were. Originally Shannon wanted to go clubbing after the game, but as we walked by the night clubs, she realized that the outfits she had brought were not dressy enough. And then she had an epiphany right there on the spot...she realized that she now enjoyed the sports bars more than going clubbing!

We finally made it back to Yonge Street. We tried going to an adult novelty store, but it closed at midnight, and it was well past midnight.

Once back in the hotel, Shannon wanted to go downstairs to the hotel's bar. She wanted to go down first and then me to go down in a few minutes and then pretend to randomly meet at a bar for a one night stand...the bar closed at 1am and, well, it was already past 1am.

Bedtime.

I remembered waking up later that morning and thinking, "Oh my God! Where the hell am I?! Wait...I'm in a hotel room. That's good....Wait...Why am I in a hotel room!?...Wait...You're in Toronto, remember? Hockey game last night...No, not really, but go on...I hope that's Shannon next to me under the covers..." I pulled the covers down and thankfully it was Shannon next to me...

By 8am, I was wide awake with a small baby headache. It took some time, but Shannon and I finally got our dupas up and out of bed. Check out was at 11am. Before checking out, we still needed to go swimming in the pool, which was located on the top floor of the hotel.

After swimming and hot tubing it, it was shower time, and then check out time.

Once we dumped our stuff off in the car, it was time to walk on down to the CN Tower for lunch. Toronto's CN Tower was erected to show the world how horny they were!

We walked our way from the hotel to the lobby of the CN Tower. At the lobby, we found the menu for the 360 Restaurant in the CN Tower. All the meals were at a fixed price, starting at $49 a plate. 360 Restaurant was a little out of our price range, so we found somewhere else to eat instead. And that somewhere else was the Loose Moose.

"When have you ever heard anyone say, 'Honey, let's stay in and order some Canadian food?'"--Smiley, Canadian Bacon

I enjoyed the Loose Moose. It looked and felt like a clean dive. And their bathrooms, besides being clean like the rest of Canada, had really cool paintings of their moose logo. For example, the moose was painted up as Jimi Hendrix, from the fro in the hair band to his 60s get up suit. The moose was also superimposed as the naked baby on Nirvana's *Nevermind* album cover.

Shannon had some Salmon salad dish. Being the kid that I was, I had the mac and cheese.

The Moose also had an awesome booze bottle display hanging from the ceiling. Every five or 10 foot section was a different bottle, such as Jose Cuervo or Corona bottles. They were all back lit and took the shape of a roller coaster track.

After food, we made our way back down to the CN Tower and paid our fare up to the observation level. I wanted to run up all the stairs, just like Boomer did in the movie *Canadian Bacon*, but I was unable to find the stairs.

Once on the observation level, I was able to convince Shannon to walk out on the glass floor. She was beyond petrified, especially when I was jumping up and down like a little kid. After I had stopped jumping, she did walk out onto the glass.

Next, we made our way outside. I asked Shannon for a penny, but she refused to give me one. She didn't want to be deported out of Canada for being an accomplice in the killing of someone with a penny.

After some more walking around, we saw that the tower had another restaurant inside it that did not charge $49 a plate. It bugged me that we didn't see an advertisement for the Horizons Restaurant in the lobby, but that didn't stop us from having Molson Canadian and cheesecake while overlooking Toronto Island and Lake Ontario.

Eventually it was time to leave Canada's largest schlong. We had to take the elevator to go back down. And yes, I did jump while the elevator was going down. On our decent from our great glass elevator, I was able to see across the street, that there was a brewery!

The elevator conveniently dumped us off into the CN Tower's gift shop…I was not surprised that our visit ended in a gift shop.

We walked past SkyDome (Rogers Center) and across the street to the Steam Whistle Brewery.

At Steam Whistle, there was a huge line, almost out the door. Soon enough, we were at the front of the line. I wanted to take the beer tour, but the next tour was in an hour, which we didn't have time for, because I wanted to take Shannon to Casa Loma. So instead we bought a 6 pack of Steam Whistle and tried unlimited free samples at their bar.

After Steam Whistle, we began the trek back to the Delta Chelsea to get our car so we could see the sights of Casa Loma.

The walk took a little bit longer than expected. Shannon wanted to look pretty for me, so she was all dolled up with make-up, a sun dress, and high heels...the heels killed her and her ankles, and toes, and gave her blisters and sliced up feet.

We finally made our way to the Bay on Yonge Street. Shannon refused to pay $20 for flip flops. I, on the other hand, had no problem paying for them. I thought: if it kept Shannon from complaining and made her walk faster, $20 sounds fine to me. I told her to think of it as a birthday present, considering her birthday was a few days earlier.

We finally made it to Casa Loma by 5pm. The sign on the door said they close their doors at 4pm. I was a bit upset that we missed out.

The last time I was at Casa Loma was about 12 years ago for my 8th Grade class trip. When I went in 8th grade, it was early June, so all the flowers were blooming and the green foliage was in full swing, as opposed to a brown and dreary late March. I told Shannon it meant that I just had to take her back to Casa Loma again during the summer.

After Casa Loma, we decided to head back home. We took the QEW back down to the Queenston/Lewiston Bridge, but before we crossed back over into the States, I had to stop off at Duty Free. I need to take a little piece of Canada home with me. Something you can only find at Canada's Beer Store or Duty Free and that would be my favorite Canadian beer...Molson Brador! Shannon bought some Alexander Keith's because that was her favorite Canadian beer. Plus it was pretty hard to find in the States.

Customs was a breeze.

Next we stopped off in Niagara Falls to Mighty Taco. There we picked up a few 3 Cheese Nacho Burritos and two cups of water. Shannon looked at me kind of weird for ordering water.

Onward we went, to Goat Island to have a little romantic dinner, overlooking Niagara Falls.

Once we got to Goat Island, then and only then, did I dump out the cup full of water. Then I filled them with some tasty Molson Brador; because you know, Molson salutes responsible drinkers.

***

The following weekend, Shannon and I were back on the road, yet again.

Saturday April 10, 5:00am, the alarm went off...snooze.

Saturday April 10, 5:09am, the alarm went off...snooze.

Saturday April 10, 5:18am, the alarm went off...snooze.

Saturday April 10, 5:27am, the alarm went off...Shannon and I finally pealed our dupas up and outta bed...it was painful.

Shannon and I had to get up bright and early that Saturday morning because we were attending her cousins Bobby and Abi's baby shower down in Philly; the same cousins we went to the Flyers game with. Though the shindig did not start until 1pm, Shannon and I still needed to wake up and get in gear. Also, I still needed to pack.

Shannon's mom, Joanie, was also going with us. Joanie was going with us because the shower was on her side of the family.

We were officially on the road a little before 6:30 am. The two women slept for the first leg.

Driving from Rochester, eastbound down the 90 to Syracuse sucked because the breaking sun was shining in my eyes and sun glasses didn't do squat. Additionally, it didn't help that I was sleepy and wanted to go back to bed.

Once we hit Syracuse, the ride got better because we took I-81 South and the sun wasn't in my eyes anymore.

We took Interstate 81 South until we were just outside Scranton, PA. That was where we hopped onto the Penna-Turn Pike, which eventually dumped us off into Philly. The ride down only took us five and a half hours.

We arrived in Philly at noon, but the shower did not start until 1pm. To kill time before the shower, we found some local diner around the corner. The joint had a feel of an extremely tacky Italian mob movie with a ton of gold accents everywhere including mirrors on the ceiling, *classy*. The cool thing was the 99 cent beers they had; we couldn't go wrong with 99 cent drafts.

For being a baby shower it was tolerable. They had some good eats and cold brews, so I was content. I mingled with Shannon's family and ogled the '70 El Camino that was a few houses down.

A lot of people asked Shannon and me when we were having kids. Before Shannon could answer, I chimed in with a Homer Simpson reference, "I can't have kids because I'm sterile from working at the nuclear power facility." After that, no one had any comment.

The party ended around 5pm. After the party, Shannon, Joanie, and I packed up my 2003 Dodge Caravan and we headed north-eastward, en route to Toms River, New Jersey.

Shannon and I had tickets for the Buffalo Sabers at the New Jersey Devils game for Sunday afternoon. The three of us were going to crash at Joanie's mom's (aka Nana) house in Bayville, NJ.

Sunday morning rolled around and the three of us went over to visit with Shannon's dad's parents.

So there we were, Shannon, Joanie, the grandparents, and me. We were eating bagels, talking, and looking at old photos.

Shannon's grandpa, Valton Parker, asked us what we were doing that day.

Shannon told them that the Sabres were in town to take on the Devils.

I knew they didn't really care about hockey, but her grandpa asked where they were playing. Shannon said, "Newark."

Grandpa Valton said, "Newark!? The hell you wanna go to Newark for?!" He then looked at us like we were crazy. He stuttered a little, trying to think of something nice or encouraging to say, but told us, "Good luck with that..."

The game started at 5pm and Toms River was an hour and a half away from Newark. Plus we had to factor in the "parking lot" known as the New Jersey Parkway. Joanie and I figured that if we left by 2pm, that would give us enough fudge time to make it to the game on time.

We said our good byes to Shannon's grandparents and then headed back to Joanie's mom's house.

Once back at Nana's house, we changed into our Sabre colors.

Shannon's three cousins, Jayson, Katie, and Tyler, were going to the game with us. But before we could pick them up, Joanie stopped off at Yesterday's Family Restaurant on Route 9 in Bayville because Joanie was planning a surprise 75th birthday party for Nana.

As Joanie and Shannon met with the coordinator picking out food items, I was belly up at the bar. I was quite surprised to find Molson Ice had made its way down there to New Jersey. Molson Ice had a special place in my heart (and liver) that I needed to have one!

Yesterday's Family Restaurant also had a beer store connected to it too, so I picked up an 18 of Miller 64. Shannon was trying to be healthy, so I bought her healthy beer.

Moments later, we had picked up Jayson, Katie, and Tyler, leaving their parents Aunt Carol (Joanie's sister) and Uncle Steve some alone time on their wedding anniversary...*giggity giggity goo!*

The jaunt up the Parkway actually turned out well; we did not run into any traffic or slowdowns.

We hopped off the Parkway and took I-95 North up to Newark. As we got closer to Newark, we could see the New York City skyline off to the right of us, which was an awesome sight.

After arriving at the parking garage and we walked up the three blocks to Prudential Center. We made it with plenty of time to spare; we arrived an hour before game time. It felt a little weird because no one was tail gating or drinking beer anywhere on the walk in. The Devils had a small outdoor party going on outside Prudential Center with a band playing and a beer tent. Shannon and I bought a round of beer, but with beer being $8 a pop, we went back to the parking garage for our next quick, couple rounds.

There were no obnoxious fans at the outside party. In fact, some dude in a Devils jersey came up to us and asked us if we were from Buffalo and I told him, "Yeah."

The dude asked me if I knew what the USS Little Rock was.

I told him, "Yeah. That's the battleship that's in downtown Buffalo at the naval park."

The dude went on to say that he served on that ship and he finally made it up to Buffalo to visit his old ship, which I thought was great.

For the Devils game, I thought that it would be fitting for me to wear my Buffalo Sabres "Goat" signed Miroslav Satan #18 jersey. Shannon felt that I looked like a traitor because the "Goat" jersey shared the similar colors to the Devils' uniforms; at quick glance they look very similar. I told her I was going incognito.

We finally wandered into the Prudential Center a little before 5pm and got our beer. We were in our seats in time for the US National Anthem. Our seats were in the nose bleeds, but I didn't mind. I actually preferred sitting higher up because the game felt a lot slower and I could see plays develop.

It wasn't even three minutes into the game when the shit heads in front of us took their seats and right from the get go, the dumbass in front would not shut the hell up. The dumbass kept on barking "Buffalo sucks!" "Go back to filthy Buffalo!" "Buffalo's the worst city in the world!" "Go back to filthy scummy Buffalo!"

I leaned down to the dumbass and said, "We're in Newark! You want filthy and scummy, you've found it 'cause you're in Newark...New Jersey, the Arm Pit of America." *At least Buffalo doesn't live in the shadow of New York City.*

The dumbass ignored me and went on to insult Buffalo's goalie Ryan Miller and how much he sucked and how he lost the Gold Medal for USA Hockey in the Olympics, and how he needed to go back to filthy Buffalo, and blaa blaa blaa.

I finally leaned down and said, "Hey Dumbass! Miller's not playing. It's Lalime!"

And well, the dumbass ignored me and went on to sound like an uneducated idiot as he whined more about how Miller sucked and how horrible he was.

I leaned down again and chirped back, "Hey! Dumbass! Miller's not playing, it's Lalime you dumbass!"

The dumbass was quick to respond with, "Don't call me 'dumbass' again!"

Without hesitation, I yelled back, "DUMBASS AGAIN!" Well, it shut him up for a little bit, but he continued on for the rest of the game.

"Dumbass again!" made it to Shannon's cousin Katie's Fakebook status because Katie thought it was the coolest thing. I think it stayed up on her Fakebook for about a week. She would have been in for a real show if my buddies came with us because we probably would have gotten into a fight and spent the night in the clink.

Shannon never got angry or upset at games, but that dumbass was really pushing her buttons; pushing them to the point where she wanted to dump her beer on him. I told her she couldn't because that would have been alcohol abuse and that she couldn't waste her $8 beer. She was tempted to pour a part of her beer on the dumbass' seat so he would have a wet ass, but she did not do that either.

The 1st Period was fairly boring. Yea, sure there were a couple scoring opportunities for both the Sabres and the Devils, but both teams played some fairly boring hockey. At first, Shannon and I were bummed out that Patrick Lalime was playing. We both thought that Buffalo didn't have a chance by starting Patrick Lalime, but Patty proved us wrong and played as if he started all season. I remember when the Sabres used to play against Lalime (when he was Ottawa's starting goaltender) it seemed like he was unstoppable. Late in the 1st, New Jersey's Ilya Kovalchuck broke into Buffalo's zone and fired a shot on Buffalo's Patrick Lalime, who came up with a big save to keep it a 0-0 game.

Eventually the 1st Intermission rolled around and Shannon and I got up to wiz and buy some beer. We have always joked around how it was good luck for us to pee during play because the Sabres would score because we were not watching. And that's what happened, 1 minute into the 2nd Period. Buffalo's Thomas Vanek dumped the puck past New Jersey's goaltender Marty Brodeur to make it 1-0 Buffalo.

Six minutes and 27 seconds into the 2nd Period, the Devils evened up the score as Travis Zajac tapped in the rebound past Patrick Lalime. The 2nd Period continued with some boring hockey. The scoring opportunities were few and far between; it just looked like no one wanted the puck or to win.

It seemed when the 3rd Period started, the Devils had a little bit of fire under their dupas. They came out hungrier than Buffalo and had a couple scoring chances, but Patrick Lalime held strong.

With just over two minutes left in the 3rd, Buffalo's Steve Montador was called for holding and with a minute to go in the period, Buffalo's Mike Grier was also snagged for holding. This gave the Devils a 5-on-3 power play advantage.

With twenty seconds left in the game, Buffalo's first penalty expired…At the time in the Eastern Conference Playoff standings, Buffalo was one point behind the #2 Devils, and Buffalo needed a regulation win against the Devils to surpass them in the standings. As Buffalo got the puck back, they skated on ward towards the Devils zone, and pulled goaltender Patrick Lalime. Buffalo ended up losing control of the puck in New Jersey's zone, and Jersey's Jamie Langenbrunner skated the puck down and dumped it into the empty net with three seconds to spare. The Devils had beat Buffalo 2-1 on the last game of the regular season.

While on the Walk of Shame, the Devils fan that was in front of me on the escalator asked me if I was a big Sabres fan. I told him, "Of Course!"

He then asked me if I had ever heard of Jim Schoenfeld.

I said, "Yeah! He's an old timer, from before my time; 1970s. He used to sell beds for City Mattress."

The Devils fan said, "Yeah! But do you remember *the fight*?"

"Yeah! When he body checked the one dude on the boards and the Zamboni doors flew open and Schoenfeld dropped his gloves and started beating the crap outta the other dude!"

"Yeah! That's the fight!" the Devils fan said.

I asked him, "Hey, how'd you know about that fight?"

"I guess you could say I'm a bit of a hockey fan...I go way back. I like your team too..." the Devils fan replied.

Once I stepped off the escalator, I finished my brew, and we received mini hockey sticks because a few games earlier, Marty Brodeur notched his 400th career win. Thankfully I didn't have that mini hockey stick and a few more beers in me during the game, otherwise Shannon and I would have gone *Slap Shot* Hanson Brothers style on the Dumbass in front of us.

After we returned the cousins to their mom, Aunt Carol, it was time to eat! Joanie, Shannon, and I were starving! Joanie ranted and raved about Pork Roll and how it was a Jersey thing. At 10 at night, we found some gas station in Bayville, NJ that was still open and we ordered three pork rolls. Tell you what, those things fit the bill for midnight drunk munchies! The pork roll consisted of fried pork, a roll, cheese, and a crap ton of mustard...mmm, wholesome goodness!

Monday morning, Shannon's Aunt Carol came over to Nana's house. From there, Aunt Carol, Joanie, Shannon, and I went out for lunch at the Sawmill on the Boardwalk at Seaside Heights. Seaside Heights was the town where MTV filmed their shitty, douche bag show *Jersey Shore*. Thankfully we didn't see any of the douche bag dill weeds from that God awful show…that show gave a bad name to Italians everywhere.

The Sawmill was home to the 27" pizza pie. It was your typical NY style thin crust, and it was extremely good; though I still preferred Buffalo Pizza like Diva's or Bocce Club Pizza.

After brunch, we walked around the boardwalk for a little bit. The boardwalk was parallel with the Atlantic Ocean. The boardwalk was full with midway games, arcades, bars, and a couple mini amusement parks; with bumper cars, Ferris wheels, and a roller coaster. Most of the attractions were not open because it was before the summer season.

However, Berkeley Sweet Shops has a sign on the boardwalk that touted that they were "open" every day, year round. My mom and Grandpa Ziggy both liked sweets and candies, so I picked them up some salt water taffy.

Once we were done with the boardwalk, we said our good byes to Aunt Carol and then began the journey back to Rochester, which thankfully only took us six hours.

2010 Playoffs

Playoff tickets went on sale the day after the Sabres/Devils game. The #3 Buffalo Sabres were facing off against the #6 Boston Bruins. I was a little late at looking for tickets, but I was able to find a pair of Game 5 tickets in Buffalo. Shannon said she had seen more Sabre away games than home games. Additionally she wanted to see a playoff game on home ice, as opposed to traveling hours away, like we had in years past to Ottawa or Carolina. I had no problem with that; I wanted to stay local too

Headed into Game 5 on Friday April 23rd, Buffalo was trailing in the series being down 3 games to 1.

I won't bore you with all the details, but the Sabres won 4-1 and forcing a Game 6 in Boston!

Needless to say, Buffalo lost Game 6 and was eliminated from the playoffs. Like every Buffalonian says, *"Maybe next year."*

2010 Offseason

During the offseason, Sabres General Manager Darcy Regier did little to improve the team…No surprise there, business as usual.

Henrik Tallinder and Toni Lydman had both left the Sabres. However, a new addition to Buffalo was New Jersey's Rob Niedermayer.

The upcoming season was going to be the Sabres 40th anniversary and in recognition of this achievement, the Sabres came out with new uniforms. The Sabres got rid of the "slug" or "Donald Trump toupee" logo and replaced it with the original Sabres logo; they had the white away and blue home jersey.

In addition to going back to the original uniforms, Buffalo added a new 3rd jersey. The 3rd jersey was a retro looking jersey that paid homage to the Buffalo Bisons, who were the AHL team that was in Buffalo before the Sabres. (Team owner Tom Golisano must have been making off like a bandit, because Shannon and I went to the season opener, and it seemed like every other Sabres fan was wearing a brand new 3rd jersey. Shannon and I looked around the arena and said, *"There's $200, there's another $200, oh, and there's another $200…"*)

During the offseason, I decided to "retire" since I hated my job so much. I was not learning anything at work, there was no advancement for me up the company maintenance ladder, and I was miserable…and all my friends and family felt it. I decided to quit my job and go back to school so I could learn something and actually use a useful degree; I went back to school for General Motors Automotive Technician through Monroe Community College.

September 2010

Sabres training camp was upon us and the season schedule was already out. It definitely seemed a lot tougher to plan mini Sabre weekend vacation getaways since I was in school during the week and doing an internship at a Buick/GMC dealership, which included me working on Saturdays at the dealership. Working on Saturdays sucked because I had to wake up early on the weekend for work. In addition to that, it cut away from potential travel time for Sabres trips, like Chicago.

Now was around the time when I stopped surprising Shannon with where I was going to take her for our Sabre trips. With our busy schedules we decided to look at the hockey schedule and plan out that season's trips.

October 2010

I checked out the Sabres schedule for October and saw that Buffalo was playing in Chicago. I had been to Chicago a few times. It seemed that every time I flew out of Buffalo, I almost always had a layover in Chicago. Even though I had been to O'Hare International, I don't consider that visiting Chicago. However, back in 2005, I road tripped out to Rosemont for a Foo Fighters concert, but I didn't get a chance to take in the sights. It was just a quick in and out trip. I knew Shannon had never been to Chicago, and I wanted to go back and check it out...

There were a few little things that needed to happen in order for Shannon and me to make the trip to Chicago happen. I guesstimated that the trip would cost around $600.

You see, there was a dilemma that occurred. I liked cars, especially my Chevys. At the time, I had a black 1987 Chevy El Camino in our front driveway. I had the car all stripped down; motor and tranny out of the car, along with the interior. For a lack of a better term, the car was a "roller" and it sat in our drive way for the better half of a year. Yea, we looked like Bo dunk white trash, fitting right in with the South, except the car was not jacked up on cinder blocks. Unfortunately the car was a rot box; it flunked New York State inspection because the frame was partially rotted. On top of that, the doors were rotted, along with the floor boards and both quarter panels. Other than that the car was solid. I was contemplating restoring the car, but the more I looked and researched, the more headaches I got and realized it wasn't worth my time and effort.

Any who, this was where the dilemma came in...I was a fan of Craigslist.com and I was always searching for old Monte Carlo SS, Camaros, Mustangs, and El Caminos. Well, the one day I was trolling Craigslist, I found another 1987 Chevy El Camino that was in way better condition than my rot box. Not only was the El Camino on Craigslist not a rust bucket, but the thing ran! And on top of that, it was only $800.

I mentioned it to Shannon, and at first, she shot back with, "No!"

Shannon knew I wanted to take her to Chicago for a Sabres game and she was really looking forward to the trip. This El Camino thing was upsetting her a little bit, and understandably so.

I told Shannon, "Shannon, don't worry about a thing. I'm like that guy in the IBM commercials that make things happen…I make stuff happen."

Shannon replied with, "Yea, you make stuff happen, you're the one who bounces the checks…"

I reassured Shannon that no checks would be bounced and that I would make everything come together. Shannon knew that one of my dream cars was an El Camino and she knew the one in the drive way was just a huge head ache for me, on top of being an enormous money pit and eye sore. I told Shannon that I would talk to the guy on Craigslist selling the other El Camino and try to chew him down to $600 for the car, and if I got the car, then the rot box in the drive way would go up for sale on Craigslist.

I drove out to Churchville, New York to see the two tone blue '87 El Camino Conquista and I bought it on the spot for $600.

As soon as I got home, I put my rot box El Camino up for sale on Craigslist, along with a frame that I had for the car.

It took a little over a week for both things to sell on Craigslist, but I did it!

Once the rot box and the frame were sold, it was time to fly out to the home town of Kevin McAlister, Wayne Campbell, Leroy Brown, Ferris Bueller, and the Blues Brothers for a Sabres game!

As I mentioned before, anytime I flew out of Buffalo, I always, without fail, had a layover in Chicago. So I figured that direct flights wouldn't be that hard to come by. So I went to Priceline.com and used the Negotiator to help me plan our trip to Chicago. The only early flights out of Buffalo had us going to Philly first, and then on to Chicago. However, the return flight back home to Buffalo was a direct flight, who da thunk it?

So I used Priceline to book the whole thing; airfare, hotel, and rental car with a grand total of $600.

Our flight from Buffalo was Saturday October 16, 2010 at 7am.

We landed in Philly around 8am or so. Our connecting flight to Chicago wasn't until 11:30am, so Shannon and I had some time to kill.

We hadn't had any breakfast yet. We stumbled across a Chickie's and Pete's and noticed it was open, so we ventured in. Tell you what, but there was nothing like having a Yuengling for breakfast to help wash down my breakfast steak and cheese sub (it had eggs on it) and Crab Fries.

It was around 11am when the airplane people came on the PA to tell us that our plane had technical difficulties and that they were being addressed.

It was around 11:30am, right when we were supposed to be boarding, when the airplane people got on the PA again and told us that our plane was going to the hanger to be fixed and we were getting a replacement plane shortly.

It was around noon when we boarded our new plane. We soon taxied out to the runway and that was where we sat for a few minutes. The pilot came on the PA and told us that this plane was having technical difficulties and that we had to go back to the terminal to get it fixed.

So, long story short, we were supposed to land in Chicago at 1:00pm and have all afternoon to explore downtown…we didn't leave Philly until 1:30pm.

During the flight, I had to piddle. Shannon and I were sitting in Row 6, two rows away from 1st Class. I felt weird walking all the way to the back of the plane to piddle because I would have everyone staring at me as I walked down the aisle; kind of like on the first day of school and you get on the bus for the first time and everyone stared at you. So I figured I would just use the 1st Class bathroom; and I did. After I finished up and washed my hands, I returned to my seat. Then one of the flight attendants got on the PA and said, "The 1st Class bathroom is reserved for our 1st Class passengers only. The bathroom for Coach is in the back of the plane…" For a second there, I felt like it was the 1960s, not 2010! I leaned over to Shannon and said, "Don't worry; you weren't missing much in the 1st Class bathroom. It's not like they had the bathroom attendant jockey with gum or cologne, or waiting to dry off your hands."

While in flight, I was lucky enough to get the window seat. We ended up flying over a couple patches of clouds. Ever since I was a little kid, I had been hoping to catch a glimpse of the Care

Bears on top of one of these clouds. I had been searching for 26 years and haven't seen them yet!

Our plane finally touched down in Chicago around 3:30-4 pm.

We hopped on the shuttle to Alamo and before we knew it, we were checking in for our rental car.

Now I was frugal, so on Priceline, I ordered the cheapest car they had, which turned out to be a Chevy Cobalt. I really didn't want to drive a Cobalt. My in-laws had one and I had driven it before. So I asked the Alamo dude if they had any new Camaros.

Alamo dude said, "It's not the Camaro you're thinking of."

I said, "Yea, I know. It's the plain Jane V6."

Alamo dude said, "Ok, let me check…nope we are all out. All the sports cars go south for the winter. I think we still have one Dodge Challenger left…nope, that one's gone too."

I asked, "Do you have anything remotely cool?"

Alamo dude said, "Um, we have a Dodge Charger."

I said, "Hemi or no Hemi, I'll take it!"

Alamo dude asked, "Do you want any insurance on the vehicle? It's only $12 a day?"

I hemmed and hawed over the insurance. I was a little bit like Ned Flanders from the Simpsons, and I too felt as if insurance was gambling.

Alamo dude asked, "Well, what are your plans here in Chicago?"

I said, "We're going to the hockey game."

Alamo dude said, "Ok, then car insurance it is…"

Shortly thereafter, Shannon and I were burning rubber in our silver 3.5 liter High Output Dodge Charger.

Before the Charger could finish fish tailing, we pulled into our hotel, the Baymont Inn and Suites, located behind one of the runways of O'Hare Airport.

The receptionist at the Baymont was Paul. He said that he was Polish, so I asked him where the best place was to get some pierogies. He said there were a few shops in the burbs where he lived and anywhere downtown. I asked him specifically where downtown and he said anywhere.

Shannon and I checked into our room and got ready for the game by putting on our Blue and Golds and we were out the door by 4:30-5ish.

Stupidly I forgot my atlas at home. Shannon and I decided that we would stop off at a gas station and pick up an atlas, along with a few brews. We ended up stopping at the first gas station we saw. Once inside the gas station, I immediately ran over to the beer cooler...there wasn't much of a selection, just the usual crap, Bud, Miller, Coors, etc. However, they did have Heileman's Old Style, Authentically Kraeusened...*whatever kraeusened meant.* The can read, "Think local, drink local." And Shannon and I wanted to blend in with the locals and not stick out; *as though our Sabre jerseys weren't a big enough dead giveaway.* I couldn't find an atlas anywhere, so when we were checking out, I asked the cashier Apu Nahasapeemapetilon, "Hey do you guys have an atlas?"

Before I could finish my question, Apu cut me off by remarking sharply, "NO!"

I was taken back a little, so I asked him, "Is it because I'm wearing a Sabres jersey?"

Apu did not answer me or make eye contact.

No atlas, no problem. It wouldn't be the first time, nor the last time, that I would be wandering around, aimlessly lost in a big city with a population ten times the size of Buffalo.

Before Shannon and I left Buffalo, I Mapquested directions from O'Hare to Baymont and Baymont to United Center. I just wanted an atlas in case we got lost; I knew that it would only be a matter of time before we were lost. And sure as shit, moments after we left the gas station, we were lost...we were cruising down the 90 and we couldn't switch lanes to get off on the exit we needed to. I figured, posh, no big deal, we'll just take the next exit. Well, the next exit put us going right into the heart of downtown, and congratulations Shannon and Adam were now officially lost!

We were trying to navaguess our way downtown with maps on the back of the brochures that we picked up in the hotel lobby. Between the Hard Rock Café, Lego Factory, Navy Pier, and Bobby's Bike Hike brochures, we made ourselves even more lost. Suddenly I spotted a bar! I knew we weren't lost! And in front of this bar was a dude in a red Blackhawks jersey with his girl. I rolled the window down on the Charger as I pulled up alongside him. Decked out in our

Sabres gear, I told the guy that Shannon and I were completely lost and that we needed to find the United Center. The dude was nice and helpful and steered us in the right direction to West Madison Street.

Well, we still ended up getting lost due to a few one way roads that dumped us back onto the 90 again.

Shannon and I soon found ourselves on North Ogden Ave. I thought that it was cool that Chicago had a road named Ogden, because Buffalo had an Ogden, so we stayed on it for good luck. Moments later, we were at the intersection of Ogden and Madison, and there was a bar on the corner! And that bar had hockey fans buzzing around it. I figured that we should park there at the bar, get a drink or two, and then get directions to United Center.

We parked a lot next to the Billy Goat Tavern and Grill. Once parked, I went to go and pay the parking attendant (who looked like a crack head) and he said that parking was free due to the city of Chicago and that donations to the parking attendant were greatly appreciated. I then looked at Shannon and said, "Man, am I glad we bought that car insurance." I ended up slipping the parking jockey a $5 wrapped around an ice cold deuce deuce of Heileman's Old Style Authentically Kraeusened, *whatever kraeusened means*. The parking attendant dude was beyond thankful.

Shannon and I visited the Billy Goat to grab a quick round. The Goat was a pretty cool place. Up in the front of the joint was a quick service take out of greasy food and along the back corner was a huge bar. The place was slammed and the atmosphere was great. Shannon and I bellied right up to the bar and grabbed ourselves a quick round.

Shannon and I didn't know if there were any other bars in the area, and we were in the mood for some bar hopping, so after our round of beer, we left.

As we were leaving the Goat, a scalper in a Blackhawks jersey saw Shannon and me in our Sabres jerseys said, "Aw no! There are more of you guys!"

"Oh yea!" I exclaimed.

"Yea, I saw I couple of your brethren already. They are already nice and drunk for the game," the scalper said.

"Yep, that sounds like us, in true, typical, Buffalonian fashion," I replied. I ended up asking the scalper where I could get some pierogies. The scalper went on to say how there was some deli on Chicago Ave or Milwaukee Ave area. He said we couldn't walk there because it was too long of a walk. He then went on to say how Chicago had the biggest Polish population outside of Warsaw. I thought that it would be a good plan the next day for Shannon and me to find some Polish restaurant and have some pierogies!

After we got done talking to the scalper, I didn't know which way down Madison to go. We had Blackhawk fans walking west and east down Madison. Now I didn't want to look like a total idiot or tourist and ask for directions. Plus we wanted to blend in, so we headed east down Madison. Before we knew it, Shannon and I found ourselves in front of Chicago's best breakfast, the Palace Diner! And on top of that, they had beer too!

Shannon and I agreed upon the Palace Diner for food. We were seated at a table, even though everyone else in the diner was wearing Blackhawks clothing. The waiter came to take our food and beer order. Beer wise, we both ordered tall boys of Flat Tire. Food wise, Shannon ordered some stir fry and I ordered up a Polish Sausage Sammy. The food and service was amazing. The owner George came over and talked to us and busted our balls and said that even though we were Buffalo fans, he would still serve us. George was extremely nice and friendly. We chit chatted for a bit and asked him directions to United Center. He informed us that United Center was west down Madison a few blocks, but after the game, George emphasized, "Head east down Madison! Towards downtown!" During our dinner, George quizzed us a few times on which way to go down on Madison...*towards downtown!*

After we paid our check at the Palace Diner, we had to walk past our car to get to United Center. So naturally, we stopped back off at the Charger to pick up a few brews so we could have some roadies. I also gave another brew to our parking attendant, and he was very grateful again.

As Shannon and I were walking down Madison, we noticed that none of the other Blackhawks fans were tailgating or pregaming with beer. "Ah, screw it," we said as we downed another Heileman's. Now I'm not going to lie, but I wasn't too sure about buying Heileman's at the gas station. I wasn't sure if it was a cheap shitty beer that tasted like shit when cold, like Steel Reserve, or if it was a cheap quasi shitty beer that tasted palatable when cold, like

Genesee "Red Heavy" beer...Well, I felt that Heileman's tasted great ice cold and half way decent warm.

Shannon and I finished pounding down the beer right in front of the main doors to United Center.

As soon as we passed through the turn styles, we hopped onto the escalator, which took us up to our standing room only seats. Shannon and I were not huge fans of the Standing Room Only seats. I thought United Center's Standing Room Only was going to be a little like Scotiabank Place up in Ottawa, where there's a ledge/bar behind the last row of seats where you can put your beer down and lean against. Chicago was a little different; it was pretty much stand where ever you can see.

I had to say that United Center had extremely nice and clean bathrooms, and there were plenty of them everywhere. They also had a nice huge bar up there in the 300s with TVs everywhere, so you didn't miss a bit of action.

By the time Shannon and I had our beers and found a nice spot that we nestled in where we could see, it was time for the American National Anthem, and then the face off!

Right from the get go, there was instant action. Soon enough, Chicago was on the power play, but Buffalo was pressing, looking for a shorthanded goal, but Chicago's Marty Turco stood tall.

Three minutes in, Chicago buzzed into Buffalo's end with a 2-on-2 rush. Chicago's Patrick Kane dumped the puck off to Patrick Sharp who blasted it past Buffalo's goal tender Patrick Lalime to make it 1-0 Chicago.

Minutes later, Buffalo bounced back to tie the game 1-1 with a goal from Drew Stafford... I was amazed that there were so many Drew Stafford fans there in Chicago. I thought it was weird that 20,000 fans were cheering "*Drew!*"

Two minutes after Stafford's goal, Buffalo skated hard into the Blackhawks zone. Buffalo's Paul Gaustad dumped the puck in front of the Blackhawk net. The puck bounced off the Blackhawk defenseman and into the net. Woo-hoo! Buffalo was up 2-1. And after Buffalo scored, I couldn't believe the number of Chicago fans that liked Paul Gaustad as well. It felt like the whole United Center was cheering, "*Goose!*"

Between the pipes, Buffalo's Patrick Lalime was playing some great hockey; making saves left and right and playing smart.

Half way through the 2nd Period, Chicago's Marian Hossa got a breakaway, waltzed into the Buffalo zone, and popped the puck past Lalime. The game was now tied up at 2 apiece. Shannon said that she liked Chicago's little chant they sing after they score a goal. I thought it was kinda lame, considering we were at a hockey game, not some Euro-trash soccer game.

Late in the 2nd Period, Buffalo regained the lead with a tough second effort goal by Cody McCormick.

Midway through the 3rd Period, both teams were playing 4-on-4 hockey. Chicago's Dave Bolland skated into the Buffalo zone, where he shrugged off the Sabres Captain Craig Rivet, before Bolland decided to score; tying up the game at 3-3.

A few minutes later in the dying seconds of the Blackhawk power play, Chicago's Patrick Sharp crashed the Buffalo net and scored to make it a 4-3 Chicago game.

Buffalo did try with a valiant effort to rebound and get another quick goal, but even on a 4-on-3 power play in the final minutes of the game, Buffalo just couldn't produce the tying goal.

After the game was over, Shannon and I had to walk "the Walk of Shame" yet again. During our walk, we ran into a couple; the wife wearing a Sabres jersey and her hubby wearing a Blackhawks jersey. I said, "Man, how does this work out? It's the odd couple…"

The chick just laughed and her hubby said, "Yea! Go Hawks! Whoo!"

I replied back with, "Hey man, you may have won the battle, but you just lost the war."

The dude seemed a little confused and asked, "What does that mean?"

I said, "You're not gonna get laid tonight bro! Your lady's team just lost to your team. You're not getting any tonight…"

About five minutes later, the four of us were in an in depth conversation. It turned out that the chick was originally from Hamburg, NY and met her hubby, who was originally from Chicago, and blaa blaa blaa they wound up living in Chicago, but the chick was still loyal to Buffalo, and she didn't sell out to become a Blackhawks fan!

Shannon and I asked the couple if there were any other bars within walking distance from the United Center. They said not really but "Don't head west down Madison!"

On our way *east* down Madison, we saw quite a few of Sabre fans walking "The Walk" too. By this point in time, Shannon was quite pissed off. She was sick and tired of road tripping all over the place to see the Sabres not show up and sucking out. And I didn't blame her. We just spent $600 to fly out to Chicago to see our Sabres lose. Shit, we could just watch them lose at HSBC Arena for cheaper, or hell, we could watch them for free on TV!

Tell you what though, we were not going to let the Sabres consistent shitty performance bring down the rest of our mini vacation in Chicago, and hell, we had all day tomorrow to wander downtown Chicago and explore, but until then, it was back to the hotel for some shut eye.

Sunday morning had sprung, and so did something else, *if you know what I mean...*

Shannon and I couldn't spend all day in the hotel because we needed to do some exploring. And the first part of our exploration journey was to find Bobby's Bike Hike, Bicycle Tours, Rentals, and Urban Adventures. We knew Bobby's Bike Hike was located on River East Docks at Ogden Slip, 465 N McClurg Court because that's what the brochure told us.

It felt weird to go exercising on vacation, but we figured that we should at least try to work off some of our beers from the night before.

We hopped in the Dodge Charger and drove to downtown Chicago.

Once in downtown, we drove around and got lost, again! We wound up going east down Illinois Street, then we had passed the intersection of Illinois Street and McClurg Court. It was around this time when I figured that we should turn the Dodge Charger around.

A few ticks on the clock later, Shannon and I were heading south down Lake Shore Drive, along with all the tailgaters to the Chicago Bears game. I tried to find some where to pull off and turn around, but it just wasn't happening. Traffic was a little heavy, plus I had no clue where we were going.

We finally found an exit to pull off onto, and hey, wouldn't you know it, we were stuck in the line for parking to Soldier Field.

Speaking about the Chicago Bears' home, I did like the architecture and location of the stadium. I liked how it has that Roman Coliseum look to it and I just loved how it was right on the water front.

No worries here; Shannon and I managed to defect from football traffic and soon found ourselves northbound on Lake Shore Drive. Our bike tour reservations were for 9am and it was around 8:45am, and we still had no idea where we were going. All we knew was that it was remotely close to Navy Pier. And all of a sudden, we saw a sign for Navy Pier, so we took that exit.

The only place that we saw for parking was at Navy Pier, so I bit the bullet and parked there, at the $27 parking garage...ouch.

Shannon and I asked some stranger for directions. We were informed that we had a seven minute walk ahead of us until we would arrive at Bobby's Bike Hike.

Shannon and I made it to Bobby's Bike Hike in the nick of time!

Hank was our tour guide and he was pretty cool and very funny.

Our first stop on our bike hike was right in front of Museum of Contemporary Art. Here, Hank checked up on us and made sure that all of our bikes were in working order. He also asked us to turn around as he showed us the Water Tower Apartments. Hank asked us if we knew who lived there, and of course no one knew. Hank gave us a hint and told us the richest person in Chicago lived there. The first person that came to my mind was Abe Froman, the Sausage King of Chicago. I was apparently wrong because it was Oprah...Oprah was my second guess. Apparently Michael Jordan owned the deluxe condo below Oprah's top floor condo, but when MJ moved out, Oprah didn't want any neighbors, so she bought MJ's condo.

Before we left the Museum of Contemporary Art, I asked Hank if that was the museum that Ferris Bueller went to. Hank informed me that he thought Ferris went to the Art Institute.

Hank seemed extremely knowledgeable about Chicago. Throughout the bike tour, he enlightened us about Chicago's history from its early inception to the Great Fire to the World's Expo.

One of the next stops on the tour was to the original Playboy Mansion at 1340 North State Parkway. Ironically enough, Hugh Hefner did not build the 69 room mansion, but rather it was built in

1899 for Dr. George Swift Isham. Hugh moved in during 1959, but eventually moved out to the mansion in California in 1974. Apparently the long, cold, harsh winters left the Bunnies with diamond cutters well into the summer months.

Our next landmark on the tour was to the Lincoln Statue at Lincoln Park. Hank told us that back in the day, Lincoln Park used to be a mass grave for all the people that died from cholera and typhoid. But eventually the bodies were dug up and moved further up north. Supposedly, scientists think there are still at least 1200 people still at rest underneath the park. Hank then mentioned that people rub Honest Abe's foot for good luck. I went up there and wished for the Sabres to start winning again...

Hank had also mentioned that early on in Chicago's history, that a lot of the garbage was dumped into the bodies of water. The contaminated garbage water eventually went down stream and made their way to St. Louis. St. Louis was extremely unhappy that they were becoming sick due to Chicago. St. Louis asked Chicago to stop dumping their garbage in the water and Chicago refused. As legend had it, St. Louis started to bottle the water and send it back up to Chicago. That water was better known as Budweiser.

From there, Hank took us to Lincoln Park Zoo, where they had free admission. Unfortunately, we only had 25 minutes to try and see everything in the zoo, because we had more Chicago sight-seeing to do. Shannon and I were able to see the birds, felines, and primates. To our dismay, we were unable to see the bears!

After the zoo, Hank led the way to and through Old Town. We biked passed Twin Anchors, which apparently was a spot that Frank Sinatra often frequented when he was in Chicago to get ribs.

Right around the corner from Twin Anchors was St. Michael's Church, which was founded in 1852 by German immigrants. St. Michael's was one of six buildings that survived the Great Fire of 1871. We would have gone in, but Sunday service was just getting under way.

Hank eventually led us to North Ave Beach. There he took our pictures with the Windy City as the back drop. Hank also mentioned that if any of us were planning to do the observatory or sky decks in the large buildings downtown, to not do them. However, he advised us that instead of paying $15 to ride an elevator to walk around on a glass floor 100 stories above the city, we could go to the John Hancock Tower and ride the free elevator ride and enjoy a $15 adult beverage at the lounge up there. Hank added that the view of the city from the women's room was spectacular, to which all of us laughed.

It must have been a little before noon because all of a sudden, Shannon and I saw two fighter jets roar right through the Chicago skyline and over the water. They must have been the jets for the fly by at the Chicago Bears football game.

I always loved watching fly byes, whether it was at Rich Stadium for a Buffalo Bills game or watching the one scene from *Top Gun* where Maverick flew by the control tower and made his commander spill coffee all over himself.

Our Bike Hike took us south down Lake Shore Drive, past Navy Pier, and back to Bobby's HQ.

Once we got done with our bike tour, Shannon and I were starving. We asked our tour guide Hank on where to go for some good Chicago deep dish pizza. He recommended going anywhere, but the closest pizza places were either Pizzeria Uno or Due on Wabash Avenue. We said, "Great, can you show us how to get there?"

From Bobby's Bike Hike, Hank told us to head down Illinois Street a few blocks and turn onto Wabash.

By the time Shannon and I reached Wabash, we forgot whether we needed to take a left or a right. We decided to take a left and we soon found ourselves standing in front of the newly built Trump Tower. Shannon and I figured that we went the wrong way down Wabash Street, so we turned around and within a few blocks, we saw Pizzeria Uno on one block with Pizzeria Due kitty corner to it.

Shannon and I opted for Pizzeria Due.

Pizzeria Due was slammed and there was a 25 minute wait for a table, but we didn't mind the wait, as we were belly up to the bar.

While at the bar, Shannon and I decided try some local brews they had. We tried Goose Island's 312 and Harvest Ale, both quite tasty.

Before we knew it, we were seated in an adjacent room, and our drinks were replenished. Shannon wanted some appetizers before we had some original deep dish pizza. Considering that

Shannon and I didn't want to end up like "Fat America", Shannon ordered a veggie platter. We were apparently starving, since we hosed the entire veggie platter.

A few minutes later, out came our authentic cheese and pepperoni deep dish pizza. I will admit that that was the first time I had ever had real deep dish pizza, and it was definitely an experience. Also, I think that that was the first time I had ever eaten pizza with a fork and knife. The pizza was delicious. The crust was different to my pizza eating pallet. The crust was almost like a croissant, where it crumbled or flaked away. Additionally, I was not expecting the sauce to be on top of the cheese, but I didn't mind, because it tasted wonderful.

After our lunch, Shannon and I wandered through downtown. We were trying to make our way to the John Hancock Tower, as our Bike Hike Tour guide Hank had told us to.

We walk our way to the John Hancock Tower and boarded the elevator which took us up to the Signature Room on the 95th Floor.

Shannon and I were soon seated and had drink menus in front of us. Shannon tried a caramel martini of some sort and I tried a different local Chicago brew, Emmett's Victory Pale Ale...it tasted a little like a Christmas tree.

As simple science theory goes, what goes in must come out. Shannon decided to break the seal first. As I waited for her, I enjoyed the beautiful skyline view of downtown Chicago and Lake Michigan. Before I knew it, Shannon was back from the bathroom and said, "Hey! Our tour guide Hank wasn't kidding! The view from the women's room is great! You walk out of the stall and wham! There's the Chicago cityscape!"

Well! After hearing that, I had to rush to the bathroom as well to check out the view too!

I came back and Shannon looked excited. "How was the view?! Wasn't it awesome?!"

I said, "Yep. Wonderful! I had a great view of the urinal that I was whizzing into!"

Apparently it was only the women's room that had the great view. However, Shannon said that she would do a quick recon in the women's room to make sure that the coast was clear, so I could see the view. I told her that I was fine and that it was probably the same view as from our table.

From our table up there in the Signature Room on the 95th Floor, Shannon and I had a great view of Water Tower. And as I peered into one of the windows on the top floor, I saw a sight that made me want to rip my eyes out! I saw Oprah making sweet sloppy passionate love sex with Stedman. Stedman was strapped down to the bed, all S&M style while Oprah straddled Stedman…Shannon and I immediately got our check and left.

(Disclaimer! That last paragraph was a joke. If you didn't laugh, then you don't know funny.)

On the elevator ride down from the 95th Floor, I just had to do it and I didn't care that there were other people aboard. Yes, that was right, I jumped a few times…it was cool. I even got Shannon to do a little bunny hop! It totally felt like we were free falling for a moment.

I did not find out until later that comedian Chris Farley lived in an apartment on the 60th Floor; he died there on December 18, 1997…Wikipedia told me that.

From the John Hancock Tower, Shannon and I strolled down East Chestnut Street to Lake Shore Drive, where we made our way to Navy Pier.

Navy Pier seemed pretty cool, but it was still a tourist trap. There were restaurants like Bubba Gump, boat tours of Chicago, a Ferris wheel, and some Shakespeare Theater.

I really had a hankering for some pierogies and since Chicago had the biggest Polish population outside Poland, I figured that Shannon and I were bound to find some sort of Polish diner somewhere.

Shannon and I drove around in the city for at least an hour and a half looking for anything Polish. We found the Polish Museum of America, but it was closed. I finally pulled off at some gas station and Apu had no clue what I was asking for. Next, I asked the cabby who was gassing up his checker. I don't think he spoke English either, but he steered me in the direction of some old dilapidated boarded up church.

Well, like any normal person having a problem, you don't go to a shrink to figure out your problems, you go and talk to your bartender, and that's just what Shannon and I did.

Shannon and I found ourselves in Bar DeVille on 701 N Damen Avenue asking our bartender where we could get some pierogies. He thought long and hard and could not think of any Polish restaurants in the area. He did tell us that there was a deli around the corner on Chicago Avenue that sold pierogies, but they were probably closed, considering it was already 6:30 pm on a Sunday. I didn't care, I wanted to check and see if they were open, so Shannon and I hopped into the Dodge Charger and drover the couple blocks around the corner and found a deli, but it was lights out. However, one block further down was Tuman's Bar, which we decided to enter. It was another fine establishment of Chicago. Shannon and I wetted our whistles there. And from Tuman's, it was off to O'Hare to catch our direct flight back to Buffalo.

Shannon and I were *supposed to* have a direct flight that left Chicago at 9:40pm and arrived in Buffalo at midnight. And from there, we were supposed to have an hour or so ride back to Rochester...emphasis on "supposed to."

Apparently American Airlines over booked the flight and were looking for people to give up their seats. Shannon and I really weren't looking forward to getting back to Buffalo at midnight and then driving for another hour. On top of that, I didn't really feel like going to work at my shitty job at the dealership, let alone go to school. Shannon didn't really feel like going to work either. And on top of that, American Air was offering $500 flight vouchers per person, along with a hotel room for the night, meal vouchers, and a flight to Buffalo the next day (Monday) at 10am...where do we sign up?!

An hour later, American Airlines had given us our flight and meal vouchers and steered us in the right direction to pick up the shuttle to our hotel, the Crowne Plaza. According to their slogan, it was the "place to meet."

Now I was thinking that we were going back downtown to stay in some huge fancy high rise hotel suite...Apparently fantasy was a far cry from reality. Don't get me wrong, the Crowne Plaza was fancy and all, but it was off somewhere 30 minutes into the burbs, in some business park; not quite the downtown high rise penthouse suite I was hoping for.

Monday morning came too quick and by 8am, we were back on the shuttle to O'Hare to pick up our 10am flight to Buffalo.

We landed in Buffalo well before noon.

I knew that Grandpa Ziggy always went to Seniors at St. Josaphat in Cheektowaga. I decided to surprise Grandpa Ziggy and drop by the church to say hello to him.

Once we got home from Illinois, *I locked the front door, oh boy. I needed to sit down and take a rest on the porch. My imagination set it, pretty soon I was singing, doot doot doot lookin' out my back door...there was a giant doing cartwheels, a statue wearing high heels. I looked at all the happy creatures dancing on the lawn, a dinosaur Victrola listened to Buck Owens...Tambourines and elephants were playing in the band...*(that's my Creedence reference).

November 2010

I had never been to Montreal before, nor did I take French in high school, nor did I teach myself French with those Muzzy cartoons from the 1990s.

I always loved going to Canada, because it was full of some great people, and because of they made great beer!

'Twas around the time that Shannon's and my beer stash of Richards, Keith's, and Molson Brador had run dry! Back in September, I took Shannon up to the Molson Amphitheater to see Alice in Chains. On the way back, we stopped at Duty Free to restock on rations. But through the ensuing months, our stock pile had evaporated! So thank God we were going back to Canada sooner rather than later.

Since I had never been to Montreal before, I decided to ask my Grandpa Ziggy for his insight and great words of wisdom; considering he's like the Man in Black, Johnny Cash, in that he's been everywhere. The Zig told me the last time he was up in Montreal was back in 1966 for the Expo. He couldn't remember any good pubs or taverns, but he did mention that Montreal had beautiful churches. Grandpa recommended "St. Joseph's, the church up on the hill."

Saturday morning of November 27, 2010 rolled around and I didn't really feel like going to work at the GMC Pontiac dealership. Considering that it was like pulling teeth the month before to get a Saturday off to go to the Sabres game in Chicago, I just decided to call in sick to work. Technically I was not lying, considering I was sick of work and all their bullshit.

Shannon and I were on the road by 9:30am. We took Route 104 eastbound to I-81 North. Soon after we hit 81, the weather became a white out. Shannon was a little nervous that it was going to be a white out the whole way up to Montreal, but I reassured her that it was just Lake Affect snow from Lake Ontario and that by the time we would hit the 1000 Islands, the snow would be gone; which turned out to be the case.

We eventually found ourselves at the US/Canadian Border in the 1000 Islands. The customs officer asked us what our citizenship was and we said, "US." He then asked us where we were going and I told him that we were going to Montreal. He asked us why and I told him that we were going because of the Sabres game…duh! He asked if we had any alcohol and I told him we had a six pack of Blue. He followed that question up by asking us if we had any guns with us. I really felt like flexing my two hell fire cannons and kissing each of them and saying, yea, just these two bad boys…I didn't feel like sitting at customs for hours, or possibly being deported back to the US, let alone miss the Sabres game. So I told the customs officer that we did not have any fire arms with us. After that, we got the green light to proceed into Canada.

After passing through Customs, Shannon and I passed by the 1000 Islands Skydeck on Hill Island, Ontario, Canada…Let me give you some background info on the 1000 Islands Skydeck though. Even before I was a born my Grandpa Ziggy, Nana, Uncle Michael, and mom have always gone up to the 1000 Islands for a summer vacation. It eventually evolved into a summer fishing trip with my Grandpa Ziggy, Nana, Uncle Michael, and me. Every year, we always stay at the same cabin on Wellesley Island at Wellesley Island State Park, which over looked the St. Lawrence Seaway and Canada. And every year we have gone up, all we did was fish. That was all the vacation was for; dedicated and devoted to fishing. I always remembered seeing a tower off in the distance, and it reminded me of the CN Tower up in Toronto. To this day, I still remember asking Uncle Michael and Grandpa Ziggy if we could go and see the Tower and they would **ALWAYS** tell me NO! The response I always got was, "we are up here to fish!" Still, to this day, all I could remember was not being able to go up in the Tower; the only thing I wanted to do up there in the 1000 Islands.

So, fast forward a few years…it was just Shannon and me and we were on our way up to Montreal. We didn't have Uncle Michael or Grandpa Ziggy with us to tell me I couldn't go to the Skydeck. I thought it would be awesome to finally go up in the Skydeck and see the vast beauty of the 1000 Islands!

As Shannon and I approached the Tower, I noticed that there were no cars in the parking lot, and then I soon realized that the parking lot was blocked off! First I was stunned, then shocked, followed by being appalled! I had waited my whole 26 years of life to finally go up the 1000 Islands Skydeck and they had the nerve to only be open seasonally! I felt heartbroken! I felt as if Uncle Michael and Grandpa Ziggy had called ahead and told the 1000 Islands Skydeck to close early because they knew I was passing through town.

Well, back to the story. After crossing over the Border, I-81 North dumped us off onto 401. We could either take 401 South to Toronto/Kingston or 401 North to Ottawa/Montreal.

It wasn't too long before we hit Quebec.

It was a little weird being in Quebec. For once, Canada felt like a foreign country to me. Now, you see, I was used to Ontario, where the road signs were in English with French subtitles. Quebec was French and French only. Don't get me wrong, I wasn't that dumb. I knew that Montreal and Quebec City were French speaking cities, along with the rest of Quebec, but I wasn't expecting almost everything to be in French. It was cool though, pretty much everyone we ran into knew English for the most part, so it wasn't like we were in a total foreign country.

MapQuest told us that it was going to take us 6 hours and 15 minutes, but in reality, it only took 5 hours and 30 minutes. I printed out directions, but we eventually got lost. We knew that our hotel, Hotel Casa Bella, was on Rue Sherbrooke Quest. Shannon and I were able to circumnavigate ourselves over to Highway 15 to Rue Sherbrooke. According to Eastern Standard Time, it was around 3:30pm, but according to my clock, it was well past beer o'clock. Considering that Shannon and I were in stand still traffic in a construction detour, I cracked open a few of Canada's finest, Labatt Blue Light, into a couple coffee mugs…*incognito was the way to go.*

Eventually Shannon and I had ourselves checked into Hotel Casa Bella. I liked our hotel. They had free parking and the rear exit to the hotel was a fire escape to the rear parking lot.

Shannon and I were starving, so we decided to find us some grub. We decided to use the fire escape due to the fact that we had never used one before.

Once we hit the streets, we had no idea which direction to meander in.

We quickly found ourselves on a corner of town that had a McDonalds and a Burger King. We didn't want either of that crap since we could get that garbage back home. However, we did notice Pizza II Focolaio, so that was what Shannon and I decided on.

The pizza, Molson Dry, and Labatt Bleue (that's how they spell 'Blue' in French) were delicious, but it was an odd experience…Shannon and I went to a brick oven pizzeria where the waiters were French speaking Indians and Asians…it just didn't fit the Italian pizzeria stereotype.

By the time we left the pizzeria, Shannon had felt that she had taught herself some French by studying the pizza menu; considering everything was written in French.

After pizza, Shannon and I traveled back through the freezing cold, back to our hotel, to change into our Sabres jerseys.

Then Shannon and I were on our hike to find the Bell Centre. For our hike, Shannon and I came prepared, like a St. Bernard. We used one of our coffee cups and loaded it up with some high octane adult beverage Tilt. The Tilt lasted the journey until we found the Bell Centre.

Hearing the Canadiens fans making fun of the Sabres and us did not sound intimidating at all, but rather comical. Shannon and I had been to enough places where we've heard, "Buffalo sucks!", "*Puck* the Sabres", "*Puck* Buffalo", etc. But just hearing, "*Boo le Sabres de Buffalo*" with the French accent somehow did not sound even remotely intimidating.

As we approached the Bell Centre, there was a Peewee hockey club that was collecting funds for their team. As Shannon and I were walking by, a couple of the squirts said, in their French Canadian accents, "*Boo Buffalo!*"

I said to myself, "Well, there goes your $2 American contribution."

Shannon and I found our seats up in the bleeders, Section 417, and we sat in the 2nd last row in the house. We were a bit early so we got to watch the warm up skate. Once the players left the ice, it was time to break the seal and buy a round of delicious Molson Canadian. As I recalled, Montreal had some nice washrooms up there in the Bell Centre. However, when it came time to buy beer, I was definitely missing those $6 beers at HSBC Arena. Bell Centre was charging $10 a pop. So needless to say, Shannon and I nursed our first round for the duration of the 1st Period.

Soon it was time to stand up and remove our hats for the American and Canadian National Anthems. Shannon and I enjoyed how the Canadian National Anthem was sung in English and French. After that, it was time for puck drop.

I was expecting to see a really good hockey game considering that Buffalo and Montreal were rivals and played in the same division.

What I was not expecting was seeing Buffalo's lack luster performance. I think they must have left their skates and hearts back in Buffalo.

Unfortunately, this game was all Montreal. Montreal showed up to play and put on a spectacle for their fans.

I do have to pause for a second and correct myself. Buffalo's goaltender Ryan Miller was the only player for Buffalo who showed up to play. Early in the 1st Period, Montreal had a break away and Miller stoned the Canadien cold. Throughout the whole game, Miller played like a champ; great save after great save.

Too bad the rest of the Sabres weren't playing with Miller's intensity or passion. Late in the 1st, Montreal ended up getting a two man power play advantage. Miller made a great save on Montreal's Brian Gionta, but Miller could not control the rebound and Montreal's Andrei Kostitsyn slammed home the puck to go ahead 1-0.

With about a minute or so left in the 1st Period, Buffalo's Mike Weber and Montreal's Mike Cammalleri collided at Buffalo's blue line, and then things just turned into romper room. Everyone on the ice skated over and crowded together and glove smeared each other's face. Montreal ended up getting another power play out of the deal, but did not produce anything.

The Bell Centre reminded me of Toronto's Air Canada Centre in that they both had the "drunk bars" in front of every seat…you know, the metal bars in front of the seats so that you have something to hold on to when you lean forward to watch play, or something to hold on to when you stumble up to go down the stairs to fetch another round.

Buffalo showed up to play a part of the 2nd Period, but didn't have anything to show for it. There were times where it felt that the Sabres couldn't even buy a goal, even on their dreaded "powerless play."

Towards the end of the 2nd, Buffalo was pressing deep in Montreal's zone when the Sabres coughed up the puck, right on to the stick of the Canadiens' team captain, Brian Gionta. From there, it turned into a 2-on-1 into Buffalo's zone. Gionta passed the puck off to Kostitsyn, who passed it right back to Gionta, who popped it right past Miller. Naturally the Bell Centre went wild with the Canadians going up 2-0.

I do have to say that I loved how the Canadiens' team captain was American born and I liked the fact that he was from Western New York…Greece, New York to be exact.

Sadly, in the dying minutes of the 2nd, Gionta got another one past Miller to make it 3-0 Montreal.

The two dudes who were sitting next to us were nice, even though they were Montreal fans. We got to chatting during the 2nd Intermission. I never got their names, but it was probably Guy and Rene. Anyway, the two dudes spoke French as their first language, with English being their second. They told us that for tomorrow, Shannon and I should see Old Montreal and Olympic Park. I asked them which beer they liked better, Labatt or Molson? I about fell out of my seat when they told me they love Buttweiser! I told them that they had the finest beer in Canada and they drink that American piss water crap! They reassured us that Bud made in Canada tasted much better than Bud in the States. Shannon, nor I, were not about to try a Canadian Bud.

I asked Guy about the Quebec Nordiques and why they left town. He said that they were not profitable. He did sound pretty upset that the South had hockey teams even though they didn't know what ice was. Guy did mention that Quebec City was trying to build a new arena to attempt to get a hockey team back there. He also mentioned to us that if we ever want to go to a real rockin' party, go up to Quebec City on June 23 and 24. The reason being was that it was the National Holiday of Quebec. I asked Guy, "Oh, so it's kinda like Canada Day, July 1?" Guy replied back with, "No! Fuck Canada! Up here, we're in Quebec, not Canada…"

In the 3rd Period, the Sabres still continued on with their sloppy play, including a turnover in front of their own net, but luckily Miller was sharp and on his game, including a couple times where he robbed Gionta of a hat trick.

The Sabres, with their shitty play, just pissed me off and infuriated the crap out of Shannon. At one point during the game, Shannon went on a "F-bomb" rant. "What the *'fudge'*?! Don't these *'fudging'* moron Sabres know how to play *'fudging'* hockey?! I mean, what the *'fudge*?!'…*'Fudging'* A!" Once the rant ended, Shannon noticed that Guy and Rene were staring at her. Shannon said, "Um…excuse my Fren…RUSSIAN!" Guy and Rene just chuckled.

Honestly, hearing the Quebecois, with their French Canadian accents, taunting Miller was just hilarious. I don't want to sound like a doofus, but hearing, *"Miller, you suck!"* in that French Canadian accent just sounded goofy and funny. Come on, does anyone take the French seriously? The only war they have ever won was the French Revolution, but either way, France was going to win! At least the French Canadians have won something…23 Stanley Cups. I don't think Guy and his buddy Rene knew, but they asked me, "How many Cups does Buffalo have?"

I said, "0…thanks for reminding me…Congratulations on your 23," as I saluted my Molson Export to them.

I know I've said it before, but I love how at sporting events, beer come in clear plastic cups. Even when I was taking a swig of beer, I could still see right through that cup and not miss a moment of play!

With 1:12 left in the game, Buffalo finally decided to show up. If you ask me, it was a day late and a buck short. At least they were able to break Carey Price's shut out. There was a face off deep in Montreal's zone and surprisingly Buffalo won a faceoff. The puck came back to Jordan Leopold, who took the screen shot, and made it past Montreal's Price.

After Buffalo's 3-1 loss, Shannon and I had to walk our usual walk. The walk that we've been known to walk oh so many times, the Walk of Shame.

Pretty much every other Canadien fan said something to us in French, which we didn't mind, mainly because we didn't know what they were saying. We both knew that it was a dis towards us and Buffalo, but as long as we had no idea what they were saying, we were fine. The French that they were chirping at us sounded so sweet and romantic. My only come back was, "Wee wee!'

Downtown Montreal was beautifully lit up for the Christmas holiday season. It seemed like every building, park, and sidewalk had Christmas lights, whether it was a tree, wreath, angel, or candle.

But regardless, Shannon and I were pissed off at the Sabres lackluster performance. And being Buffalonians, the only thing we knew to uplift our spirits was some spirits!

Finding a bar in Canada would seem like an easy task, but apparently Shannon and I walked down the only street or rue in Canada that did not have any bars. Shannon and I must have walked miles before we finally found a convenience store that was actually open! There was a whole bunch of overpriced beer, so we settled on a $7 40 ounce bottle of Molson Dry…7.5% alcohol to be exact, and in case you are keeping score of our drinking habits, the Molson Dry I had at the pizza joint was only 5.5%.

Soon afterwards, Shannon and I were walking down Rue Sherbrooke, with me nursing my baba of beer. That's when we stumbled upon the Holiday Inn's Restaurant Ace. It was still open, so we went in for a round of beer. $20 later, Shannon and I only had two beers to show for our bar tab.

I enjoyed how the bar did not look like your average hotel bar, but I did not like how expensive it was.

Eventually some of the beer caught up with me and it was time to piddle again. Somehow I managed to find the washroom. Once I was relieved, I washed my hands. Next I had to dry off my hands under the blow dryer. Beside the blow dryer was a rubber machine! The rubber machine had banana flavored condoms. I tried to think if I ever had a banana flavored condom before, but like any other alcohol induced night, I couldn't remember shit. Well, the rubber only cost $2 and I knew that I would have no use with a

Loonie back in the States, so what the hell, I decided to buy Shannon a surprise!

Shannon and I soon left the bar to find our hotel. Our hotel was just a few short blocks away.

It was the first time in weeks that I could finally sleep in for a change, and there I was, wide awake at 7am!

Shannon and I eventually showered and got ourselves ready and we were out the door before 9am...9am on a Sunday in Montreal was very quiet.

Shannon and I had no idea on where to go so we just ended up meandering towards the water. We enjoyed the fact that we weren't running into people or in a rat race to get anywhere.

We soon found ourselves in Chinatown. Chinatown was pretty cool, even the Holiday Inn. The Holiday Inn blended right into the surrounding area because it had the stereo typical Chinese architecture incorporated into the building of the hotel.

After Chinatown, Shannon and I stumbled upon Old Town and Notre Dame Basilica. The Basilica looked grand and beautiful. Shannon and I probably spent the next two or three hours walking up and down the streets of Old Town, just marveling in how that section of town looked old, clean, and pure. In my head, Old Town is what France looked like. We did some window shopping, saw an exorbitant amount of art galleries, and a vast amount of restaurants that we wished we could sample.

After exploring downtown, Shannon and I went back to the hotel so we could do some more exploring with our van.

Shannon and I found hopped back on Rue Sherbrooke to find our next destination, Olympic Park and the Botanical Gardens.

I would have liked to have seen the botanical gardens during the spring or summer, when they were in full bloom. When Shannon and I were there, there was a dusting of snow and all the foliage was tarped off.

Shannon and I walked through the Japanese Garden. Right before we entered the Japanese Gardens, we were greeted by a life size statue of a lion. At first, I had flashbacks to *Ghostbusters* when lion statues in Central Park were chasing Louis Tully around before they finally possessed him. Needless to say, I kept on looking over my shoulder, making sure we weren't being pursued any lion statues! The Japanese Garden looked nice even though it was covered in snow. There were a few buildings, a couple ponds, hibachi trees, and snow!

We walked our way through some other parts of the gardens before we decided to walk across the street to Olympic Park.

The Olympic Stadium looked like a huge concrete UFO. The UFO looked similar to something out of *ET* or *Close Encounters of the Third Kind.* Shannon and I walked into the Olympic Stadium. We liked that a part of the stadium had been turned into a fitness centre, *something that most Americans are unfamiliar with.* While Shannon and I were walking around, there were tons of people swimming laps in the Olympic pool, synchronized swimming in a side pool, people playing badminton, water polo in another pool, while scuba lessons were being taught in a side pool. If it is one thing Montreal had that America didn't have, it was skinny people…that meant that we didn't see any fat people up in Montreal because they were swimming, walking, riding a bike or playing hockey!

After walking over half of Montreal, Shannon and I were a little tired and hungry. The one thing up there in Canada that I had an appetite for was poutine! It's like I always say, "When I'm in Canada, I always want some poutine before my pootang!" Or was it "some pootang before my poutine."

For poutine, Shannon and I set forth back to Old Town! Our destination was Montreal Poutine. In the heart of Old Town at Montreal Poutine, Shannon and I ordered a single order of original poutine, a Sleeman beer, and La Fin du Monde (End of the World) beer…all three were wonderful!

From Old Town, Shannon and I needed to make our pilgrimage to St. Joseph's Basilica…or as Grandpa Ziggy called it, "The church up on the hill."

At the time, Montreal had a lot of construction going on, which made it hard to navigate the city. And on top of that, every other street is a one way street with no left or right hand turn. But none of those obstacles stopped us. It took us some time, but Shannon and I finally made it to St. Joseph's Basilica

It felt weird; as soon as we turned the corner into the main gate into St. Joe's and I looked up, I began to get vertigo. It was a little tough to drive with vertigo, but through some divine intervention, I managed.

There was a windy, twisty road up to the top of the basilica.

After Shannon and I parked, we walked to the edge of the parking lot, where we just looked out over the extraordinary landscape.

Shannon and I continued on with our pilgrimage into the basilica.

As we entered, we were greeted with some wonderful stained glass murals. After we turned the corner, there were huge concrete pillars leading to the base of the alter. Mass was not in session, but there were many people paying homage and praying.

Shannon and I made our way down stairs to the Crypt. Down in the Crypt, there were candles to light for prayer; leave it to the Catholic Church to charge you money to light a candle and to say a prayer…$5 a candle/prayer! Since Shannon and I were broke, I just decided to say a prayer. My mom had always told me to say a prayer every time I go into a church that I had never been in before. I decided to say a prayer to my Nana (my mom's mom). I told her that I still missed her and that I love her. I told Nana that I took Shannon up to Montreal to watch the Sabres play the Canadiens, but unfortunately the Sabres missed the ride up and lost 3-1…Yes, I liked to keep Nana updated on the Sabres and the Bills because I didn't know if she was getting the updates up there in Heaven…Grandpa Ziggy had always forced Nana to watch the Sabres, even though she said she "disliked" hockey. I think she said that because she wanted to watch something else on TV.

Down there in the Crypt was where Brother Andre's tomb was located. There were many pilgrims walking by, praying, and paying their respects.

I'm not going to lie, it was extremely creepy that they had Brother Andre's heart on display for people to view and pray to…It was especially creepy to me considering that road kill and mannequins scared the poop out of me.

Eventually it was time for us to depart for Western New York.

From St. Joseph's Basilica, Shannon and I found Highway 15, which lead us to 20 East towards Toronto/Ottawa.

As Shannon and I pulled up to the US/Canadian Border, we were well below the red line for gas.

Once we got to the customs shack, the customs officer wanted to shoot the shit, which made matters worse. We had to sit there at customs with the van running on fumes, chit chat with some schmuck about how we traveled five hours to watch our Sabers lose. All the while, I still had to drive another three miles and hope to make it to the 1000 Islands Bait Store before they closed. God or Baby Jesus must have been watching over us or helping to scoot our van over the bridge to make it to the 1000 Islands Bait Store to reload on petrol! Hallelujah! Praise the Lord!

Shannon and I finally puttered back into Western New York by 9pm…just in time to shower, go to bed, and wake up the next morning for another thankless week at work at that horrible dealership…

December 2010

The following weekend, Shannon and I were back at it; *on the road again.* This time it was to Ottawa.

Now Shannon and I had been to Ottawa before. Back November 5, 2006, we saw the Foo Fighters open for Bob Dylan at Scotiabank Place. We also caught a couple Sabre/Senator games; including the Game 4 of the 2006-2007 Stanley Cup Eastern Conference Finals, where Buffalo won and prevented Ottawa's sweep of the series. But after experiencing all of that, Shannon and I have never fully experienced Ottawa.

The Sabres game up in Ottawa was the following Saturday after our Montreal trip. I thought that it would have been a little too suspicious if I called in sick two Saturdays in a row at the dealership. So instead I went to miserable work at the miserable Buick GMC dealership.

I would rather have not worked on that Saturday of December 4, 2010, but what could I do? I didn't think that work was too bad though, considering that I only had to work until noon and that Ottawa was only five hours away.

So like a typical guy, I am always shot gunning things, and doing stuff at the last minute. After I got out of work, it was time to pack, remember the tickets, clean the van, and check its fluids. Grandpa Ziggy always reminded and harped on me to "check the water and oil" before road trips. He was always looking out for his children, grandchildren, and great grandchildren.

When everything was all said and done, Shannon and I were packed and ready to go by 12:45pm...plenty of time to get up to Ottawa.

Shannon and I took the same route up to Canada as we had done the week before. Luckily for us, we didn't run into any snow storms on the way up. However, on our drive on Route 104 through Oswego, I think I hit every single red light in town...I think there were at least 25 stop signals in town that we got stuck at. It probably took Shannon and me 15-20 minutes to drive through Oswego.

Customs up in the 1000 Islands went well, but surprisingly we had to sit in a huge line of cars, probably 10 cars deep in every open lane. The wait at Customs felt like forever.

After all that waiting, it only took 30 seconds to tell the customs officer what he wanted to know.

"Hello, citizenships?" asked the Customs Officer.

"U.S.," Shannon and I replied.

"What are you doing up in Canada?" the officer asked.

"Sabres game up in Ottawa," I answered.

"Staying the night?" the officer asked.

"Yep," I said.

"OK," the officer said.

From there, Shannon and I only had an hour and a half ride ahead of us to Ottawa, which, contrary to what Boomer from *Canadian Bacon* said, is actually the Capital of Canada...but we'll see about that...

We finally hit downtown Ottawa by 5:30pm and we soon found our hotel, Chimo Hotel. After we checked in, we went upstairs to our room.

Now once we got to our room, I had to poop, so I did my business. After my business, I had to shower. I had this thing that whenever I pooped I had to shower right after, and this was my reasoning behind it. First of all, I did not like seeing skid marks in my undies. Secondly, I wanted to feel clean down there in the nether region...I never knew when something would spontaneously happen, just like in them boner pill commercials.

So once I pooped and showered, it was time to get dressed in my Sabres gear. I decided to spice things up a bit and wear my #18 Miro Satan Sabres jersey. Shannon rocked her blue and gold jersey.

By the time we arrived at Scotiabank Place, it was around 6:30 pm. No matter when Shannon and I visited Ottawa, it was always freezing! I think we were half frozen by the time we walked into Scotiabank Place.

Shannon and I grabbed a couple Molsons before we found our seats up in Section 320.

After we found our seats, I noticed that the one dude next to us was wearing a Sabres jersey! Woo-hoo, more Sabres brethren!

I asked the dude, "Where in Buffalo are you from?"

The dude said, "I'm not. I'm from Windsor, Ontario."

I paused for a second, "Wait, you're from Canada and you are a Sabres fan?!"

The dude said, "Yea, well, you see I'm a huge Doug Gilmour fan. I liked him in Calgary, Toronto, New Jersey, Chicago, Buffalo, and Montreal. But I just really liked it when he played for Buffalo…"

I just found so much gratification in finding and meeting actual Canadians who were Sabre fans! It felt like bonus points, a Canadian cheering for an American team!

It soon became time for the American and Canadian National Anthems, and just like up in Montreal, they raced right through the American National Anthem…I think it was a new world record of 43 seconds. However, on the other side of the puck, I think they had the world record for the longest Canadian National Anthem of 10 minutes…

With Molson at hand, it was finally time for some hockey and puck drop!

I was expecting a real great game to be played, considering that Buffalo and Ottawa were in the same division and were pretty big rivals.

Right from the puck drop, I could tell that it was going to be a high intensity game. Buffalo stormed into the Ottawa zone and had a great shot on net, but the Ottawa Senator goaltender, Brian Elliot, wasn't letting anything in.

A few minutes later, Ottawa was on the power play and in Buffalo's zone. Buffalo's Mike Grier intercepted a pass from the point and skated the length of the ice, all alone on a breakaway. The only thing keeping Grier from scoring was Elliot. Grier took a wrist shot and rang it right off the post and into the glass...as in the great words of Disney's *Mighty Ducks*, "Two inches to the left, and it would have gone in...yes, but two inches to the right and I would have missed completely..."

For that night's game, Ottawa was wearing their 3rd jerseys. I thought they were kind of ugly looking. They were a black jersey that had in white "SENS" across the chest and red down the arms, they weren't visually stimulating.

The opening period was scoreless.

During intermission, Shannon and I replenished our drinks because we were parched.

The 2nd Period was filled with end to end skating and action. Buffalo had a chance to score point blank in front of the net. Buffalo's Paul Gaustad ended up digging at the puck while it was under Ottawa's Elliot. The puck did dribble over the goal line, but the whistle had already been blown for a stoppage in play; no goal.

Play bounced around both ends, Buffalo had a "powerless play" and obviously did nothing on it. There were a few odd man rushes, and Ottawa's Sergei Gonchar even cranked one off the post, but after two periods of play, the score still remained 0-0. I remember back in the 1998 Eastern Conference Finals when the Sabres played the Capitals, Gonchar was a thorn in the Sabres side.

It was just amazing how my beer kept evaporating during the game! After the 2nd Period, Shannon and I needed to refuel again.

The 3rd Period started and there was still plenty of action and scoring opportunities, but at the end of the 3rd, it was still tied 0-0.

Time for overtime!

Midway through 4-on-4 overtime hockey, Buffalo had a good scoring opportunity. Buffalo's Derek Roy skated into the Ottawa zone. Buffalo's Thomas Vanek skated toward the net. Roy dumped the puck off to Vanek for the shot, but Ottawa's Elliot was there to foil any goal scoring ideas.

Overtime was still exciting even though neither team scored.

Now Shannon and I were really getting our money's worth because we were going to the shootout! Yea, we've seen the shootout on TV, but we've never seen it in person at the game, so we were pretty excited.

Ottawa elected to go first.

Alexei Kovalev picked up the puck from center ice and skated in on the Buffalo goaltender Ryan Miller. Kovalev went for the back hander, but Miller, in the sprawled out butterfly position, stopped him.

Buffalo's Jason Pominville took the puck from center ice and skated in on Ottawa's Elliot, who came up with the big save to keep it 0-0.

The next shooter for Ottawa was their captain, Daniel Alfredsson. Alfredsson skated in on Miller, but Miller blocked the shot.

Then it was Thomas Vanek's turn. Vanek skated into the Ottawa zone and took a slap shot from in between both face off circles and the puck found the back of the net! Buffalo was up 1-0.

Ottawa's last chance to try and tie the game came down to Jason Spezza. Spezza came flying in on Miller and lost control of the puck. The puck wound up in the corner of the rink with Buffalo winning 1-0!

Woo-hoo! Shannon and I finally didn't have to walk the walk of shame!

After the game, Shannon and I decided to hang out and savor the moment while we waited for traffic to die down. We came across the Hockey Country Lodge, a bar that was underneath our section at Scotiabank Place. Shannon and I figured that we could sober up by splitting a beer and listening to the live band.

I tipped the band $2 so they could play *Freebird*. The guitarist said he didn't know *Freebird*. I hated it when live bands didn't play *Freebird*. And yes, I am *that guy* at every rock show who yells, "*Freebird!!*"

To the table next to us were some Ottawa fans, two guys and a girl (*but I don't think they worked at a pizza shop*). We asked them where in Ottawa we should go. They mentioned that we should go to the ByWard Market Square in downtown. They said while we were there, we should go to the Heart and Crown. They also said Parliament and the Mint were down there.

After Last Call, Shannon and I got the boot from the Lodge. From Scotiabank Place, it was time to head downtown.

We soon found Parliament via Metcalfe Street. Parliament looked extremely beautiful with a Christmas light display.

Parliament was lit up with red and green lights with huge snow flake lights all across it. Downtown also had Christmas tree lights up on almost every building and tree. It looked like a winter wonderland with the snow sprinkling down.

From Parliament, Shannon and I made our way over to the ByWard Market Square.

Once we parked, Shannon and I needed to find some sort of establishment that served food. The first sort of establishment that we saw was a strip joint, which Shannon objected to. We soon found the Hard Rock Café. The Hard Rock had a sign in front of it that said it was closed for a private party, but that didn't stop me from waltzing right in to check out the situation.

As I entered the Hard Rock Café, I was not greeted by any one; no host or hostess or bouncer. The first thing that I saw was horrible white people dancing. The party and dancing reminded me of a 20 year high school reunion or a business Christmas party because everyone looked awkward and didn't want to bump and grind. I knew I stuck out like a sore thumb with my Sabres jersey, so I knew it was a matter of time before I got caught. I tried to make my way to the open bar, but before I knew it, I was cock blocked and asked to leave.

After getting kicked out of the Cock Block Café, I met up with Shannon outside. I thought that if we dropped our jerseys off at the car, we could go back into Hard Rock all incognito style and crash the party, but Shannon felt like that was too much work. Also she was really hungry, which meant we needed to get a move on.

The next block up was Pub 101. I made a decisive decision and decided to go in. From the windows, all I saw were neon beer signs, a bar, and dining tables, so I figured why not...*Man was I wrong*. We should have left that dump as soon as they hit us with a cover charge, but Shannon was very hungry. When Shannon got hungry, she got cranky and angry; hangry. When she got cranky, you did not want to be around her. The only remedy to make Shannon not cranky was food. I sucked it up and paid the b.s. cover charge.

The first floor seemed a little crowded so we went upstairs to the second floor. There we found a table. We were eventually greeted by our waitress; some blond ditz. I ordered a Molson Canadian and Shannon ordered a Rickards Red. 10 minutes later we got our drinks. 10 minutes later our waitress took our order. We ordered sweet potato poutine and a margarita pizza. 10 minutes later our waitress came back and said they were all out of pizza. I told our waitress that just the poutine would be fine. 10 minutes later we got our poutine...our poutine and poutine only. Apparently our waitress forgot forks and napkins. Shannon walked into to the kitchen to find forks and napkins!

Shannon and I soon realized that the reason for the cover charge was that there was a night club up on the 3rd floor...we were watching a steady march of fat chicks in hoochie mama skirts walk up to the night club. Pub 101 had some douche bag bouncer, who was obsessed with playing with an empty water bottle and checking non-existent texts on his phone. I really wanted to see what this "bouncer" was bouncing or guarding. So, I got up from my seat and waltzed past the fartknocker, like I owned the joint. As I reached the 3rd floor, I had flashbacks to all the nightclubs I use to get hammered at up in Clifton Hill, Niagara Falls, Canada. But this night club was a lot different from what I remembered. Maybe I was older, or maybe I was more sober, but it was the hugest collection of fat, ugly broads wearing clothes that were 15 sizes too small! I wanted to gouge out my eyes!

By the time I got back to Shannon, we had been waiting another 10 minutes for our waitress to come with the check. We thought about dine and dash, but the waitress had our credit card. Eventually the ditzy waitress came back with our check and she couldn't remember which credit card was ours. We soon found it and it took another 10 minutes for her to run the card.

Once we left Pub 101, Shannon and I were determined to have fun and find the Heart and Crown. We didn't really know who to ask, but the first people that I saw who might have known were two cops.

I asked the one cop, "Excuse me, but I was wondering where a bar was?"

The cop said, "Yea, what bar would that be?"

In my infinite wisdom, I said, "The Crown Royal!"

Shannon, standing a few feet away, said, "That's not it, the Heart and Crown..."

So I said, "Yea, the Heart and Royal...what she said..."

The cop said, "Oh yea, eh, the Heart and Crown. Go down that road and take a left. It will be one block down on your right."

I told the cop, "Thank you, and PS, don't go to that bar," as I pointed to Pub 101. The cop asked why and I told him, "Because it sucks!" The cop asked why, and I told him, "The service is horrible and they are slow."

The other cop chimed in, "Hey, that's not bad. At least they will make our job a little easier..."

Moments later, Shannon and I found the Heart and Crown. Too bad for us, there was one problem; there was a huge line of at least 25 people deep, trying to get into the place. Shannon and I decided to cut our losses and find a half way decent bar that we could just chill in.

As we were walking back to our car in the freezing cold, we walked past Chateau Lafayette of Ottawa. I said, "You know what, let's go in here. This will be the last place we attempt before we call it quits and hit the hay..."

The Chateau was an enjoyable establishment. It was fun and had a great atmosphere, a normal man's bar with normal people. There was loud music with tons of people talking and having fun; not an empty seat in the place. I made my way up to the bar and asked for a Labatt Blue. The barkeep asked, "Small or large?"

Like I always said, go big or go home; so I ordered a large! Shannon and I noticed that the bar patrons wore every color and shade of flannel possible, but we didn't mind.

After the Chateau, Shannon and I made our way back to Chimo Hotel.

It felt weird to finally be able to sleep in as late as we wanted. At the time, if I wasn't at work at the Buick GMC Dealership by 8am, then I was at auto school by 8am. I was glad that the hotel's check out wasn't until noon. So there I was at 7 am on Sunday morning, wide awake! Shannon and I eventually made our way down to the indoor pool and sauna.

After Shannon and I checked out of the hotel at noon, it was time to get some grub. Shannon wanted to see ByWard Market Square during the day, so we traveled back downtown. The market looked a lot different during the day. There were people selling Christmas trees and holiday wreaths along with other vendors selling winter apparel. There were also Christmas Carolers singing in French.

I was really in the mood for the Hard Rock Café since I was denied the night before, and I didn't want to be defeated. I also had a huge hankering for their Ultimate Mac and Cheese. Shannon opted for a Veggie Burger. Any who, I needed to wash down my mac and cheese with something, and that something was Molson Stock Ale. It had been years since I had the Stock Ale. Some of the allure was that I could not get it back in the States. Also, I grew up with it on the annual June fishing trips in the 1000 Islands with Nana, Grandpa Ziggy, and Uncle Michael. Shannon's beverage of choice for lunch was Rickards Red.

After the Hard Rock, Shannon and I wandered around the corner and we stumbled upon the Heart and Crown. That time, there was no line out front, so we jumped on the opportunity to go in. As we entered the Heart and Crown, Shannon and I could see why everyone we met recommended this place. It looked and felt like an Irish pub, right down to the Celtic music and soccer and rugby on the TVs. Shannon had a pint of Alexander Keith's Harvest and I rocked a pint of Kokanee.

I'll tell you why I had Kokanee. As a kid, Grandpa Ziggy occasionally had some cans of Kokanee left over from the fishing trips. As a kid and sneaking beers, I couldn't wait a half hour to chill the beer. Up until that point in time, I had only experienced warm Kokanee canned beers. At the Heart and Crown, I finally got to try a fresh, cold bottle of Kokanee, and it was good!

From the Heart and Crown, Shannon and I meandered around the ByWard Market until we reached our next destination, Parliament.

Shannon and I did the usual tourist thing and we took pictures in front of Parliament.

Eventually, I decided to see whether or not Parliament was open or not. Shannon seemed a little nervous, just waltzing in, but I reassured her that we are Americans, so we had the right to do whatever we wanted because we were arrogant, snobby, know it all's...and those were the comforting words that Shannon was hoping I wasn't going to say.

As we approached the front door to Parliament, Shannon got more nervous, and said "What if we're not supposed to be here, what if we get shot?"

I reassured Shannon, "Posh, it's Canada, they don't have guns! Just beer and hockey sticks!"

Shannon then said, "Well, it's 3pm on a Sunday, they are probably closed..."

"Posh," I said as I opened the door. As we entered Parliament, there were security guards everywhere, thankfully their hockey sticks weren't drawn, but Shannon was still nervous.

We were greeted by a girl who asked us, "Are you here for the tour?"

Shannon and I said, "Yes...how much is it?"

"Free," the girl said.

"Yes, that's our kinda price," we said.

Our tour did not start until 3:20pm, so we had some time to kill. We were informed that we could ride the elevator up to the clock tower and take in the Ottawa skyline and surrounding scenery, which we did.

The view from the clock tower was amazing. The entire top of the tower was windows, so we were able to take in a 360 view of downtown Ottawa and neighboring Quebec.

Soon enough, Shannon and I had to shoot back down the elevator because our tour was starting!

The first leg of our tour took us right outside the House of Commons. In the lobby, our tour guide talked about the architecture, painting, and stained glass before we entered into the House of Commons.

While in the House, our tour guide discussed what order of business went on in the House and who in government sat where. Our guide showed us the chair that the Speaker sat in and then she asked us who the Speaker was. I thought it was Wayne Gretzky...apparently I thought wrong because the actual Speaker was Peter Milliken.

From the House of Commons, the tour led us to the Library of Parliament. The Library was a beautiful thing to see. The Library itself was a circular building with three levels of book cases, which were built into the perimeter of the building. The fine detail in the ornate wood was just visually pleasing; a lot of time and craftsmen ship was put into this room. Our tour guide told us about the 1916 Fire that almost destroyed the Library, but thankfully the Library's thick iron doors told the fire to simmer down!

From the Library of Parliament, the tour concluded at the Senate. The Senate Chamber was interesting as well, though a lot smaller than the House of Commons. The walls of the Senate Chamber had eight murals of Canada during World War I.

After seeing the Senate, the tour was over. Our tour guide said we were actually able to see more of Parliament because it was the weekend.

Once we left Parliament, it was around 4pm and we didn't know what to do. Shannon and I ended up walking across the street to a visitor's information building. I remembered from the night before at the hockey game, that a few people told us to check out the Mint. So I inquired at the front desk about the Mint. The lady working there said that we were too late for any Royal Canadian Mint tours.

Shannon and I didn't know what to do or where to go then. In the meantime, the snow had picked up, so we decided to high tail it on outta there before we got stuck in a blizzard.

The entire way back from Ottawa to WNY was like driving through a snow globe. Though it took us about four and a half hours to drive up to Ottawa, it took us five and a half hours to get back home, and that was including a stop at the 1000 Islands Duty Free so I could restock my Molson Brador and Shannon on her Alexander Keith's and Rickards.

***

Christmas eventually rolled around and my older sister Sarah got me a Christmas present. Sarah gave me NHL 2K10 for PlayStation2. Up until then, I was still rocking out to EA Sport's NHL '94 for SEGA Genesis. And in case you were wondering, yes, the Buffalo Sabres had won the Stanley Cup like 50 million kazillion times when I played it! Even as a little kid, Mom and Sarah would yell at me to let some of the other teams on the game win the Stanley Cup once in a while. I always told Mom and Sarah, "If the Sabres can't do it in real life, then I have to do it vicariously through the video game!"

I had to say one of the best parts of NHL '94 was knocking out Wayne Gretzky at center ice and seeing his body twitch before his head exploded with 32 bit graphic blood onto the ice…oh the memories of my youth.

The Sabres have not won the Cup yet on NHL 2K10, but I will tell you when they do!

January 2011

Though there was no Sabres game on Sunday January 2, 2011, there was *Forty: The Sabres in the NHL* exhibit going on at the Albright Knox Art Gallery in Buffalo. The exhibit started back in November 2010, but starting on January 2nd, the Stanley Cup and other NHL trophies were going to be on display. I know I had never seen the Cup before in person, nor had Shannon or Grandpa Ziggy, so I decided to take all three of us to the exhibit.

The three of us arrived at Albright Knox at 1pm and there was already a line out the door. We waited in line amongst the plethora of Sabres fans, some donning jerseys. Shannon and I noticed some teenaged pimple faced dork wearing a Pittsburgh Penguins #87 Cindy Crosby jersey. Shannon and I thought it was weird that he wore Pittsburgh gear to a Buffalo exhibit.

Grandpa Ziggy decided to treat us and paid for the tickets to the Sabres exhibit. The Stanley Cup was a different exhibit from *Forty: The Sabres in the NHL*. Both exhibits were conveniently located on opposite ends of the art gallery…perfect for an 85 year old man.

We decided to see the Stanley Cup first. It took us a while to get to the exhibit considering we had to walk down a few corridors and walk up half a dozen flights of stairs. Grandpa was a little upset that he didn't make it to the spa that morning, but I told him he was getting his work out in.

Finally, at the end of a huge flight of stairs, there it was, the Stanley Cup!

You know the saying, "TV adds 10 pounds," well I think it was true because the Stanley Cup looked small, like three feet tall. On TV, it looked like a huge, ginormous trophy that hockey greats have lifted over their heads. On the boob tube, the Cup looked like it was four or five feet tall.

Grandpa Ziggy, Shannon, and I eventually had our picture taken with the Cup. And for the record, the three of us **DID NOT** touch the Cup because it was bad luck to touch it if you had never won it before. But tell you what, there were a crap ton of Buffalo Pollocks posing with and touching the Cup! I felt like stopping them, but I didn't want to make a scene.

Also on display were other NHL trophies.

I thought it was pretty cool to see Dominik Hasek and Ryan Miller's names on the Vezina Trophy (former Sabres Tom Barrasso, Don Edwards, Bob Sauve were also on the trophy, but they were before my time).

It was great seeing the President's Trophy because the Sabres won it in the 2006-07 season.

I enjoyed reading Dominik Hasek's name twice on the Hart Trophy. The Hart Trophy was awarded to the League's Most Valuable Player.

Also on display was the King Clancy Memorial Trophy, which Sabre great Rob Ray won back in 1998-99.

The Frank J. Selke Trophy was also on display. Former Sabre team captain Michael Peca won (Craig Ramsey also won it, but he too was before my time).

Once we were done looking at the 15 or so trophies, we had to hike back to the other side of the Albright Knox to see the Sabres exhibit. On our journey to the other exhibit, we walked passed some pieces of art by Georgia O'Keeffe, Andy Warhol, Roy Lichtenstein, Jackson Pollock, Giacomo Balla and other famous dead people.

We eventually made our way to the Sabres exhibit. The exhibit consisted of at least 200 photos, both in black and white and color. The photos pretty much chronicled the team from 1970 to 2010. There were photos of the French Connection and the "Fog Game" from the 1975 Stanley Cup Finals in Buffalo. There were too many photos to describe. On top of that, there was a TV that played Sabre highlights and hockey fights. One of the highlights obviously included Sabre great Rob Ray beating the shit out of some guy at center ice. Other highlights included one of many Sabre/Flyers all out ice brawls. One clip in particular that was being shown was a playoff game back in Buffalo on May 3, 1997 where Sabre goaltender Steve Shields was duking it out with Flyer goaltender Garth Snow.

NHL in 360 was another part of the exhibit. *NHL in 360* was a film that showed that fast pace of the game. There were cameras mounted on a couple Sabre players' helmets, including goaltender Ryan Miller. The film was projected onto a 10 foot by 30 foot screen and as I watched it, it made me feel as if I were a part of the game...it reminded me of a Disney ride or attraction.

I was a little bummed out with the exhibit because there was no memorabilia. I was hoping to see some game worn jerseys that were ripped up due to a fight or Sabre goaltender Clint Malarchuk's bloodied jersey from when he had his jugular cut wide open from a skate. I was hoping there were going to be some net minder helmets on display. Goalie helmets almost always had cool artwork painted on them. Oh well, maybe they'll have it for the 50th Anniversary.

Afterwards, I took Shannon and Grandpa to Mighty Taco for lunch. And yes, we had the three cheese nacho burritos.

***

A few weekends later, Shannon and I were back *on the road again*. This time, we were headed to the land of *Weekend at Bernie's*, Long Island.

It was Saturday January 15, 2011 at 4:30am when the alarm went off. I slept like crap that night because I was fighting off a cold and I was too excited to sleep. Shannon only got three hours of sleep because the past week at work, she worked the evening shift of 4pm-midnight. Needless to say, Shannon slept for half the car ride.

The two of us were finally packed and on the road by 5:30am.

We finally reached our general area of destination before 11am.

Shannon and I knew that we definitely wanted to be tourists and visit Ellis Island and the Statue of Liberty. We ended up parking at Liberty State Park in New Jersey.

Shannon and I had packed lightly for our night in New York. We each had a back pack with our Sabres jersey, a change of clothes for the next day, and we each had a 24 ounce can of Tilt, which was 12% alcohol...Oh yea, and we had two bottles of Sprite, which we dumped half of it out and refilled with apple vodka...We knew New York was expensive and we didn't want to break the bank on buying drinks, so we planned accordingly.

Well, anyway, back to the story...We bought our tickets and the next ferry left in a few minutes, at 11:40am. Before we could board the ferry, we had to go through a security check point. The security check point for the Statue of Liberty and Ellis Island were just like at the airport.

I plopped my bag onto the conveyer belt to be x-rayed. As sure as shit, they needed to open up my bag and search it! One of the security personal saw a "spray can" in my back pack.

Moments later, the female security guard had my back pack opened and was rifling through everything, including my Homer Simpson underwear. I felt like telling the female security guard that the pair of undies in her hands was soiled, but I didn't think it was the time or place for that. The broad found the two cans of Tilt. I reassured her that they were not "spray cans." She ended up calling over her supervisor to deal with me. She started yelling at me, stating that I could not bring alcohol with me. I told the broad and her supervisor, "Hey, you don't need to throw those out. I'll just go in the lobby and shot gun them..."

The supervisor dude was pretty cool and told me to just run the cans back to my car.

As I exited the ferry terminal, I did not feel like walking the half mile back to the car to drop off the two cans of Tilt, so I just said, "Dah, *puck* it..." and I cracked one open. The first one I pounded, the blue flavored one, went down extremely smooth. However, by the time I cracked open the second 24 ouncer, purple flavored, the bubbles and sugary goodness caught up to me and started to give me a stomach ache.

Then the dilemma ensued. I thought about dumping the can in the garbage, but that would be alcohol abuse! I tried to choke down the purple Tilt, but I just wasn't happening. Considering the Tuesday before the trip, I got laid off from the Buick GMC dealership, a $3 can of booze was a lot of money to me. So then it became a moral dilemma over wasting $3. Eventually my stomach ache told me to cut my losses and I dumped the brew.

I went back into the ferry terminal and I cleared security. The "spray can" that the security broad was looking for was a deodorant spray can of Axe Kilo, which she found when I was pounding down the Tilt.

PS-those two cans of Tilt were considered my breakfast!

Soon Shannon and I hopped onto the ferry to Ellis Island. Even though Shannon had been to New York City many times, she had never been to either Ellis Island or the Statue of Liberty.

Ellis Island was fun and fascinating; a lot of American history washed up through there.

We walked around the whole museum and through the Great Hall. As Shannon and I were walking on the upper level of the Great Hall, I let out a deep, dark, grumbling, *"Winston!"* like in *Ghostbusters 2* and to both of our amazement, it echoed throughout the Great Hall. Then Shannon smacked me in the stomach for acting like a doofus.

From Ellis Island, we hopped the ferry to Battery Park on Manhattan. Shannon and I were going to save the Statue of Liberty for the next day because we were a little strapped for time.

It was around 2pm when we landed at Battery Park. Even though the Sabres @ Islanders game started at 7pm, Shannon and I still had to find some food and check in to our hotel at the Hotel Pennsylvania, before we crossed the street to meet up with Shannon's co-worker/friend Carolyn and her hubby JJ at Penn Station, to catch the 4:30pm train out to Nassau Coliseum.

So with that being said, Shannon and I walked up Broadway because we wanted to eat in Chinatown.

On our walk up to Chinatown, we passed by Wall Street, where all the white collar crooks worked. It upset me walking down Wall Street, knowing that banker CEOs that got millions of dollars in bailout money from us tax payers in 2008. The slap in the face was when those evil bankers gave themselves million dollar bonuses at the end of that year at the expense of us hard working people!

Before long, Shannon and I had stumbled into Chinatown. Shannon said that she wanted to try cat, so I told her to try the General Meow.

We weren't picky, so we stopped into the first restaurant we saw. I did not recall the name of the place but the cat and dog tasted great! Shannon had some tofu cat crap and a Taiwan beer and I had the General Meow with a Chinese beer.

After the quick bite to eat, it was 3:30pm, and off to the subway, bound for our hotel.

By the time we got off the subway and to the Hotel Pennsylvania's lobby, it was 4:10pm. Shannon was on the phone with Carolyn, telling her that we were going to try our hardest to make the train, but if for some reason we didn't make it on time, to leave without us.

Before we knew it, we were checked in and had our keys to our room up on the 13th floor.

Shannon and I were sprinting down the halls, trying to find our room, so we could drop our luggage and change real quick, to be able to meet up with Carolyn and JJ.

We soon found our room, room 1373.

I swiped the card to our room and as I opened the door, I realized that there was a person in our bed!

The lady immediately shot up and put a blanket over herself. Don't worry, she wasn't hot or naked. She gasped, "Dah!"

I said, "Uh...hi...what are you doing in my room?"

She said, "Uh...you're not my husband and this is my room."

I replied, "Um...ok."

She said, "Are you sure you have the right room?"

"Um...yep. 1373." I said.

She said, "I think the hotel made a mistake. I'm going to call down to the front desk..."

I said, "That sounds great. Hey by the way, I'm Adam and this is my wife Shannon. We are from Buffalo and we are here to see the Sabres play the Islanders tonight."

She said, "Hi, I'm Debbie from California..."

I asked to Debbie from California, "Hi Debbie. Do you mind if we change real quick? We actually have to meet some friends next door at Penn Station. We are going to the game with them and we are trying to catch the same train with them. The train leaves at 4:20 and I know we are cutting it a little close. Is it alright if we change really quick?" as I took off my shirt to put a fresh shirt on before I put my jersey on.

Debbie said, "Yea, no problem, feel free to use the bathroom if you need it."

I asked Debbie, "Hey, do you mind if I look out the window? The front desk said there was a great view of the Empire State Building from this room?"

Debbie said, "Not at all."

I quickly looked out the window and saw the Empire State Building. It was an alright view, nothing special.

By the time Shannon and I got back down to the lobby to iron everything out, we had missed our 4:20pm train with Carolyn and JJ. The front desk issued us a new room; that hopefully did not have anyone sleeping in it. Our new room was also on the 13th floor.

As we stood in front of room 1330, I knocked on the door and said in my best David Spade impression from the movie *Tommy Boy* , "*Housekeeping…*knock knock, *Housekeeping…*knock knock…*Housekeeping, you want towel?...Housekeeping, you want me fluff pillow?...Housekeeping, you want me jerk you off?*"

As I swiped my card, the light on the lock turned green. I opened the door handle slowly and flung the door open.

Shannon and I stood in the door way. The room was dark, nothing was visible.

I wasn't taking any chances. I entered the room with arm circles flailing! If there was anyone in there, I would have clearly knocked 'em out!

Shannon walked in behind me and flipped the light switch on and noticed no one was in there.

My response was, "I knew that! Chivalry isn't dead! I just wanted to protect you if there was anything in here!"

Shannon and I dropped our bags and made ourselves conferrable. Since the next train for the game out to Hempstead did not leave until 5:40pm, I had enough time to poop and shower.

A few minutes later, Shannon and I were out the door and headed across the street to Penn Station.

Once we bought our tickets, it was time to play the waiting game. Shannon and I had about 50 minutes to kill before our train departed. I was amazed that one of the venders was selling the big bubba cans of Molson XXX! So I bought two, one for Shannon and one for me. Shannon and I enjoyed our beers while we listened to a Celtic Irish band; though all the members of the band were Asian.

After a few songs, Shannon and I decided to wander around Penn Station a little.

As we walked through the terminal, I heard someone "boo" at our Sabres jerseys. With my Molson XXX at hand, I swung around, pointed my finger, and said, "Who is booing my Sabres?!"

To my surprise, I saw three NYC police officers, two of which were rocking riot gear and machine guns on their chest. The one cop yelled out to us, "Go Rangers!"

I discretely stopped pointing and slowly hid my can of Molson XXX behind my back. I said, "The Sabres are playing the Islanders tonight."

To that, the cops said, "Oh, OK. Go Sabres! We don't like the Islanders!"

Eventually it was time to catch our train for the game. I could not remember the last time I was on a train, but I was pretty sure the last train I was on was the old fashion "steam powered" one at Martin's Fantasy Island on Grand Island, NY.

Shannon and I met other Sabre brethren on the train; they were from Alden, NY.

Shannon and I had a layover in Jamaica, NY. We waited a while in the freezing cold for our connecting train to Hempstead. In the meantime, we had finished the Molson XXX and started working on the last bottle of Sprite/apple vodka.

Our train eventually came and picked us up and eventually dropped us off in Hempstead at 7pm. We ended up taking a cab from the train station to Nassau Coliseum.

Our cabby asked us where we were going.

I said, "To the Nassau Mausoleum for the Sabres/Islanders game!" Our cabby was a cool dude. During our drive, I said to our cabby, "Hey, it's 7 and the game starts at 7…"

As the cabby was burning through amber and red lights, he reassured us, "No worries man, I'll have you there before puck drop."

And no lie, 90 seconds and $11 later, we were finally at the Nassau Coliseum!

Them beverages had caught up to Shannon and me, so we quickly peed, and grabbed another round.

By the time we made it to our seats, we had missed maybe 10 minutes of play, but nothing had happened because it was still 0-0.

I was quite optimistic for that night's game. So far during the season, the Sabres had been playing sub-par and were struggling to stay at .500. The Islanders, on the other hand, sucked more than we did. So I figured we would win, not that I was counting my chickens before they hatched…

Towards the end of the 1st Period, the Islanders took advantage of a Buffalo mistake and had a 2-on-0 breakaway into the

Sabres zone, but the Buffalo goaltender, Ryan Miller, stoned the Islanders cold!

In the dyeing minutes of the 1st, Buffalo turned the puck over multiple times in their own zone, but the Islanders just couldn't capitalize. So at the end of one period of play, the game was tied 0-0.

In the beginning of the 2nd Period, Buffalo went on the power play, and something amazing happened. The Buffalo Sabres actually scored on the power play for once! And to make it even better, that over paid bum Thomas Vanek finally scored! I'll tell you why I thought Vanek was one of the biggest bums currently on the Sabres. Vanek got paid millions of dollars a year to be the top goal scorer on the Sabres. Half way through the season, he had only scored 18 goals. If you ask me, he should have double that. But why should he care how many goals he scores, considering that he already got his millions.

After Vanek's goal, it was all Islanders…

New York's John Tavares had a hat trick during the 2nd Period while New York's Blake Comeau put the icing on the cake to go up 4-1.

In the beginning of the 3rd Period, Buffalo found themselves on the power play again, and to our surprise, Buffalo's Tyler Ennis scored to make it a 4-2, New York lead.

With just a handful of minutes left in the 3rd, Buffalo found themselves on the power play again and I was going to be optimistic. I knew we were down by two goals, but I figured the Sabres had it in them to tie the game; I had seen it done before…

Well, was I wrong. Buffalo coughed up the puck in the offensive zone and New York's Michael Grabner picked up the puck, skated down the ice, and scored a shorthanded goal to make it a 5-2 Islander lead.

Minutes later, with Buffalo in the offensive zone again, Buffalo's Jochen Hecht scored to make it a 5-3 New York lead, but by then, it was a day late and a buck short, the damage had already been done. There was no way Buffalo could come back.

The gamed ended with the Islanders winning 5-3.

Shannon and I were quite pissed off at the Sabres lack luster performance. You know what grinded my gears? It was that in any other profession, if you screwed up and sucked out like the Sabers did, you would be fired from your job. Oh, you're a doctor and your patients died because you gave a halfhearted effort...you're canned. You're a mail man and you stop delivering mail to a few houses consistently day in and day out...you're canned. You're a firefighter and you don't put out the fire because you are lazy that day, well you're shit canned. But when it comes to professional sports you still had a job at the end of the day.

I feel that professional sport athletes are overpaid. I also think that their pay should be performance based. If you play well and helped your team win, you should be rewarded and get paid more. If you played like crap, you get a small check (or cheque if you're French Canadian). But that was just my theory.

After the game that ended in such misery, Shannon and I were planning on catching up with Carolyn and JJ again. We were to meet them in the Nassau Coliseum and take the train back to Manhattan together.

As Shannon and I walked through the arena, we started to hear heckles on how much Buffalo sucked. Shannon got angrier and angrier with each and every heckle. Her fists started to clench until I could see the veins bulging. Shannon hissed through her teeth, "The next person that tells me that Buffalo sucks is going to get their *pucking* ass beat!"

I thought to myself, "Oh hell yea! It's been a long time since we've had a hockey fight after a Sabres game! Nothing like being on the road and being out numbered...I still like our odds..."

Then some douche bag broke my concentration when he yelled, "Sabres suck!"

I turned around to him and chirped back at him and told him in a roundabout, G rated version, "Yea! Well, you know what?! You're just a cotton headed ninny muggings!" I barely finished my statement as Shannon and I bumped into Carolyn and JJ. I said to Carolyn and JJ, "Duh...That guy was lost. I was just helping to give him directions on how to go screw himself..."

Moments later, the four of us found ourselves in a taxi headed back to the train station. My brilliant, genius self-asked our cabbie if we were on *Taxi Cab Confessions* but to our dismay, we were not, even though we were good material for the show!

By the time we hit the train station, the windows in the cab were nice and foggy. And there is only one thing to do with foggy windows and that is to draw sets of cock and balls on the windows!

We finally got our train, which took us directly back to Penn Station.

While we were on the train, the four of us struck up a conversation with a couple other hockey fans. We discussed about how we don't really like the New York Jets or Giants, and that actually, the Buffalo Bills were the only NFL team in New York State.

At one of the train stops, some dude wearing a polo shirt got up and approached the us. He informed us that our Bills sucked and that the Jets were the best team.

A pet peeve of mine was when the top button of a polo shirt was buttoned; it does not need to be buttoned! I looked at the gentleman and asked, "Sir! Did you know that your top button is buttoned?!"

Everyone burst out laughing hysterically because I said what everyone was thinking.

The dude was flabbergasted and extremely embarrassed and didn't say anything as he got off the train.

From Penn, Carolyn, JJ, Shannon, and I meandered across the street to Blarney Rock Pub. There we grabbed a quick round. Before we knew it, it was around midnight, and we were all exhausted. We said our good byes and parted ways.

7am came quite fast! Shannon and I were supposed to meet up with my cousin Andrew, who was a NYC cop; I'd like to think of him as my own personal John McClain. Our breakfast plans were to meet Andy up on 96th and Broadway at 8am. He was going to show us where he worked and then out to breakfast.

It was very difficult waking up that morning. Something about 12 solid hours of drinking eventually caught up to me. Shannon opted to skip out on breakfast because she was exhausted, and rightfully so. We packed a lot in the day before and she did not get much sleep either.

Minutes later, I was showered, dressed, and on the subway up to 96th Street. The whole subway ride I was a little nervous. There weren't many people on the subway and I thought as if I was in a remake of *Friday the 13th Jason Takes Over Manhattan*. I felt alone, vulnerable, and unarmed as I waited for Jason Voorhees to step into my subway car! Thankfully I made it to 96th Street before Jason could meet up with me.

I soon met up with Andy, who drove me past his precinct and then through a brief part of Harlem that he patrolled.

Andy decided to take me to breakfast at Tom's Restaurant. Tom's Restaurant was better known from the outside as the restaurant from the TV show *Seinfeld*. There Andy and I had the Lumberjack breakfast as we talked and got caught up on things.

After breakfast, Andy asked me, "Hey, do you want to see Grant's Tomb?"

I asked, "Um, is this a joke?"

Andy replied, "No, he's right around the corner…"

So we went to see Grant's Tomb. To be honest, I had no idea that Grant's Tomb was in New York.

A few short blocks and we were at Grant's Tomb.

Grant's Tomb was an interesting place. Grant was there and so was his wife. There were artifacts of Grant, along with some history about him. The Tomb was a nice looking architectural building. We were only there for maybe 15 minutes before we left. There was not too much else to do at the tomb.

After that, Andy drove me back to the subway station and we parted ways. Andy was headed back home because he had just worked an overnight shift. I headed back to the hotel to see if Shannon was stirring.

By the time I got back to the hotel room, the coffee from Tom's Restaurant was kicking in and doing its job…*I had to pop my bing winger…take the Browns to the Super Bowl…drop a duce…*

Once I was done pooping, it was time to wipe myself.

From the bed room, Shannon heard me shout out, "WOW!"

Shannon queried, "Did you amaze yourself in there?"

I said, "Oh hell yea! You gotta come check this out! I need some confirmation but I think my poop is green!"

And green it was; bright neon green! And yes, Shannon and I had reached a new level in our relationship as she looked in the bowl at my green turd and then to the TP which had a little green stain on it from my bum. In retrospect, I should have taken a picture of it!

After I flushed away my little green poopies, it was time to shower.

Shannon and I were all packed up and out the hotel's spinning door by 11am.

Andy mentioned that Shannon and I should hit up McSorley's Old Ale House, New York's oldest saloon. Shannon and I figured that we would hit it up for lunch.

Well, Shannon and I got lost on the way trying to find it, but we did stumble across the World Famous Jekyll and Hyde of Greenwich Village. Jekyll and Hyde was a fun place. It was set up all dark and spooky inside. There were also animatronics that came to life and had conversations with the patrons. The food was good too, which was always a plus.

Our waiter was a cool dude. He asked why we were in New York and I told him we were there for the Sabres/Islanders game. He asked who won and I told him the Islanders did. Our waiter was astonished that the Islanders won. He told us that any minor league team or even a beer league team could beat the Islanders. I told our waiter that it was a shitty time to be a Buffalo fan considering that the Sabres and Bills both sucked.

After Jekyll and Hyde, Shannon and I continued down 7th Avenue South until it turned into Varick Street. As we wandered down Varick Street, we came across North Moore Street, and all of a sudden, I realized that Shannon and I were not lost any more. We had stumbled across the Ghostbusters Firehouse again!

I said, "See Shannon, we're not lost! It's the Ghostbusters Firehouse!"

Shannon said, "Oh yea!"

As we approached the Ghostbusters headquarters I noticed it was all locked up, no way to enter the joint. Suddenly, I came up with a brilliant plan to sneak into the Ghostbusters headquarters...I was going to call 911 and tell them there was a fire around the corner, and when the fire truck would leave the firehouse, I would seize the opportunity and sneak in through the open doors and have the whole place to myself! Well, on paper it looked like a great idea, but Shannon pulled me back to reality. So needless to say, I did not execute my plan.

Shannon and I were en route to Battery Park. We were going to take the ferry to the Statue of Liberty, and then back to Liberty State Park.

On our way to Battery Park, we walked past the former sight of the World Trade Center Twin Towers. We paid our respects and viewed the progress of the 9/11 Memorial and new Trade Center building.

Moments later, Shannon and I were on the ferry to the Statue of Liberty. Shannon leaned over to me and asked, "Are you prepared to go inside a woman's head?" as she pointed to Lady Liberty.

I told Shannon, "I was up there when I was 13. Don't worry, it's like any other female's head. There's nothing in there..."

I got smacked in the arms, stomach, and head a few times for my peanut gallery comment.

Alas, Shannon and I were standing before the Statue of Liberty. I leaned over to Shannon and asked her, "Kinda makes you wonder?"

Shannon questioned, "Wonder what?"

I replied, "Whether she's naked under that toga. She *is* French...You know that..."

Shannon just shook her head as she led the way inside the Statue.

The Statue of Liberty museum was fun and also quite informative and educational. It contained the history of Lady Liberty from its conception in France to her 1980s restoration.

When we were finished with the educational part of the tour, Shannon and I made our way up to the pedestal, and what a work out that was! Shannon and I had to climb some 100+ stairs to get to the top of the pedestal. Unbeknownst to us at the time, we needed a special Crown Pass to walk up the spiral stair case to the crown. And to get our paws on the Crown Pass, we needed to obtain them three months in advance. Oh well, we'll know for next time.

Shannon and I made our way to outside the pedestal and took in the NYC skyline. We also looked up at Lady Liberty, and almost got vertigo.

After touring Lady Liberty, I could safely say that I had been *up inside* Lady Liberty. After that, it was time to catch the ferry back to New Jersey, hop in the 2003 Dodge Caravan shaggin' wagon, and head home.

The following weekend, the Sabres were back on the Island to finish up a home-at-home weekend with the Islanders. That game the Sabres won 5-3. I was a little upset, and I wanted to hop into my flux capacitor powered 1981 DeLorean and go back in time to buy tickets for that game, so Shannon and I could see a winning game on the road for a change. The only problem I had was I was fresh out of Uranium, the key ingredient to help power the flux capacitor and time travel. I checked my rolodex for the closest Lebanese terrorists, but they were all out of town.

February 2011

Well, during the month of February, there weren't any road trips that worked for our schedule. The away games that Buffalo was playing were already cities that Shannon and I had previously visited, and we didn't want to repeat a trip.

Regardless, a lot had gone on in Buffalo during the month of February. The Sabres were struggling to reach .500 and were floating around the 9th and 10th spot in the Eastern Conference, just trying to make their way into the playoff picture. On top of that, Buffalo struggled to string more than two wins together. Up to that point in the season, the Sabres had not won more than two games in a row, and the fans were getting quite upset. Even worse, Buffalo's home record had more losses than wins.

Towards the end of the month, the Sabres put Captain Craig Rivet on waivers and eventually Columbus Blue Jackets picked him up; thank you Columbus for picking up our sloppy seconds! I was glad that Buffalo dropped Rivet, mainly because he didn't produce for the Sabres. He rarely scored or assisted on goals, and half the time he was a healthy scratch. It was about time the Sabres cut some dead weight.

Another monumental event that added to a new chapter in Sabres history was billionaire Terry Pegula purchased the Sabres from billionaire Thomas Galisano. Pegula, who was from Pennsylvania, was a huge Sabres fan and a Sabres season ticket holder for 18 years.

Former Sabre great and French Connection member Gilbert Perreault joined Terry Pegula's side at a heartfelt press conference. Pegula reassured Buffalo fans that, "Starting today, the Buffalo Sabres reason for existence will be to win the Stanley Cup." Pegula went on to say that money was no option, the community deserved to win the Cup, and by three years, the Sabres will have won a Stanley Cup...I was skeptical. As much as I wanted to buy in and drink the Kool-Aid, logic and reality got in the way.

The day of the trade deadline, Sabres GM Darcy Regier finally made a trade to get a new face into the locker room. The Sabres had acquired Brad Boyes from the St. Louis Blues for a draft pick the following year.

March 2011

As March roared in like a lion, we had our next road trip…

Now I couldn't really remember the last time I was in Pittsburgh, but I did know the Steelers were still playing at 3 Rivers Stadium and the Donald and I toured the USS Requin (SS-481), a WWII era submarine.

Anyway, enough reminiscing and back to the story! The trip down from Rochester to Pittsburgh was a little boring; though it only took three and a half hours…there wasn't much scenery on the 90 or I-79.

Shannon and I made good time and pulled into our hotel before 3pm. I used the "name your own price" on Priceline.com and got a good deal on Spring Hill Suites by Marriot on Pittsburgh's North Shore. The Marriot was wonderful and the service was superb. From our hotel window, we could see PNC Park, where the Pittsburgh Pirates played baseball. Off in the distance, we could see Heinz Field, where the Pittsburgh Steelers played.

After Shannon and I checked in at the front desk, the concierges asked us if we needed any help with anything. We asked them what the quickest way to get to the Penguins game was. Concierges told us they had a shuttle that left every 30 minutes and that they could drive us and pick us up after the game. Since we had no idea where we were going, that was music to our ears!

By 3:30pm, Shannon and I were on the Marriot's shuttle bus to Market Square to begin our bar hop to the Consol Energy Center…Consol Energy Center did not roll well off the tongue. But you know what sounded awesome? The Igloo! I thought that it was so cool that the Penguins played in the Igloo, and that Mellon Arena looked like an igloo. Unfortunately, I never saw a game there. However, I did see *Sudden Death* where volunteer firefighter Jean Claude Van Dam saved the day and Game 7 of the Stanley Cup Finals!

Everyone Shannon and I talked to recommended that we go to Primanti Brothers.

When we arrived at Primanti Brothers downtown location, Shannon and I were hungry, so we asked our waitress what she recommended. She told us to try the Capicola Sandwich. We were told they were big sandwiches, so Shannon and I decided to split one.

Minutes later, Shannon and I were served a huge sandwich on big slices of Italian bread. The thing had coleslaw on it along with French fries, capicola, and other stuff on it. We washed our sandwich down with a Yuengling Draft, and a couple local brews; Iron City Light and Penn Pilsner.

Once we finished our lunch, I leaned over to Shannon and said, "Oh boy, coleslaw and draft beer, tomorrow is gonna be a fun ride back up to New York..."

After we left Primanti Brothers, we walked around Market Square a little bit. I noticed that there was an enormous skyscraper that appeared to be made out of glass and looked like a castle. I just thought it was cool, a castle looking skyscraper.

The next establishment that Shannon and I found ourselves in was Courthouse Tavern on Forbes Avenue. We enjoyed the bar. It was a quiet bar, off the beaten path. It had a kitchen, but Shannon and I were still full from Primanti Brothers. However, we were parched as usual. They had Yuengling Bock beer on draft and I was feeling a little adventurous, so I ordered a round. The Bock turned out to be tasty.

Normally I drank light beer, like Labatt Blue Light or Molson Canadian. I liked light beers because they tasted good and went down easy. With a light beer, I could easily pound them down with no worries. Now on the other hand, a dark or heavy beer was like eating a meal, like steak and potatoes. If I had two heavy beers, like Guinness for example, then I would be full on beer. Not to mention it was difficult to chug a heavy beer...just like the time my buddy Jason and I were playing beer pong. We were all out of Blue, so we used his last two bottles of Guinness...big mistake. It was almost impossible to chug that crap. After that game of beer pong, Jason and I made a beer run to pick up some more Blue.

Anyway, back at Courthouse Tavern, the Yuengling Bock tasted so good that Shannon and I decided to have a second round of it.

After we left the Courthouse, we wandered our way over to 5th Avenue because that was the street that Consol Energy Center was on.

Shannon and I soon found Consol Energy Center and we still had an hour and a half to kill.

We walked into Souper Bowl for a quick round. Shannon and I were the only Sabre fans wearing our jerseys there. There were a few Buffalo fans, but they were afraid to wear their colors and I didn't know why. All of the Penguins fans were nice…maybe they felt sorry for us because our team sucked and we had never won a Stanley Cup before. But whatever, all the Penguins fans were nice, and we had great conversations with a few of them.

From Souper Bowl, Shannon and I made our way to Café 5th Ave. There, Shannon and I split a deuce deuce of Corona. The fans there were nice and we met a few transplants from Western New York who moved down there for work. After Shannon and I pounded our Corona, it was time to head over to Consol Energy Center for the game.

It was the inaugural season for the Consol Energy Center and it was a very nice looking arena; even the bathrooms were nice. Another great thing about the Center was they had Labatt Blue on tap.

Shannon and I found our Standing Room Only seats in Section 227. I liked the Standing Room Only section at CEC a hell of a lot better than at the United Center in Chicago. At least at the Consol Energy Center, you had a specific "seat" or place on a bar that you could lean up against.

It was the 33rd home game for the Penguins on that Tuesday night on March 8th. Soon the National Anthem was sung and then it was time for puck drop!

I was really excited about the game. Pittsburgh's two big top guns, Cindy Crosby and Evgeni Malkin were out with injuries. Cindy had a yeast infection and Geni had a broken nail. Since Pegula bought the Sabres, Buffalo was all of a sudden hot again; 6-0-1 for their last road games. I thought Shannon and I were going to be in for a good game…

It wasn't even three minutes into the game when Buffalo's Rob Niedermayer decided to break the ice and scored the first goal of the game. Niedermayer single handedly took the puck over the blue line, into Pittsburgh's zone, out muscled the Penguin defenseman, and slipped the puck past Penguins goalie Marc-Andre Fleury!

Though Shannon and I were not counting our chickens before they hatched, I did mention that if the Sabres won the game, then we would take our good luck to Rivers Casino.

Half way through the 1st Period, Pittsburgh found themselves on a 5-on-3 power play advantage. Pittsburgh gave Buffalo a run for their money…

As the first power play expired for Pittsburgh, the Penguins lost control of the puck, and it dribbled out into the neutral zone. Buffalo's Tyler Ennis was fresh out from the penalty box, scooped up the free puck, skated in to the Penguins zone on a breakaway, and got stonewalled by Penguins goalie Fleury. After that play, the Sabres stopped playing and decided to pack up and go back home…

Minutes into the 2nd Period, with a face off deep in Buffalo's zone, Pittsburgh won the draw, and James Neil snuck the puck past Buffalo goaltender Ryan Miller to make it a 1-1 game.

Two minutes later, with a shot from the point, Pittsburgh's Zbynek Michalek scored to give the Penguins a 2-1 lead.

During the 2nd Period, both Pittsburgh and Buffalo had their chances on the power play, but the two juggernaut power play squads couldn't seal the deal to score.

With just under seven minutes left in the 3rd Period, Michalek's bad angle shot hit his teammate Mark Letestu, and the puck was redirected by Buffalo's goalie Ryan Miller, to give the Penguins a 3-1 lead.

Buffalo did pull their goalie, but it was too little too late.

After the game, Shannon and I had to walk the dreaded Walk of Shame yet again. We didn't get booed by Penguins fans after the game, which surprised us.

Shannon called the Marriot for our shuttle and a few minutes later it arrived.

On the way back to the Marriot, Shannon and I decided that since our Sabres sucked out, that maybe we might have the same luck as well if we went to Rivers Casino. We figured we would cut our losses and skip the casino.

Back at the Marriot, Shannon and I had the midnight munchies, so we went to SoHo, which was the bar and grill located on the lobby floor of the Marriot. There we had a smorgasbord of food. We had some Buffalo Pierogies, pizza skins, and a steak and cheese sub with a Miller Lite.

Soon bedtime beckoned.

The next morning, Shannon and I were in no rush, so we slept in until 9am or so. We showered and got ready and packed.

As we were checking out, we asked the front desk if they had directions to the Beer Church. The lady working opened up a rolodex and found Church Brew Works. She gave us the paper that had the name, phone number, and directions from the Marriot to Church Brew Works.

Shannon and I then sat down and had our continental breakfast. I noticed that the Marriot also had a pool. I was a little bummed out that we didn't get to use the pool.

After Shannon and I finished breakfast, we loaded up our Dodge Caravan and walked the two blocks down General Robinson Street to the Andy Warhol Museum.

Since I had a BS in Art from Daemen College, I had to take my fair share of art history classes. One of the many people who I learned about (many of whom I don't remember) was Andy Warhol; better known as the Campbell Soup guy.

I'm not going to lie, but I personally thought the Andy Warhol Museum sucked. Yea, there were some interesting things, but for most part, it flat out sucked.

I'll start with the interesting parts first. I thought it was cool that the museum was seven stories high. Yes, they had the Campbell Soup cans, probably about 12 or so. Yea, they had Elvis 11 times in there along with the Marilyn Monroe and Jackie O screen prints. There were screen prints of other people as well. That was all fine and dandy.

What sucked was they had seven floors of absolute dog shit. I bet if they had Andy Warhol's used toilet paper, they would have hung that shit up in there too and would have called that art! There was a painting where Warhol used a copper based paint that would oxidize. So once he finished painting this copper paint on a 5x20 foot canvas, he pissed on it so the paint would oxidize. Big deal! My dog poops in my neighbors' front yard, but I don't call that art!

There was an entire floor dedicated to "home movies" that Warhol made. Apparently back in the 60s, he acquired a camcorder and video recorded everything and I mean everything. He recorded himself being dressed up in drag, an interview with Dennis Hopper in a hotel, himself painting a hammer on the floor with a mop, a dripping faucet, and rambling conversations with nothing and nobodies. The stupid ass art world ate that crap up and considered it art!

There was a taxidermy lion that Warhol titled *Lion*...I was extremely unimpressed.

There was a whole floor dedicated to screen prints of a human skull. And you know what all 15 screen prints of the skulls were called?! If you guessed *"skull"*, you won! *It was ground breaking artwork!*

There was early Warhol work where he drew shitty cartoon versions of fat, ugly, naked cherubs.

I felt like taking a dump in the middle of one of the rooms and calling it *poop* but I didn't want people to think that Warhol did it and get all the credit for my poop!

Tell you what, if you thought about going to the Warhol Museum, save your $15 and your time and look up the garbage on the internet.

After the Warhol Museum, Shannon and I hopped into our minivan to head over to drink and dine in splendor at the Church Brew Works.

Church Brew Works was a cool place. It used to be St. John the Baptist Church until it was renovated into a restaurant and microbrewery. The Church still had the original Douglas Fir hard wood floors, along with the stain glass windows. Even the pews were saved and turned into benches for the tables. The alter was converted a little bit to house the six or so beer vats. Along with the seating area, there is a bar there as well. The bar and dining area was located where the congregation would sit for Mass. It was a really cool place and kinda motivated me to go back to church. The Church's atmosphere was great and the place smelled like hops.

The appetizer that Shannon and I ordered was the beer sampler. The sampler included eight 5oz glasses of the Church's brew. They had four seasonal brews and four brews that they kept in normal rotation; Celestial Gold, Pipe Organ Ale, Bell Tower Brown Ale, and the World Beer Cup award winning Pious Monk Dunkel.

For lunch, Shannon ordered French onion soup and a sandwich. I on the other hand tried their signature pierogie dish, both were decadent.

After lunch, Shannon and I hopped back into the shaggin' wagon and cruised on through the Strip District and did some quick window shopping.

From there, Shannon and I were trying to make our way across the river to Station Square, but we got lost through all the one way streets. We found ourselves driving around the Duquesne University campus for a little bit before we got back on track. We finally saw the entrance for the bridge over to Station Square, but I couldn't get over into the next lane. Instead we were forced onto 279 where we traveled over the Fort Pitt Bridge and then into the Fort Pitt Tunnel. Eventually the tunnel spit us out on another side of a mountain. Shannon and I thought about trying to turn around to navaguess our way back to find Station Square, but traffic was heavy and the rain was coming down pretty good, so we decided to save it for the next time we went back down to Pittsburgh.

Once Shannon and I got back into town, our buddy Karl told us that we should stop going on road trips, because lately the Sabres have been losing whenever we go see them.

April 2011

As April rolled around, the Sabres hopes for the playoffs were still up in the air. The Sabres, New York Rangers, and Carolina Hurricanes, were all fighting for the last two playoff spots in the Eastern Conference. However, on Friday April 8th, the Sabres, who were playing their final regular season home game, beat the Philly Fliers in 4-3 in OT and solidified a playoff spot. The next night, the Sabres were playing in Ohio against the Columbus Blue Jackets, and that was where our story continued...

Months ago, Shannon and I asked our friends Brian and Teri if they wanted to go on a mini road trip with us to see the Sabres take on the Columbus Blue Jackets and they said, "Oh H-E-double hockey sticks yea!"

A few years ago, Brian and Teri and a few other friends went down with Shannon and me to New Burn, North Carolina for Spring Break. We conveniently timed that trip around a Sabres/Hurricanes game. It was an enjoyable experience, but that trip had too much driving. From New York to North Carolina alone was a 14 hour drive and New Burn to Raleigh was another two or three hour drive; plus the ride back home to New York.

Columbus wasn't too far away and it was still under my six hour limit. I had a six hour road trip limit. If a road trip was shorter than 6 hours, then I would drive. If the trip was longer than six hours, I would fly or teleport.

Shannon had that Friday off from work and I only had morning classes at school. The plan was to drive down that day to Youngsville, Pennsylvania where Brian and Teri lived. We would spend the night and leave bright and early Saturday morning for Columbus.

The whole week leading up to our trip was torture. I didn't feel like doing any work or going to school, I just wanted it to be the weekend! Shannon had the same problem.

Friday finally came, and even though my morning class got out early, it was still painful to wake up and go to school. Thankfully I was out well before noon. Shannon and I packed and cleaned the house before we hit the road early that afternoon.

Shannon and I drove the Dodge minivan down the 90 to the Fredonia exit and headed towards Jamestown, the home of Lucile Ball. Youngsville was about 20 minutes south of Jamestown, New York.

Shannon and I arrived at Teri's place midafternoon. Brian was still at work, but we were going to pick him up and hit up the big city of Warren, Pennsylvania.

For dinner, Brian and Teri took us to Corner Stone, who brag that they have the best wings in Warren, PA. Their delicacy wings, which I had, were called Old Granddads. Old Granddads were deep fried, and then mixed with pepper, garlic powder, and medium sauce. The wings were deep fried again, and then shaken with Cajun, butter, and lemon pepper. The end result was a great tasting wing. Brian informed me if you added some beer to the equation, that about 30 minutes later, you got some stank ass smelling burps that last the whole night.

After dinner, we went back to the *big city* of Youngsville where the four of us hit up the huge night life scene for a Friday night...bowling at a joint within walking distance that had 8 lanes and a BYOB policy.

At the bowling alley, we tried to find the Sabres/Fliers game, but all we could get was the Penguins/Islanders game. However, the Pens game was giving updates to the Sabres game.

Bowling was fun, and as midnight approached, we had closed the joint down. We were going to hit up the American Legion, which was across the street, but we had not finished our 18 pack of Rolling Rock. So instead, we just walked back to Brian and Teri's.

I woke up at 5:30am on Saturday April 9 because I had to pee, and then I could not fall back to sleep. I was so excited about our road trip that lay ahead of us.

The four of us were finally showered, packed, and on the road by 10am. According to the GPS, it was going to take us 4.5 hours to get to our hotel in downtown Columbus.

It was around noon when all four of us started to get hungry. I asked Brian if he could look up on his phone or GPS if there was a Sonic or a White Castle nearby. Though there was nothing on the Pennsylvania/Ohio boarder, Columbus did have both and I got a boner! I said, "Holy shit! I'm gonna knock so much stuff off of my bucket list this weekend! I've never been to Columbus, never been to White Castle, and even though I was at a Sonic in Raleigh, I still needed to go back again..."

Brian and Teri were thrilled about the idea of going to Sonic because they too have seen the commercials for Sonic but have never gone because there weren't any in their area either.

It was close to 3pm as we pulled into Downtown Columbus. My first impression was, "Yep, this is kinda how I thought it was going to be, a small town just like Buffalo...and hey, it looks like a ghost town in downtown, just like in Buffalo!"

Minutes later, we had driven past our hotel, the Hyatt on Capital Square. As we drove around the block, I noticed that there was a park that was broken up into grass quadrants. I told Shannon, Brian, and Teri that after the game, when I was nice and sloppy drunk, that I would go streaking though the quad...

Eventually we checked in and found ourselves in our hotel

room. We had opened our 18 pack of LionHead Light and Brian checked on his phone for things to do in Columbus. He came across an establishment called Elevator Brewery and Draught Haus. Not only did the place sound cool, but it was on the way to Nationwide Arena.

We arrived at Elevator Brewery a little before 5pm, though Elevator did not open until 5. As we were standing outside, we made some small talk with a few locals and we asked them what there was to do in Columbus. The locals told us that on the weekends, nothing in downtown opened until after 5pm. The couple recommended German Town and the Arena District. They also said there was a shopping center that was the equivalent to 10 city blocks or something like that. I'm not gonna lie, I did not drive five hours just so I could go to a mall, even though there was apparently three Victoria's Secret stores at that mall.

Any who back to Elevator. Our waitress came around and gave us our menus and asked if we knew what we wanted to drink. Since it was a microbrewery, and they had a lot of brews, we ordered the sampler platter, which included about 12 different kinds of beers. They ranged from hoppy, to stouts, to pilsners, and everything in between.

For dinner I ordered the Sauerkraut Balls and pizza, both of which were delicious. Shannon had scallops and Teri ordered a sandwich and fries. However, Brian ordered Elevator's signature dish, The Rock Filet. The Rock Filet was awesome to look at. One could order either 7oz. filet or Ahi Tuna. Brian ordered the tuna. The meal was served on a big wooden tray with a sizzling hot 450 degree Finnish Tulikivi firestone. One would cut up the meat or fish and cook it for however long he or she wanted to on the sizzling hot stone. It also came with three different dipping sauces.

Elevator had some history with its building. It was built back in 1897 in the historic Columbia building and it used to be Bott Brother's Billiards and Saloon. The building still had the original mosaic floor, decorative ceiling, and stained glass windows. Also, their bar had won the blue ribbon for craftsmanship at the 1893 World Columbian Expo in Chicago. And if that wasn't cool enough, the building is supposedly haunted! *Who ya gonna call? Ghostbusters!*

After dinner, it was time to race over to Nationwide Arena,

because we only had a half hour to spare until puck drop.

On our walk over to the arena, we did not see any Columbus Blue Jackets fans, and even when we entered the arena, it was mainly dominated by Sabres fans. Honestly, it felt like a Sabres home game.

As we walked past the beer concession stand, I noticed and pointed out that they had Labatt Ice. That was followed up with, "Who's gettin shit faced tonight? This guy!" as I pointed to myself.

Once we found our seats and beer, we waited the 8 minutes for the National Anthem to start.

As the house lights went out, the place went crazy and you could distantly hear "Let's go Buffalo!" being chanted.

Soon the Columbus Blue Jackets hit the ice and their fans cheered.

Then the Sabres hit the ice and the place erupted with a mix of boos and cheers.

Next the National Anthem was sang and then it was time for the last regular season game of the 2010-2011 season!

The 1st Period was incredibly boring and nothing much happened. A few of the Sabres and a couple of the Blue Jackets threw their purses at each other, but that was about it.

It wasn't until the 2nd Period when things became interesting. It was about five minutes into the 2nd Period, when Columbus's Derek Dorsett came skating into Buffalo's zone and scored a wraparound goal on Buffalo goaltender Ryan Miller. Columbus had gone up 1-0. I had to say that I thought it was pretty cool, because when Columbus scored, Civil War reenactors fired off an old cannon; boom, fire, smoke, and all!

Midway through the 2nd Period, Buffalo was pressing down in the Columbus zone, when Jason Pominville took a one timer shot from the slot, which made it past the Columbus goaltender Steve Mason, to tie the game at 1-1.

A few minutes later, Columbus had a breakaway, but the Blue Jacket couldn't sneak the puck past Sabre goalie Ryan Miller.

Midway through the 2nd, Ryan Miller was pulled and Jhonas Enroth was put in net.

Towards the end of the 2nd Period, with Buffalo deep in the Columbus zone, the puck popped back to the point, where Sabre defenseman Chris Butler wound up and slapped the puck past the

Columbus goalie to make it a 2-1 Buffalo lead.

With just under five minutes left in the 2nd Period, Columbus was farting around with the puck behind their net. Buffalo forward Drew Stafford came flying in and bumped the Blue Jacket off the puck. The puck dribbled out of reach of the two, but Sabre Steve Boyes came and swept the puck towards the front of the net, where fellow teammate Tyler Ennis dumped the puck into the net to make it a 3-1 Sabre lead.

Columbus wasn't dead or out of the contest. After the third Buffalo goal, Columbus came roaring back and Jared Boll dumped one past Enroth to make it 3-2 Buffalo.

During the 2nd Intermission and during stoppages of play, a live band was playing all the "pump you up" kind of music like G-n-R's "Welcome to the Jungle" Harvey Danger's "Flagpole Sitta" and Green Day's "Basket Case." Also, the dude on the PA said that if Columbus scored three goals in that night's game, then everyone would get free chili from Wendy's the following day...

As the 3rd Period started, Shannon, Teri, and I had still been nursing our cans of Labatt from the 1st Period. The beer was a little warm, and I'm not a Brit nor do I like warm beer, so I pounded mine so I could get myself a cold beer.

With just two and a half minutes into the 3rd Period, Columbus' Kristian Huselius scored to tie the game at 3 and the whole arena started to chant, "Chili! Chili! Chili!"

Just after the half way point in the 3rd Period, former Sabres captain, and current Blue Jacket Craig Rivet cross checked Sabre Tyler Ennis. That drew a huge crowd and players from both sides grabbed tango partners. When it was all said and done, Rivet received a five minute major for cross checking, two minutes for roughing, and a game misconduct.

Now with the Sabres on the power play for five minutes, everyone saw a rarity among the Sabres...Drew Stafford and Paul Gaustad both scored on the same power play series! The "powerless play" finally had some power!

With under a minute left in regulation, the Sabres were up 5-3. However, the Blue Jackets were on the power play and pulled their goalie. Brian leaned over and said, "Oh yea, we got this one..."

I told Brian, "I wouldn't be too sure. You know last week the Sabres were at home and up two goals with under two minutes left in the game and the Nashville Predators came back to win it 4-3 in OT..."

Well needless to say, with 22 seconds left in regulation, Columbus' Kristian Huselius wrist shot made it past Buffalo goalie Enroth to make it a 5-4 Buffalo lead.

The game would end in a 5-4 Buffalo win and all the Buffalo fans went wild! It was just like a home game.

After we exited the arena, we entered a huge mob of Sabre fans chanting and cheering and shouting the Bills Shout song. There were even people yelling, "We're going to the Super Bowl!!"

We found a piano bar that we wanted to go into, but there was a huge line out the door. We were all a little bummed out that we didn't go to the piano bar, especially me because I wanted to hear Lynyrd Skynyrd's *Freebird*.

Luckily for us, there was another bar right around the corner. They had tables on the patio that were empty, so we sat there. The bar was 343 Front Street and it quickly became a huge Sabre after party hang out. About every five minutes, we saw a steady stream of security guards escorting a Sabres fan out of the bar...*You can take the boy outta Buffalo, but you can't take the Buffalo outta the boy!*

Nationwide Arena looked cool at night. They had a huge light that shot up into the sky. It looked a lot like the Batman spot light, but without the Batman logo.

Midway through our beer drinking festivities, Brian and I had to break the seal. We navigated our way through the huge mob of people, finally finding our way to the bathroom. I was surprised to find a Bathroom Jockey in the men's room...You know, one of those dudes that hung out in the bathroom ready with paper towels, gum, and cologne.

After three pitchers of Molson, we decided that the four of us were going to take one of those bicycle taxis back to the hotel. The four of us had never been on one, so we figured why not?

Well, our bike rider was some petite college girl who struggled to cart our fat asses the 0.7 miles back to the Hyatt. She got us about half way and was sweating and out of breath. The four of us decided that we could walk the rest of the way.

When we finally got back to the Hyatt, Brian and I decided that we would grab one last quick round at the sports bar that was located in the lobby of the Hyatt. As we walked into the bar with our

Sabres jerseys on, one of the patrons told us to not even bother because the bartender was a dick and the bar was "closed." Brian and I looked at each other in disgust! What the hell kind of sports bar closed before midnight on a Saturday?

So we went upstairs to the room where we found the girls naked and making out in the hot tub...wait, nope, that's what I dreamt about.

The four of us hung out for a little bit before calling it a night.

We checked out Sunday morning at10am.

As we left the parking garage and drove past the Hyatt, we noticed across the street were Civil War reenactors getting ready to fight. We would have stayed, but watching Civil War reenactors was not on my bucket list; Sonic and White Castle were. Plus, I already knew who won the Civil War, the North!

Brian looked up the address to the closest Sonic on his phone and before we knew it, we were there. It was a wonderful and glorious experience for all of us. I had a chili pie with cheese and Fritos, tater tots with chili and cheese, a junior chili Fritos cheese wrap, and a strawberry slushy. It was advertised that the slushy was made with real fruit, so that it meant it was healthy. I was not sure what everyone else got, but they loved it. As I recall Brian's exact words were, "They got Sonic, White Castle, Chick-fil-A, and hockey...yea, I think I can move to Columbus..."

Once we finished our breakfast, I was in a food coma, but we weren't done yet. We still had to stop at a White Castle!

Brian found a White Castle that was en route on our way home. A half hour later, we were pulling into a White Castle. Our White Castle meal was on the Columbus Blue Jackets. At the hockey game the night before, the team gave out free coupons that were good for the Original Slider, chicken sandwich, or BBQ pulled pork slider. Shannon and I both tried the Original Slider. Even though I was in a food coma I still found room for the slider. The slider was good and worth the wait. However, when we were at the game, I took at least 15 of the free slider coupons and the coupons said 1 sandwich per person per visit. Fortunately enough for me, there was no expiration date or region restrictions, so I was saving those coupons for when I plan the next Sabres road trip that has a White Castle.

We got back to Youngsville, PA around 5pm. Shannon and I said our good byes to Brian and Teri before we started our trek back up North to New York.

2011 Playoffs

The Sabres opponent in the 2011 Stanley Cup Playoffs was the Philadelphia Flyers, with Philly having home ice advantage. Sabre home game tickets went fast the day they went on sale. The cheapest I could find on Stub Hub were $125 apiece. I checked ticket prices for down in Philly and the cheapest was $65 a pop. Shannon and I contemplated road tripping back down to Philly, but our work and school schedules weren't that flexible. Additionally we could not repeat cities that we had already been too!

Game 1 was on Thursday April 14 down in Philly. I won't bore you with the details, but Buffalo's own Patrick Kaleta scored the only goal during the 3rd Period to give Buffalo a 1-0 win and 1-0 lead in the series.

Game 2 was still in Philly, but the outcome was a little different. That Saturday April 16th game was more of a shooting gallery. After the 1st Period, the game was tied at 3 apiece, but the 2nd Period was all Flyers, as they scored two more goals. Buffalo did try to come back in the 3rd Period, but fell short. The Flyers had won 5-4 and the series was tied 1-1. Game 2 sucked because the entire 2nd Period, Buffalo was in the penalty box.

Game 3 moved up to Buffalo. Game 3 was on Monday April 18, and since my birthday was April 17, I was hoping for a Sabres victory as my birthday present. I forgave the Sabres for not winning on my birthday eve, but they needed to make up for it on my birthday post. I figured that if the Sabres could give Shannon a birthday win, they why not me? Well, needless to say, Buffalo lost at home 4-2 and Philly went up in the series 2-1. That was two birthdays in a row for me where the Sabres lost playoff games!

Buffalo was host to Game 4 on Wednesday April 20th. Like every other game in this series, Philly laid it on thick and tested Buffalo goaltender Ryan Miller mentally and physically. Thankfully Buffalo went back to playing their style of play and it paid off in a 1-0 Buffalo victory. Jason Pominville scored the lone goal midway through the 1st Period. The series was all tied up again at two apiece.

Game 5 traveled back down to Philadelphia on Friday April 22nd. Buffalo shot out to an amazing 3 goal lead in the 1st Period, and as usual, they blew the lead. Philly came back and scored two goals in the 2nd Period and one late one in the 3rd Period to send the game to overtime. The hero of overtime was Buffalo's Tyler Ennis, to make it a 4-3 OT win for Buffalo.

Game 6 was back in Buffalo on Sunday April 24th, or better known as Easter Sunday. That Sunday, my mom was having Easter Dinner. I had told her earlier in the week that Shannon and I were going to try to make it to Party in the Plaza.

Party in the Plaza was an event the Sabres put on during the Playoffs for Sabre fans who didn't have tickets for the home game. Right outside of HSBC Arena, the road was blocked off and two huge big screens were set up. There were also vendors selling beer and food. It was like an over flow of the Arena. And unlike Dallas Cowboys owner Jerry Jones, who charged $200 a ticket to stand outside Cowboy Stadium for the 2011 Super Bowl, this was totally FREE!

Even though the game started at 3pm, Shannon and I arrived in downtown at 2:30. We parked in the Early Bird parking garage next to Pilot Field (It's now called Coca-Cola Field, but I'm still stuck in the 1990s, which I still call it Pilot Field), where the AAA baseball team Buffalo Bisons play. In the parking garage Shannon and I had a few beers and some of Mr. Tracy's Cherry Herrings.

Shannon and I soon found ourselves walking down Washington Street towards HSBC Arena. We and 20,000+ other fans, were confronted by Bible Thumpers, telling us how all of us are going to Hell and we must repent because we are watching hockey on a Sunday. You know what, if I am going to Hell for watching a hockey game on a Sunday, at least I'll know somebody there…I'll be there with 20,000+ of my closest friends!

We soon navigated our way to the Plaza and joined probably 2,000-3,000 other Sabre fans. Shannon and I soon found the beer line and purchased two Labatt Blue Lights and enjoyed the atmosphere. A lot of people had signs that were pretty funny. One sign read, "Philly sucks so much that the Fresh Prince left" and another read, "Philly Cryers" with a tear drop in the middle of the Flyer logo. Some other dude had a picture of Jesus with Ryan

Miller's head superimposed that read, "Jesus Saves!" There was a lot of energy and enthusiasm in the crowd.

Right after puck drop, Buffalo came out with intensity and before the 10 minute mark of the 1st Period, Buffalo was up 2-0. Once the 1st Period had ended, Buffalo held a 3-1 lead.

Party in the Plaza was a lot of fun until Philly won the game in Overtime 5-4, forcing a Game 7 in Philly.

Sadly, the Flyers won Game 7 at home, knocking the Sabres out of the playoffs.

Every spring for the last 27 years of my existence, my heart had been broken; the Sabres would inevitably be eliminated from the playoffs. You would think that I would have gotten used to it and that the pain wouldn't sting as much, but it never got easier...I wasn't pouting, I was just frustrated!

I should be happy though, because earlier on in the season, I did not think the Sabres would make the Playoffs, let alone go 7 games with Philly. So in that respect, yes, I was happy and proud that the Sabres were able to turn things around.

If I've said it once, then I've said it a thousand times before...*Well, maybe next year...*

2011 Offseason

There was a lot of activity happening during the 2011 Off Season.

First of all, Buffalo based fine dining restaurant Mighty Taco announced that they were expanding outside of the Buffalo market and opening the first store in Rochester, to be opened by Summer 2011! That was good news and music to my ears.

Second, there were some changes in the NHL. It turned out that Shannon and I were not going to go to Atlanta to see the Thrashers host the Sabres. Yep, that was right, the Atlanta Thrashers had been sold and were moving, north of the boarder, *up Canada way, that's where I fell in love where the stars above, came out to play...*

The NHL was finally returning to Winnipeg after a 15 year drought. Back in 1996, the Winnipeg Jets moved down to Arizona and became the Phoenix Coyotes.

I was a little bummed out hearing that the Thrashers were moving because I was really looking forward to visiting Atlanta. I had never been to Atlanta and I was extremely excited to meet Atlanta's best defense lawyer, Ben Matlock. On top of meeting Matlock, I thought that it would have been really cool to hang out with Matlock's associate Conrad McMasters. If anyone knew of a great BBQ Pit to go to, it would have absolutely been Conrad McMasters. Additionally, Conrad would have driven us in style in his 1965 red convertible Ford Mustang.

I heard Atlanta was a great city and there was so much to do there. I would have liked to have seen Olympic Park, since Atlanta was host to the 1996 Summer Olympic Games. Coca-Cola has their headquarters down there as well. Since the Thrashers were moving to Winnipeg, I guess I would just have to postpone my trip to Atlanta for another time.

Friday June 24, 2011 was the first night of the NHL draft. The draft was being held at the Xcel Energy Center in Minnesota. Eventually Winnipeg took the podium to announce their 1st round draft pick, "On behalf of the Winnipeg Jets…" So it was official, the Jets were back in business, and playing in the Eastern Conference, South East Division for the upcoming 2011-12 season…weird!

Third, some rumors surfaced in Buffalo, that new Sabres owner Terry Pegula wanted to buy the AHL Rochester Americans.

I'll give you a quick history lesson…For 29 seasons the Rochester Americans were the Sabres farm team. However, for a few seasons, the Sabres ended up sharing the Amerks with the Florida Panthers. In 2008, the Sabres and Americans cut their ties and got a divorce. The Sabres new farm team was the Portland Pirates. Once the Sabres weren't affiliated with the Amerks, everyone in Rochester stopped showing up to the AHL team's home games and attendance dropped to like 8 people per game. Plain and simple, no one cared about the Americans since they weren't affiliated with the Sabres any more.

If you ask me, and anyone else in the Western New York area, the Sabres/Americans marriage was a match made in heaven. The two cities were only one hour apart, and if the Sabres needed to call someone up from Rochester for a game that night, it was no big deal. On top of that, you could see the future Sabres evolve in

Rochester. A lot of great Sabres have played in Rochester at one point in their career, including Ryan Miller and Rob Ray.

On Friday June 24, 2011, that wet dream became a reality and the Sabres signed a purchase agreement with the Rochester Americans. Subsequently, the Sabres announced their departure with the Portland Pirates.

Additionally, Terry Pegula opened the check book for free agency, something the Sabres had never done in their history. The Sabres acquired Villie Leino from Philly, Christian Ehrhoff from Vancouver, and Robyn Regher from Calgary. Every sports news feed said that the Sabres were gonna be the next hot team for the upcoming season, and possibly a Stanley Cup contender...

Fourth, before the upcoming season, the Sabres were to take part in the NHL Premiere Series in Europe with a game in Berlin and another in Helsinki. On the Sabres website, they had travel packages set up by AAA if you wanted to go. I briefly researched it, but opted not to go. Now I was a huge Sabres fan, and I know that I've dragged Shannon all up and down the east coast to see the Sabres play, but it came with a reasonable price tag. However, to watch the Sabres play in Germany came with a little bit bigger price tag. The six day trip to Germany cost roughly $1700, and that wasn't including the $1250 plane ticket per person. On top of that, it only included tickets to the Berlin game. Tickets and accommodations for the Helsinki game were extra. And then there are the added costs of food and beer and souvenirs and all that stuff. But it was okay, I had already been to Germany, at Disney's EPCOT. *Maybe next season...*

During the summer, the Sabres home changed names. The former HSBC Arena was now renamed First Niagara Center.

New owner Terry Pegula paid the bill for some renovations to First Niagara Center. The Sabres locker room was gutted and had a total make over. There were some fresh coats of paint added to the First Niagara Center as well.

Lastly, I landed a job and got off unemployment. I was able to use my future automotive degree and got a job at an automotive research and development company. That was a good thing because now Shannon and I could afford our mini hockey vacations.

October 2011

Friday, October 21, 2011, it was 5:40am and the alarm clock was going off. I rolled out of bed and hit the snooze.

Friday, October 21, 2011, it was 5:49am and the alarm clock was going off. I rolled out of bed and hit the snooze.

Friday, October 21, 2011, it was 5:58am and the alarm clock was going off. I rolled out of bed and hit the snooze.

Friday, October 21, 2011, it was 6:00am and Teppo puppy was barking because my father in law Jimbo was at the front door, ready to pick up Shannon and me for the airport.

I didn't get much sleep the night before because Shannon and I had stumbled home from the Bay Side Pub earlier that morning. The night before, Shannon and I watched the Sabres/Panthers game from the Bay Side and then we hung around to watch the rest of Game 2 of the World Series, while we had a few more drinks.

I think by the time we made it back home, it was at least 1am and we still needed to pack for our mini Florida trip. So there Shannon and I were, drunk packing in the wee hours of the morning.

We were finally loaded up in Jimbo's Ford Taurus by 6:10am.

I was a white knuckle flyer, so I normally had a drink or two, or got shit faced before I flew. I didn't drink this time because I was still rockin' a buzz from the night before.

We needed gas, so Jimbo stopped off at Delta Sonic. I decided to gas up his car since he was taking Shannon and me to the airport. Jimbo thought it was thoughtful and wanted to know if I wanted a coffee from the gas station. I told him, "Thanks, but no thanks. I don't want to wreck my foggy buzz that I've got going on right now..." Jimbo just laughed.

Shannon and I got to the Rochester airport and checked in without a problem. Thanks to Priceline.com, we were flying a direct, three hour flight via Air Tran.

Once we boarded the plane, I closed my eyes for half a second and when I opened them, we were in sunny Tampa, FL...*The local time is 10:30 and the local weather is sunny and 72 degrees Fahrenheit.*

Shannon and I navaguessed our way over to the Hertz car rental kiosk. When I was booking the flight, hotel, and rental through Priceline, I chose the cheapest econo-box car. The sales clerk dude said that I had my choice between a Nissan Versa or a Toyota Yaris.

I laughed out loud and said, "Ha! I'm not gonna drive around in that crap…can you do something better for me?"

The Hertz dude asked, "Well sir, what were you looking for?"

I answered, "I dunno. Do you guys by chance have something cool like the new Camaro or a Mustang? I'll even do the new Challenger."

The Hertz dude said, "Let me make some phone calls," as he picked up the receiver to call up to see what they had available. After a couple of "uh-huhs" on the phone, the Hertz dude said, "We do have a brand new Mustang GT convertible."

I whole heartily and enthusiastically said, "Sounds great! Sign me up!"

The Hertz dude asked how much I was willing to spend on the GT. I said, "I dunno, maybe an extra $100?"

The Hertz dude said, "Unfortunately I can't do that."

I inquired on how much the upgrade would be. After he told me it would be an additional $500, I exclaimed out loud, "Good Lord that's a lotta money!"

We ended up settling on a brand new V6 hardtop Mustang, and if you were wondering, the pony was silver.

I will make an admission that may upset some people; even though I was a Chevy guy I was still excited to drive the Mustang. Actually when it came down to it, I honestly liked the Mustang a little better than the Camaro. The thing that didn't fly well with me was that the Gen5 Camaro was made up in Oshawa, Ontario, Canada. I had nothing against Canadians (except they won the Gold Medal by beating out Team USA on our own turf back in Salt Lake City, and then they beat us again for the Gold up in Vancouver), but the Camaro was an iconic piece of America. It was just another prime example of America selling out its own sovereignty. At least the Mustang was still built in America!

As we were leaving the Hertz parking garage, I drove past a couple Dodge Chargers that fired up as I passed by them. I tore ass leaving the parking garage, trying to do my best rendition of Steve McQueen in *Bullitt*.

Shannon and I soon found ourselves on I-275 headed towards downtown Tampa. We had no real plans for Friday. Our

Sabres/Lightning game wasn't until Saturday night, so we had the whole day to hang out and do whatever we wanted.

As we were approaching downtown, I realized that we needed some beer. So all race car driver/Steve McQueen style in my V6 mustang, I ripped it across all three lanes and took the exit ramp on two tires, with burning rubber in my wake.

I soon found a nice gas station that sold beer. The gas station was classy looking, right down to the metal bars on the windows and doors. We picked up an 18 pack of Modelo, a 12 of Tecate, and big bottle of Corona.

Minutes later, Shannon and I pulled into the Sheraton River Walk Hotel.

As I put the Mustang into park, the valet greeted us. I popped the trunk and Shannon and I grabbed our bags and cases of beer. The valet attendant looked at all the beer and then at our Buffalo Sabre shirts and said, "Huh, you guys must be here for the game..."

Once Shannon and I got into our room, I opened her Corona for her and grabbed a Tecate before heading towards the bathroom because I had to poop and then shower, because that's what I do.

The shower was pretty cool because they had an arm level beer holder tray. Shannon later informed me that it was to hold shampoo and conditioner, but I'll let her believe what she wants to believe.

The hotel room had a tour guide book of stuff to do in Tampa. As Shannon and I leafed through the book, we saw that there were sunset pirate cruises. Since Shannon was a huge pirate junkie, we had to go! Shannon called up Captain Memo out there in Clearwater, Fl. and booked the two of us on a sunset cruise for 6pm.

From there, Shannon and I migrated our way down to the pool to check it out before leaving the hotel to go explore.

Next, Shannon and I found ourselves walking down River Walk. River Walk was nice and was exactly like what it sounded like; a walking park along the river. There were a couple parks for kids and even a puppy park.

After walking for a bit, we began to work up an appetite. Since we were still close to the hotel, we decided to try out its bar and restaurant, Ashley Street Grill.

For lunch, I decided to branch out of my circle of chicken wings and pizza. Instead I tried Gator Gumbo and a Shrimp and

Crab Sandwich which I washed down with local brew Florida Avenue Ale...I had two ales to be exact.

Then it was time for Shannon and me to take a cat nap before our cruise.

Shannon and I made it just in time to board Captain Memo's pirate ship before it set sail. Right after we boarded, we had our picture taken with a pirate and a treasure chest. We were quickly ushered towards the open bar! I was excited about the open bar until I found out the only beer they had was Butt Light or red label Bud Heavies. I could not drink Bud Heavy because after two of them I would get a viscous head ache. I was not a huge fan of Butt Light because it tasted like seltzer, which also tasted like crap. However, looking on the "bright side" of Butt Light, I could drink as many of them as I wanted without getting headaches.

Captain Memo's cruise was awesome. The ship puttered around Clearwater and headed towards the Gulf of Mexico. On our voyage out to the Gulf, there were a couple of dolphins that swam along the ship and jumped out of the water a few times. Both Shannon and I thought it was pretty cool. I told Shannon, "These are *Clearwater* Dolphins, not *Miami* Dolphins, so they are ok in my book..."

Besides the open bar, the cruise was a lot of fun. The pirates had games and activities and drunk dancing from the conga line to the chicken dance. The pirates also handed out pirate hats and face painted pirate beard and goatees on everyone.

It was around this time that the Butt Lights were kicking in. I remember it quite vividly *because I looked to the sea, reflections in the waves sparked my memory; some happy, some sad. I thought of childhood friends and the dreams we had. We lived happily forever, as the story goes, but somehow we missed our pot of gold, but we'll try the best we can to carry on! A gathering of angels soon appeared above my head, and they sang me this song of hope, and here's what they had to say...They said come sail away, come sail away, come sail away with me!...*

I soon realized that there were no angels singing above me. In fact, I was the only one singing. And the only angle above my head was Shannon, and she was trying to cover my mouth, trying to stop my tone deaf singing and butchering of the Styx's classic song.

Midway through the cruise, Shannon and I made our way to the bow of the ship. I wanted to reenact that horrible James Cameron movie *Titanic*. Shannon refused to put her arms around me, but I still reached out and shouted, "I'm king of the world!" I then asked the one of the pirates, "Do many people reenact *Titanic*?"

The pirate said, "Yes!"

I had a follow up question, "I noticed the 'poop deck' sign...Which pirate swabs the poop deck?"

The pirates smiled.

I asked, "Do you get that a lot too?"

The pirate said, "Yes."

Shannon and I ended up talking to the pirate and he said he was originally from Washington. We asked him what brought him to Florida. Our new pirate friend told us he left Washington for Nashville and spent some time there before he packed up and drove out to Florida. Shannon and I told him that we were going to Nashville that upcoming December for a Sabres/Predators game. So we inquired on where to go. Our pirate friend told us that we needed to hit up South Broadway.

It was 8pm and our pirate cruise had ended. I still had a Butt Light to drink and the pirates wouldn't let me leave the ship with it. I tried to choke down the Butt Light, but it wasn't happening. I poured out the Butt Light into the water, thinking that I was helping out the fishes by giving them a buzz too.

Once Shannon and I were on the mainland, we had no idea what to do. We ended up running into two fellow pirates from the cruise, Mike and Melissa from Illinois. They were headed for Frenchy's to try out their Stone Crab Fest. Shannon and I had nothing better to do, so we asked if we could crash their party, and they said, "Yeah, why not?!"

Mike was on a mission because he needed to take a leak very badly, which was understandable, considering we all came from an open bar.

We stumbled across a Wings beach shop, so we all wandered in. Mike asked the employee if they had a bathroom and the woman said no. Mike promptly asked, "Well, where do you go when you have to pee?"

The employee said, "We don't have a public bathroom..."

A few establishments down was a bar, so Mike ran in really quick to take a squirt.

A short walk later, we finally arrived at Frenchy's!

The place was a lively and happening joint. They even had a live band.

I had to squirt again, so I ran off to the bathroom; I think I inherited my mother's bladder. In the meantime, Shannon, Melissa, and Mike got a table, but I didn't know that.

After I got out of the bathroom, I made a lap around one of the bars, trying to find my party. As I started my second lap, I decided to make a pit stop at the bar, grab a beer, and continue the search for my party.

The bartender asked what I wanted and I requested a Corona. I don't know what it is about Corona, but every time I have one, it tastes like I'm on vacation.

While I was waiting at the bar, I heard some dude bitch about how horrible his Tampa Bay Buccaneers were that current season (which turned out to be 4-12). Apparently winning a Super Bowl, a Stanley Cup, and a World Series did not make that guy happy.

There was some older lady sitting next to me at the bar. I asked her if she was a local and she told me yes. I told her that I wasn't from Tampa and I was wondering what some of the hot spots were. She told me that I was already at one of them. She asked what I was doing down there in Clearwater and I told her that Shannon and I had come down for the Sabres game. She gave me the evil eye and jokingly grumbled, "Oh, you're one of them...the enemy. Just because you invaded doesn't mean you're gonna win..."

I jokingly said, "Hey, that's a nice way of telling me to go screw myself"

She replied, "Honey, you're down here in Tampa, we don't tell foreigners that...The correct terminology is 'Go Buck Yourself!'"

I told her that I liked that and it was pretty creative.

Just then Shannon found me and I told her how I met a new friend, Ann.

We told Ann that we were staying in downtown Tampa so we could walk to the game and stumble back to the hotel afterwards.

Ann said that if we wanted to, her son worked at the Tampa Aquarium and he could get us some discounted tickets for Sunday.

Ann also mentioned that the Clearwater Aquarium was home to Winter the Dolphin from the new movie *Dolphin Tale*. We told her that both sounded like great ideas, and we gave her our number.

Shannon and I then met back up with our new friends Melissa and Mike.

Evidently our table was right next to the live band, Sweet Spot. The band was decent; they played a lot of covers.

I waited for my chance. It came in between songs, when it was kind of quiet, and I shouted, **"FREEBIRD!!! PLAY FREEBIRD!!!"**

The lead singer immediately looked over at me and spoke into his mic, "Ok, ladies and gentlemen, right here is a no-no, and I'm glad we're getting it out of the way early. We *do* take requests, but we **DO NOT** play *Freebird* or *Stairway to Heaven*…"

I asked, "What about *Big Balls* by AC/DC?!"

The lead singer answered back with a quick, "NO!"

Since Frenchie's was having their Stone Crab fest, we decided to partake. Shannon and I ordered just one basket and they were delicious!

The table next to us noticed that Shannon and I were wearing our Sabres gear and they wandered over to strike up a conversation. Apparently the party of eight was from Lackawanna and East Aurora, NY. I told them that I was from South Central Grand Island originally, then I married Shannon, and she moved me down the road to Rochester.

Eventually Shannon and I were ready to check out the rest of Clearwater's night life. We told Melissa and Mike that we were going to wander across the parking lot to the Palm Pavilion and that they were more than welcome to join us. Shannon and I closed out our tab and ventured out.

One of Shannon's coworkers told us that we needed to go to the Palm Pavilion because his sister was the hostess there. By the time Shannon and I made our way over to the Pavilion, we found out that we missed the hostess by 10 minutes.

Shannon and I grabbed a drink at the bar and then migrated towards the beach to enjoy our bevies.

I tried to convince Shannon to go skinny dipping but my efforts turned out to be fruitless. I tried to tell her that the water was warm and that it was dark enough that no one would see.

Since Plan A didn't work, I tried convincing her that we should shag in the sand dunes, up in the tall grass, hidden from everybody.

Plan B didn't work since Ms. Buzzkill said that we are not allowed in the tall grass because they were endangered and we could not disrupt the natural habitat and blaa blaa blaa with that eco-weenie jargon.

After we finished our beers, we aimlessly wandered around some more before coming upon a bar that had a grand piano!

At first, Shannon and I thought it was a piano bar, but it was more of a cocktail lounge. The name of the place was Lobster Pot Bistro. We decided to go in any way. The pianist was in between songs, so I asked him if I could make a request and he said, "Yes." I asked him if he could play the Charlie Brown theme song. So moments later, there were Shannon and me, dancing like the Peanuts gang to the Charlie Brown theme in a fancy black tie restaurant.

After our dance, the two of us realized we were still hungry, but we weren't in the mood for lobster.

We found a pizza shack a few steps down the block. Shannon and I had slices of pepperoni pizza and a Coke.

Then it was bedtime.

We were up by 6am on Saturday because we had our deep sea fishing trip aboard the Queen Fleet.

Shannon and I were checked in, on the boat, had our reels and seats picked out by 7:15am. Our boat was not departing until 8am, so we just shivered in our seats...Yes, it was cold out. Go figure, it was the same temperature in Florida as it was back home in New York! It felt like 60^0F with a steady wind ripping off the water, so it was a bit chili.

Finally 8am rolled around and we puttered out to the Gulf of Mexico. Shannon and I were still tired from the night before, so we went into the mess hall and passed out.

Once the boat was about 8-10 miles away from shore, it was time to fish!

It was about 20 minutes into fishing and Shannon caught a fish, a Grunt to be specific.

The deck hand asked Shannon is she wanted to keep her fish.

Shannon told him that she would like to.

He told Shannon that she needed to pick a number so he could keep track of the fish we caught.

Before Shannon could answer, I shouted out, "69!"

The deck hand said, "69 it is!"

Shannon just stared at me and shook her head.

A few minutes later I caught a small silver looking fish. It was too small to keep so I threw back.

We fished for about another hour and then I began to get sea sick. The boat was bouncing around in every direction; bow to stern and port to starboard.

I got up to hit the head.

Once in the head, I had to do the tripod to pee correctly (the tripod was when you put your hand against the wall to balance yourself when you pee so you don't hit everything; 2 feet on the floor and one on the wall, hence the tripod). The awful smell of stinky poopy diapers in the garbage can and the rocking of the boat almost made me toss my cookies all over, but I chocked them down.

After I finished up and washed my hands, I went back out onto the deck to tell Shannon that I was calling it quits and that I was sea sick. We both caught our $40 fish (fishing tickets were $40/person) so I figured that the trip paid for itself. At least we weren't coming ashore empty handed.

I made my way back to the mess hall where I joined a couple other sea sick seamen.

It was about an hour and a half later when Shannon and I were land lubbers again! Oh thank God!

One of the deck hands cleaned our fish for a nominal fee.

Our captain recommended that we wander down a few slips to the Bait Shop and they would cook up our fish into fish tacos. I thought about for a bit and decided, "Why not, I've never had an actual genuine fish taco before."

Once we got to the Bait Shop, our waitress told us that our fish would only make two fish tacos, which was fine with us. Shannon and I ended up ordering Buffalo Shrimp and tuna steak cutlets. And everything tasted wonderful!

After we left the Bait Shop, we headed towards the beach.

We quickly found ourselves upon Pier 60, which was loaded with people. The area was really cool because on a section of the white sands were organized volleyball courts; with at least 15 games being played. Shannon and I walked down the pier, but we didn't stay too terribly long because the parking meter was about to expire.

By the time we got back to the hotel, it was time for another poop and shower, and yes I had another beer while I was on the can. In the meantime, Shannon went down to the pool to catch some rays and Vitamin D. Once I finished with my poop and shower, I went down to join her.

We stayed at the pool for a little bit, but we figured that we needed to sneak in another quick cat nap before the game. We needed our energy because if the Sabers won, we were going to go to the Hard Rock Casino in Tampa. So we quickly scurried off to bed.

We woke from our cat nap at around 5pm. Our plan was to be walking to St. Pete Times Forum by 5:30pm with roadies in hand. Surprisingly we stuck to our agenda. We figured that since we weren't in Buffalo, the local law enforcement would probably frown upon us for walking around with open beer cans through the streets of Tampa. Luckily enough for us, our hotel supplied our room with paper coffee cups…

By the time Shannon and I had finished the 6 block trek over to St. Pete Times Forum, our beers had evaporated and we were still thirsty. As we looked at St. Pete Times Forum, we noticed that there was an outdoor bar on the upper deck! Thusly we did not hesitate to go in an hour before puck drop.

Shannon and I found our way to the Butt Light Party Deck, and seconds later we were next in line for beer. Unfortunately all they were serving was Butt Light or Butt Red Heavy. Shannon and I opted for two 20oz Butt Lights that totaled $18! *Highway robbery!* I felt like we were back at Ralph Wilson Stadium; where you needed to take out a second mortgage to buy a round of beers.

Thankfully our bartender told us that if we liked the Tampa Bay Lightning on Fakebook, then we could get a free 20 oz. draft beer! After being told that great news, we hopped onto our cell phones to try to find this free beer coupon. All we needed to do was to "like" the Lightning and then a coupon would show up on our phone. Lastly we would need to show our phone to the bartender to redeem our free beer.

The two dudes standing next to us told us that there was a glitch in the software system. Apparently you could sign up to get the free beer coupon, but there was no way for the bartenders to collect the coupon from our phone. So our new friends told us to hit up the one bar before the game, and then during the 1st Intermission to hit up the other bar on that party deck…$40 worth of free beer?! I could handle that!

It was 6:45pm when Shannon and I finished that last of that piss water Butt Light. Then we wandered back up to the bar to redeem our first free round of Butt Light. Once we got our round, we ventured into the Forum to find our seats in Section 328.

Shannon and I got to our seats just in time for the pregame video up on the jumbotron. They played the typical pump you up music to get the fans ready for the game. At the same time, there were two Tesla coils that were hung from the rafters. It was a cool sight to see those Tesla coils being energized! It looked like 10 feet long lightning bolts shooting out from it. That really got the crowd going.

Moments later, we removed our hats for the American National Anthem. The color guard for the National Anthem was from the MacDill Air Force Base. Also joining them was 1980 Team USA Men's Hockey gold medal winner, goaltender Jim Craig.

Once the crowd finished singing the Anthem, the Tesla coils were lit up again!

After the Tesla coils calmed down, it was time for some hockey! Buffalo was wearing their classic whites and Tampa was rocking their "Bolts" 3rd jersey.

The Sabres came out of the gate strong and had some quick shots on the Tampa goaltender Mathieu Garon, but Garon was up for the challenge. Buffalo had a couple odd man rushes, but couldn't produce anything. Tampa also had their chances, but Buffalo's goalie Ryan Miller was playing pretty well.

Buffalo had everything going for them in the 1st Period. They had some great offense and shots on net, but nothing went in. It didn't help Buffalo that Garon was playing great.

At the end of the 1st Period, it was tied 0-0

After the 1st Period buzzer rang, Shannon and I got up and headed out to the Butt Light Party Deck to retrieve our 2nd round of free Butt Light.

Tampa came out strong at the start of the 2nd Period and it paid off for them. Almost 5 minutes into the 2nd Period, the Bolts'

Pavel Kubina put Tampa on the board with a slap shot from the Buffalo blue line.

In the last minute of the 2nd Period, Buffalo found some offense again, but they just couldn't score. Buffalo had great puck movement and multiple shots on goal, but they just couldn't squeak one past Garon. After two periods of play, Tampa Bay Lightning was still up 1-0.

There were quite a few Sabre fans down there at the game. The arena was about ¾ full, with about half the fans cheering for Buffalo. Shannon and I met a few Buffalo transplants. The one guy we met was from Cheektowaga. He moved his family down to Orlando a few years back. He said every time the Sabres played in Tampa, the whole family would road trip out to see their beloved Sabres.

Buffalo had a power play chance during the early stages of the 3rd Period, but the Sabers "powerless play" showed its true colors, and the game remained a 1-0 Lightning lead.

Midway through the 3rd Period, Buffalo got sloppy in their own zone as they were clearing the puck. Tampa stole the puck back at the Sabres blue line and threw the puck towards the Buffalo net, where Tampa's Martin St. Louis was waiting. St. Louis was all alone, facing Buffalo goalie Ryan Miller. St. Louis deked, pulled Miller out of position, and dumped the puck past Miller's stick side, and scored. St. Louis made it a 2-0 Tampa lead.

With just over 90 seconds left in the game, Miller was pulled for the extra attacker. It went for naught because Tampa's Victor Hedman scored an empty netter, making it 3-0 Tampa.

It was an aggravating game to watch. Buffalo couldn't even buy a goal. On top of that, it upset us that Shannon and I had to walk the "Walk of Shame" again. It was just so infuriating. It upset me that Shannon and I traveled long distances to show up and see our Sabres play, yet they couldn't be bothered to show up; they didn't even make an attempt.

Regardless, Shannon and I sucked it up and walked the few blocks back to the Sheridan. On the walk back, we agreed that our luck would be similar to the Sabres if we hit up the Hard Rock Casino. Getting shut out 3-0 was a buzz kill and spoiled the mood for any partying. Shannon and I agreed upon getting back to the room, cracking a cold one, and then going from there.

Once in our hotel room, we cracked our beers and debated on what we wanted to do that evening. It was only 10:30pm, so the night was still young. We thought about hitting up Ybor City or finding a bar close by...

It was 10:45pm and we passed out. I felt like the big loser...years ago, 10:45pm on a Saturday night meant that we were just getting ready to go out and party, not fall asleep! I hated to say it, but I thought I might be getting old. One of the first signs that I was getting old was when I noticed that all the bands I grew up listening to in high school were coming out with greatest hits albums...Foo Fighters, Alice in Chains, Rob Zombie, Godsmack, Collective Soul, Nirvana, Korn, Smashing Pumpkins, Red Hot Chili Peppers, Green Day, Soundgarden, the Offspring, Stone Temple Pilots, Pearl Jam, Stained, Goo Goo Dolls, Limp Bizkit, need I go on? I felt even older when I heard Metallica on a classic rock radio station!

Anyway, I was awoken at 11pm to the chants of a mob. I was startled and had no idea what was going on. I sprang out of bed and opened up the sliding glass door to our balcony. It turned out to be the Wall Street Protesters marching around the block of the Bank of America building.

After I drifted back off to sleep, I was woken up a couple more times because some car pealed out at 2:00 in the morning and a police car siren screamed by at 3:00 in the morning.

I finally pulled myself out of bed Sunday morning around 8:30. I was still frustrated about the game and still licking my wounds. I felt that Johnny Cash put it just right in *Sunday Morning Coming Down* by singing, "Well, I woke up Sunday morning with no way to hold my head that didn't hurt. And the beer I had for breakfast wasn't bad, so I had one more for dessert..."

So, on my way to the bathroom for my morning poo, I grabbed a beer out from the ice filled sink before I plopped my dupa on the can. Before I finished my poop, I already cracked open another can for dessert.

I had to say that even though Shannon and I were on a mini vacation, we surprisingly ate relatively healthy; a steady diet of fish and libations...*just like Jesus and his disciples.*

Shannon and I decided to head on out to Ybor City for breakfast since we missed out on the night life there the evening before.

We boarded the hotel shuttle and we arrived there in no time.

One of Shannon's coworkers told us that we needed to go to the Columbian, so Shannon and I started our course in that direction.

A lot of the establishments were still closed at 10am, but that was understandable because it was Sunday morning.

Shannon and I both liked the buildings, architecture, and the cool fun vibe that it gave off.

We soon made it to the Columbian and we were ready for breakfast! We opened the doors to the Columbian and walked into an empty restaurant. We looked around the place and it looked gorgeous. Even though the place was dead, we could tell that would have been a great place to hang out. Shannon and I waited a minute or two to see if a host or hostess would greet us but nothing. As I looked around the bar, I got a weird and eerie felling from *The Shinning*...**REDRUM!** Shannon and I decided to get breakfast somewhere else.

We walked past Gaspar's Grotto and it caught Shannon's eye because it had Captain Morgan and chick pirate statues in the lobby. That got us in the door and we had breakfast at Gaspar's Grotto.

Shannon and I both ordered the New Mexico Eggs Benedict, and they were scrumptious. Instead of an English muffin, Gaspar's used a fried Polenta wedge...it was delicious! I washed down my Benedict with a mimosa and Shannon with a Bloody Mary.

After breakfast, Shannon and I were picked up by the hotel shuttle.

Once Shannon and I checked out of the hotel, we headed back out *on the road again*. Soon we were on Bay Boulevard, en route to the beach!

On our way out to the beach, we stopped off at the original Hooters! Shannon had never been to Hooters before. I decided to take her because she needed to get it off her bucket list.

We sat on the porch and grabbed a couple drinks. I was thoroughly unimpressed with their beer selection. It was the same crap ass, shit beer served everywhere else; Butt, Butt Light, Coors, Coors Light, Miller, Miller Lite...They had no local beers at all. I ended up settling on a Sam Addams Oktoberfest.

Shannon was quite surprised on how tame the Hooters girls' outfits were...she thought they were going to be sluttier.

The outfits looked they had not changed since their 1983 inception. The girls were still wearing the scrunched down tube socks with white sneakers.

On a side note, apparently the reason why Hooters was started was because six dudes down in Clearwater wanted chicken wings from Buffalo. The dudes knew they couldn't get a weekend pass from the women to go up to Buffalo, so they decided to bring the wings down to Clearwater...and the rest was history...the back of the menu told me that!

After Hooters, our next stop was to Clearwater Marine Aquarium (Rescue*Rehab*Release) and home to Winter the Dolphin; star of Dolphin Tale.

As soon as Shannon and I entered the aquarium, we rushed upstairs to see Winter's 1:30 show.

We couldn't really see Winter too well because there were a ton of people around the deck to see Winter; it was least five people deep. One of the trainers was talking to the crowd on her PA set and giving some fun facts about Winter; such as how they found her. The trainer had told us that the true story of Winter varies quite differently than the Hollywood version, go figure.

Winter's actual story was that she became tangled in crab traps off the coast of Florida. She ended up losing her tail because the line had wrapped around her tail, cutting off circulation. She was eventually rescued and sent to the Clearwater Marine Aquarium for rehab. Winter compensated for her missing fin, which in return, was going to cause stress on her spine. Special people came in to help and created a special prosthetic tail fin for Winter to help correct her swimming...So in layman's terms, Winter was the Nemo to the dolphin community.

Winter was cool. She could do everything else a normal dolphin could do, except survive in the wild. Winter would perform jumps and give high five.

After the show, Shannon and I migrated our way to the Third Level where Nicholas the Dolphin was. Nick was the only boy dolphin currently at the aquarium. He seemed pretty cool. As Shannon looked at Nick, she observed a lot of funky discoloration the entire way down his back. Shannon asked me what I thought was wrong with him. The only thing I could come up with was that Nick got in the way when the Buffalo Bills squished the fish! After that comment I felt a sharp pain in my rib cage area. Later I found out that baby dolphin Nicholas and his mom Noelle were found off the coast of Florida on Christmas Eve 2002. Noelle and Nicholas were rushed to Clearwater, but unfortunately Nick's mom did not make it. Attention was then focused towards Nick, who pulled through. All of the scaring on Nick's back was due to sever sunburn, not the Buffalo Bills' stampede.

The aquarium was also home to a couple Mother Sharks, stingrays, Hope (the baby dolphin), Panama the Dolphin (probably named after the Van Halen song), otters, and sea turtles. The aquarium even had a Turtle Intensive Care Unit!

The aquarium was fun, but it was just swamped with people wanting to see Winter and everyone else.

After we left the aquarium, Shannon and I drove around the surrounding neighborhoods for a bit. The houses seemed nice, but it looked like there wasn't enough property. The houses looked small and stacked side by side; pretty close to each other. Now I was the kind of guy who wanted my space. Yes, I like my neighbors, but I also like to pee in my own back yard without anyone looking at my massive moose cock. On top of that, the houses down there were lucky to have a garage, let alone a two car garage. And the driveways were only one or two car lengths deep. Now I am a car guy. If I were to live there, how was I going to work on my Camaro Z28, El Camino, and future 1980s Chevy Monte Carlo SS with T tops, on top of having Shannon's Jeep Wrangler in the drive way!? There wasn't enough room!

So after cruising' around town, Shannon and I finally found a spot to feed a parking meter and run off to the beach.

Shannon and I soon found a plot of sand, out of reach from a bocce ball game. After we finished off our first round of Modelo, we decided to go for a sea foam walk up and down the coast, all romantic and all.

Shannon and I ended our walk back where the trouble all began...Palm Pavilion!

Shannon and I ran into Palm Pavilion for a quick drink because we only had nine minutes left on the meter. Also, Shannon wanted to see if her coworker's sister, the hostess, was working. It turned out that the sister was not working that day.

At the bar, I asked the bartender what they had on tap, and I got the stupid rehearsed regurgitated line of, "Buttweiser, Butt Light, Miller, Miller Lite, Coors Light…"

I asked the wench, "Do you have anything local? Like Florida Ale? Florida Avenue Blueberry Ale?"

The bartender answered back, "No, we don't have Florida Ale…"

I inquired, "Well…what local brews do you have?"

The bartender said, "Yuengling!"

I looked at Shannon and then the bartender. I said, "Really?! How is Yuengling a local brew when they are based out of Pennsylvania?"

The bartender informed me that Yuengling just opened up a brewery in the area.

Shannon ordered a Sam Addams Oktoberfest.

Shannon and I got back to the meter with no ticket…SCORE!

Our next mission was to hit up the one of the two Polish restaurants we saw in Clearwater on Gulf to Bay Boulevard.

Pierogi Grill was the winner!

Our hostess, who also spoke fluent Polish, seated us at our table…She was authentic and had a nice dupa as well; not that I was looking.

The whole place was cool, not only did the waitresses speak Polish, but so did the patrons (mind you the 80 year old patrons probably just came from bingo at the local Catholic church).

Shannon and I studied the menu….We both opted for two draft Okocims…they also had Warka and Zywiec.

Shannon ordered the Polish Prince Platter which included some sauerkraut, a kielbasa, four strawberry pierogies, and a cabbage roll. I ordered up the 12 piece Pierogi, half cheese and potato and half sauerkraut.

Before our food came, Shannon and I wandered around the Polish deli they had. It was filled with candies, jams, spices, cold cuts, and frozen pierogies!

Our meals were wonderful and everything tasted great.

After we closed out our check, Shannon and I hopped back into our Mustang. I Steve McQueen-ed it around the corner to the gas station, filled her up before we gently returned her to Hertz.

Shannon and I chugged the last two beers of our trip on the gangway to the airport...nothing like chocking down warm beer; it did not go down smoothly.

Well, Shannon and I breezed through the pat down and the "turn to the left and cough" check point.

Our next mission was to find our gate.

On the way to our gate we found a bar...

We both did a shot of Jose Cuervo with training wheels and chased it with a beer. We made our flight without a problem.

November 2011

My buddies Brian and Travis began to hated it when Shannon and I went on the mini Sabres vacations because the Sabres almost always ended up losing. I thought about it, and I devised a plan to make the Sabres win, or at least make money off of them losing...

Any Buffalo fan knew not to bet with their heart; otherwise they will lose. On our road trips, the Sabres were always losing. So all I need to do was to call my bookie every time we went on our vacations and put $50 down on the opposition. It was going to be a win/win situation. If my Sabres lost, I would have more beer money to drown my sorrows in. But if my Sabres won, well then it was a good $50 invested. Now I just needed to test out my theory...

It was Friday November 11, 2011 and the entire work day dragged. It felt like forever before 4:30pm rolled around.

I had a couple errands to run before running home and packing for our Boston trip.

I ran to the grocery store because I had to pick up a bag of dog food for Teppo Numminen.

Next to the grocery store was the liquor store. I wanted to pick up some chocolate liqueur for the trip.

I told Grandpa Ziggy that last month when Shannon and I went deep sea fishing in Tampa, I got sea sick. Grandpa told me that when he was in the navy during World War II, the government used to hand out chocolate to help ease sea sickness.

That weekend in Boston, Shannon and I had a whale watching excursion planned for 12:30pm on Saturday. I was going to take every precaution and home remedy to not get sea sick. So I had it all planned out. I would buy a bottle of Godiva chocolate liqueur to mix in with my hot chocolate.

I got to the liquor store and it was packed. I tried looking around for the Godiva stuff, but I couldn't find it. However I did stumble across some chocolate whipped cream flavored vodka. I thought about it for half a second...*whipped cream goes well with hot chocolate. Chocolate goes well with chocolate. Vodka goes well with everything...* So it was settled. I bought the bottle of chocolate whipped cream vodka to put into my hot chocolate before the whale watching excursion!

On my walk up to the cashier counter, I stumbled across a bottle of watermelon Pucker liqueur, which I obviously bought as well.

I got home a little after 5pm. I pooped and showered and then packed.

Shannon and I were off to the hometown of one of my favorite rock bands, Godsmack, and one of her favorite rock bands, Aerosmith.

We hit the road before 6pm, en route to Bean Town!

From Western New York, it was pretty much a straight shot to Boston. All we had to do was hop on the 90 and head east.

On the ride out to Boston, I still had one small errand to make.

We pulled off the Verona exit on the 90 to stop off at Turning Stone Casino so I could place a bet on tomorrow night's game.

I was sure that Turning Stone was going to have sports betting because it was a casino. And on top of that, Turning Stone had all kinds of gambling from slot machines to table games and keno to bingo; certainly they must have had sports betting.

Shannon and I canvassed the entire gaming floor, trying to find sports betting. I finally asked an employee if they have sports betting.

She told me that they do not.

I was upset! It must have been Murphy's Law c-blocking me from trying to help the Sabres win!

Also, I thought about it briefly. That was probably the first time a casino had ever said no to free money, but oh well.

Shannon and I piled back into the minivan.

We finally arrived at our hotel, Waltham, at 1am.

I slept like poop that night because I was battling a cold and kept coughing throughout the entire night. Shannon also slept like poop.

On Saturday morning, we got our dupas out of bed and in gear by 8:30.

The first thing scheduled on our Boston tour was to hit up the Samuel Adams Brewery. From there, it was whale watching, then hanging out at Quincy Market, followed by the hockey game, and finishing up the night bar hopping around town.

According to Sam Adams' website, tours filled up quick, so we needed to get there early for tickets.

Shannon and I were all ready and out the door by 9am.

We made a quick pit stop at CVS to pick up some meds for Shannon. Shannon wasn't feeling too hot that morning. Don't worry, it's not what you think, it wasn't morning sickness. Shannon thought she might have had an ulcer or some medical thing like that. I thought all she needed was some free beer from the brewery.

We somehow navigated the minivan through the city streets of Boston to the Sam Adams Brewery. Those streets in Boston sucked, especially since I had never been to Boston and had no idea where I was going. Shannon and I had MapQuest directions, but those were screwed up too. While we were trying to not get lost, the areas we drove through looked beautiful; nice old houses and parks.

Shannon and I strolled into the brewery at 9:45am and got our tickets for the 10am tour! Woo-hoo, we made it on time.

Shannon was still feeling like poop and she wasn't sure if she wanted to go on the beer tour. I got her a cup of water, but that didn't help.

Soon enough, 10am rolled around and Shannon mustered up the will power to attempt the tour.

She made it about 20 minutes into the tour before she needed to go back out to the lobby to sit down and take a breather.

During the tour, I received a phone call from the whale watching company. They were calling to inform me that the tour was canceled due to the weather. They told me that I could have a refund or reschedule.

In the meantime, I continued on with the tour. Before I knew it, the tour was over and it was time to drink free beer samples! I knew I was under a lot of pressure because since Shannon wasn't there to drink, I was now drinking for two...nothing like beer for breakfast at 10:30 in the morning!

Our tour group and I were on our second pitcher of five beer flavors when Shannon texted me that she wanted to go to the hospital. As I filled my empty glass, I texted Shannon that I would be right there.

I met up with the wife in the lobby and we walked back to the minivan.

I soon saw a sign for a hospital and took that route. I drove and drove and drove. I drove for at least 10 minutes without finding a hospital. In the meantime, all the hospital road signs vanished.

We drove past Park School, which was having a craft fair. They also had a cop directing traffic. Since we were lost, I figured I'd ask the cop for some directions.

I pulled the minivan over and illegally parked it right behind the illegally parked squad car.

As I walked up to the cop, I thought to myself, "Ah, this is great, you just left a brewery at 10:30am, you wreak of beer, and now you are going to ask a cop for directions...just breath in when you talk, the cop won't be able to smell the beer on your breath that way...wait a minute, you're in Boston; isn't everyone always drunk?"

The cop gave me adequate directions and asked if Shannon needed an ambulance. I told him no, but thanked him.

After driving a few blocks down the road, Shannon and I arrived at Faulkner Hospital. I dropped Shannon off at the Emergency Room entrance and then parked the minivan in the parking garage.

I had learned that hospital visits were never short and I knew we were gonna be in it for the long haul. I had no idea how long the long haul was going to be, so I cracked open that bottle of Pucker watermelon and poured it into a coffee cup that I had in the van.

By the time I got back to the ER waiting room, Shannon had been admitted. The receptionist told me that the doctor was currently meeting with Shannon and that I would be allowed back there in a few minutes.

I thanked the receptionist.

The receptionist asked why Shannon and I were in town. I told her that we were there for the Sabres game that night. The receptionist opened her vest to reveal her Bruins shirt and said, "I'm a Bruins fan...Don't worry, you'll be out in time for the game..."

A few minute later, I was allowed back to see Shannon in her room. She was in Room 16, and my mind instantly went to, "Oh, Shannon's in the room with Pat LaFontaine's number!"

As I entered the room, Shannon was on a gurney, all curled up in a ball, with an IV in her.

I told her that I called her mom to inform her of the current situation.

Shannon said, "*Great*! Get my mom all riled up and nervous..."

I said, "Hey, you know, damned if I do, damned if I don't. I just want your parents to be informed in case anything goes wrong...like if you can't make it to the game, your dad still has enough time to race out here to make it with me while your mom sits here at the hospital and sit at to your bedside..."

I noticed that Shannon was in her hospital gown and that her pants were on the floor in the corner (hehe). So I got up to check out her dupa to see if she was going commando or not...she had red undies on; no commando.

Shannon did mention to me that while she was waiting for the doc to show up, some dude on a drug over dose was rolled in. I thought that was pretty interesting, and then I told Shannon that I was slightly hungry, considering that I only had a few glasses of beer for breakfast.

Shannon noticed my coffee cup and asked, "When the hell did you get McDonalds coffee?"

I answered, "Last night at the rest stop outside Albany."

Shannon inquired, "Why are you drinking last night's coffee?" I gave her a look and she said, "OOOHHH! Gotcha."

"Watermelon...Pucker," I said.

Just then another nurse came in to whisk Shannon away for her ultra sound. I told Shannon that I was gonna wander upstairs to the cafeteria.

For lunch, I decided to have a salad and a cup of minestrone soup. I wanted to play it safe and attempt to eat healthy. I did not want to be another number in the "Fat America" stats.

After lunch, I was tired and ready for a nap. I wasn't sure if I was in a food coma, or the lack of sleep from the past week, or the early morning beers, but Nappy Poo Time was calling my name, "*Adam…Adam…Come to bed! Take a nap…Adam…*"

I responded back, "Yes Nappy Poo Time! I know I'm tired. Where do you want me to sleep? The chairs in the waiting room suck and I don't want to hop on a gurney in the ER because I don't want them to think that I'm a stiff because if they do, they'll send me down to the morgue. And I don't like the morgue. There are dead people there. And if they bring me down to the morgue, they will probably put me on one of those trays and shove me into a dead person holding cell and slam the door shut! And then I would wake up! I'll scream and shout for someone to let me out! But no one will hear, and I will suffocate to death before anyone finds me!"

Nappy Poo Time said, "You idiot, just crawl back into your minivan to take a cat nap!" and so I did.

It was around 3pm when I woke from my slumber. I refilled my coffee cup with some more Watermelon Pucker and headed back into the ER.

Shannon was snoozing when I got back into her room, so I just parked my dupa on the chair and waited for her to wake up.

Moments later Shannon woke up and she was still in a bit of pain. She had just come back from getting the ultra sound done, so we waited for the results.

I asked Shannon what was wrong with her and she said the doctors thought she had Gall Stones. Shannon said she was a bit relieved because she thought it could have been appendicitis.

In the meantime, the crazy dude who had overdosed earlier was coming down from his high. The dude went ape shit and tried making a break for it. The dude looked like Grizzly Adams. Grizzly Adams barreled around the corner and sprinted past Shannon's room. He then slammed into the ER's double doors in a last ditch effort for freedom, but to his dismay, the doors were locked. A few security guards and EMTs quickly tackled Grizzly and brought him back to his room.

A few minutes later, Grizzly had a talking to by security and a cop. They threatened to strap him down to his bed. This sparked my curiosity, so I decided to do a recon...you know, check things out.

In the hallway by the nurses' station, there were about 20 security guards, paramedics, and nurses all huddled around Grizzly's room. One of the nurses came back over to me and asked me if I would go back into Shannon's room, just in case there was another outburst from Grizzly.

Sometime later, the nurse and doctor came back and said that Shannon's ultra sound checked out and there were no other problems. The nurse gave Shannon some crackers and peanut butter to make sure she could hold down some food.

About a half hour later, the doctor came back in and gave the green light for Shannon's discharge. The doctor told Shannon to follow up with her primary back home and if the pain persisted, that she might need to have her gall bladder removed. The doc hooked Shannon up with a script for some Percs (that's street talk for Percocet).

By 4:30pm we left the hospital, in search of a CVS to get Shannon's script filled.

It was a bit after 5pm when Shannon got her script filled. We soon found ourselves on South Huntington Ave, headed towards downtown.

I had another quick shot of Pucker to take the edge off. I was a little nervous that we weren't going to make it to the game in time. First of all, I had never been to Boston, so I had no idea where the hell we were going. Second of all, we were driving around downtown Boston on a Saturday night with a whole bunch of traffic. Third of all, I was driving in downtown Boston...need I say more?

It felt as if every street I was on turned into a one way street, with me going the wrong way! We must have driven in circles at least five times. However, we got a nice tour of downtown at night. We got to see Chinatown, Paramount Theater, Boston Common and Public Garden.

Shannon and I found parking at the Massachusetts General Hospital parking garage. I grabbed my McDonalds coffee cup again and filled it up with some more Watermelon Pucker. Next we huffed the five blocks over to TD Gardens.

We came upon TD Gardens from the back side and it looked like a huge concrete brick, like a convention center or a warehouse.

TD Gardens was pretty cool inside because it also served as a hub for the public transportation.

Shannon and I must have ridden five escalators to get up to the upper deck to where our seats were in Section 312.

Surprisingly we got there a bit early, so we got to watch both teams skate around and warm up.

TD Gardens was nice. I had never been in an arena that had yellow seats. It gave the entire building a different feel or atmosphere. It reminded me of a bee hive, not that I had ever been in a bee hive, but that's probably what it would look like inside.

Shannon had not eaten yet, so I ran down to the concession stand real quick. I picked her up a pretzel and a Coke. I got a Molson Canadian for myself.

After the National Anthem was sung, the PA announcer told the crowd that tonight's game (on Veterans Day) was being dedicated to the parents of a soldier from the Boston area. The parents were called down to the ice and a little number about their son was shown upon the jumbotron. The soldier was serving in Afghanistan for over a year. The PA announcer said the Boston Bruins had a special gift for the soldier's parents. The Zamboni doors were opened and their son, the soldier, came walking out onto the ice to surprise them! TD Gardens was already on its feet in the first place, but once the soldier stepped out onto the ice, the entire place went crazy with cheers.

Buffalo's Thomas Vanek opened the scoring five minutes into the 1st Period by sneaking the puck by Boston goalie Tim Thomas…Thomas mishandled the puck and it squirted through his pads for an ugly Buffalo goal.

Boston was playing strong and had a few chances on Sabres goalie Ryan Miller, But Miller was playing rock solid, even when Buffalo was on the penalty kill.

During the 1st Period, Boston's Milan Lucic was skating towards Buffalo's zone. Lucic couldn't reach the puck that he passed foreword for himself. The puck dribbled into the face off dot to the right of Miller. Miller skated out of the net to play the puck, so that Lucic wouldn't have a breakaway opportunity. Lucic made no attempt to play the puck. Lucic raised his arms and just unloaded on

Ryan Miller, knocking Miller's goalie mask off in the process. Miller dropped right to the ice and the refs blew the whistle as the Sabres bum rushed Lucic into the boards. Lucic got two minutes for goaltender interference and Miller stayed in the game. Naturally, the Boston fans started to taunt Miller, but Miller played strong for the rest of the 1st Period.

Buffalo led 1-0 after the 1st Period.

Boston got on the board roughly 8 minutes into the 2nd Period. Boston's Rich Peverley waltzed into the Buffalo zone and past three Buffalo defenders, before he popped the puck though Miller's five hole to make it a tied 1-1 game.

Midway through the 2nd Period, Buffalo had a horrible give away at their own blue line. Boston waltzed in the Buffalo zone with 2-on-1 and Boston's Tyler Seguin slapped a one timer past a defenseless Miller.

Needless to say, Boston's Nathan Horton scored 16 seconds later to make it a 3-1 Boston lead.

For the start of the 3rd Period, Buffalo's head coach Lindy Ruff put back up goaltender Jonas Enroth in net for Miller.

I'll avoid the boring and gory details of Boston's Chris Kelly, Tyler Seguin, and Brad Marchand goals, but Boston quickly jumped ahead 6-1.

Late in the 3rd, Buffalo's Marc Andre Gragnani scored a meaningless goal.

The final score to that crappy and exhausting day was Boston-6 Buffalo-2.

Throughout the entire game, the Sabres had their chances to make a statement to Boston for Lucic hitting Miller, but no one on the Sabres bench did a damn thing! They were all pussy chicken shits who were too afraid to stand up for one of their own!

In the post-game interviews, someone asked Miller what he thought of Lucic. Miller said that Lucic was, "a piece of shit." It turned out that Miller suffered a concussion and was put on injured reserve. Buffalo would be without Miller for a few weeks.

The NHL's new "police man/safety watch dog" Brendan Shanahan did not suspend Lucic for his hit on Miller.

After the horrible and miserable performance by the Sabres, Shannon and I prepared ourselves for the Walk of Shame...yet again. It was another *pucking* away game that Shannon and I showed up to, but not the Sabres.

On the walk back to the minivan, we came across another CVS. Shannon and I ran in real quick to pick up some microwaveable Campbell's Chicken Noodle Soup.

As we made our way to the parking garage, we noticed that every road way was a parking lot with fans leaving the game. We knew that we would sit forever in traffic, waiting to get back to the hotel. We dropped off our chicken noodle soup at the van and decided to navaguess our way over to Cheers.

We walked over to Charles Street and headed towards Beacon Street. Walking down Charles St. was nice because it was filled with shops and eateries. Some restaurants were in the basements of buildings; so you had to walk down a few stairs to enter each establishment.

Shannon and I finally reached Charles and Beacon and we didn't know which way to go, left or right. I didn't want to stick out like a tourist and ask for directions; not that our Sabre jerseys didn't make us stick out like sore thumbs. We decided to go left down Beacon. Shannon and I huffed it for a few blocks until we realized we went the wrong way, but we didn't mind. We were getting another free tour of downtown Boston, and the weather was nice. It was a clear sky and 65^0 F.

As we were walking back down Beacon, Shannon was a little nervous because she didn't know if we were in a bad section of town. I looked around us and said, "I think we're in a good section of town."

Shannon asked, "Why do you think that?"

I pointed to a car parked on the street and said, "Well, someone thinks it's safe enough here to park their Maserati. And there's a Yukon Denali, and Audi…"

"Oh, okay," Shannon said.

We noticed that even at 10:30 at night downtown Boston was still busy with people wearing their Sunday Best, out for a night on the town. Even earlier in the day when we were trying to find the brewery, all the city streets in Boston were filled with people; cyclists, runners, walkers.

Shannon and I found our way to Cheers, and bellied up to the bar with two Sam Adams Winter Ales.

Cheers had live music there; it was some dude and his guitar. He was pretty good, but sounded even better after each beer. He played *Pumped up Kicks* by Foster the People and *"Forget" You* by Cee Lo Green. I took out a dollar and scribbled something down on a napkin and dropped it off on the table next to the musician. Moments later I heard the first couple notes of *Freebird* being plucked out of the acoustic guitar! The dude played about half of *Freebird*; all the way up to the fast part of the song.

Shannon and I were getting sleepy, so we decided to leave.

Across the street from the hospital parking garage was another CVS. Shannon and I agreed that the two cans of chicken noodle soup wouldn't hold us over, so we stopped in to pick up some microwaveable pizzas…that was our fourth trip to CVS in one day.

I had the hardest time trying to find our way back to the 90. I could not find any entrance ramps for the 90 westbound. We ended up taking Route 20 all the way back to Waltham…Tell you what, there were a shit ton of bars on Route 20. I wish we could have stopped at all of them.

Shannon was feeling a little better Sunday morning. I wish we could have had more time to explore Boston, but I needed to get Shannon back home because she had play rehearsal at 6pm. As it was, Shannon was already missing the noon rehearsal…Shannon was in a community theater production of *Oklahoma*.

My Best Man Jason informed me that up until that point of the Sabres season, they had only lost two road games…the same two road games that Shannon and I had gone to…

December 2011

December 3rd was a Friday night. Shannon and I had just finished packing up the minivan for our latest road trip. Shannon and I were venturing down to the Music City to watch our Sabres get beat by the Nashville Predators.

That Friday before I left work, I decided to make a friendly bet with my co-worker Ryan. I said, "Hey Ryan, do you wanna make a bet on tomorrow night's hockey game?"

Ryan replied, "Maybe. Who's playing and what's the stakes?"

I answered, "My Buffalo Sabres are playing down in Nashville against the Predators. Pretty much every time Shannon and I go anywhere to see our Sabres play, Buffalo loses. Last month I got denied by Murphy's Law when I tried betting against Buffalo, because the casino I stopped at didn't do sports betting…I'm trying to get Murphy's Law back, bro. I'm telling you it's a 'win-win situation' going on here."

Ryan hemmed and hawed a little bit.

I said, "Hey Ryan, I'm 0-5 with Buffalo bets this year…"

Ryan said, "Oh I see how it is. You're about due for a win…"

"No, no, no," I said, trying to reassure Ryan that it would be a win-win situation.

Ryan inquired, "Well, okay. What do you want to bet?"

I responded, "I'll bet you $2 that Nashville wins."

Ryan asked, "Could we change the stakes a little bit?"

"Sure, why not," I said. "What were you thinking?"

Ryan said, "Well, I'm running a little bit low on Jack Daniels…"

I said, "Perfect! Sounds good to me! If Buffalo wins, I buy you a one liter bottle of Jack Daniels. If Nashville wins, I'd like a 28 pack of Labatt Blue Light with the specially marked package that comes with the Buffalo Sabres bottle opener!"

Ryan shouted back, "Ugh! You're on!"

I shot back with, "Oh it's on, like Donkey Kong!"

It was finally 8pm on that Friday night when Shannon and I were all packed up in the minivan. We had a 12.5 hour car ride ahead of us. The goal was to drive about half way and sleep over night at a rest stop…yep, that's right, we were going to kick it old school.

It was 3:45am when we were about 20 miles outside Cincinnati, Ohio. I decided to pull into a rest stop to take a cat nap. Shannon had already been snoozing off and on since we left the house. I crawled in the back bench seat of the minivan and tried to fall asleep.

It sucked. When I was driving, I could barely keep my eyes open and I was ready for bed. I finally pulled off to take a nap and I was wide awake.

I eventually managed to drift off into sleep.

I was wide awake by 7am. "Great," I thought to myself. "I only got three hours of sleep after being awake for close to 24 hours...this should be fun..."

It was around 9am when Shannon and I puttered into downtown Louisville, Kentucky. I figured that since Louisville was on the way down to Nashville, why not stop off at the Louisville Slugger Museum and Factory.

The factory tour was fun. During the tour, one employee showed our tour group how they used to make baseball bats. Up until the 1980s, bats were hand crafted on a lathe, as the employee demonstrated. Now, bats were made by robotic machines that cut, sanded, and trimmed the bats. Louisville Slugger made wooden bats for Major League Baseball, Minor League Baseball, and Little League. They also made composite bats at a different location. MLB bats were made on special lathes separate from the other bats.

The tour showed us how they branded the Louisville Slugger name onto the bats. Right next to the branding station was an open flame, which give some bats a more natural look. The bats were rotated through an open flame to help bring out their natural wood grain.

Also, there was an employee who was dipping bats into a black acrylic paint, to give the bats a black finish.

At the end of the tour, Shannon and I (along with everyone else on the tour) got a mini Louisville Slugger baseball bat souvenir. Shannon and I then proceeded to beat the crap out of each other with our new bats!

From there, we toured the rest of the museum.

They had batting cages there, so we tried them. I used the Derek Jeter style of bat.

After that, we looked at the Charlie Brown Christmas exhibit that was on display there. One could even write a letter to Santa, so I did...

Dear Santa Clause,
This year for Christmas, I would like the Buffalo Bills to win the Super Bowl. If that is too big of a task, I would like the Buffalo Sabres to win the Stanley Cup. Whichever is easiest. Thank you.

--Adam

From there, Shannon and I headed south toward Nashville.

As we drove, we listened to Louisville's Only Real Classic Rock Station, 95.7 QMF...I felt old because apparently Nirvana was now considered "classic rock." Yea...that's all I gots to say about that.

We finally arrived at our motel, an outdated Howard Johnson.

Before long, I was dressed up in my blue and gold jersey and Shannon and I were ready to take on Nashville!

We really hadn't eaten anything substantial all day, except for a bag of kettle cooked salt and vinegar chips; which we had polished off earlier in the day.

I still had White Castle coupons left over from our Columbus trip. I was saving those coupons for a moment like this.

We got an original slider, two bacon cheeseburger sliders, two jalapeño sliders, sweet potato fries, and chicken rings.

Shannon was a little grossed out by the chicken rings. She said, "Doesn't that creep you out? Chicken rings?! What part of the chicken is this from?"

I answered, "The cock."

Shannon just shook her head and rolled her eyes as she mumbled, "Good Lord, I married a thirteen year old..."

After dinner at White Castle, we drove over to the Bridgestone Arena and parked the minivan.

We kicked off bar hopping at Margaritaville. Shannon was a huge fan of their Perfect Margarita. I had a Gerst Beer on draft. I had never heard of it before, so I attempted it. It was good; reminded me of George Killian's.

As we were leaving Margaritaville, Shannon insisted on stealing a salt shaker because she wanted to be the woman to blame.

From there, we hopped down to The Second Fiddle. There, Shannon had a Blue Moon while I had a tall boy of Pabst Blue Ribbon, as we both enjoyed the live band.

Nashville was awesome. Every bar we went into had a live band! Now I am not a huge fan of country music, but hearing it live is a different story.

Shannon and I hopped on over to The Stage. The effects of not enough sleep were catching up to me and I was fading quickly. Shannon and I got a round of vodka Red Bulls as we watched another live band. Even though they were playing country music and not Polka, I still think Grandpa Ziggy would have enjoyed the band because the lead singer was a nice looking blond...and Grandpa Ziggy likes blonds.

Next, Shannon and I hit up the other side of Broadway and went to Nashville Crossroads to order another round of vodka Red Bulls and see another country band play. Before we knew it, it was time to head into Bridgestone Arena.

That night's game was Sabre goalie Ryan Miller's first game back since his concussion he suffered from Lucic in Boston last month.

Before the game started, the Bridgestone Arena's lights went down. Some stuff was played up on the jumbotron, but when the lights were turned on, there was a huge Predator head in front of the Nashville bench. The huge Predator head had been lowered from the rafters. The Nashville Predators hockey club skated off the bench through a life sized logo. Shannon and I were entertained by Nashville's entrance.

Buffalo's rookie Luke Adam opened the scoring midway through the 1st Period with a point blank shot from in front of Nashville's goaltender Anders Lindback.

Nashville had their chances and tested Miller early, but Ryan was up to the task.

A few minutes later, Buffalo's Zack Kassian picked up the puck at center ice and skated past the Nashville defender for a breakaway.

Kassian deked once.

Kassian deked twice.

Kassian deked a third time.

Kassian snuck a back hander past Lindback to make it a 2-0 Buffalo lead!

In the 2nd Period, both goalies, Miller and Lindback, played well.

With a little over four minutes left in the 2nd Period, the Predators' Jordin Tootoo skated with the puck into the Buffalo zone. Buffalo's defenseman Christian Ehrhoff defended Tootoo all the way to the net. Tootoo then made a leaping lunge towards Buffalo's goalie Ryan Miller. The puck never made it toward the net as Tootoo made a run at Miller. At the first sign of contact with Miller, Miller dropped his glove and started to throw punches at Tootoo. The ref immediately called the play dead and everyone played pile on.

Both linesmen were in the thick of it as the refs watched.

Miller eventually whipped his mitt off as his other fist had some more say to Tootoo.

Both teams quickly paired off and tangoed with each other. The refs broke up most of the fights, but a few sucker punches from both sides were thrown and landed.

Buffalo's Paul "Goose" Gaustad was fit for a straight jacket, as three officials needed to secure him.

Tootoo and Goose were both personally escorted to their respective benches. As Goose was escorted to his bench, he was clearly chirping to Nashville's goaltender Lindback...Goose was probably telling him that he was next. Tootoo was given a major penalty for charging and a game misconduct.

In the dying seconds of the 2nd Period, it was 4-on-4 hockey. Buffalo dumped the puck into the Nashville zone. Nashville's goaltender skated out to shoot the puck away from the pressing Buffalo foreword. However, Nashville's goalie missed the puck and Buffalo's Tyler Ennis had a chance to make a shot at the open net. Nashville's defense was able to collapse and block off Ennis' shot. The 2nd Period ended in a 2-0 Buffalo lead.

During the 2nd Intermission, Shannon and I grabbed a couple beers to enjoy our meager 2-0 lead. Shannon and I noted the huge Sabres fan presence at Bridgestone Arena, there were a lot of us Buffalo fans there!

When I came back with the beers, I told Shannon, "I met a man who lives in Tennessee."

Shannon said, "Oh, ok? Was he a Sabres fan?"

I replied, "He was headin' for Pennsylvania."

Shannon asked, "Ok, why?"

With a smirk, I answered, "For some homemade pumpkin pie."

Shannon rolled her eyes and called me a dork.

Early in the 3rd Period, Nashville was trying to generate some offense in the Buffalo zone, but Miller stood tall. Nashville popped a puck up high, but Miller was able to swat and snatch it away before Nashville could score. Nashville had definitely thought they scored a goal on Miller because they had the lights and music going off, but before the puck had crossed the line, Miller had snatched it away to keep it a 2-0 Buffalo game.

Nashville had a perfect one timer, a point blank shot at an open net and Miller dove back and threw his trapper out and caught the puck; preventing yet another goal. I'm a little biased, but it was definitely highlight footage.

Minutes later Buffalo found themselves shorthanded. Buffalo has always had a good penalty kill, but that night they let one slip by. The Preds' Craig Smith ripped a wrist shot off from the faceoff circle from Miller's left side, to cut Buffalo's lead in half; 2-1 Buffalo.

After Nashville's goal, the Preds gained some momentum and started shooting more on Buffalo.

With just under five minutes to go in the 3rd Period, Buffalo was pressing in the Nashville zone. Buffalo's Tyler Ennis skated into the Nashville zone and received the puck at the blue line. Ennis skated in and snapped a wrister past Lindback to make a 3-1 Buffalo lead!

Being down 3-1, Nashville pulled Lindback as a last ditch effort.

Nashville's last ditch effort proved fruitful with a sloppy goal by David Legwand, to make it a 3-2 Buffalo lead.

By that point, Shannon and I were nervous and antsy; thinking we drove umpteen hours to watch, yet again, another Sabres loss...

The faceoff was at center ice. The puck was dropped and the Sabres somehow found a miraculous way to kill the waning seconds to win the game!

The Sabres had beaten the Predators 3-2! It was awesome! *We were going to the Super Bowl!*

It was amazing! The Sabres finally won a game that we traveled to see! The last road win we saw was last December back in Ottawa!

Outside Bridgestone Arena, it felt like a Sabres home game. I was high fiving Sabres fans and telling them, "Yea! We won! We're going to the Super Bowl!"

After the game, Shannon and I wandered into Nashville Crossroads to listen to some more live music and to grab another quick round.

From there, Shannon and I experienced the night life up and down Broadway. On our tour of Broadway, we came upon Hard Rock Café. We had midnight munchies, so we grabbed an order of potato skins.

Sunday morning, Shannon and I piled back into the minivan to venture further west. We got onto I-40 west, with Graceland being our next stop. The three and a half hour ride from Nashville to Memphis was a nice ride. It was scenic but a bit of a haul. Plus it rained the entire ride. During the drive, I was able to find the Tennessee Titans @ Buffalo Bills football game on the radio.

We arrived at Graceland early afternoon.

As Shannon and I arrived at the front door of Graceland, I noted that Elvis had a pretty cool pad.

As soon as we walked in through the front door, Shannon and I were hit with an awful odor. It smelled like a mix of funeral home and old person, but we eventually got immune to the smell.

The interior was tacky from the get go, and it screamed 70s.

We got to see the living room and Elvis' parents' bedroom.

We got to see the stairs that led to the second floor, but visitors were not allowed up there. Even when Elvis was alive, he would greet guests down stairs. Elvis' rule was that upstairs was off limits and the estate still kept it that way in his honor.

The tour then led us into the dining room, and from there, we entered the kitchen.

Ah the kitchen! What could I say about it other than it had carpeting on the floor. It did not seem like a good idea, especially when something spilled or dropped. Tile, hardwood, and linoleum seemed like easier things to clean than carpet.

We were able to look into the family room, better known as the Jungle Room. It was called the Jungle Room because it looked like a jungle. The room had green shag carpet on the floor as well as the ceiling.

The tour led us down stairs into Elvis' TV room. The TV room had a bar and three TVs in it. It also had mirrors on the ceiling...*classy!*

From there, we entered Elvis' pool room. The pool room had floor to wall to ceiling hideous carpet. I leaned over to Shannon and said, "Hey, this house is already furnished for your grandmother to move into..."

The tour led us down another hallway to a stairway that had even more carpet on the walls.

Once Shannon and I got to the top of the stairs, we could see the rest of the kitchen and Jungle Room.

Next, the tour lead us outside to the Smokehouse, Trophy House, and then down to the Racquetball House. After that, we were led to the Meditation Garden, where we paid our respects to the King. He was buried there alongside his parents and grandma.

As in the great words of Forrest Gump, "Some years later, that handsome young man who they call the King, well he sung too many songs. Had himself a heart attack or something...must be hard being the King."

Afterwards, we went back across Elvis Presley Boulevard to check out the rest of the exhibits.

We saw Elvis' car collection and went aboard his two jets, *Lisa Marie* and *Hound Dog II*.

From Graceland, Shannon and I headed off to downtown Memphis to check out Beale Street.

As we entered downtown and took the ramp for Riverside Drive, we could see the Mighty Mississippi River flowing.

After finding parking, we strolled up and down Beale Street. It was late Sunday afternoon, so it was very quiet, but we didn't mind.

Shannon and I ate at Blues City Café and had ourselves some BBQ ribs. Once we were done with dinner, we wandered through the Cadillac Room and down into a room with live music.

There was a nice band playing with three older guys. One was playing an upright bass, one playing a red electric guitar, and the lead vocalist had an acoustic guitar.

Up on stage was a photo of the Million Dollar Quartet. The band talked about each member of the band; Elvis Presley, Carl Perkins, Johnny Cash, and Jerry Lee Lewis. The band played their favorite songs of each performer and gave some background info to the songs.

As Shannon and I were leaving Memphis, we decided to drive across the Mississippi River and on into Arkansas, just to say that we had been to Arkansas.

We didn't get back to the crappy Howard Johnson until midnight. If you are wondering why the HoJo was a dump, well let me tell you. The TV didn't really work. I could turn it on, but the volume didn't work. It was like watching a silent film. And there was no hot water in the showers. When we got back from the hockey game, there were pan handlers waiting for us in front of the hotel rooms. And lastly, the bedding was full of cigarette burns. Hotel staff did not seem concerned about my concerns.

Shannon and I were up bright and early Monday morning. We were on the road by 7am. We had a hot date that morning. We were trying to get to the Corvette Factory in Bowling Green, KY before 8:30am. I wanted to do the factory tour and the first tour for the day was at 8:30am. The next tour wasn't until 11:30am.

Shannon and I made it in the nick of time. We got our tour tickets with literally five minutes to spare.

The factory tour was awesome and informative. Our tour guide Parker said that the first Corvette ever built was in Flint, Michigan. It was a white Vette with red interior. Production of the Corvette moved to St. Louis, Missouri. In 1980, GM bought the Bowling Green facility from Chrysler. At the time, Chrysler was using it to make air conditioners. In 1981, the factory opened to make Corvettes.

The tour took us through start to finish of a Vette's assembly. Big huge machines carried partially painted Corvette frames/bodies down from the ceiling. Then the assembly line started. UAW employees were putting on rear bumper fascias onto the different colored Vettes as they passed by. We got to see entire Corvettes being put together; from doors being installed to dropping the body onto the drive train.

I leaned over to Shannon and said, "I wonder if this is like the Louisville Slugger tour, where instead of getting a free baseball bat at the end, you get a free Corvette!"

Shannon shook her head and rolled her eyes.

I said, "I really like the yellow one...the silver one is pretty cool too!"

Our tour guide Parker told us that the factory averages about 8 Corvettes every hour and 80 Corvettes a day.

The base model and Grand Sport Corvettes' motors were made in St. Catherine's, Ontario, Canada, which was located just across the border from Buffalo. Parker also informed us that the motors for the Z06 and ZR1 were made up in Michigan. He said that if I ordered a Corvette from the dealer, I could actually come down to the plant to see my baby being made. From start to finish it took three days for a Corvette to be birthed.

Also, the Cadillac XLR was assembled at the Bowling Green Facility. I did not understand why people would have bought the XLR. The XLR cost more money than the Vette and compared to the Vette, it was well under powered. And lastly, as a third strike, the XLR was only available with an automatic transmission.

It was after 10am when our tour ended. Shannon and I left the Corvette factory and we decided to skip the Corvette Museum because we still had at least an eleven hour car ride ahead of us.

We picked up some breakfast at Sonic which we enjoyed even though their food was so unhealthy. It just tasted so good!

Driving back through Kentucky, there were several road side attractions that we wanted to stop at, but we didn't have any time to spare. We figured, the next time we traveled down to Nashville for a Sabres game, that we would stop at one of the many Kentucky State Parks, tour Kentucky Speedway, visit Abe Lincoln's birthplace, Fort Knox, Jim Bean, Makers Mark, and of course Dinosaur World!

We were right outside Cincinnati when Shannon and I got a little hungry again. Shannon's parents recommended that we stop at Skyline Chili.

Shannon and I were on I-71 northbound when we saw a sign that said Skyline Chili was the next exit. Also, that happened to be the same exit for Big Bone Lick State Park, *hehehe*.

Unfortunately we did not have enough time to go to Big Bone Lick State Park, just Skyline Chili.

Once there, we were advised to try the spaghetti chili. It was spaghetti noodles with chili dumped on top; with a crap ton of shredded cheddar cheese on top of that…it was delicious!

We got back home around 11pm. Shannon told me that she had fallen in love with Nashville and that she had started to dream about the day we would go back.

***

Mr. DeRose Goes to Washington…it had a nice ring to it, just like that Jimmy Stewart movie that I never saw. Yep, that's right; Shannon and I were headed down to our Nation's Capital!

The last time I was in Washington D.C. was back in the 1990s. I was a young, innocent lad. My family had parked right across the street from the horniest statue in America, the Washington Monument. We took a trip up the Washington Monument and it was fun. The part about the trip that wasn't fun was when we got back to our Plymouth minivan, some thug broke the driver window and ransacked the van! They stole my younger sister's backpack that had about $100 in it. They also stole my older sister's CD player. Unfortunately the perp did not steal my backpack that had my Spanish text book in it. That was my first memory of Washington D.C., getting our van robbed.

Yep, that was my only memory of our Nation's Capital.

I was hoping my next visit would be a little bit better…

According to the White House's website, to get tickets for a tour, "Requests must be submitted through one's member of Congress…Tours are scheduled on a first come, first serve basis. Requests can be submitted up to six months in advance and no less than 21 days in advance"

So like the slacker I was, I waited until the end of November to write my elected official about tickets to the White House…

November 18, 2011

> *Dear Senator Schumer,*
>
> *Hi Chuck, how are you doing? I'm good, thanks for asking. I am taking my wife Shannon to our Nation's Capital on December 30th to catch a Buffalo Sabres/Washington Capitals hockey game. I figured that since we were going to be down there, that it would be cool to tour the White House. According to the White House's website, it says I need to contact you for*

tickets. I know you are a busy man, but from one New Yorker to another, I was wondering if you could get us some tickets for the morning of December 30th. If not, I understand. Thank you for your time.

    Sincerely,
    (I signed my signature here)
    Adam DeRose

P.S.-GO SABRES!!

Even though it was a holiday week (Thanksgiving), my boy Chuck got back to me!

Chuckey-poo told me that he received my request, but he couldn't make the tour happen because in order for my request to have been processed, I needed to give him four to six months' notice. However he did say that if I was interested, he could hook me up with a tour of the Capital Building, which sounded good to me.

I informed Shannon of our Washington D.C. plans. She seemed more excited to see the Capital Building than the White House.

Shannon told me that she already been on a White House tour and that it was pretty boring...*Here's the Green Room, it's green. Here's the Red Room, it's red...*

I tried explaining to Shannon that the White House tour would have been cool because they were self-guided tours.

Shannon reassured me that the tour still would have sucked.

I asked Shannon, "Would the self-guided tour still have sucked if we snuck off and did it in the Lincoln Bedroom!?"

Shannon said, "Yea, I don't think so. That wouldn't happen..."

I came back with, "I see, you want something more provocative and kinky. You probably want to re-enact things in the Oval Office..."

Shannon looked at me and said in her best Dana Carvey impression of George Bush, "Not gonna happen, not gonna do it..."

"Damn! Shot down again!" I exclaimed!

So on the morning of Thursday December 29th, Shannon and I hopped back into the 2003 Dodge Shaggin' Wagon, bound for

Baltimore. Yes, that was correct, Baltimore, because, you see, Shannon and I were spending Thursday night with Shannon's Aunt Betty, Uncle Warren, and their family.

From Western New York, Shannon and I took 390 South to the Pennsylvania border where we picked up Route 15.

I enjoy driving through Pennsylvania, especially Route 15 because it is so entertaining. For instance, there was a town just across the PA border called Buttonwood, or as I pronounced it, Butt-On-Wood.

Also, another entertaining thing about Route 15 is the sheer amount of "video outlets" and "dance studios."

The drive along Route 15 was scenic because we drove through the mountains and followed the Susquehanna River.

For years, my favorite part of the Susquehanna River was trying to find the white colored Statue of Liberty. It was located around Pennsylvania's capital, Harrisburg.

Shannon and I made it to Aunt Betty's late that afternoon. We hung out for a little bit and talked. Aunt Betty and Uncle Warren's kids Dustin, Britney, and Amber (with hubby Chris) were all there. Aunt Betty fed us some awesome raviolis.

Shannon and I were up fairly early on Friday morning because our tour of the Capital building started at 9:50am. We were unsure how DC traffic was going to be, so Shannon and I left Aunt Betty's at 7:30am.

Uncle Warren told Shannon and me to take the back roads into D.C. to avoid traffic. Uncle Warren led us down 295 to 50 and that would take us right into downtown D.C.

I had to say that the drive down 295 was quite nice and pretty. The overpasses, bridge abutments, and guard rails looked nice because they were all built out of cobblestone. On top of that, there was no traffic at all.

Shannon and I were checked into our room at Courtyard by Marriott Convention Center by 8am and by 8:15am, I had pooped and showered while drinking a beer at the same time. In case you were wondering, it was a Labatt Blue Light that I was drinking.

It was a little before 9am when Shannon and I left the Marriott, headed onward on foot to the Capital Building for our tour.

When we got to the Capital Building, we had to go through a security screening. After the security check, we were allowed inside. Next we went to the main desk and got our tickets for our tour.

Even though our tour was slated to start at 9:50, it did not begin until after 10am.

Eventually Shannon and I were let into an auditorium, where we watched a brief movie about the history of the United States of America. The video was about the formation of our government and its three branches (the Judiciary, Legislative, and Executive) and how they work. The video talked about different laws and acts that were passed through out America's History, such as civil rights, work place rights, and going to war.

Once the video was over, we were ushered up to the basement of the Rotunda. There our tour guide rattled off a whole bunch of dates and facts and dead people's names throughout America's History. One of the things our tour guide mentioned was during the War of 1812, Congress was burned down when the British invaded Washington DC. The Congress Building has obviously been rebuilt since, and had some additions throughout the years.

Our tour guide showed us a spot in the floor that had a glass marker. It was to be the final resting place for America's first President, George Washington. When the tomb was completed, the Washington Family prevented the government from reburying Washington. The Washington Family told the government that Washington's body was going to stay at Mt. Vernon. To this day, the Crypt remains empty.

From there, the tour took us to the original chambers of the Supreme Court. From 1860 to 1935, the United States Supreme Court held business in the Capital Building. In 1935, the Supreme Court moved across the street into the United States Supreme Court Building.

Next, our tour led us up into the Rotunda. There is a lot of art work in the Rotunda. In the top of the dome is a painting, *The Apotheosis of George Washington*, which depicted George Washington ascending into Heaven with 13 Maidens. The 13 Maidens signified the original 13 Colonies.

Also, there were many marble and bronze statues of famous Americans. Each State in the Union was to send two statues of someone from their respective state. These statues have been placed in the Capital Visitor Center, Rotunda, Crypt, and some other places in the building.

Unfortunately our tour did not go into the rooms of the Senate or the House of Representatives because one of them was in session. Also, we needed a special ticket to get in there.

After our tour ended, Shannon and I took a tunnel over to see the Library of Congress.

The Library of Congress was a grand sight to see. In the lobby, there is one of the original copies of the Bible printed on the Gutenberg Press. We were able to go to an observation deck and overlook the Library of Congress, but we were not allowed in. We spent a few minutes wandering around there before we left. We still had to meet up with Aunt Betty, Uncle Warren, and Britney so Shannon and I didn't want to waste all our time at the Library.

Shannon called Aunt Betty and we were to rendezvous at the Museum of Natural History. On our walk over to Natural History, Shannon and I were a little hungry, so we decided to have breakfast at one of those food vendor carts. The first vendor I saw was advertising Polish Sausage. They also had egg rolls. Shannon liked egg rolls and I enjoyed Polish Sausage, so I figured that I was a convenient place to stop and eat.

It turned out that the Polish Sausage was just a glorified, oversized hot dog and Shannon's egg roll tasted like shit.

Before long, we had met up with Aunt Betty, Uncle Warren, and Britney.

Since we were in front of the Museum of Natural History, we decided to venture in there. We ended up looking at most of the museum.

The Marine Life exhibit scared the shit out of me because there was a whole bunch of dead fish everywhere! The reason why dead fish scare the crap out of me was that fish don't have eye lids. I remember as a kid, being up in the 1000 Islands and helping Grandpa Ziggy clean the fish. I was so creeped out and disgusted because the dead fish were looking at me! It would be like going to a wake and the stiff in the box is staring right back at you!

We went through the Neanderthal and Cave Man exhibit, which led into another exhibit with a whole bunch of taxidermy animals, which were freaky.

The dinosaur exhibit was nice, but I thought it could have been a lot better. They had the skeletons of a T-Rex, Stegosaurus, and Brontosaurus; a couple of the skeletons were just casts, not the real McCoy. I figured that since the Smithsonian was America's National Museum, why would they chintz out and have fake dinosaur bones? We paid enough in taxes that we should have real dinosaur bones, but oh well.

The gang and I went upstairs to see the Hope Diamond, which was 45.52 carat. I saw the diamond and I was a little unimpressed...I thought, "Yep, that's a diamond."

We walked a little more through the rock display there before we turned around. I could only look at rocks for so long before they all looked the same...I thought, "Yep, that's a rock. Yep, there's another rock."

We left Natural History and walked down the Mall towards the Washington Monument.

The Washington Monument was still closed because back in August there was an earthquake in Virginia. The earthquake was so powerful that it cracked parts of the monument, and some of the cracks were visible.

From the Washington Monument, Aunt Betty, Uncle Warren, Britney, Shannon, and I walked down to see the World War II Memorial. It was nice and it was my first time seeing it. There was a pool in the center of the memorial that was having maintenance work being done on it.

As we walked down the Mall to the Lincoln Memorial, I noticed that the Reflecting Pool was all torn up. The Pool was under construction. A huge fence along the entire perimeter of the Pool blocked people from all the construction vehicles.

I was extremely bummed out because I wanted to reenact the scene from *Forrest Gump* where Forrest, who had just arrived back from Vietnam, was reunited with his love Jenny. I wanted to play the part of Jenny, as she ran through the Pool shouting, "FORRREESSSTTTT!!! FORREST!!"

Shannon said that she did not remember that part of the movie. I told Shannon what part of the movie it was, but she claimed that she didn't remember. I think Shannon didn't remember that scene on purpose because she didn't want to get arrested by some unknown Federal agency.

As I finished climbing the stairs to the Lincoln Memorial, I wanted to turn around and yell, "Hey Adriane!" but I knew that it was the wrong set of stairs and the wrong city, so instead I said nothing. Plus, I was out of breath.

The Lincoln Memorial was awesome. Seeing a larger than life statue of Lincoln just chilling out in his easy chair was pretty memorable.

Back in the day when I used to watch Ren and Stimpy, there was an episode where Ren and Stimpy were hired to be security guards for the Lincoln Memorial. In the episode, Ren got stuck in Honest Abe's nose. Stimpy needed to find a way to free Ren. Stimpy saw that next to Lincoln was a 5 cent machine to see President Lincoln pick his nose. Stimpy dropped in a nickel and Honest Abe picked his nose, and in the process, freed Ren...I looked all over that statue and memorial to try to find the nickel slot so I could see Abe pick his nose, but I was unsuccessful.

As we left the Lincoln Memorial, we could see the Vietnam Memorial and the Korean War Memorial.

We soon made our way to the newly opened Martin Luther King, Jr. Memorial, which was nice. As we approached the MLK Jr. Memorial, we entered through two enormous white stones. Through the stones, we could see across the Tidal Basin at the Jefferson Memorial. Once we walked past the two great stone entrance way, we came upon the missing stone that has Martin Luther King Jr. The stone wall in the background of the memorial has inspirational quotes from Martin.

We spent some time there to sit down and take a break from all the walking.

I really wanted to see the Air and Space Museum, so after a few minutes of relaxing, we all continued the voyage.

Once we got to the Air and Space Museum, we had to go through a security check point. After that, we started our tour off with the Space exhibits. We walked through one of the space capsules. We walked through an exhibit of the Gemini and Apollo Missions and we saw a couple rockets.

We were a little pressed for time, so we scurried over to the aviation section of the museum.

The Amelia Earhart exhibit was interesting.

There was an old black and white cartoon of Mickey and Minnie Mouse that I got sucked into.

We saw some old war birds from WWII as well.

The Smithsonian even had an old plane that was built by the Ford Motor Company. I had no idea that Ford used to build airplanes; I knew they had built one of the first WWII Jeeps and had also built farm equipment, but had no idea they use to be in the aviation business.

Once the museum closed, we walked Aunt Betty, Uncle Warren, and Britney back to the Verizon Center. They had taken the Metro into DC and the Metro Station was inside the Verizon Center. Uncle Warren showed us that our hotel was two blocks away and wished us luck before we parted ways.

After Shannon and I got back to the hotel room, I had to poop again. All that walking got the food inside of me moving. I quickly grabbed a Labatt Blue Light from the mini fridge and plopped my dupa on the can. Once I was done doing my duty, I grabbed my beer and hopped into the shower.

As Shannon and I were getting ready, we kicked back a few brews and popped back a couple of Mr. Tracy's whiskey cherries. Shannon noted that she did not see anyone with an open container walking up to the Verizon Center, so we did not bring any roadies with us.

At the Verizon Center, or the Phone Booth as some people called it, we quickly found some beer and then our seats. Shannon and I made it in time to watch the opening warm-ups.

Before we knew it, it was time for the American National Anthem and then puck drop.

It only took Buffalo 27 seconds to find themselves on the penalty kill due to a two minute boarding call against Buffalo's Mike Weber.

A few moments later, Washington's Alex Ovechkin capitalized on the power play. Ovechkin skated into the Buffalo zone and tried to pass the puck to a teammate, who was crashing the net. Ovechkin's pass ricocheted off the Buffalo defenseman's stick and flew past an out of place Ryan Miller.

Washington kept up their play throughout the 1st Period; pressing in the Buffalo zone for most of the opening period and testing Sabres goaltender Ryan Miller.

With a little over three minutes left in the 1st Period, the Caps had the puck in the Buffalo zone. Buffalo defenseman Christian Ehrhoff skated towards the pressing Capital foreword. Washington's Troy Brouwer set a pick as he jumped and led with his elbow towards Ehrhoff's head, right inside the faceoff circle. Ehrhoff did not take too kindly to it. Ehrhoff cross checked Brouwer and the two of them popped their gloves off to fight!

The fight turned out to be nothing exciting, but rather a grappling match. A few punches were thrown, but nothing really landed. The tango ended as they wrestled each other down to the ice right in front of the goalie's crease.

Both players received five minutes for fighting. Ehrhoff did not return to the game because he suffered an injury…way to go genius. It wasn't like Buffalo was already down six players due to injury.

Buffalo had zero offense in the 1st Period. They were outshot 11-2! I was amazed that the game was still 1-0 at the end of one period of play. Miller had some great saves even though he got no help from his D.

And another thing! When did America sell itself out and become bitches? What the hell happened to the America of the early 1980s that I was born into?! The America that was still fighting the Cold War and wouldn't take *pucking* crap from the damn Commies, especially Communist Russia!

I felt as if I didn't know my America because Red Russia's Alex Ovechkin played for our Nation's Capitals, the Washington Capitals!

I bet Alex was a secret covert spy, doing recon work for his Mother Country. I bet during his off nights, he and his dumb yellow ice skate laces snuck into highly guarded government buildings, took pictures of top secret documents, and sent them back to the KGB!

The Washington Capitals had a second logo on the shoulders of their jersey. It was an image of a spread eagle, but this logo looked just like the El Camino Royal Knight emblem.

Minutes into the 2nd Period, Buffalo got caught playing Bee Hive Hockey; where all the Sabres were chasing the one Capital player who had the puck. This left the four remaining Capitals wide open.

With some razzle dazzle puck passing, Washington's Nicklas Backstrom scored to make it a 2-0 Caps lead.

Buffalo did show some signs of life during the 2nd Period; getting 15 shots on goal, one of which, became Buffalo's first goal.

Normally it was good luck for either Shannon or me to pee during play because then the Sabres will score a goal because one of us is not watching the game.

This held true for me, because as I was piddling, Buffalo's "Stone Hands" Jochen Hecht scored an ugly goal off a miss managed rebound from the Washington goalie Tomas Vokoun. Hecht's goal brought Buffalo within 1 goal of Washington.

At the start of the 3rd Period, Shannon and I had high hopes for Buffalo. Buffalo had a strong 2nd Period of play and was only down 1 goal.

We gave up hope with about 4 minutes left in the 3rd Period because Washington's Alex Ovechkin slapped a one timer past Miller to make it a 3-1 Washington lead.

In the dying minutes of play, Buffalo pulled Miller for the extra attacker, but it was useless. Buffalo had earned their 5th straight road loss.

Some may say that I was bad luck for the Sabres. That was not the case...the Sabres were just horrible that season. It was looking a lot like that season was going to be another "rebuilding year."

Once the game was over, we went back to the hotel to figure out what to do.

I filled up one of the paper coffee cups with whiskey cherries and said to Shannon, "Let's just go spelunking." Spelunking was a term used by Michelangelo in *Teenage Mutant Ninja Turtles II* and it meant the hobby or practice of exploring (caves).

So with cherries at hand, Shannon and I were off to spelunk downtown D.C.

During our spelunking, we walked past Ford's Theater, where Lincoln was shot by John Wilkes Booth. Across the street we saw the house Lincoln died in.

Shannon and I sauntered our way towards the Mall. We popped the whole cup full of cherries as we approached a security check point. I think the check point was there to prevent cars from driving past the White House so we were able to get a decent view of the back of it.

We also wandered around the Ellipse and looked at the huge Christmas tree. There was also a huge train display there. Additionally, each state had a decorated Christmas tree.

The beer munchies had begun to settle in, so Shannon and I started to wander back to the hotel to find a place where we could grab some grub.

Right next to our hotel was District of Pi Pizzeria, and they were still open, so that's where we had dinner. Shannon and I ordered a deep dish pie and it was delicious. I'm not sure what beer Shannon ordered, but I didn't like it. Her beer was too hoppy for me. I tried the local beer DC Brau Rotating Selection. Whatever I had, I didn't like it either because it was way too hoppy. I did not want to waste the beer so I choked it down.

Shannon and I were pooped, so after dinner, we decided to call it a night.

The next morning, Shannon and I had a breakfast date with her family again. We all met up at Bob Evans outside Ellicott City off of Route 100.

Shannon and I couldn't stay too long at breakfast because we had plans that night for New Year's Eve. Shannon and I needed to get back to Buffalo because we were going to see the Sabres play host to the Ottawa Senators and after the game, we were going to watch the Ball Drop at the Mohawk building right in downtown Buffalo.

From the D.C. area, Shannon and I took the second star to the right and drove straight on 'til morning.

Shannon and I arrived at the Adam's Mark Hotel in downtown Buffalo by 6:45pm. We were on a tight schedule because the Sabres game started at 7:05pm; so that gave us roughly 20 minutes to check in, change, and run the few blocks over to First Niagara Center.

Shannon and I were finishing our 24 ounces of beer as we approached First Niagara Center. We could hear the Canadian National Anthem, so we knew we were on time. After getting our tickets scanned, we hopped on the large escalator up to the 300 Level. We grabbed two Labatt Blue Light Limes and found our seats.

Early in the 1st Period, Buffalo found themselves on the power play. For once, Buffalo had good puck movement in the Ottawa zone. Buffalo's Jordan Leopold took a slap shot from the Ottawa blue line. The shot hit Ottawa's goaltender Craig Anderson right in the mask. The puck deflected onto Buffalo's Brad Boyes' stick. Boyes was looking at a wide open net, and thankfully he put the puck in the net, making it a 1-0 Buffalo lead.

The goal didn't take any spark away from the Senators. The Senators kept playing hard and had some great shots on the Buffalo goaltender Jhonas Enroth.

Late in the 1st Period, Ottawa found themselves on the power play. They did everything right except putting the puck in the back of the net.

During the 1st Period, Ottawa suffered from "Coach Gordon Bombay Syndrome." Ottawa had at least three shots that rang off the pipe, but never went in for a goal.

It was 1:22 into the 2nd Period when Ottawa's Matt Carkner put Ottawa on the board with a shot the just snuck underneath the cross bar on Enroth's glove side.

A few minutes later, Buffalo's Paul Gaustad answered back with a goal. It was an ugly one. Goose, who was in front of the net, deflected a shot from the point. Buffalo had gotten their one goal lead back, making it a 2-1 Buffalo game.

The whole 2nd Period was entertaining. Both teams were playing well and it was back and forth hockey.

A little over six minutes into the 2nd Period, Ottawa's Chris Neil skated into the Buffalo zone on a breakaway. Neil was bothered from behind by a Buffalo defenseman, but Neil shrugged him off and she shot the puck past the Buffalo goaltender Enroth, tying that game at 2 apiece.

Later on in the 2nd Period, both teams found themselves on the power play, but neither team could find the back of the net.

Since it was the 2nd Intermission and we have the time, I have a small little story. The story is about chicken wings and it is quite fitting since we were in Buffalo, birthplace of the chicken wing...

Now I have been working on this theory about Buffalo...If the sports teams don't give you a heart attack, then the food will. And the food in Buffalo is so delicious! So I have come up with this theory so us Buffalonians (and others) don't die from heart disease…so just hear me out. I know that chicken wings are cooked in the fryer basket and deep fried food is some of the unhealthiest stuff out there. Yea, no big deal, we have to die some time. Anyway, the plan is to order your wings hot. Why you ask? You have probably had spicy food before and the hotter it is the quicker it runs through your system. The faster it runs through your system, the less grease and fats your body can absorb. On top of the hot sauce, you need to trade off drinks between beer and pop and I'll tell you why. In case of an emergency and you almost do have a heart attack; you should have a beer on hand. Beer will act like liquid Coumadin; it will thin your blood. And the reason why you need to drink pop? Well pop is an acid and acid eats away at stuff, like grease, but more importantly, chicken wing grease. The acid in the pop will break down and dissolve the grease from the wings and also help eat away at the plaque buildup in your arteries. And if you don't want to be pissing like a race horse all night long, a Jack and Coke would kill two birds with one stone…your welcome.

During the 3rd Period, Buffalo skated into the Ottawa zone and crashed the net hard. In doing so, there was a huge collision in front of the net. Bodies went flying and the puck crossed the crease as the net was thrown off its moorings. The ref instantly called it "no goal."

By the end of three periods of play, the game was still tied 2-2…Overtime!

With just seconds remaining in OT, there was a face off deep in Buffalo's end. Right as the ref dropped the puck, the two centers dove on top of it. The four wingers joined the mosh pit. Punches were thrown as the refs pulled players off of each other. Buffalo's Robyn Regehr received two minutes for roughing, while Ottawa's Chris Neil got two for roughing and Zenon Konopka got a 10 minute misconduct.

Overtime was exciting, with both teams having chances to win the game, but after five minutes, it was still tied 2-2.

Time for the shoot out!

Last December, Shannon and I went up to Ottawa for a Sabres game. The Sabres ended up winning that game in the shootout. I was pretty sure that all 18,690 fans in attendance at First Niagara Canter were hoping that the Sabres would repeat that shoot out win.

I never liked it when Buffalo shot first in the shootout, but Head Coach Lindy Ruff liked it for some reason. I would prefer if Buffalo went second.

Buffalo's Thomas Vanek went first for Buffalo. Vanek missed the net. Was I surprised? No, that was why Vanek got paid the big bucks, to consistently miss the net in critical situations.

Milan Michalek shot first for Ottawa, but Buffalo's Enroth blocked the shot.

It was Buffalo's Brad Boyes' turn and he shot the puck past Ottawa's Anderson to put Buffalo on the board 1-0.

Ottawa's Jason Spezza countered with a goal, tying the shootout at 1-1.

In the 3rd round of the shootout, Buffalo's Captain Jason Pominville scored to give Buffalo the lead back.

However, Ottawa's Captain Daniel Alfredsson responded by getting a goal of his own, to tie it yet again.

Buffalo's Derek Roy skated in the 4th round of a tied 2-2 shootout. Roy shot and Anderson saved.

This was why I preferred Buffalo shot second in the shootout. It was a lot like baseball, in the manner that I would like to be the home team in the 9th Inning because you go second. You got to play defense and see what your opponent threw at you. Ottawa's Eric Condra had a chance to win the game for Ottawa. Now I did not doubt Enroth's capabilities as a goaltender, but I just got nervous in situations like that. Thankfully Enroth saved the shot from Condra.

Drew Stafford shot for Buffalo in the 5th round of the shootout. Stafford shot, and Anderson saved.

Ottawa's Bobby Butler skated next. Butler preformed the Triple Deke and pulled Enroth out of position, and scoring the shootout game winning goal.

First Niagara Center was dead silent. You could hear a pin drop.

After the heartbreak, Shannon and I walked in silence with the rest of the other 18,000+ Sabres fans.

Shannon and I stopped back off at our room at Adam's Mark. There we peed and reloaded on beer, roadies to be exact. Our next stop was the Mohawk Building.

On our walk over to the Mohawk Building, we walked past the Hyatt. I told Shannon that we needed to go inside so I could show her the enormous ginger bread man in the lobby.

Probably about 20 years ago, my grandparents took my two sisters and me to the Hyatt's restaurant during the Christmas Season. For a couple years, the kitchen would bake a larger than life Ginger Bread Man cookie. Back then, the Ginger Bread Man looked massive! He could have given the Stay Puft Marshmallow Man a run for his money.

So after Shannon and I walked through the spinney door at the Hyatt, we were greeted by a security guard. He asked us if we were guests of the hotel. I told him no but we were there so we could see the really big Ginger Bread Man. The security guard looked puzzled and informed me that there was no ginger bread man there. I proceeded to tell him the same story I just told you. The security guard chuckled and insisted that there was no such man in the restaurant or lobby. I left feeling bummed out and defeated.

Shannon and I soon had our spot, front and center of the Mohawk Building with 45 minutes to spare until the New Year. Since we had 45 minutes to kill, there was only one thing for us to do, so Shannon grabbed one of the Blue Lights from her purse and we cracked it open.

There was a live band playing some shitty ass music on a stage in front of the Mohawk. Also, there were two huge screens that were showing downtown Buffalo and New York City.

Finally it was time for the 97 Rock Ball Drop count down!

10...9...8...7...6...5...4...3...2...1! Happy New Year!

Once the clock struck midnight, Shannon and I kissed...*awe, so romantic!*

There was a fireworks display from the Mohawk Building that lasted for at least 15 minutes.

Once the show was over, Shannon and I decided to hit up the bars on Chippewa Street.

Chippewa was a zoo, but that was to be expected. There were so many people that the fuzz ended up closing down Chippewa Street to traffic. Shannon and I walked past quite a few bars and clubs that had lines of 20 people deep. I told Shannon that I wasn't going to wait in any line or pay any stupid cover charge.

We turned off Chippewa onto Delaware Avenue and found a bar that had no line and didn't seem like a club either.

As we approached it, the two bouncers asked to see our IDs, so we showed it to them.

The bouncers said that we were ok to enter, so I proceeded in.

The other bouncer said, "Whoa, hang on buddy. It's a $5 cover."

I looked at Shannon and said, "I'm not paying $5 to go in their shitty bar to buy their overpriced beer…"

Shannon and I were hungry, so we made our way back to the bar/restaurant at the Adam's Mark.

There we ordered a round of Molson draft and a sampler platter to go.

We munched on our unhealthy, greasy smorgasbord board of food as we watched Dick Clark.

We woke up too late Sunday morning to utilize the pool at Adam's Mark.

Once Shannon and I checked out of the hotel, it was time for breakfast. Well, by that time it was noon; so I guess it was time for lunch.

For Lunch, I took Shannon to Charlie the Butcher on Wehrle Drive, right behind the Buffalo Niagara International Airport.

Shannon and I both ordered Beef on Weck. I also ordered one to go for Grandpa Ziggy, since we were going to pay him a visit after lunch.

The Beef on Weck is one of many Buffalo staples. It is a sandwich which consists of thinly cut, still mooing roast beef on a Kimmelweck Roll. The sandwich is garnished with a lot of horseradish. I washed my Beef on Weck down with a nice Aunt Rosie's Loganberry.

To top off the experience, Mr. Charlie the Butcher was there at his restaurant, in person…white hard hat and all.

Grandpa Ziggy was excited to see Shannon ("Wifey" as Grandpa Ziggy call her) and me. He was even more thrilled about the Beef on Weck we got him.

We stayed at Grandpa's for a little while. We caught the first half of the Buffalo Bills @ New England Patriots game…I should say we caught the only good part of the game. By the end of the 1st

Quarter, Buffalo had a 21-0 lead. Thankfully we didn't watch the rest of the game, but surprise, Buffalo shit the bed and lost 49-21.

January 2012

The Sabres started off the season on fire with an 11-6 record. However, as of late, the Sabres had been playing horribly. They had been 0-10 on their last 10 road games and their home record wasn't looking too good either. The Sabres were pretty rock solid in 11th place in the Eastern Conference.

I was pretty sure that this wasn't going to be our Stanley Cup season that new owner Terry Pegula promised us...*maybe next year*.

Terry Pegula's attempt at pulling a "George Steinbrenner" wasn't working out as well as fans in Buffalo had hoped. Ville Leino, Christian Ehrhoff, and Robyn Regher have all been flaccid duds, who hadn't produced. Yea, I know they were injured throughout the season, but if they were making millions of dollars a year, they should be producing and scoring goals, not freaking pussy farting around! The three of them had a combined total of 6 lousy goals!

Anyway, back to the story.

It was the night of Friday January 20, when Shannon and I boarded a plane at the Rochester Airport. Our destination was St. Louis to watch the St. Louis Blues beat my Sabres.

Shannon and I had to walk out to the tarmac to board our twin prop plane, bound for Cleveland.

Our seats were located right next to the propeller engines, so every time we said something to each other, we sounded like Darth Vader.

While en route to Cleveland, we experienced some turbulence. Now I am not a huge fan of turbulence on a plane because it makes me nervous. The plane is not supposed to dip and drop like a roller coaster. Anyway, we made it safely into Cleveland.

As we were boarding our connecting flight to St. Louis, we met a couple that was from Buffalo originally; Derby, New York to be exact. They too were going down for the Sabres game. Our connecting flight from Cleveland was a straight shot to St. Louis.

After landing in St. Louis, we boarded the Metro Link. We took the Metro from Lambert Airport all the way to the 8th and Pine stop. Shannon and I huffed it the few blocks to 4th and Pine, where we found our hotel, the Crowne Plaza.

It was 11pm once we were all checked in and situated in our room. We were pretty hungry and the hotel kitchen had just closed. Shannon and I noticed that Lumiere Place Casino was just a few blocks away, and since casinos never close, we figured they might have a restaurant open.

On our journey over to the casino, we came upon The Landing. The Landing was full of bars and night clubs.

Shannon and I settled on Joey B's because their kitchen was open. For dinner (at 11:30 at night) Shannon and I ordered a sampler platter and a small cheese pizza. The sampler platter was pretty good. It came with chicken fingers, deep fried raviolis, and crab Rangoon. The pizza, on the other hand, wasn't what we thought it was going to be. It was thin crust, but thinner than New York style. It had tomato sauce and a mix of American and provolone cheese…we were not fans of it. It tasted like a saltine cracker pizza, like the Oscar Meyer lunchables I got when I was a kid.

Once we closed out our bill, Shannon and I headed down the brick road to Lumiere's. Shannon quickly found a spot at the video poker as I found a spot at the roulette table.

The table I was at was a $5 minimum bet, which I was fine with. I like the $5 tables better than the $10 tables. I tossed a $20 onto the table and got 20 orange $1 chips.

My rule of thumb is that I only play $20. If I lose my $20, well then I'm shit outta luck. I normally play with a strategy when it came to roulette, which is play until I run out of chips or until I hit my 0s.

I always bet the 0/00 split, then I am left with four chips to bet elsewhere on the table.

I had played roulette enough times to see that the ball sometimes landed in 0 or 00 and bounced out and rested in the slot right next to the 0 or 00. That was why I bet the numbers next to 0 and 00.

For instance, the numbers next to 0 are 2 and 28. The numbers next to 00 are 1 and 27.

On the roulette table, I would place a $1 chip on the four corners of 1, 2, 4, and 5. I will place my 3rd dollar chip on four corners of 27 and 26. For my 4th chip, I normally put that on a corner of 28. I like to try to incorporate #26 in my bets because even though #26 Thomas Vanek never came up big during the hockey game, his number always came through for me on the roulette table. Lastly, I had one last chip to place anywhere else on the table that I was feeling.

More times than not, my strategy worked for me; as was the case that Friday night. Shannon won $5 on the video poker and I won $28 on roulette. Before we could lose any money, we decided to call it a night. As I got up from the Roulette table, I ran into a group of Sabres fans, who were also going to the following night's game. They were originally from Kenmore, NY, but left town to find a better life in St. Louis. We didn't chat for too long because Shannon and I had a lot planned for the next day.

On our walk back from Lumiere's, Shannon and I came across The Big Bang Bar on The Landing. The Big Bang Bar was a dueling piano bar. Shannon and I stayed for a few songs as I nursed my local beer, Michelob Amber Bock.

Shannon and I didn't get back to the hotel until 2am.

The alarm woke us up bright and early at 8am. Shannon and I had the Brew Masters Tour at the Budweiser Brewery just down the street.

Even though our tour was scheduled for 10am, Shannon and I had to leave pretty early because we were walking the two or so miles from our hotel all the way down to the Budweiser Brewery.

Shannon and I left the Crowne Plaza and headed down Pine until we hit 7th St. We hung a left down 7th and walked the next two miles or so. On our walk, we got to see the Arch, Busch Stadium (Home of the St. Louis Cardinals), Purina Headquarters, and the Soulard section of town.

During our morning walk down 7th St through Soulard, we came upon a Gentlemen's Club. It didn't open until 11am, but it had a sign in the window that advertised that they were bringing bingo back to the bar the following weekend! Now I was curious how Bingo worked at a strip joint. Who called the balls? Was it the stage announcer or was it one of the dancers? Or was there a volunteer from the Knights of Columbus or old folks home? If only the hockey game was the following weekend, our questions could have been answered!

Shannon and I made good time on our morning exercise walk. We arrived at the brewery around 9:30am.

After we checked in for our tour, we walked around the lobby a little bit. There was a whole bunch of Budweiser displays from their history, to their product line, to their place in sports.

In the lobby, Shannon and I ran into some more Sabre fans, who were obviously down for the game.

Our tour started in a private VIP room that was furnished with plush pleather couches and two pub tables. That was where our tour guide greeted us and went over the main ingredients of beer. Our tour guide said that German Law for beer ingredients was hop, barley, and yeast. However, Budweiser broke the rules and added rice.

The first part of the tour took us into a large building that housed enormous beer vats for Primary Fermentation. There were a minimum of 12 vats, and they were at least three stories tall.

The next leg of the tour took us into the Beechwood Aging Cellars. There we were able to sample Bud Light before it went through the filtering process. I had to say that the unfiltered Bud Light tasted a hell of a lot better than the filtered and purified Bud Light. The unfiltered Bud tasted better because it had some body, flavor, and taste to it.

Our tour led us through the Bevo Packaging Facility. Even though the packaging line was down for maintenance, it was still interesting to see where all the bottles were cleaned, filled, capped, labeled, born on dated, and packaged. The facility did both bottles and cans. We were able to see the machines that put the Bud Light stickers on the glass bottles along with the paper labels for Budweiser. They even had a machine that shrink wrapped labels onto bottles, but we were told that that line had not been used since a 2010 Minnesota Vikings promotion.

From the packing facility, we boarded a trolley that took us to the Clydesdales. There was a small pasture that had two Clydesdales in it. Our tour guide was rattling off some facts about the horses, but I zoned her out. I was just amazed at the size of a Clydesdale's schlong! Man, for only being 30°F, that Clydesdale was half-mast! The size of the horse's half chub was at least the size of my forearm! I nudged Shannon and pointed out the well-endowed

Clydesdale, and she was amazed. Before we could take a picture of the Clydesdale's crank, we were ushered into the Stables.

The Stables housed some more Clydesdales and a few Budweiser carriages. We even got to see King the Dalmatian!

After touring the Stables, we were led into another building, where we were able to sample some fresh Bud and Bud Light from the Finishing Tanks. Our tour guide informed us that each tank housed 3600 barrels of beer. We were told that for one person to drink all the beer in the tank, that person would have to drink one beer every hour, for the next 130+ years…that sounded like a challenge that I was willing to take!

Once the tour was over, we went back to our VIP room. There we were able to sample more beer. Shannon tried a Raspberry Shock Top and I tried the new Bud Light Platinum, just days before it hit the shelves for the public. Bud Light Platinum was a 6% beer, as opposed to the 4.2% Bud Light. We received our Honorary Brew Master Diplomas, and that was the end of the tour.

Shannon and I didn't want to walk the two miles back to the hotel, so we took a cab back.

By the time we got back to our room, we were both a little tired and hungry.

Tigin Irish Pub was a couple blocks away from us, so we went there for lunch. We had some Cheese Dip Wedges, Smoked Salmon Bites, and Smithwick's Mini Burgers. We washed all that down with some Schafly and a Bell's Brew.

Shannon and I couldn't spend too long at Tigin because we had reservations for the Arch at 2:30pm.

After Shannon and I passed through the security check point, we hopped into an egg shaped gondola, which took us to the top of the Arch. The Arch was pretty cool. One set of windows overlooked the Mississippi River and Illinois while the other set of windows had a beautiful view of downtown St. Louis.

Shannon and I met some more Sabres fans up in the Arch, Mike and his girlfriend Kyla. Mike was from Holley, New York but had moved out of the Western New York area. Mike and Kyla had just recently moved to Nashville and they drove up the night before for the game. It turned out the Mike and Kyla had gone to the same Buffalo/Nashville game back in December that Shannon and I went to!

The four of us talked for a good half hour before we all decided to go back down.

Before parting ways, we exchanged numbers because both parties wanted to meet up before, during, and/or after the game to party.

Shannon and I returned to our hotel room. We wanted to go swimming before the game, but we couldn't. The hotel's pool was located on the roof, and it was closed for the winter. Instead, we took a catnap.

The alarm went off at 6pm.

Within minutes, Shannon and I had our blue and gold jerseys on and it was time to huff the few blocks from 4th Street to 14th Street to the Scottrade Center.

Before we got to our seats, I decided to grab a beer. They didn't really have a good beer selection, so I went with the local brew, Bud Light.

Charles Glenn led us in the American National Anthem. Chuck had a great voice and hit every note on key and just sounded good.

Soon it was time for some hockey.

After puck drop, one of the St. Louis Blues fans asked out loud, "Hey, didn't Brad Boyes use to play for us?"

The friend replied, "Yes he did."

I turned around and remarked, "Yes, and you are more than welcome to have him back!"

The Blues fans laughed and one of them asked, "Has Brad learned how to find the back of the net yet?"

I said, "No, why would he when he has all that glass to shoot at?!"

Everyone laughed.

One of the Blues fans asked me if Shannon and I were from Buffalo.

I said, "Yea!"

He asked, "Do you live here?"

I said, "No, we flew down for the game."

With shock and astonishment in his voice, "Wait, you mean to tell me that you flew all the way from Buffalo to St. Louis!?"

"Yep, that's what we do. Shannon and I want to see the Sabres play in every arena," I answered.

The shocked Blues fan said, "Yea, but it's St. Louis! You flew all the way to St. Louis! There's nothing to do here!"

I told him that Shannon and I had enjoyed our visit thus far.

Buffalo had a great 1st Period with several opportunities to score, but just couldn't cash anything in.

Finally, with some 4-on-4 play late in the 1st Period, Buffalo's Mike Weber put the Sabres on the board, 1-0. Weber's shot beat the Blues goaltender Jaroslav Halak. After all the Buffalo fans stopped cheering about the goal, the Blues fan behind me noted that there were a "shit ton of Sabres fans" at Scottrade Center.

Since Buffalo got the first goal, it meant that they could fall asleep and not show up for the rest of the game…status quo.

The Blues looked a lot like the Sabres of the Midwest. The Blues team colors and jerseys were quite similar looking to that of the Sabres. Plus, the Blues played like crap on the power play. Additionally, the Blues had players, like the Sabres, who didn't like to shoot at the net, but rather the glass. So needless to say, there were a lot of boring parts during the game.

St. Louis got on the board midway through the 2nd Period by a shot from BJ Crombeen. Buffalo was playing some Bee Hive Hockey again and left Crombeen wide open. Crombeen slapped the puck past the Buffalo net minder Ryan Miller.

A few minutes later, Buffalo got caught again playing Bee Hive Hockey and St. Louis' David Perron took advantage of it by scoring the Blues' second goal of the night. St. Louis scored on the exact same play as they did for their first goal. The Blues skated into the Buffalo zone, shrugged off every Buffalo defender, skated behind the Buffalo net, and dumped the puck towards the front of the net, while everyone of the Sabres watched and marveled.

Towards the end of the 2nd Period, there was some exciting 4-on-4 play, but neither team could score. Buffalo's goalie Ryan Miller was playing great and so was St. Louis' Jaroslav Halak.

Looking around the Scottrade Center, I had forgotten about the good players that had played in St. Louis; such as Wayne Gretzky, Al MacInnis, Adam Oates, Keith Tkachuk, Curtis Joseph, the infamous Brett Hull, and former Sabres Pierre Turgeon and Grant Fuhr. I'm not including Rod Brind'Amour in the list because he's a dingle berry.

Speaking about former Sabres, former Sabre head coach and GM Scotty Bowman used to coach the Blues back in the day. Scotty took the Blues to the Stanley Cup Finals three times. Sadly Bowman never took Buffalo to the Cup Finals, ever.

In the 3rd Period, Miller kept the Sabres in the game. Unfortunately the Sabres juggernaut offense could only muster three shots on net!

The Sabres weren't helping out Miller that much in the 3rd Period. Miller could only hold St. Louis back for so long and it was a matter of time before St. Louis would get another goal.

St. Louis extended their lead to 3-1 mid way through the 3rd Period on a power play goal by David Backes. Miller blocked the shot originally, but the puck dribbled past him and across the line.

With almost four minutes left in the game, the Sabres found themselves on a four minute power play! St. Louis' TJ Oshie got two minutes for cross checking and two for unsportsmanlike conduct.

The Sabres screwed around in their own zone with the puck for the first part of their power play...no surprise there.

With a minute left, still on the power play, and an empty net, Buffalo's Tyler Myers finally scored on the Blues goalie Halak to bring Buffalo within one goal of St. Louis' lead.

With less than a minute remaining in regulation, Buffalo had won the face off and brought the puck deep into the St. Louis zone. Then Buffalo turned the puck over and St. Louis' Backes scored an empty netter.

Buffalo lost 4-2.

Once the game was over, Mike, Kyla, Shannon, and I decided to drown our sorrows in beer at Maggie O'Brien's.

The four of us celebrated the Sabres new franchise record of 12 straight road losses with a few pitchers of Butt Light.

Maggie O'Brien's had a live band playing, White Noise. White Noise was playing everyone's favorite and over played classic rock songs by 80s bands such as Foreigner to AC/DC. And judging by the looks of the band, I think they had been playing those classic rock covers since the songs were new!

After a few pitchers of beer, Mike and Kyla and Shannon and I parted ways.

Shannon and I made it back to our hotel, where we hopped onto a shuttle, back to Lumiere's Casino.

Shannon and I were hungry again, so before we hit up the gaming area, we decided to dine at Burger Bar. We had a couple burgers and zucchini fries. The zucchini fries tasted very good.

After dinner, we hit the gaming floor. Shannon played her video poker again. The only roulette tables I could find had a $10 minimum bet. I wasn't feeling too confident about it, but I played my $20 anyway.

Needless to say, Shannon and I suffered the same fortune as our Sabres...we lost. We lost everything we won the night before, and then some.

It was after 2am when the Crown Plaza shuttle dropped us back off at the hotel.

Shannon and I did not have any plans for Sunday morning. The pool was closed so we didn't have any real motivation to get up. We were going to go to the spinney restaurant on the top of the Millennium Hotel, but there was a huge fog over the city. We could barely see the buildings across the street from us, let alone the Mighty Mississippi. We figured that it was useless to go up in a 360 restaurant if we couldn't even enjoy the skyline.

As we were checking out at the front desk, one of the receptionists was bitching about how the St. Louis Rams sucked. I was pretty sure he was referring to the Rams' 2-14 season. I asked him, "What do you have to complain about? Didn't Kirk Warner win you a Super Bowl like 10 years ago? Did your St. Louis Cardinals just win their 11th World Series Title? I'm failing to see your dilemma here..."

The receptionist was just dumbfounded and didn't really know what to say because he realized that he was being the village idiot.

On our walk over to the Metro Station, Shannon and I walked right past the Arch again. The Arch was barely visible through the fog.

It was a little afternoon when Shannon and I decided to make like a fetus and head out. Our flight to Cleveland wasn't leaving St. Louis until 3:40pm. However, the Metro rail system was closed from Wellston to North Hanley on Saturday and Sunday due to maintenance repairs. That meant that the train wasn't going to the airport. Shannon and I had to allot ourselves some extra time because we needed to board a bus to take us to the airport.

When we finally arrived at the airport, there was a 45-60 minute wait at security. We were glad that we gave ourselves the extra time.

We didn't land in Rochester until 8pm.

February 2012

It was late February and Shannon and I were suffering from a very hardcore case of Cabin Fever. All we wanted to do was to try to shake that disease away. All we wanted was to see some palm trees. All we wanted was to live beside the ocean and leave the fire behind. We could swim out past the breakers (and skinny dip) and watch the world die (that's my little ode to Everclear).

Shannon and I got onboard a westbound 747 and *we didn't think before deciding what to do...*

All we knew was that were flying out to sunny CA to watch our Sabres and for a much needed actual vacation...

As we flew out to California, Shannon wondered aloud to me, "Are our Sabres going to disappoint us and loose, yet again?"

I broke into verse, "It never rains in California, but girl, don't they warn ya? It pours, man it pours!"

Shannon said, "I'll take that as a 'yes.'"

I carried on, *"Will you tell the folks back home we nearly made it? But please don't tell them how they found us, don't tell them how they found us! Gimme a break, give me a break!...it pours, man, it pours..."*

Though Shannon and I joked about it, it was true, our Sabres played horrible and lost almost every time we watched them on the road! Oh well, we weren't going to let the Sabres miserable performance disrupt our vacation!

It was Saturday February 25, Shannon and I had a 3pm flight from Rochester Airport.

We had a quick layover at Chicago's O'Hare Airport.

By 5pm, Shannon and I were back in the air and headed to LAX!

The flight was boring. The only cool thing that happened was that I had a window seat. I entertained myself by watching the sun set. Just before we took off from O'Hare, I saw the sun set behind the runway. Once we were up in the air, I could see the sun again, but not for long. For most of the flight, we kept up with the sun, so I got to watch about a two hour long sunset…it was a hell of a lot better than watching the in-flight movie, that crappy Justin Timberlake flick *In Time*.

We finally landed at LAX at 8pm Western Standard Time; 11pm Eastern Standard Time.

It took a while for us to get our luggage. In the meantime, Shannon and I people watched…there were a lot of weirdos in LA, but then again, they probably thought I looked weird wearing my Sabres gear.

We waited a while for the Hertz rental bus to pick us up.

Once we were dropped off at Hertz Rental, we stood in line for a while. Eventually we got a set of keys to a Toyota Corolla. Believe me, the Corolla was not my first, second, or third choice of car. I was originally promised an econo-box Chevy, but wound up with a ball-less Toyota.

Shannon and I pulled into the Travelodge in Anaheim around 10pm. After we checked into our room and unpacked, it was time to find food.

We drove down Ball Street until we found Ralph's Grocery Store. We picked up a couple microwave pizzas and a 30 pack of Caguama. Caguama caught our eyes because it was packaged in a bright yellow box with blue sea turtles on it. On my walk up to the cash register, I noticed they also sold hard liquor! I picked up a 750ml bottle of Jose Cuervo for $8!

Now I have a quick little story about Jose and myself.

Back in the day, Jose and I use to be best buds. I remember meeting Jose for the first time. *Fade in harp music.* I was 19 years old and just lubricating my drinking wheels in Niagara Falls, Canada. At the time, the legal drinking age in Canada was 19, a beautiful thing for a young lad who lived across the river from the True North. It seemed like a match made in heaven. By the time I turned 21, I had no reason to visit the bars in Canada again. I could get drunk in the States, and so Mr. Cuervo followed me over the border. Jose and I hung out that entire summer of my 21st birthday. Well, long story short, Jose liked to party hard and kick my ass the next morning. Jose and I had a lot of fun nights, but he also got me into some trouble too. I think I was 22 when I finally told Jose we couldn't hang out any more. Yes, I broke up with Jose. There was a long time where we didn't speak, but every now and then, I would see him at a bar, and we would say "hello" but that was about it...I had "retired" from drinking Jose Cuervo, but once in a blue moon, I would get my feet wet and come out of retirement.

So long story short, I bought the bottle of Jose. I figured he could help Shannon and me in a few days after the Sabres future loss to Anaheim.

After we checked out, Shannon and I went back to the hotel for our marvelous dinner of beer and microwave pizzas.

Shannon and I did not sleep that well that night. We were way too excited to sleep because the next morning, we were going to Disneyland!

We were wide awake by 6am. Disneyland did not open until 8am.

We were showered and walking down Disneyland Drive towards Disneyland by 7:30am.

Shannon and I bought our 1 Day Park Hopper Pass.

Disneyland opened at 8am, but California Adventure did not open until 10am. That evening, California Adventure closed at 8pm, but Disneyland had extended hours and was open until midnight!

After Shannon and I walked through the turn styles, we walked past the train station and straight on to Main Street, USA.

Shannon and I stopped at City Hall so we could pick up our "1st Visit Disneyland" buttons.

As we proceeded down Main Street, Shannon and I were both amazed at how small Sleeping Beauty's Castle was! We thought it was going to be huge like Cinderella's Castle at Magic Kingdom in Florida, but it wasn't. Sleeping Beauty's Castle was still cool.

Shannon and I made a bee-line towards Tomorrowland.

The first ride we went on was Buzz Lightyear Astro Blasters and it was awesome! We rode around in little pods and we had laser guns. We needed to shoot Zurg's henchmen and eventually defeat Zurg at the end of the ride, which we did! We made Zurg our bitch!

After Buzz, we quickly raced over to Space Mountain! Space Mountain was freaking awesome! We hopped into the space ship roller coaster and clicked up to take off. All of a sudden, we were whipping around and flying through space.

Shannon and I avoided the Captain EO attraction because I did not want to get molested by a 3D image of Michael Jackson.

Shannon then drove Miss Daisy (that would be me) around in a green car in Autopia.

Then we ran over to Finding Nemo Submarine Voyage, formerly 20,000 Leagues Under the Sea. Shannon was quite excited to ride the Submarine Voyage. Years ago when she was at Magic Kingdom in Florida, they closed down 20,000 Leagues Under the Sea, and she was bummed out that she never got to experience it. Well, I helped make Shannon's dream come true by going on Nemo with her!

By the time we got off the Nemo ride, it was 10am, and time to head on over to California Adventure!

As we walked through California Adventure, there were a few sections of the park that were walled off due to construction. I read one of the signs and said to Shannon, "Radiator Springs is coming Summer 2012! That means we need to come back! Thank goodness we have to come back to see Buffalo play the LA Kings next season!"

Shannon and I made our way over to the Twilight Zone Tower of Terror and we each got a Fast Pass.

We had about an hour or so until we could use our Fast Passes, so Shannon and I walked around the corner. We went to the attraction Turtle Talk with Crush. Crush was the sea turtle from *Finding Nemo* and he was a blast. A group of about 30 people were ushered into a small theater room where we could interact with Crush. We were able to see him through the ocean window and he could see us through the "human tank window." He had a little Q&A session with the little children in the front row. He also taught everyone how to talk turtle…*Duuuudddddeeeee!*

Crush asked if there were any older kids that had any questions.

Since I still behaved and acted like a kid, I quickly raised my hand because I had a question for Crush, "Crush, who is your favorite Ninja Turtle?"

Crush inquired, "*Duuudddeee!* What's a Ninja Turtle?"

I informed Crush that Ninja Turtles were crime fighting turtles from New York.

"Dude!" Crush said. "Who's your favorite Ninja Turtle?"

Like an anxious kid, I blurted out, "I *love* Michelangelo!"

Crush said, "Yea, I like Michelangelo too. He's my favorite..."

Crush and I chit chatted a little bit more before moving on to someone else.

A few minutes later Crush had to say good-bye.

After Shannon and I parted ways with Crush, we found an Animation Academy. Since I was an artist (2007 Daemen College BS in Art), I decided to become educated by a professional Disney artist.

In that class, our instructor taught us how to draw Mickey Mouse.

Shannon and I ended up keeping both of our Mickey pictures. We figured that they were souvenirs from our $100 art class lesson (park admission tickets were $100 per person).

Once our class was over, our instructor told us that if we wanted to come back in a few minutes, that we would be learning how to draw Winnie the Poop. Believe me, I'm a Poop fan, but there was still more Disney magic to see and experience!

The time had come for Shannon and me to use our Tower of Terror Fast Passes!

We headed to the Fast Pass line at the Tower of Terror, and gave our passes to the bell hop of the 1930s Hollywood Tower Hotel and marched right to the front of the line. A receptionist greeted us in the lobby and escorted us to a study.

While we were in the study, the power went out and the room was pitch black. Suddenly, in the corner of the room, an old black and white TV turned on. Rod Serling, from *The Twilight Zone,* greeted us from the boob tube. Somehow Disney had brought Rod back from the dead. Rod informed us that that evening's atmosphere was eerily reminiscent to the one of that one fateful day back in 1939, when the hotel was abandoned after five elevator passengers mysteriously disappeared!

Moments later, Shannon and I found ourselves in the boiler room of the Hollywood Tower Hotel. Another bell hop led Shannon and me into the only working elevator in the hotel.

SLAM! The elevator doors were shut, we could feel the spooked elevator move us backwards, and then up a few flights.

As elevator abruptly came to a stop, the doors swung wide opened, and we were staring down a dimly light hallway of the hotel. We soon heard Rod Serling's beyond the grave voice. He broke the bad news to us and told us that we were "the passengers in the most uncommon elevator about to ascend (us) into our very own episode of *The Twilight Zone!*" Suddenly we saw the five apparitions of the victims from 1939! The elevator then shot us up 10 stories and instantly dropped us down to the boiler room! The possessed elevator shot us back up to the 13th Floor and dropped us again. The elevator dropped us a few more times before we crash landed back in the boiler room. There the doors were opened and we were spared from death! The bell hop greeted us and escorted us out of the hotel.

After Tower of Terror, Shannon and I migrated over to Muppet Vision 3D. There we got to see a 3D movie of Kermit, Gonzo, Rizzo, and the whole gang. Unfortunately Miss Piggy was there as well. I was not a fan of Miss Piggy. I thought she was a bitch and Kermit could do better. Also, I was not into heifers or "hogging."

Next, Shannon and I enjoyed Disney's Aladdin—A Musical Spectacular.

Now let's take a moment here, a TV time out if you will. I am a guy, and a hetero for that fact, which yields me to not being a fan of the theater. I can't nor do I understand theater or "jazz hands." Once a year, I suffer and have to take Shannon to one theater show, normally one of my choosing. So, I decided to take Shannon to the Aladdin theater performance. I figured that Disney never screws anything up and everything they do is awesome, so how bad could their theater be?

Disney Theater was awesome and I'll tell you why...Disney was able to take their 90 minute long animation feature and transform it into a 45 minute long show. There were no stupid intermissions either. The only thing that could have made it better was if they sold beer or if I had a flask with me...*Note to self, next time we go back for Aladdin Theater, bring a flask.*

Thereafter, Shannon and I trudged through A Bug's Land...*Note to self, DO NOT bushwhack through A Bug's Land, even if it looks like a short cut. Too many damn strollers, kids, traffic jams, and it was a cluster!*

By the time we exited A Bug's Land, Shannon and I were quite tired and hungry.

We came upon Sonoma Terrace at the Golden Vine Winery. Shannon and I purchased our dinner and received tickets to World of Color, which was an evening water and light spectacular show. Our World of Color tickets were for 8pm, and at the time, it was only 3 or 4pm, so we still had plenty of time to explore the rest of California Adventure and wander back to Disneyland.

After dinner, Shannon and I crossed over a boardwalk and entered Paradise Pier. We coasted up to California Screamin' roller coaster to get our Fast Passes.

Once we received our Fast Passes, we marched on down the Toy Story Midway Mania!

Next on our agenda was Mickey's Fun Wheel!

Now I was not a fan of the Ferris wheel, but then again, who is? To me, the Ferris wheel was a big dumb, boring ride that just went in a circle.

On top of that, I had a fear of Ferris wheels. Back in the day when I was a wee young whippersnapper, my mom took my sisters and me to McDonalds on Grand Island Boulevard in Grand Island, NY. It was a nice summer evening. The old McDonalds overlooked one of Western New York's amusement parks, Fantasy Island.

As I was munching on my cheeseburger Happy Meal, I gazed across Grand Island Boulevard and stared at the Ferris wheel at Fantasy Island. Moments later, I saw a huge slew of fire trucks, cop cars, and ambulances! It was like a little kid's dream! Lights and sirens and action! Well, long story short, a kid slipped out underneath the lap bar of the Ferris wheel and plummeted to his death! I was petrified of Ferris wheels ever since then!

Years later at WNY's other theme park, Darien Lake, my friends tried to convince me to go on that park's Ferris wheel, so we could throw "I Got It" balls from the top of the Ferris wheel, but I was too fearful to go up…and that was in high school.

Like I mentioned earlier, Disney didn't really screw anything up. While Shannon and I were eating dinner at Sonoma Terrace, I had a great view of Mickey's Fun Wheel and it looked awesome! Each gondola rode on its own oval track; it was not on a fixed axel. So when the Ferris wheel moved, your gondola would swing around on the track and whip you side to side; it looked bad ass!

Since I was 27, I decided to face my fear...

Shannon and I were seated in the gondola with another couple and their teenage daughter. As the cast member slammed the gondola door shut, it sounded quite reminiscent of a jail door...not that I've ever been locked up before.

My Spidey senses soon began to tingle! I reverted back to "Young Adam" at the unripe young age of seven from St. Stephens Grammar School and thought about that kid that died at Fantasy Island! Now 27, I thought my time was up, I was next! It was going to be like *Final Destination!*

I was a little surprised that there were motion sickness bags onboard. I really wanted a barf bag with Mickey ears for my collection, so I asked the dad if he could pull one out for me. As the dad pulled the bag out, I could see that there were no Mickey ears on it, let alone a "Disneyland" logo on it. I had the dad put the bag back because it was just a generic glossy plastic barf bag.

I'm gonna pause for a second for station identification...A little known fact about Adam DeRose is that I have a barf bag collection.

I was still nervous that the gondola would break off from the Ferris wheel and that we would plummet into Paradise Bay, and that we would all drown because there would be no way out of the locked, caged gondola that we were in!

I tried to face my fear and once the ride ended, I was still petrified! I thought about kissing the ground, but I did not. That facing your fears crap did not work for me with that ride!

Shannon and I doubled back around Paradise Pier.

Golden Zephyr was the next attraction that Shannon and I were in line for. During our wait, a voice over head told us that the ride might be canceled due to high winds! The hell with high winds! We were on vacation! There should not be any hang ups!

Somehow, Mickey farted some magic pixy dust and Shannon and I were able to ride the Golden Zephyr!

We got to ride in the front seat of one of the Golden Zephyrs... I do not want to spoil anything for any children, but the Golden Zephyrs were actually silver in color.

The ride actually was fun. When I originally looked at the ride, I looked a bit boring, but once I actually hopped into it and rode it, it was a blast! The Zephyr whipped us around and over the Paradise Pier water!

After we got off the Zephyr, a Phinneus and Furb Float/Parade went by.

Once the parade ended, Shannon and I made a bee line towards Goofy's Sky School roller coaster. We saw that the wait line was 45 minutes and we were bummed out; we did not want to wait that long.

As we turned around to head back towards Disneyland, Shannon and I saw Goofy!

Goofy was dressed up in his aviator suit! Shannon was dressed up in her "I'm with Goofy" T-shirt!

Goofy was excited to see Shannon's T-shirt and the both of them got their picture taken.

After chillin' with Goofy, Shannon and I high tailed it on outta there, back to Disneyland.

As we were exiting California Adventure, we walked past a kiosk that was selling Mickey ears. One set of ears they had was a graduation cap with ears. I decided to get it because I was graduating from Monroe Community College in a few months with an automotive technology degree. I figured I'd wear the Mickey ears as I crossed the stage to get my diploma.

Once we entered back into Disneyland, Shannon and I rushed on over to Shannon's favorite ride, the Jungle Cruise.

As we boarded our boat, our captain looked at me and saw my graduation Mickey ears cap. He commented in the most boring, dull, and monotone voice, "Congratulations Class of 2012, you may be the last class to graduate…"

Our Jungle Cruise Captain did not disappoint. He dropped all the classic lines, such as, *"Welcome to the wonderful backside of water!" "That rock over there is made of marble, but people take it for granite" "Everyone, watch out for Ginger. Ginger snaps. Yup, she's one tough cookie." "Aww, look at that. Those lions are protecting that sleeping zebra." "That's a Bengal Tiger folks. They can jump up to 20 feet, but don't worry; we're only 15 feet away. He'll jump right over us."*

Once our Jungle Cruise boat docked, Shannon and I watched our step as we exited from the boat. I did not want to bump my head, because I would have had to watch my language because we were in a family place...

Shannon and I kept with the adventure theme and hopped in line to the Indian Jones Adventure or as the Jungle Cruise captain called it, "The Indiana Jones Adventure and the Temple of the Four-hour line."

As we waited in line for Indy, I got Aqua's stupid song "Doctor Jones" stuck in my head...*Doctor Jones, Jones, Calling Doctor Jones! Doctor Jones, Doctor Jones, Get up now!"* I all knew was the refrain so I sang that for the entire 45 minute wait in line.

The Dr. Jones ride was quite the adventure. There was fire and brimstone and snakes! A ton of snakes actually and I am petrified of snakes. The ride was fun, and at the end of the ride, we helped Indy save the day!

As we parted ways with Indy, Shannon and I were still in a thrill mood, so we quickly scurried towards the Haunted Mansion. On our way we came upon Tarzan's Treehouse, formerly known as Swiss Family (Robinson) Tree House.

Shannon and I quickly explored the tree house because we wanted to try to get in all the Disney in one day. Once we were done exploring, we continued on over to the Haunted Mansion!

Shannon and I loved the Haunted Mansion in Florida; it was one of our favorite rides. The Haunted Mansion was exactly what it sounded like, it was a haunted mansion.

Shannon and I hopped into our Doom Buggy and prepared to see some spooks and specters!

As the ride ended, Shannon and I had a stowaway! One of the ghosts hopped in our Doom Buggy and came home with us!

By the time we left the Haunted Mansion, it was time to head back to California Adventure. It was 7:40pm and our World of Color show was starting at 8pm.

Shannon and I got our front row seats on Paradise Bay and excitedly anticipated the start of the water and light show.

World of Color was much like the Bellagio water show, but better. World of Color incorporated a water and laser light spectacular that was choreographed to Disney music. As opposed to Bellagio's 5 or 10 minute water show, Disney's show lasted well over 30 minutes.

At the conclusion of World of Color, Shannon and I shot back on over to Disneyland to take advantage of their extended park hours.

While walking back down Main Street, USA, we caught Sleeping Beauty's Castle fireworks display. We even saw Stinker Bell flying overhead. The fireworks lasted for a good 15 minutes.

When the fireworks finished, Shannon and I ran like light speed over to Star Tours. There, R2-D2 and C-3PO greeted us and prepped us for our journey in the StarSpeeder 3000. Apparently it was C-3PO's first time driving the StarSpeeder 3000, but I think he did quite well considering the circumstances; we were being chased by Darth Vader's henchmen!

After C-3PO successfully got us out of harm's way and landed the StarSpeeder 3000, Shannon and I took a romantic stroll up to Sleeping Beauty's castle.

As we walked, we could just barely see the summit of Splash Mountain! Shannon and I promptly rushed on over to it.

Within moments, Shannon and I were in a carved wooden water vessel. As we floated down the river and water falls, we watched Br'er Rabbit try to elude Br'er Fox and Br'er Bear.

The finale of the ride was a huge water fall drop. Thankfully for us, we came away un-soaked from the ride.

The next ride we saw and rode was The Many Adventures of Winnie the Pooh. I had to say that the best part of that entire ride was when it ended. Like any other Disney attraction, once the ride was over, they dumped you into a gift shop. Winnie the Pooh was no exception, but in this case, that name of this gift shop was "Pooh Corner!" I was not the only one taking a picture of the gift shop sign!

My parents had told me from a ripe young age that poop was not funny, nor will it ever be funny. Well shit! I think they were full of crap because at the age of 27 I still thought that poop was one of the most hilarious things. Even the word "poop" was awesome. I could spell "poop" frontwards or backwards and it's still "poop!"…it's a palindrome!

Disney security stopped me before I could poo in Pooh Corner…I think their sign was misleading.

Shannon was a huge Pirates fan, so in short order, we found our way to the entrance of Pirates of the Caribbean.

I thought it was a cool idea that there was a restaurant inside overlooking the first scene of the Pirates ride.

Pirates of the Caribbean was a fun experience. We got to boat through a battle between a fort and pirate ship! Also, we got to motor though a town with all the drunken seamen and saw a wench auction! And yes, we even got to see that dreamy Captain Jack Sparrow.

When we finished up with Pirates, Shannon and I bolted on over to Big Thunder Mountain Railroad! I loved the idea and concept of the runaway train in the gold rush of the Wild West.

Fantasyland was our next destination after Thunder Mountain.

By the time we made it over to Fantasyland, it was 11pm. That meant we only had one hour of magic left before we turned into pumpkins!

Shannon and I saw that there was a short line for Dumbo the Flying Elephant.

The last few times Shannon and I were at Magic Kingdom in Florida, Dumbo was broken and down for repair. I knew that it had to be destiny that Dumbo was alive and working that night!

Shannon and I hopped into a green clothed Dumbo. We chose a green one because green is Shannon's favorite color.

Once we had lifted off with Dumbo, I jerked him up and down. I was hoping to get some "Disney magic." I thought that Dumbo would come to life and fly around the park with us. Shannon made me stop jerking Dumbo up and down because she thought I was going to break him. I thought it was pretty hard to break a Dumbo because elephants are pretty resilient. Shannon thought that maybe the Dumbo ride was constantly broken was due to big kids like me.

When the ride ended, Shannon took my picture with me inside Dumbo.

Next we hopped aboard Pinocchio's Darling Journey.

I was never really a big fan of Pinocchio. In fact, the movie kind of scared me as a child, and even as an adult. The one thing I remember from the movie was that they said "jackass!" When my sisters and I were kids, we could not say "jackass" because it was a swear word. I tried to argue with mom and told her it wasn't because Disney was able to use it...I never won that fight.

I even argued with mom that they use that word in the Bible!

Matthew 21: 4-7: This happened so that what had been spoken through the prophet might be fulfilled: "Say to daughter Zion, 'Behold, your king comes to you, meek and riding on a jackass, and on a colt, the foal of a beast of burden.' The disciples went and did as Jesus had ordered them. They brought the jackass and the colt and laid their cloaks over them, and he sat upon them."

I never won that argument with mom either…

I even mentioned to mom that they used "ass" in Peter Pan, staring Cathy Rigby…Stinker Bell didn't like Wendy, so Stinker Bell called Wendy an "ass."

I didn't win that argument either.

And speaking of Peter Pan, Shannon and I saw Peter Pan's Flight! We really wanted to ride Peter Pan, but when we saw that there was a 45 minute wait, we opted for another ride…quick side note for the Peter Pan ride. Back in the day, Shannon's parents took her and her brother Kyle to Magic Kingdom. It was a young child's dream come true to go to Disney World, and to make it even better, Shannon's parents Jim and Joan bought the kids ice cream for lunch! What kid wouldn't want to have ice cream for a meal!? After Shannon had her meal of ice cream, the family went on the Peter Pan ride. Shannon got a little motion sickness from the ride, and she ended up ralphing on the fight scene between Peter Pan and Captain Hook on Hook's ship! Needless to say, the ride was quickly stopped and closed for cleaning.

Shannon and I then picked out our next ride, Mr. Toad's Wild Ride! She was beyond thrilled. Years ago, back on that same trip with her parents when she puked on the Peter Pan ride, the Magic Kingdom used to have Mr. Toad's Wild Ride, and it was one of Shannon's favorites! A few years later, Shannon went back to Magic Kingdom on a school trip. By then, Magic Kingdom had closed and changed the ride to Winnie the Poop. So of course Shannon was ecstatic to ride Mr. Toad again! She couldn't yank my arm hard enough to drag me over to Mr. Toad's ride!

Once Shannon and I were secured in our shiny red motor car, our journey with Mr. Toad began!

Mr. Toad kicked off our journey at Toad Hall.

Mr. Toad was joy riding us through his library, where we saw MacBadger at the top of a ladder, screwing around with a load of books.

Mr. Toad was so obsessed with his new motor car! He told us, *"Ain't nothing like it, my shiny red machine! Got the feel for the wheel! Keep the moving parts clean! Hot shoe, burning down the avenue! Got an on ramp coming through my bedroom!"* and with that, Mr. Toad drove us down the hallway, through the double door into his bedroom, through his bedroom, and out the window!

Mr. Toad's shiny machine crashed out onto the ground. The motor car was old enough that it didn't have air bags, so we ate the dashboard.

Then Mr. Toad drove us through some other houses in the English country side. Mr. Toad blurted out, "Tally ho!" and we were soon driving merrily, merrily, merrily, merrily, merrily on our way to nowhere in particular! Mr. Toad drove us to Nottingham to Brittingham to Buckingham and to any hammy hamlet by the sea! We were on our way to Devonshire, Lancashire, and Woostershire!

I leaned over to Mr. Toad and asked him where he was taking us.

Mr. Toad blurted out some gibberish of, "I'm not so sure! We'll have to wait and see!" Mr. Toad took his eyes off the road, and in a weird demonic look, he said, "We'll have to wait and see!" As his eye balls twisted in his sockets, he asked, "Are we on our way to Dover? Or going merrily over the jolly old road that goes to Plymouth? Ho!"

Shannon and I both agreed that Mr. Toad probably had too much "pond water" before we got into his shiny red machine.

I asked Mr. Toad if he wanted me to drive. He just looked at me and said, "We're merrily on our way, through the roads, are perpendicular!"

Shannon shouted out, "Maybe Adam should drive!"

Mr. Toad rambled out, "We're always in a hurry! We have no time to stall! We gotta be there!"

Shannon and I didn't know what the hell Mr. Toad was carrying on about, but we were getting a little nervous.

After touring the English country side, Mr. Toad soon had us upon the city limits of London!

I asked Mr. Toad, "Hey Bud, where are you taking us to?"

Mr. Toad slowly took his eyes off the road to look at me. In the meantime, we blasted a pothole and Mr. Toad bounced up in his seat. Without taking his eyes off me, he calmly said, "We've gotta be there, we've gotta be there!"

"Yes! Ok! Where is there Mr. Toad!" I shouted!

Mr. Toad quietly and calmly replied, "But where I can't recall…"

Shannon blurted out, "Ah *puck*! He's gonna kill us!"

As we blew into downtown, Mr. Toad mooned a couple Bobbies. Mr. Toad was amused because his shiny red machine was faster than the Bobbies' flat feet.

Mr. Toad was burning down the avenues of London; we could barely see the road from the heat coming off it.

Before we knew it, we headed down the wrong way of a "One Way!" We almost had a head on collision with a truck!

Luckily for us, Mr. Toad swerved toward Winkie's Pub!

Split seconds before we crashed into Mr. Winkie's Pub, Mr. Toad, Shannon, and I all made eye contact with bar keep Mr. Winkie! We could all see Mr. Winkie pouring three beers for a bunch of Weasels!

SMASH!

Mr. Toad had crashed his new shiny red machine into Mr. Winkie's establishment!

After all the dust had settled, Mr. Winkie was nowhere to be seen, but we saw the three beers still spinning in the air!

Shannon, Mr. Toad, and I quickly hopped out of our burning wreckage and grabbed the three mugs before they hit the ground. We couldn't bear to watch the three brews hit the floor because that would have been alcohol abuse!

Suddenly Mr. Winkie popped his head out from behind the bar and he was a pissed off mofo! He instantly started yelling at us, "Look at my bar! Look at my window!"

Once Shannon, Mr. Toad, and I finished a quick, long, hard chug, we turned around to look at the aftermath and assess the damage; we didn't think it was that bad.

I said, "It doesn't look that bad…it's just cosmetic…"

Mr. Toad weighed in and said, "Don't worry; I'll give you Toad Hall for it!"

Instantly Shannon and I knew where this was going and it wasn't good; it was like déjà vu!

I said, "Hey Mr. Toad! Watch this!" I quickly grabbed my beer and chugged it. My college frat boy like actions totally side tracked Mr. Toad from the ensuing events. Mr. Toad and Mr. Winkie were so mystified that I was able to pound a 40 ounce stein in one fell swoop…honestly it didn't really take much practice…

Before Mr. Toad could resume giving the deed of Toad Hall to Mr. Winkie, I quickly cold cocked the beer stein over Mr. Toad's head. Mr. Toad was knocked out cold and the stein shattered everywhere.

Mr. Winkie was not happy with us. Mr. Winkie said, "You owe me for that drink and for that stein!"

I told Mr. Winkie, "Hey Winkie…"

Mr. Winkie snapped back and yelled at me, "Don't call me 'Winkie!'"

I said, "Ok, One Eyed Willy!?"

"Blah!" Mr. Winkie choked out.

I said, "OK Dick, You don't need to worry. Everything is fine. It already looks like you have the makings for a Planet Hollywood franchise on your hands with the car in the wall and the Mr. Toad stuff up on the walls…"

Mr. Winkie wasn't having any of it. He grabbed a shiny Saturday night special from behind the bar. As he cocked the gun, he picked up the telephone, and said, "That's it! I'm calling the cops on you guys!"

Shannon and I weren't ready to go to jail, let alone Disney jail! I couldn't bare thinking about being in a holding cell with Jafar, Zurg, Captain Hook, or Stromboli! Especially Stromboli! I'm a weak young lad with a virgin bunghole; I could only envision how Stromboli would tear my shit up with his Stromboli! Quickly thinking on my feet, I instantly remember a scene from *Back to the Future Part 2* when Marty McFly asked Biff about the Sports Almanac…

I exclaimed, "Yea, but Mr. Winkie, you're just forgetting one thing!"

Mr. Winkie looked puzzled as he lowered his gun and said, "What's that kid?"

I pointed behind Mr. Winkie and shouted, "What the hell is that!?"

As Mr. Winkie turned around to look at what I was talking about, I picked up a metal spoked ash tray up from off the bar and whipped it towards Mr. Winkie.

I'm going to take another quick TV time out here. First of all, Hollywood never depicts life. Second of all, I sucked at hand eye coordination. That is why I ran cross country at St. Joseph's Collegiate Institute and Daemen College....*I'd like to thank our sponsors St. Joe's and Daemen for producing this outstanding graduate and tax paying member of society. Now back to your regularly scheduled programming...*

I did not reenact the scene from *Back to the Future Part 2* perfectly...

I clipped Mr. Winkie in the jugular! As he was bleeding out, Shannon and I could hear the 911 operator calling out on the receiver from the phone, asking if everything was alright. Shannon quickly grabbed the phone and said, "Everything is fine here. Just another drunk patron, hehe."

With his right hand, Mr. Winkie grabbed towards his neck, where the ash tray was protruding out. Blood was just gushing out of his neck and blood foamed out of his mouth, like a canned beer that had just been opened after being dropped! With Mr. Winkie's other hand, he reached towards me, trying to strangle me. Acting quickly, I pounded Mr. Toad's beer. Once I polished it off, I whacked the empty beer stein over Winkie's dome, knocking him unconscious.

Everything came to a pause as Shannon and I looked at each other briefly...

We climbed over the bar and grabbed a handful of top shelf liquor.

As we climbed back over the bar, we grabbed a sham-wow cloth (as seen on TV) and whipped away our finger prints! Just then, Mr. Winkie's chumps, the Weasels, came in from the back room with pieces out. The Weasels were acting ill because they were so full of 8 balls. Gunshots rang out like a bell.

Shannon and I decided to make a break for it.

We both grabbed Mr. Toad by his arm pits and dragged him outside like a wounded soldier or football player.

Once outside the pub, Shannon and I were both disoriented and confused.

It was around that time when Mr. Toad came to. He woke up from his stupor and pointed out that his buddy Cyril was waiting around the corner in the canary yellow carriage.

The three of us scurried over to Cyril and hopped onto the carriage.

Moments later, Cyril was galloping down the concrete roads of London. We could see the Weasels were in hot pursuit, their gun fire racing past us faster than Cyril could run!

All of a sudden, Cyril hit a bump and the glove box to the carriage popped open! Out popped a 9mm that Mr. Toad quickly grabbed...and all we heard were shells falling on the concrete, fast.

Cyril wanted to hit the gas, but he was only a horse. It was a matter of time before the Weasels were bumper to bumper with us!

The avenue we were on was packed!

We could hear Disney security closing in quick!

The Weasels had disappeared.

Before Mr. Toad, Shannon, and I could try to get away before being jacked, Disney Security pinched us.

Mr. Toad, Shannon and I were arrested by Disney Police. After we were cuffed, we were dragged to town hall where we were finger printed and had our mug shots taken. Disney decided to call our parents and tell them what kind of trouble we were in.

Though Shannon and I were in Disney jail, we were not placed in common population. Because we were husband and wife, we were placed in solitary confinement together, inside of one of the towers in Sleeping Beauty's Castle!

Though we had been in jail only minutes, Shannon and I were allowed visitors.

A guard told me that my Grandmother Cyril was there to visit me.

Shannon looked puzzled and asked me, "You have a Grandma Cyril?"

Grandma Cyril gave Shannon and me "old lady clothes" so we could try to sneak out of Disney Jail...

Shannon and I decided to put on the old muumuus and blue bonnets.

Somehow we were able to sneak past the Sleeping Beauty Castle Security.

Once the three of us were outside the castle limits, we heard the Code Red!

All three of us looked at each other. Shannon and I thanked Cyril and wished him best of luck! We told him that he should get back to the Mr. Toad Ride before he got into more trouble.

Cyril wished us luck and Godspeed.

To elude Disney security, Shannon and I dumped the granny garb and we hid on Storybook Land Canal Boats ride. Storybook Land was an alright trip. The canal boat just took us through different villages from Disney movies, such as Pinocchio's town, Aladdin town, and Ariel's underwater town.

By the time we got off Storybook Land, it was 11:40pm! We only had 20 more minutes of magic left before we turned into pumpkins!

Shannon and I had put our next ride on hold for the entire trip. We were a little nervous to go on it because spinney rides always make us sick and dizzy. We figured that since the park was almost closed, that even if we got sick on this ride, it wouldn't really matter too much, because we would just go back to the hotel and sleep it off...

Yes, that was correct, Shannon and I hopped on the Mad Tea Party, better known as the Tea Cups!

When the ride had ended, Shannon and I were not dizzy at all; no motion sickness! So what did we do next? We went back on the Tea Cups for a second round!

We were still in a time crunch, there was still 8 minutes left with our Disney extended hours!

The next closest ride to us was Alice in Wonderland. Alice had a short line, so we hopped in.

Alice in Wonderland was one of those other Disney movies that always scared the crap out of me as a kid. The movie and plot just seemed too weird for my little pea brain to grasp the concept and follow what was going on...the Alice in Wonderland ride scared me as well.

After we got off of Alice, there were only 5 minutes left until Disneyland closed!

Our very last ride we rode in the park was a ride that was guaranteed that no one would be riding on, It's a Small World.

Yea, we decided to torture ourselves with that horrible ride…

The ride was about 10 minutes too long and by the time the ride was over, I was singing "*It's a Small World*" in every language!

Shannon and I could not escape quickly enough from that ride. Once we had escaped, our magic hours were over and the park was closing. Surprisingly enough, the only things that were still open in the park were souvenir shops and the Peter Pan ride still had about 50 people in line waiting for it. Shannon and I thought about sneaking into the back of the line, but Disney Security was guarding the entrance to the ride. We didn't want to make ourselves known to Disney Security because we weren't sure if there was still an APB out for us. We swiftly hid behind a large family that was exiting the park via Sleeping Beauty's Castle.

Shannon and I successfully escaped Disneyland without being captured by Disney Security.

I still wanted to go back to Disneyland and California Adventure because there were still more rides that we didn't get to go on! Like I said earlier, I was glad we had to come back next season for the Sabres/Kings game.

That same day that we were at Disney was also the same day as the Oscars. I could care less about the stupid Oscars and the Hollywood Elite that went along with it.

On top of that, the Oscars were being held at Highland/Hollywood Theater, not Kodak Theater. The month before, Kodak had filed for bankruptcy and requested to take their name off the venue in an effort to cut costs. The people in charge of the show ended up putting blankets over anything with "Kodak" on it, but they eventually took the blankets down because it looked too tacky! You're in Hollywood and having blankets on Kodak Theater was tacky?! Did you take a look around town at all?!

Shannon and I woke Monday morning with only one thing on our list to do, and that was the Late Late Show with Craig Ferguson. Taping did not start until 3pm, so we had some time to putz around.

We finally got our butts in gear by 11am. We hopped into the Corolla and headed to Downtown Disney.

We wandered around downtown for a bit. We decided to have breakfast at Wetzel's Pretzels. I had a jalapeno pretzel and

Shannon and a salt covered one. The pretzels may have cost a lot, but the mustards were free! I think I ate more mustard than pretzel...

After breakfast, Shannon and I wandered into California Wilderness Hotel to check it out.

The lobby was amazing. Disney left no detail unfinished. The lobby looked like a wilderness lodge. The huge ceilings were accented with large, wooden carved tree trunks. They even had a huge fire place.

Shannon and I checked out the pool. We wanted to go in, but it was locked. We needed a room key to get in and our Econo Lodge key would not work.

A short while later, Shannon and I hopped back into our rental and headed out to CBS Studios for Craig Ferguson!

For those of you who didn't know, Craig used to be Drew Carry's boss on the Drew Carey Show, until Drew Carry got the job to host The Price is Right.

Shannon and I were able to get our FREE tickets to the Late Late Show with Craig Ferguson by going to 1iota.com. I signed up to have an account and picked the dates we wanted to see Craig. Within a week, I had confirmation on tickets to a show.

I had requested tickets for Monday February 27th and Tuesday February 28th. Before we left New York, we were granted tickets for Monday's show, but nothing for Tuesday's show.

On our electronic tickets, it said check in time was 3:15pm. The ticket also said that we needed to arrive 30 minutes prior to the check in time stated on our ticket.

So there Shannon and I were, standing in line at 2:45pm, with about 25 other people, lined up on the side walk on Fairfax Avenue, that over looked CBS Studios.

Finally around 3:30pm the rookie warm up guy came out and hyped us up for the show.

A couple people associated with the show came by and checked everyone's tickets to make sure they were all legit.

After waiting around some more, the line started to move. We had our IDs out with our tickets. We got a cool wrist band and eventually walked through a metal detector.

Once we passed through the metal detector, we sat on freezing cold bleacher benches.

Then Dukes came out to warm us up for the show. Dukes informed us that Craig used profanity, so if we didn't like words like "shit" "damn" or "fuck" then "you need to get the *fuck* out!"

Eventually we were ushered into CBS Studios. We had to huff it up four flights of stairs to the Late Late Show's studio.

I was amazed at how small the studio was! It was probably the size of two classrooms! Half of the studio was the stage and the other half was seating for the audience. It was tiny and cozy. They crammed about 100 of us in the seats.

Before the show started, we got another warm up guy, Chunky. Chunky told us a whole bunch of lousy jokes. Chunky informed us that we were "show enhancers" and that even if a joke sucked, we all still need to laugh really hard; just to prove to America that it was a funny joke.

Once Chunky got done with his bit, it was time for the show to begin!

The PA guy said, "Ladies and Gentlemen, please welcome Craig Ferguson!" And as "show enhancers" we went crazy; clapping and cheering, hooting and hollering!

Craig came out and did his monologue.

Craig thanked everybody and mocked out the Academy, and thanked them as well. Then Craig mocked out Angelina Jolie with her leg posing thing she did at the Oscars.

Now Shannon and I both missed the Oscars the night before, but the word on the street was that all Angelina did the entire night was strutted and flashed her leg as if she was a panty hose model.

Craig tried his hand at leg posing like Angelina.

He followed his Angelina rant up with his tag line, "It's a great day for America everyone!"

Craig mentioned that yesterday's Daytona 500 was canceled due to rain, so the race was run on Monday. He dropped a couple Dick Trickle jokes. He also went on to say that LA had their own version of NASCAR, and "It's called the high speed police chase…same winner every time though…"

Craig chit chatted with his robot skeleton side kick, Geoff Peterson. We even saw Craig's other sidekick, Secretariat. Secretariat was a horse that did not speak, but still communicated to Craig with yes or no answers.

Craig said that after last Friday's show, he went out for a late night snack. He went to a restaurant in the San Fernando Valley and had a stir fry chicken dish...he thought to himself, "Is this chicken a little under cooked? Naw! No, it's fine! It's a little pink, whatever!" Craig didn't want to go on in detail, but he did mention that all available routes for the food to exit were used. Craig went on to say that he felt like he was in LA too long because in the aftermath, he thought to himself, "Hey, at least I lost some weight!"

Craig read some emails from fans (however, when the show aired, the email bit was cut and pasted at the end of the show).

The first guest was Eric Idle from Monte Python.

Eric was there to plug his new theater show *What About Dick*.

After every interview with his guests, Craig gave the option to the guest whether they wanted an awkward pause, BIG Cash Prize, or to play the mouth organ.

Eric chose to play the mouth organ and he played it so well, that he won the Golden Mouth Organ.

Craig's second guest was actress Sarah Paulson. Sarah was there to promote her new show *Game Changers* on HBO.

When Sarah came out onto the set, she looked emaciated. Hanging from the ceiling were a whole bunch of TVs, so us "show enhancers" could see how the show looked on TV. No joke, but Sarah actually gained 10 pounds on TV!

As Sarah was talking to Craig, she noticed his hands and caressed them because they were smooth. Sarah asked Craig, "Do you cream?"

Craig looked at Sarah and gave her a look before saying, "I just did!"

Sarah mentioned that she was from Tampa, Florida, which led into a conversation about sharks.

Sarah ended the interview with the BIG Cash Prize! $50 in quarters! There were two ways to win, she had to answer a question or guess what was in Craig's box, but Geoff was the only one that knew what was in Craig's box. Sarah opted to guess what was in Craig's box.

Craig said, "Geoff, I'm imagining a box..."

Geoff grinned and giggled.

"Geoff do you feel the box?" asked Craig.

Geoff grinned and giggled.

Sarah guessed that there was a "crow" in Craig's box.

Craig asked Geoff what was in his box.

Geoff said, "We would have accepted 'cream' but 'crow' is the correct answer!"

After the show ended and Sarah left the stage, Craig came over briefly to say "hello" to everyone and thanked us all for coming. Craig then introduced the voice of Geoff Peterson, Josh Thompson. Then Craig left the set and we were escorted out of the studio.

Once we left CBS Studios, Shannon and I hopped back into the rental and decided to go cruising around Hollywood!

We soon found our way onto Sunset Boulevard, where we drove up and down it, taking in the sights. We passed by a couple famous places, such as the Whiskey a Go-Go, the Comedy Store, and the Roxy, just to name a few.

We soon got the munchies, so we stopped off at a small diner…actually it wasn't a small diner, it was a big yellow train car! We had dinner at Carneys, Express Limited. I had a Spicy Polish sausage with a Bud. Shannon had the Orient Express wrap and Bud. We split a small cup of pineapple slaw and sweet potato fries. The meal was good. The atmosphere was also good. The diner was a converted luxury box car. The kitchen was a smaller box car as well.

When we finished wolfing down our food, the food coma kicked in. We waddled back in the rental car and took back off again, down Sunset Boulevard.

We quickly came upon Beverly Hills. Shannon and I had to do the touristy thing and pull off to the side and get our picture taken with the Beverly Hills sign. Naturally there was no place to park, and where there was a spot, there was a "no parking" sign. Well, I had always been an exception to the rules, so I parked the car anyway, and took a snapshot with Shannon's Kodak digital camera, thus making it truly a "Kodak moment."

We coasted on through Beverly Hills and stumbled upon Bel Air!

I made the right hand turn off Sunset into Bel Air. I wanted to try to find the Uncle Phil's house from the Fresh Prince of Bel Air, but it was a little difficult because it was dark out. As we were trying to find the house, I thought to myself, "Maybe the Fresh

Prince moved out? That's ok, because Carlton still definitely lives at home! I wouldn't mind saying "hi" to Carlton."

Did you know that there are a ton of houses in Bel Air!? After about five minutes of looking, Shannon and I got bored, so we turned back around and headed back down Sunset Boulevard.

As we headed back to Hollywood, we saw Rodeo Drive, so we made the right hand turn onto it.

We drove down a couple blocks and saw some rich foo-foo houses. Then we came upon the shopping district. We were quite amazed that the shopping district was so short; it was only a few blocks long. We did drive past the one clothing store that the Mighty Ducks kids got thrown out of in *D2, Mighty Ducks Part2*.

Rodeo Drive ended, so I took a left hand turn. The next road I saw was El Camino Drive! I thought that was an awesome road sign, but unfortunately I did not bring my Milwaukee sawzall.

Shannon and I found our way back to Sunset Boulevard.

On our drive back to the hotel, my mom called me. That day was the NHL trade deadline. Mom informed me that the Sabres actually wheeled and dealed some players! The Sabres ended up trading center Paul Gaustad to Nashville for a 1st round pick. Also, Buffalo traded Marc-Andre Gragnani and Zach Kassian to Vancouver for Cody Hodgson and Alex Sulzer.

I was a little bummed out to hear that Buffalo peddled Gaustad because I had one of the Goose's jerseys. He was good at face-offs, a tough gritty player, and he was American born! Buffalo dumped him partly because his contract was going to be up at the end of the season.

Shannon and I got back to the hotel around 9 or 10pm. We tried our hardest to stay awake to watch the Late Late Show with Craig Ferguson. We made it through about half of the show before we passed out.

As Tuesday morning rolled around, so did the beer, hot sauce, and sauerkraut from the Polish sausage from the night before.

While I was on the can blowing out my O ring, I checked my email on my phone. It turned out that 1iota.com found an extra pair of Craig Ferguson tickets for Shannon and me!

When I finished pooping, I hopped in the shower. After I finished showering, I got dressed, and went down to the lobby. There

I used the hotel's guest computer and printed out our tickets to that afternoon's Craig Ferguson show.

Not long afterwards, we were back *on the road again*, headed towards Hollywood.

Our first destination was to find the Hollywood sign.

Shannon and I were not sure on how to find a good view of the sign, so we drove around Hollywood for a bit.

We drove up and down some windy and narrow streets. Eventually we came upon the entrance to Griffith Observatory.

As we drove up North Vermont Avenue, we approached a tunnel. Right before we entered the tunnel, we took a deep breath; we held our breath for good luck. As we approached the end of the tunnel, I stopped the car a few feet before the opening, and then Shannon hit me because she knew I was messing with her.

We eventually made our way up to the parking lot for the observatory.

From Griffith Observatory, we got a wonderful view of the Hollywood sign and the skyline of downtown LA. We also noted that there were many hiking trails around the park. We took our fair share of pictures before heading out of the park.

Hollywood Boulevard and the Walk of Fame were next on our list.

We parked the rental in a parking garage just off Hollywood Boulevard, and then we began our touristy activities…

We started our Walk of Fame a block away from La Brea Gateway gazebo; but commonly known as "The Four Ladies of Hollywood." There we saw the stars of Elvis and the Beatles. Some of the most notable stars we came across were those of Charles Schulz, Walt Disney, Bob Hope, George Eastman, Victoria's Secret Angels, Jim Henson, Dr. Seuss, Mickey Mouse, and the Rugrats.

There were plenty names that Shannon and I did not recognize. However there were a few names we did recognize and we were dumbfounded that they even had stars; Judge Judy, Nick Cage, Kenny G, the Osmonds, Keanu Reeves, Rush, and Joan Rivers! Don't worry, the horrible list went on, but I just wanted to highlight the turds.

Chuck Norris has a star on the Walk of Fame, but I am not going to say anything bad about that, otherwise he'd kick my ass.

You know, Godzilla even had his own star! You gotta be kidding me! They gave Godzilla a star but God forbid they give Jason Voorhees, Freddy Krueger, or Jaws a star! Thankfully Mike Myers had a star!

During our Walk of Stars, Shannon and I took a tour of Grauman's Chinese Theater.

The tour was interesting. We got to learn about Sid Grauman and the history of the theater. The lobby of the theater looked like your average Chinese food joint with all the red and gold accents everywhere. The lobby also displayed gowns and dresses from famous actresses.

Our tour guide took us down into the ladies restroom. There we were shown the bathrooms where Marilyn Monroe, Audrey Hepburn, Judy Garland, and other Hollywood's famous damsels got prepared before their premiers.

We also got to see a Chinese mannequin that was standing next to a red and gold throne. Apparently, back in the day, Sid purchased both items from China. Supposedly, if you rub the mannequin, it brought good luck...I don't like mannequins, we established that already, so I did not touch the mannequin, let alone look at that creepy ass thing.

The tour guide would have shown us what the theater looked with the lights on, but one guy was watching a movie. We were able to walk around a part of the theater to see its huge ceiling, balcony, and other crap.

Next, the tour went outside, where we looked at a few famous footprints and the stories behind them. We got to see the footprints of Marilyn Monroe, Jane Russell, Judy Garland, Adam Sandler (with his DK sneakers), Shirley Temple, John Wayne, and John Travolta.

The tour concluded by going upstairs and looking at photography of other dignitaries and famous people.

After the tour ended, Shannon and I peed.

After peeing, we walked around the outside of Kodak Theater.

We continued walking down Hollywood Boulevard and looked at the Stars.

I wanted to stop into the Frederick's of Hollywood, but we were running out of time because we needed to get in line to the Craig Ferguson Show!

A short while later, Shannon and I were back at CBS Studios. There was not enough parking in CBS's lot, so I had to park elsewhere. I dropped Shannon off in line and I parked the car a block away at the Original Farmers Market.

I quickly met up with Shannon. We waited in line again, for what felt like forever.

Time had finally passed and the line began to move. We went through the same routine as we did the afternoon before...we showed the security dude our tickets, got wrist bands, went through the metal detector. Dukes went through his routine, we were introduced to Chunky and he went through his routines. After flapping his lips for 10 minutes, Chunky got tired, so we got to go inside the studio. We still had to walk up the same four flights of stairs and wait in line to get into the studio.

That evening's show was a little different than the previous night's show...

As we got our seats, Shannon and I noticed that the stage was set up for a band! Shannon and I were hoping that is was going to be some awesome, cool, kick ass band like the Foo Fighters!

By the time we got seated, Chunky got his breath back. He informed us that we were "show enhancers" and went through the same spiel as he did the night before. Thankfully Chunky kept it to a minimum. He did so because the show needed to record the band.

Hereafter, the PA guy announced to the crowd, "Ladies and gentlemen please welcome the Light Brigade!" The Light Brigade played "Til the Wheels Come Off." The show pre-taped the Light Brigade's song, and it was to air on March 2nd.

Once the band finished their song, the audience cheered. Once the cheering was over and the band was done waving to us, they left the set. Then stage crew came in and I watched the fastest set breakdown in the history of the world!

Chunky came back out and continued to warm us up for Craig.

The moment finally came when the PA guy came on again and said, "Ladies and gentlemen, please welcome Craig Ferguson!"

As Craig walked onto the set, everyone cheered and clapped louder and harder.

Craig came out and whipped candy up into the audience and thanked the crowd. Craig started his monologue with is trademark saying, "It's a great day for America."

Craig went on to make fun of Lady Gaga and stated that she had a role in the new *Men in Black 3* movie as a creepy alien who can only breathe through her tentacles.

Craig went on to make some political jokes about that day's Republican primary race in Michigan. Craig went on to talk about how Mitt Romney had trouble in his home state of Michigan. Craig said that, "Losing your home state would be unthinkable. Could you imaging being rejected from the place you call home? That'd be like Bill Clinton being thrown out of a strip club..." In his best Slick Willy impression, Craig said, "*I didn't even get to fondle the buffet...*"

Then Craig brought up an old story about Mitt Romney...Years ago, to save money on a family vacation, Mitt put the family dog in a crate and tied it to the top of the car and drove for 600 miles! There were people in the audience gasping in disbelief! Craig followed it up with, "That's no way to treat a dog! That's...that's for cats!"

There were a few more jokes made at the former Massachusetts governor and US Presidential Candidate.

Craig ended his monologue with making fun of Angelina Jolie by showing off his leg. He got a little risqué when he lifted his pant leg and we saw some skin and a whole lot of black sock.

Then we went to an imaginary commercial break.

During the imaginary commercial break, Craig saw that a female in the front row was wearing a shirt that read 'Scotland' and had the Scottish flag under the font.

Craig asked the girl to come on stage because he wanted to do a bit with her.

One of the producers asked Craig what the girl's shirt said.

Craig shouted over, "Scotland!"

The producer said, "Well we just need to make sure it wasn't free advertisement for anything."

Craig barked back in his Scottish accent, "What!? Advertisement?! Advertisement for really bad teeth?" The audience lost it and laughed.

Craig went behind his desk and pulled out one of his puppets, a rabbit to be precise.

When we came back from our "commercial break" a rabbit puppet of Craig's was interviewing the girl about her Scotland shirt.

The bit was funny. Rabbit made fun of the girl because she was not from Scotland but New Hampshire...It was one of those things that was funny if you were there...It was on YouTube.com so in your free time, you can look it up and watch it for yourself.

After the interview, Craig went to his desk and read a couple emails. Unfortunately for our viewers at home, that bit was cut out of the telecast because the interviews with Dr. Oz and Carrie Keagan ran a bit long.

Yes, Dr. Oz was Craig's first guest.

At first, I was a little bummed out to hear that Dr. Oz was the first guest. I never watched Dr. Oz's TV show, and if I needed medical advice, I just asked Shannon or my mom.

To my surprise, Dr. Oz was quite entertaining...

Craig hit Dr. Oz up for some doctor advice. Craig told Dr. Oz about the rotten chicken he had the previous Friday, food poisoning.

Craig told Dr. Oz about how he went to his doctors for an annual physical and got a clean bill of health. He also stated that his doctor shoved his finger up his butt for a quick prostate check.

Craig's doctor told him that his prostate was a little enlarged but it was normal for a man his age.

Craig rebutted with, "I don't think it's enlarged. I think it just gets bigger when you put your finger in there."

Dr. Oz and Craig made some more poop and prostate jokes. They were good and funny! Poop is funny.

The two talked some more and then went to a "commercial break." The "commercial break" lasted about 15 seconds. Craig and Dr. Oz continued to talk during the break.

After the break, Dr. Oz and Craig continued to talk about more poop related stuff; colonoscopies.

Somehow it came up and Dr. Oz brought up why testicles were shaped the way they were. Dr. Oz said that one testicle hung lower than the other; otherwise they would bang against each other.

Craig started to make the gesture of the toy monkey clapping the cymbals.

Dr. Oz picked up on it and stated knocking his hands back and forth like a paradigm.

Dr. Oz. said that one testicle is supposed to naturally hang lower than the other. He then informed us that avocado was Aztec for testicle because they are shaped like that.

Craig exclaimed in his Scottish accent, "Avocado!? I love you man! That is fantastic! So when you say 'avocado' you're really saying 'testicle?' Farmers markets just became fun again!"

Craig informed Dr. Oz that they were out of time and that they needed to end with Dr. Oz's option of an awkward pause, mouth organ, or Big Ca$h Prize.

He went for the mouth organ and took it out of its box. As Dr. Oz whipped the germs off the mouth organ on his knee, he asked Craig if the harmonica was clean.

Craig grabbed a bottle of hand sanitizer from his desk and offered it to Dr. Oz.

Dr. Oz said he would try to play *Oh Susanna*.

Dr. Oz put that mouth organ up to his face and played *Oh Susanna* without skipping or missing a beat! He was dead on!

Once he finished his song, angelic music was played over head, and the stage hand came out with the Golden Harmonica on a red silk pillow. Craig grabbed the pillow and presented Dr. Oz his new golden harmonica.

After our "commercial break," Craig came back to introduce Carrie Keagan.

Now I had never heard of Carrie Keagan before, let alone knew what she looked like. But when she walked out on stage, I about creamed myself. She was a tall blond bomb shell, in a low cut, skin tight yellow dress, with long legs and high heels! It was instant bone prone!

The studio had TVs set up in the rafters for people who couldn't see the stage. I'll tell you this, Carrie had a large chest to begin with, but TV added 10 pounds to her boobs…it was a beautiful sight, motor boating worthy!

Carrie was watching Craig's interview with Dr. Oz, so they continued with some "produce" conversation.

In case you were wondering, Carrie was the host of VH-1's morning show. I never knew that VH-1 had a morning show.

Carrie and Craig's conversation was pretty much sexual innuendos.

Carrie touched on how she had not had any dates in a while because of her hectic schedule. She had to be up for work by 4am and she was in bed by 8pm. She touched on how she had "lunch" while the early bird special was going on. She said that she had lunch with old people like Craig.

Craig eventually told Carrie that he was distracted and trying to not look at her breasts! I didn't blame him, I was staring too.

The poop talked continued when Carrie mentioned that her mom went for a colonoscopy too. Her mom was on the can and tried too hard to poop. She passed out, fell off the can, and broke her nose and part of her face!

Craig got on the topic of what Carrie was looking for in a man.

Carrie soon started to hit on Craig's sidekick Geoff Peterson.

She talked some more while Craig, Geoff, and I stared at her boobies.

Eventually Craig asked Carrie if she wanted to do the awkward pause, mouth organ, or Big Ca$h Surprise.

Carrie went for the Big Ca$h Surprise because Dr. Oz did the mouth organ.

Craig stated the rules of the game, "Two ways to win. You can either answer a question or guess what's in my box. Here's how that works. I imagine a box within my head. I don't know what's in it. Only Geoff knows what's in it. You tell me what's in it. If you're right, Geoff tells me 'yes or no.' If you're wrong, something awful will happen."

Carrie asked, "Is your box clean? Has it been…"

Craig inquired, "Do you want to go for the box?"

Carrie replied, "Hmm…it scares me."

Craig responded, "Sometimes exciting things will scare you!"

Carrie reluctantly said "Let's go for the box."

Craig spoke, "Ok, let's go for the box…Geoff…I'm imagining…I'm imagining a box, Geoff…"

In a creepy turned on voice, Geoff answered Craig, *"Okay."*

(The audience giggled)

"Okay," said Craig.

Carrie asked Geoff, "Okay, what's in the box Geoff?"

The audience laughed as Craig interrupted and said, "No! Wait! No. You can't..."

Then Craig and Carrie bickered about the rules and questions to the game.

Carrie finally guessed that there was a hamster in Craig's box.

Craig seemed a little surprised and shocked, "A hamster?!" Craig asked Carrie, "A gay thing?"

Carried said, "That's a gerbil. That's totally different! Not that I would know that..."

Craig followed that up with, "That's just a rumor though...Geoff, what's in the box?!"

Geoff looked at Craig and Carrie and answered, "I'm so gonna spank you...it's a hamster!"

Carrie won the Big Ca$h surprise of $50!!

Sadly, Carrie left the stage after the interview was done.

Craig then met up with Geoff for the closing monologue. After the show ended, Craig came out to thank us all. The producer came up to Craig and told him that the show needed to record another bit for a future show.

It turned out that we got see another act, comedian Geoff Tate. Geoff was pretty funny and clean. Craig was already off the set when Geoff did his routine. Geoff had some good jokes and his bit lasted about five minutes. When Geoff finished, everyone clapped, and gave him a standing O.

Then the show was over and we had to get off CBS property in 30 seconds, otherwise they would have released the hounds!

Once Shannon and I were off CBS property, we headed back towards the Farmers Market.

Shannon and I needed to wander around the Farmers Market because we needed to buy something so we could get our parking pass validated.

Shannon and I both enjoyed the Farmers Market. It reminded me of the Broadway Market back home in Buffalo, only it was outside and people actually went to it at all hours of the day. There were butcher stands, flower stands, candy stores, nick knack shops, and restaurants. Shannon and I were there around 6pm, so there weren't many people and we were able to take it all in.

Shannon and I were a little hungry. We thought about eating at one of the stands at the Farmers Market, but the night before I saw a restaurant on Sunset Boulevard that appealed to both our likings, Pizza and Wine Bar.

We drove around for a little bit and found parking around the corner from Pizza and Wine Bar.

Shannon's big thing she wanted to do on the trip was to have an actual glass of real Californian wine, so we thought we found the place...well we found the place where a glass of wine costs as much as a pizza pie did.

I told Shannon that we could just order a pie and have water. After dinner, we could pick up a bottle of cheap wine from the corner store, and that was what we did.

After dinner and picking up a cheap bottle of Yellow Tail, Shannon and I decided to head back to the hotel.

Shannon and I enjoyed those Hollywood nights, in those Hollywood hills, but we were pretty tired. Upon arriving back to our room, we were both whipped and ready for bed, but it was only 9pm, west coast time. We forced ourselves to put on our swim suits and we hopped in the hot tub.

Once we got all pruned from the hot tube, we knew it was time to head back to the room.

Shannon and I tried to stay up to watch Craig Ferguson, but we both passed out before 10pm.

Wednesday, February 29, 2012...besides that day being Leap Day, it was also game day; Buffalo Sabres @ Anaheim (Mighty) Ducks!

Our game did not start until 7pm, so Shannon and I had a whole day to go spelunking!

Shannon and I took I-5 to I-10, towards Santa Monica. Once in Santa Monica, we headed north bound on the Pacific Coast Highway to Malibu.

Once in Malibu, we filled up the car and drove around for a bit and saw the Pacific Ocean. We were going to stop at a winery and partake in some wine tasting, but the winery was closed from 11am-1pm.

Instead, Shannon and I headed back towards Santa Monica.

After we arrived in Santa Monica, we made a straight shot towards the beach.

We made our way down the beach line and saw Muscle Beach and strolled on the Santa Monica Pier.

The Santa Monica Pier was nice. There were restaurants, shops, and a mini amusement park with a Ferris wheel and roller coaster. We walked down to the end of the pier and saw a few fishermen; one fisherman was cleaning sardines.

It was quite windy and chilly on the pier, so we decided to head back to the mainland.

Shannon needed her ocean fix, so we walked down to the beach. Shannon and I dipped our toes into the freezing, ice cold ocean.

When we finally got feeling back in our toes, we realized that we were hungry. Shannon and I stumbled upon Cha Cha Chicken, which was where we had lunch. Shannon and I weren't used to authentic Caribbean cuisine, so it was quite the flavorful experience.

Shannon and I wanted to have some fun and watch the sun come up Santa Monica Boulevard, but we couldn't. We had more sights to see and a hockey game later that night. After lunch, we drove down to Venice Beach. From there, we drove down Venice Boulevard and picked up I-10, back to I-5.

We sat in traffic on I-5 for about an hour or so. Before our hockey game, we hit up the Disney Discount Store to buy some souvenir crap for the folks back home.

Back at the hotel room, I cracked open a beer, plopped my ass on the can, and did my duty. Soon after, hopped in the shower.

Moments later, Shannon and I were dressed in our Sabres jerseys and we did a couple shots of Jose Cuervo for good luck!

As we pulled up to the Duck Pond, we noticed that every Anaheim Police Officer on the squad was directing traffic. We had the foot patrol, cop cars, cop trucks, and biker cops…it looked like they were ready for a riot.

We paid for parking and found a spot for the car.

Shannon and I were about an hour early for the game, so we grabbed a couple Caguamas and polished off a 6 pack.

Once the beer evaporated, it was time to head into the Duck Pond…I do not like Hondas, so I will not be referring to the Ducks' home arena as the Honda Center, but rather the Duck Pond.

As we approached the Duck Pond, we had to pass through a security check point. After the metal detector wand was waved over us, we were allowed to pass through the turn styles.

My buddy Brian only had one request. He wanted a Mighty Ducks goalie mask; like from the Ducks' original logo. Shannon and I came upon a souvenir stand and they had the mask! I told Shannon that I did not want to jinx our Sabres, so we would buy the mask after the game.

Before taking our seats in section 444, we decided to grab a round of beer-verages. For a round of beer, it cost us almost $25! If it was one thing we learned in California, it costs a lot of denero to get a buzz on. Shannon and I made that one round of beer last the entire game, which was a feat in of itself for us.

The Duck Pond was very nice inside, right down to their coral marble floors and tiled marble walls.

Now, the week before, Shannon and I had to brush up on our hockey a little bit…we watched all three Disney *Mighty Ducks* movies, just so we had all the quotes down right.

When the time it came for the game to start, I was amazed that the Duck Pond was half full. And on top of that, half of the fans were Buffalo fans!

Buffalo started the 1st Period off playing strong. They had a few chances in the early minutes, but Anaheim goaltender Jonas Hiller, or Goldberg as I liked to call him, was playing pretty well.

About 7 minutes into the 1st Period, Buffalo found themselves on the power play, and Derek Roy yelled, "*It's Knuckle Puck Time*" as he beat Goldberg, and score a power play goal to make it a 1-0 Buffalo lead!

A few minutes later, Buffalo was back on the power play. However, Buffalo fumbled with the puck and turned it over at the Anaheim blue line. One of the Anaheim players pounced on the puck, blew by the Buffalo players, and was off to the races. Ryan Getzlaf, the Duck's captain, skated in alone on Buffalo goalie Ryan Miller. Miller came up big and protected the 1-0 lead by making a kick save.

During the opening period, as Buffalo skated with the puck out of their own zone, I yelled, "Flying V Buffalo! Flying V!"

Some kid a few rows away shouted back, "Hey man! You're stealing our thunder!"

At the end of the 1st Period, Buffalo was nursing a 1-0 lead.

Averman: Hum, Batter-batter-batter! Hum, Batter-batter-batter, Hey, Batter-batter-batter. Hey, Batter-batter, batter! Swing, Batter-batter-batter. Hum, Batter-batter-batter!

Coach Bombay: Averman! IT"S HOCKEY! There's no batter! Idiot!

A few minutes into the 2nd Period, Buffalo found themselves on the power play. And yet again, they putzed around with the puck, and turned it over, all while being deep in their own zone. Anaheim had a glorious opportunity to tie the game with a wraparound shot by Corey Perry, but Miller made a kick pad save.

Minutes later, Buffalo was back on another power play! Shannon and I were a little nervous due to Buffalo's last few power play performances and turn overs. Fortunately for us Buffalo fans, the Sabres did not turn the puck over on that power play. The Sabres did one better, they scored! Buffalo's Christian Ehrhoff took a slap shot from the blue line and Buffalo's Brad Boyes, who was parked in front of the net, tipped the puck in past the Ducks' Goldberg. Buffalo now led 2-0.

The Ducks were certainly not out of the game. The Ducks had several scoring opportunities, but Sabre goalie Ryan Miller was on fire!

In the last few minutes of the 2nd Period, Buffalo's Corey Tropp and Anaheim's Matt Beleskey dropped the gloves for a quick and entertaining fight. Right after the puck was dropped at the Buffalo blue line, the two took off their helmets, tossed their sticks aside, and dropped the gloves. Tropp back peddled into his own zone as Beleskey pursued him. The two danced around inside one of Buffalo's face off circles before Tropp reached out and grabbed Beleskey by the jersey. Tropp landed two quick blows to the head! Beleskey came back with a few head shots and an uppercut! The two ended up losing their balance and taking a spill into the boards. The linesmen had then swarmed the two to break up the fight as they still rolled around, giving each other jabs.

Did you really Quack at the Principal?—Gordon Bombay

In the 3rd Period, the Ducks came out strong and gave it everything they had at Buffalo and Miller, including 20 shots on goal!

During the 3rd Period, it was quite apparent that Buffalo was playing to protect their 2-0 lead.

Miller's stellar performance and the Ducks lack of scoring took a toll on the Ducks, and tempers began to fly.

With under a minute to play in the game, Buffalo's Mike Weber and Duck's captain Ryan Getzlaf dropped the gloves to bear hug. A couple fists were thrown, but nothing major landed. The "fight" came to an end when Getzlaf fell to the ice.

After the refs divvied up the penalties, it was time to play the remaining few seconds of the game.

Anaheim had pulled their goalie again, in the hopes to break the shut out. To my happiness, there was another fight! This time Buffalo's Robyn Regehr and Anaheim's Corey Perry took their turn to tango! The sad excuse for a fight happened in front of the Buffalo net, with only a few punches landed by Regehr.

As the horn blew to signify Buffalo's 2-0 shutout victory, more fights broke out!

Buffalo's Pat Kaleta was in the mix of things as he had five Ducks dive bombing at him. Within seconds the sticks came up and players were soon picking dance partners.

At one point, there were four fights going on, and the two refs and two linesmen had no idea which one to break up first.

Buffalo's Tyler Myers was paired up with Anaheim's Sheldon Brookbank. The two of them fought along the boards, with Brookbank landing head shots. Myers was still nursing a broken hang nail, so he didn't really drop any bombs.

Buffalo's Derek Roy and Anaheim's Saku Koivu joined the huge mosh pit in front of the Buffalo bench.

In the meantime, Myers and Brookbank got tired and called it quits. The refs then focused their attention to the huge melee in front of the Buffalo bench.

The fans loved it and we all hooted and hollered.

Eventually the refs had created order and sent players back to their respective benches. Penalties were handed out, but they were just a formality considering that the game was over.

After all was said and done, Shannon and I thought that we finally got our old Ryan Miller back! He was back to playing his game and he was on fire. Not only did he shut out the Ducks, but he blocked 43 shots!

Once the game ended, Shannon got our picture taken with the rink in the background. Then Shannon and I bought the Duck goalie mask for Brian. Shannon wore the Duck mask and posed with it, while wearing her Sabres jersey.

I was a little bummed that I did not see any Ducks fans wearing Averman, Goldberg, Banks, or Conway jerseys!

Though the Duck Pond was only two miles away from our hotel, it took us one hour to drive down Ball Street! There was bumper to bumper traffic down the entire road.

By the time we got back to the hotel room, it was almost 11pm. Shannon and I wanted to walk on over to Downtown Disney and party it up. I really wanted to get shit faced with Mickey, Donald, and Goofy. Unfortunately we turned in for the night because we had to wake up early the next day. Tomorrow morning, Shannon and I were headed up to the Bay Area to meet up with Shannon's cousin Jen and her husband Chad. The four of us were going to the Buffalo Sabres at San Jose Sharks game that night.

While at the Sabres/Ducks game, a fellow Sabre fan who lived in the area told Shannon and me that LA morning rush hour traffic sucked. We were advised to get on the road before 6am to play it safe.

March 2012

Thursday March 1st...it was 5am when the alarm went off. After the second snooze, Shannon and I finally got our dupas up outta bed.

As we got ready, I had the news on. Apparently, the reason why there was a huge traffic jam after the hockey game the night before was because Disneyland had extended hours for Leap Day. Every Leap Day, Disney parks were open for 24 hours! On top of that, Disney had reached maximum capacity, 65,000 people! It was reported that Disneyland and California Adventure had to refuse people at the gates!

Shannon and I were on I-5 by 6am. We only got stuck in LA traffic for about 45 minutes.

The drive on I-5 out of LA was nice and scenic because it was through the mountains.

Once the mountains ended, the terrain was flat and boring. At first, we saw a bunch of oil wells, and then orange groves.

On the drive up I-5 to the Bay Area, I popped in Soundgarden's *Live on I-5* into the CD player…I wanted to be "that guy."

Shannon's cousin Jen was working until 4pm and Chad was working until 2pm. By the time we got to the Bay Area it was noon. Since Shannon and I had some time to kill, we went to the Winchester Mystery House in San Jose.

I first learned of the Winchester Mystery House on the Travel Channel. Every year around Halloween, Travel Channel went across America in search of haunted houses and documented them. One of the houses was Sarah Winchester's mansion.

So here was the quick nutshell story about the Winchester House…Sarah Lockwood married Mr. Winchester, the gun guy. The two of them had a child, who died shortly after birth. A few years later, Mr. Winchester died and Sarah inherited the company and all of Mr. Winchester's fortune. Sarah went crazy and became intrigued with the occult and spirits. Sarah went to a soothsayer. The soothsayer told Sarah that she was haunted by the spirits of the victims of the Winchester rifle. The spirits told Sarah that she needed to find an unfinished house and continuously build onto the house, so she could escape the spirits. Sarah left New England for San Jose, where she bought a farm house. For almost 40 years, there was 24 hour construction, transforming the farm house into a mansion. Construction on the mansion ceased when Sarah died. Supposedly Sarah still hung around and haunted her mansion…Tell you what, I saw more haunts at the Haunted Mansion at Disneyland!

Once our tour was over, we walked around the property and through the well-manicured gardens. After that, we hopped in the rental, towards Jen and Chad's place in Dublin, CA.

We arrived at 3pm. Chad welcomed us in and made margaritas for us. Jen arrived home around 5pm.

I offered Jen and Chad Sabre jerseys to wear to the game. Jen took one, but Chad was hesitant. Chad said, "They're pretty crazy around here when it comes to sports…last year, there was a preseason football game. San Fran was playing in Oakland and a gun fight broke out…" I tried to reassure Chad that hockey was a little different, but I could not persuade Chad to wear a jersey.

The four of us soon piled into Jen's pregnant roller skate (a 2 door Toyota Yaris) and we were off to San Jose for the Sabres game!

I asked Jen, "Do you know the way to San Jose?"

Jen looked back at me through the rear view mirror and simply answered, "No I don't Dionne Warwick, but I do have a GPS on my phone."

We found parking kitty corner to the Shark Tank (aka HP Pavilion) about an hour before the 7:30pm puck drop.

The four of us tail gated inside the roller skate. We cracked open that bottle of Yellow Tail, that Shannon had bought a few days earlier. A few minutes later, we cracked open the other bottle of Californian wine. Once both bottles were dry, we began our march on into the Shark Tank!

The ladies went up to find our seats in Section 224 as Chad and I went to go find some drinks. Chad and I bought some wine for the ladies and beer for us.

Soon it was time for the game to begin!!

A huge shark head was lowered from the rafters. Eventually a voice was heard over the PA, telling the fans to welcome their San Jose Sharks. The team walked out of the locker room, to the bench, and through the mouth of the shark onto the ice.

After the American National anthem, the Sabres and Sharks took their respective spots at center ice for the opening face-off!

Buffalo goaltender Ryan Miller was tested in the early minutes of the opening 1st Period. San Jose was pressing deep in the Buffalo zone, but Miller came up big and stopped a one timer that was shot a few feet away from his net.

Miller came up big for Buffalo all throughout the 1st Period, blocking all 11 shots that came his way.

With just a little over a minute left in the opening period, Buffalo's Tyler Ennis intercepted a Sharks pass at the Buffalo blue line. The play soon turned into a 3-on-2 for Buffalo. Ennis dropped the puck off to teammate Drew Stafford, who took a slap shot, and beat the Sharks net minder Antti Niemi! It was a 1-0 Buffalo lead.

I struck up a conversation with the fella sitting next to me; he too was a Sabres fan. I don't remember the dude's name, but Shannon and Jen thought he looked like Dr. Carlisle Cullen from *Twilight*. So Dr. Cullen was originally from the Southtowns of

Buffalo and played hockey with Buffalo's own Pat Kaleta. For whatever reason, Dr. Cullen left Buffalo for the West Coast.

I asked Dr. Cullen where he lived and he told me, "Tahoe, CA."

My follow up question was, "Are there a lot of people in Tahoe that drive Chevy Tahoes?"

Dr. Cullen laughed and said, "No, not really. A lot of people drive Subarus...but a buddy of mine does have a Tahoe."

In the meantime, Shannon and Jen were just drooling over Dr. Cullen. Jen convinced Chad to take a picture of her, Shannon, myself, and Dr. Cullen.

Later on in the game, I mentioned to Dr. Cullen, "The girls secretly wanted to take your picture because they think you look like Jacob from *Twilight*."

Dr. Cullen shook his head and rolled his eyes while saying, "Come on!" Dr. Cullen's girlfriend/wife asked what was going on. After Dr. Cullen informed her, the girl giggled in agreement.

The Sharks came out strong in the 2nd Period. The Sharks skated hard, made some razzle dazzle plays and shots, but just couldn't get anything past Miller.

In the dying minute and a half in the 2nd Period, Buffalo was on the penalty kill. Miller tried to clear the puck out of the Buffalo zone, but ended up putting the puck right on the stick of a Shark forward. The Sharks' Joe Thornton and referee had thought the Sharks had tied it up 1-1, but upon further review, the goal was not counted. In fact, no goal had been scored, even though the ref had thought one was scored. It turned out that as Thornton crashed the net, the puck bounced off Thornton's hand, and the Buffalo defenseman cleared the puck out of the crease before anything could happen. The ref had thought the puck made it in the net, but he was wrong. The 2nd Period had ended with Buffalo leading 1-0.

For the 3rd Period, San Jose gave it everything they had. They ended up out shooting Buffalo 17-5, but Buffalo's Ryan Miller was playing like a brick house! Even when the Sharks crashed the net with five men, and even with all the Sharks' odd man rushes, and shots through traffic, Miller still denied the Sharks a goal.

The final horn rung out and Miller and the Sabres had shut out the Sharks in the Shark Tank! Miller had managed back to back shutouts! It was a good day to be a Sabres fan on the West Coast!

Once the game ended, Shannon had to pee.

We waited a bit for the mass exodus to die down before we headed out.

By the time we got back to Jen and Chad's, we were all tired so we hit the hay.

Friday March 2nd rolled around. Shannon and I finally awoke from our slumber around 9am. Jen and Chad had a big day planned for us!

About an hour later, the four of us were on the BART (Bay Area Rapid Transit) with downtown San Francisco as our destination!

One of the stops on our train ride was the Coliseum, where the Oakland Raiders and Oakland Athletics played. The Coliseum looked like a huge concrete bowl.

We finally got off the BART at Powell Street. Jen, Chad, Shannon, and I took an escalator up to the city streets. San Fran was alive and buzzing with people, street vendors, and musicians everywhere!

The four of us soon hopped onto a Cable Car and rode around the city!

I had been to San Fran probably about 15 years earlier, but I never got to ride a Cable Car. I thought it was quite interesting how the cars worked. The conductor had a cool job, managing all the levers while trying to avoid dip shit drivers on the road.

Our Cable Car took us through parts of Chinatown. Our final destination was Fisherman's Wharf. We walked around Fisherman's Wharf before stepping it on over to Pier 39.

We stopped off for lunch at Wipeout Bar and Grill. I had the Blackened Mahi Mahi Bowl. I am not a fish kind of guy, but the Mahi Mahi was good. I was not sure what everyone else ate, but we all drank Anchor Steam, the local beer.

The bathrooms at the joint were a little weird. Not only were they done up to look like beach tents, but they were also unisex.

After lunch, we walked around Pier 39. We got to see all the sail boats and yachts in the marina. We took a couple pictures of Alcatraz. And of course, we got to see Pier 39's best guests, the Sea Lions!

As we were leaving Pier 39, I noticed a ship sailing in the San Francisco Bay with 73 seamen on it. They soon rolled off their ship and here's what they had to say, *"We're callin' everyone to ride along to another shore. We can laugh our lives away and be free once more!"* I would have rode with them upon their magic mystery ship, but I told them that we were en route to Lombard Street. I bid them farewell and watched the 73 men sail off into history.

We left Pier 39 in search of Lombard Street; however we became side tracked when we saw Jacks Cannery Bar. They advertised that they had nearly 100 beers on tap, so naturally we were drawn to it.

After having a few rounds at Jacks, we still needed to find Lombard Street. The wonderful GPS took us the wrong way, so I whistled for a cab, and when it came near, the license plate said "Fresh" and it had a dice in the mirror. If I could say anything, this cab was rare, but I thought nah forget it. As we piled into the cab, I yelled, "Yo, home to Lombard Street!"

Jenny asked our driver if he could take us by Lombard Street and then back to the Powell Street BART Station and our cabbie said, "Yup!"

Not only did our cabbie take us to Lombard Street, but he drove us down it too! Our cabbie gave us an interesting history lesson about San Fran as well…the reason why Lombard Street was so windy was because back in the 1800s, horse drawn carriages could not go straight up hills. The roads needed to be windy to make it easier on the horses.

After driving down Lombard Street, our cabbie drove us to the next block down and stopped the car at Filbert Street. He said to us, "Now look up that street, you can tell that it's very steep because they have steps built into the sidewalk!"

Our cabbie told us more historical factoids about his town, but I wasn't really paying attention because I was taking in all the scenery. Also, the cabbie was driving a little bit like a maniac; he had the pedal to the metal as we flew over those hilly SF streets. It was almost like a scene out of *Death Pool* where Dirty Harry was being chased by a remote controlled car that was packed with C4.

As our cabbie approached our train station, I asked him if we were on *Taxi Cab Confessions.*

The cabbie said, "No."

I followed my initial question up with, "Have you ever been on *Taxi Cab Confessions.*"

The cabbie said, "No."

Shannon just rolled her eyes and Jen and Chad laughed (probably at me).

There were still so many other things to see down there in San Fran, but Jen and Chad wanted to take Shannon and me to their favorite German restaurant for dinner that night. I told Shannon that since we didn't get see everything we wanted to in San Fran, that that just meant that we needed to come back!

Later that evening, we had dinner at Speisekammer in Alameda, California.

Speisekammer was a nice German restaurant. I thought that all the employees were going to be in authentic lederhosen, but they weren't. However, the restaurant did have a German feel to it with the big wooden tables and beer steins lining the perimeter of the bar.

For dinner, I had Weiskohlrolade, which was two cabbage rolls stuffed with seasoned ground beef and topped off with onion sauce and mashed potatoes. I quenched my thirst with a Weltonburger Asam Bock; just a half liter…the bock alone was a meal in itself.

After dinner, we went back into the bar because it was Pirate Night with a real pirate band. The pirate band was entertaining. They were all dressed up in pirate garb, right down to their swords. There was even one dude in the band who was rocking out with a recorder. A recorder! I have never heard anyone play a recorder outside of 5th grade music class, but that pirate was doing one hell of a job with it.

The pirates ended their set at 10pm, and that was when we decided to head back to Jen and Chad's place for the night.

The next morning was Saturday March 3rd, the last day of our trip. We were leaving that night from San Francisco. We had a red eye that was departing at 11pm and landing the next morning at JFK at 8am. From JFK, we had a 9:30am flight to Rochester.

Jen had a nice day of wine tasting planned for us.

First we went to Trader Joe's to pick up some supplies: cheese, crackers, and all that other crap that went along with wine tasting. Trader Joe's had buffalo jerky. I never had buffalo jerky before, just venison jerky. So we bought a bag of it, and well, buffalo jerky tasted just like venison jerky.

We did our wine tasting tour in the Livermore Valley Wine Region. Jen said Livermore was better than Napa because we didn't have to pay $25 to do wine tasting.

We started off our tour at Bent Creek Winery. We had a light lunch of cheese and crackers and some wine tasting. I liked the winery because the owner had a couple old Chevy pickup trucks and a 1957 Chevy Bel Air.

Next, we hit up Eckert Estate Winery because their advertisement slogan read, "We dare you to find us!" Jen plugged Eckert Estate into her GPS and we found the winery. It was nice and we sampled some more wine.

The following winery we visited was Garre Vineyard and Winery. We chose Garre because they advertised that they had bocce ball courts!

As we pulled into Garre, we could see their two bocce ball courts. As we walked up to the courts, we could see the one court was occupied by a few children. The other court, however, looked open.

As the four of us walked up to the court, I exclaimed, "I claim the blue balls!"

Shannon rolled her eyes and Jen and Chad giggled.

Chad picked up a green ball. As he threw the ball, he asked, "How do you play this game?"

I picked up another ball and tossed it and said, "You have to get your ball as close as you can to that small white ball…"

Right after I threw my ball, some broad on a picnic table started to yell at us, "Whoa! Whoa! Whoa! We're playing a game here!"

Apparently Chad and I screwed up somebody's bocce game, but if you asked Chad or me, the four people sitting on the picnic table didn't look as if they were playing bocce…you know, considering that they were sitting on a picnic table!

Jen said, "We're sorry. We didn't know that you guys were playing. We could put the balls back…"

"Whoa! Whoa! Whoa!" was all the dumb broad could say to us.

Jen stopped, looked at the broad, and said, "Wait! Nobody 'whoas' at me!"

Before things could escalate, Chad ushered Jen into the wine tasting room; that was right around the corner.

As we were sampling wine, Jen could not get over that bitch broad's attitude about the bocce ball game. She said, "Nobody 'whoas' at me! Let me back out there! I'll kick her (expletive) ass! What a bitch…"

Well needless to say, karma came around and bit that bitch in the ass because she ended up spilling her entire glass of wine all over her shirt. Unfortunately she was wearing a black shirt, so we could not see all the red wine. The four of us just grinned and snickered.

The last winery we went to was Les Chenes Estate Vineyards. We sampled more wine there. That winery had artisan mustards to sample. The wife of the winery made probably 10 different mustards. Shannon and I bought a jar of Tequila Jalapeno Mustard and Syrah and Chocolate Mustard.

Once wine tasting was done, Chad and Jen decided to bring us to one of their other favorite bars, Tap 25 Craft Beer.

At Tap 25, we ordered the sampler paddle, where we got four small glasses of the beers of our choice.

Time flew by, and a little while later, I had finished my fourth paddle of high octane beer; all on an empty stomach.

Jen mentioned to Shannon and me, "Oh, we have to get going soon because you guys need to get ready to go to the airport…"

My response to Jenny was, "The airport? Why the hell do we need to go to the airport?!"

Jen said, "Um…because you guys are going back to New York tonight."

"Doh! Shit!" I blurted out. "I forgot about that…Huh, I don't think I can drive…maybe I need some food in me."

In a blink of my eye, I found myself in line with Jen, Chad, and Shannon at In and Out Burger.

Chad was about to order food. I asked him what was good, and he said, "Everything."

Once Chad ordered, it was time for Shannon and me to order. The cashier asked what we wanted, so in my drunk stupor, I said, "I'll just have whatever Chad ordered."

That was probably the best damn cheeseburger and fries I have ever had!

In the meantime, Jenny was on the phone with American Airlines, trying to see if she could reschedule our flight for the next morning. A few minutes later, American came back and told Jenny that for an extra $800, the flights could be changed to tomorrow. Shannon and I looked at each other and we both shook our heads no.

Jen and Chad were sober enough that they could drive us and the rental car to the San Francisco Airport.

Before we left for the airport, we had to stop back at Jen and Chad's place because Shannon and I still had to pack up our luggage.

Back at their apartment, Chad was able to convince me to finish the last of the Jose Cuervo. I caved into the beer-pressure and polished off the bottle of Jose. Man as soon as that Jose hit my lips, I felt just like Popeye the Sailor Man when he popped open a can of spinach!

Jen and Chad got us safely to the airport and Shannon and I checked in without a problem.

In our drunkenness, Shannon and I somehow managed to find our way to the correct gate.

Shannon and I had about 30 minutes until boarding. In the meantime, I had to pee again. I had broken the seal hours earlier.

When I got done peeing, Shannon asked me, "Did you enjoy yourself in there?"

I slurred, "Yea I guess so, why?"

Shannon said, "Because I could hear you singing the *Ghostbusters* theme song…"

I said, "Yea, when you're peeing, if you wiggle your wiener back and forth, your pee looks like the stream from proton pack!"

Shannon and I made it safely back to Rochester.

April 2012

By the time April rolled around, Buffalo's Playoff hopes were hanging by a thread.

Unfortunately, the Sabres did not make the playoffs. It was probably a good thing because I would have been upset and let down again because they would probably have been bumped out of the first round.

Well, the Sabres had one full season of the Terry Pegula ownership and we did not win the Stanley Cup, or ever make the playoffs. Well, Terry had two more seasons to come through with his promise of bringing a Stanley Cup victory to Buffalo... *Well, maybe next year...*

Offseason 2012

The Sabres had a busy off season.

The Sabres saw the departure of forward Brad Boyes. Apparently there was bad blood between coach Lindy Ruff and Brad Boyes.

Surprisingly, Sabres General Manager Darcy Regier made a big trade. Darcy traded Sabres forward Derek Roy to Dallas Stars in exchange for forward Steve Ott and defenseman Adam Pardy. Hopefully these two guys would pan out, but then again, anything would be better than Roy's lack luster performance for the last two seasons.

The Sabres also acquired forward John Scott. Scott was an unrestricted free agent. Scott was a tall glass of water, 6'8" and weighing in at 270 lbs. He would definitely add some force and fight to the wimpy Sabres.

A blast from the past came knocking at 1 Seymour H. Knox III Plaza that summer as well. That 47 year old Dominik Hasek came crawling back to Buffalo. The Dominator wanted back into the League and he thought that Darcy and Lindy would take him back with open arms. Thankfully Darcy and Lindy told Dom something along the lines of, "Thanks, but no thanks. We already have Miller and Enroth..." See, every now and then Darcy made a good decision.

On top of all this action during the off season, one major black cloud loomed overhead. Would there be a 2012-13 NHL Season!?

NHL owners and the NHL Players Association were bickering about the Collective Bargaining Agreement again. The two sides were arguing about profit shares, again. The last time they pulled this crap was back in 2004 and that resulted in a full season lockout, where there was no NHL hockey! In my opinion, the 2004 Lockout almost killed the League. Hockey was not that big of a sport in America. People cared more about football, baseball, and basketball. And some people even cared more about NASCAR! After the 2004 Lockout, the casual hockey fans were pretty much gave up on the sport.

Regarding the 2012-13 Lockout, both sides, the League and Players Association, needed to get their act together. Neither side could afford another lockout, because it would have pretty much killed what the League had built up from their last lockout.

The looming lockout was just another prime example of how the owners and its players honestly did not really give a hoot about their community or fans. Both sides were money hungry and greedy, but they forgot the sole fact that they were only there because the community supported them.

It was just aggravating that the NHL, as a whole, was giving the middle finger to all its fans. The League probably knew us true fans were diehard fans and we would come crawling back.

As of Monday August 6, 2012, the labor negotiations had not been resolved and that was upsetting. The upcoming schedule was already out and we were already making our possible road trip plans

September 2012

As of September 1, 2012, the NHL Players Association and Gary Bettman still could not agree on terms to a new Collective Bargaining Agreement. The deadline for the CBA was Saturday September 15, 2012. As hockey fans, we would have to wait and see if there would be an upcoming 2012-13 Season.

Now here was what I thought would happen. I thought that there would have been a lockout for a few months, and then both sides would have realized that they were losing out on millions of dollars. Once both sides felt the pain in their pocket books, then a new agreement would have been hammered out. It would play out like what happened last year in the National Basketball League. The NBA had a lockout until December, and then both sides got their act together.

In case there was a season long lockout in the NHL, I did have a backup plan...

I knew that Shannon and I were going to be chomping at the bit for hockey and beer. Thankfully the Sabres minor league affiliate, Rochester Americans of the AHL, would be playing a full season!

Just because the National Hockey League was having a lockout did not mean that the American Hockey League was locked out. As horrible and desperate as it sounded, Shannon and I would travel locally to see the Amerks play.

***

September 15, 2012…Let the lockout begin!

October 2012

It was no surprise that the lockout continued into October. The NHL had canceled the season thus far, but I didn't care. Let the owners and players fight over one of the Seven Deadly Sins, Greed! Both sides obviously didn't care about us fans.

Mid way through October, the owners offered the players a 50/50 split of revenue and tried to salvage the 82 game season, but the Players Union, rejected Gary Bettman and the owners' offer.

Anyway, while the two sides fought over money, Shannon and I continued on with our hockey trips. As I mentioned earlier, while the lockout was in effect, Shannon and I were going to follow the Buffalo Sabres AHL minor league affiliate, the Rochester Americans.

It was 10am on Friday October 19, 2012. I had the 2003 Dodge Caravan all packed up and ready for our trip. Even though my baby had 200,403 miles on her, I was extremely confident that she could get Shannon and me down to Hershey, PA! That's right, Shannon and I were going down to Hershey to see the oldest rivalry in the AHL, Rochester Americans vs. Hershey Bears!

By 10:30am, Shannon and I had left the Greater Rochester Area. We took 390 South to the state line, and that was where we picked up Route 15 (Future I-99 Corridor). The drive down 390 was scenic and colorful; we got to see the changing colors of the leaves; all the greens, reds, oranges, and yellows. Once we hit 15 in Pennsylvania, we drove into some rain clouds up in the mountains, so we couldn't see the fall foliage too well.

It was 1:30pm when we pulled off Route 15 into the parking lot of Clyde Peeling's Reptiland in Allenwood, Pennsylvania. Allenwood was a few miles south of Williamsport, which was Home of Little League Baseball.

Anyway, I was so excited that I was finally going to Reptiland! It had been a dream in the making for the last 28 years of my life!

Let me give you a little background story about Reptiland. Ever since I could remember, my family and I would drive from Buffalo, New York to York, Pennsylvania for the DeRose family reunion. Every time we drove down and back, we **ALWAYS** passed by Reptiland. As a kid, I was a huge fan of turtles and of course the Teenage Mutant Ninja Turtles! For years, I would always ask mom and dad if we could stop. Every year, I got the same response out of my father, the Donald, "No! We can't stop!"

I would inquire, "Well, why can't we stop?"

The Donald would answer, "Because I said so!"

I would say, "That's not a good answer. You yell at me whenever I use that excuse."

The Donald would snap back, "We can't stop because we are racing the clock!"

I had no idea what the Donald was talking about, so I always asked, "What clock are we racing? This isn't NASCAR or rally racing…"

The Donald would shout back, "It cost's money! We can't afford it!"

Normally that would be the part where I would get smacked upside the head because I would say something along the lines of, "Well if you hadn't spent over $1000 on a stupid camera, then you could afford to take the family to Reptiland!"

After I got smacked or had the everlasting shit beat out of me, mom would be pissed off at the Donald for beating the shit out of me and for blowing so much money on himself.

The Donald was pissed off at me then because the 10 year old Adam had narked him out.

Poor me cried the entire three hours to our destination.

In the meantime, my sisters Sarah and Katie sat in silence because they knew if they spoke up or even farted, they were going to get the same punishment from the Donald…*Father of the Year!!*

There are a lot of morals to this story. First, don't tell secrets to a 10 year old. Second, don't hid money from your spouse (you're supposed to be in this together!). But most importantly, **TAKE YOUR KIDS TO REPTILAND!**

So that was the 1990s, but this was 2012, and before the World was supposed to end on December 21, 2012, Adam Donald DeRose was finally going to see and experience Reptiland!

For those of you who did not remember, some soothsayer or gypsy or loony minister or Mayan Indians predicted that the world was going to end on December 21, 2012. Some people bought into it, but most didn't. Only time would tell if the world was going to end…

Upon seeing Reptiland, I quickly pulled into the parking lot. I don't think the van had stopped rolling before I threw her into park.

As Shannon and I approached Reptiland, I ran up real quick and opened the door for her because chivalry was not dead.

After I paid for our tickets, Shannon said, "This better be worth the $14 admission."

I said, "Just stepping foot inside has already been worth it!"

The cash register chick said that there was a 1:30pm live show in one of the adjacent buildings. Shannon and I quickly scurried over to catch the show.

Shannon and I missed the opening minutes of the live show, but we didn't miss a whole lot.

The lady giving the presentation was talking about how birds are actually modern day dinosaurs! I was a little skeptical at first, but she gave us three supporting facts. Our guide mentioned that birds and dinosaurs both had wish bones. Secondly, both had the same type of foot structure, with three toes pointing forward and one pointing back. And thirdly, both animals shared the same walking style, where the legs were underneath the body. Our guide mentioned that some dinosaurs even had feathers. Our guide had a live chicken on stage to demonstrate all the features.

Once the guide put the chicken away, she brought out a live baby alligator. Our guide rattled off some quick fast facts on how gators were related to dinosaurs. She walked around the audience and let people touch the baby alligator. I did not touch the alligator. I am not a germ freak, but I did not want salmonella or e-coli.

After everyone was done petting the baby alligator, our guide put it away.

Lastly, our guide pulled out a Boa Constrictor! I won't lie, I was a little nervous! Then the guide lady put the Boa around her neck and I about pooped myself! The guide said that she was perfectly fine and that she was too big of a meal for the Boa Constrictor, but I didn't believe her. I looked at our guide and then at the Boa Constrictor. That Boa was eyeing up our guide for lunch!

Our guide told us that there were three things that differentiated snakes from lizards. Snakes did not have limbs, eye lids, or ears. Other than that, snakes and lizards were quite similar.

The guide lady talked some more about snakes, but I didn't really pay attention to what she was saying. I was more focused on the Boa constricting around our guide's neck. Plus, the snake was trying to get fresh with the guide because it kept poking its tale into the lady's vajayjay.

At the end of our tour guide's spiel, she asked if there were any questions. I asked her, "Have any of the animals here ever broken out? Like the alligators or the snakes?"

Tour guide lady said, "None of the big animals have ever escaped."

After the Q&A session, the guide let people touch the Boa Constrictor if they wanted to.

Shannon double doggie dared me to touch the Boa. I do have to say that it felt extremely weird to touch a snake other than my one eyed trouser snake.

The Boa Constrictor felt nothing like I've ever touched before. It had a weird texture, but it was not slimy. It was not a leathery feel, and it did not feel like the scales on a fish. It just felt different; I couldn't describe it.

After the show was over, Shannon and I migrated our way to another building, which was home to many wild creatures!

The main building had two species of tortoises and at least five varieties of turtles such as an Alligator Snapping Turtle and a Snake Necked Turtle.

The exhibit had a chameleon that was trying to blend into the green foliage.

Reptiland also had a Beaded Lizard, one of two types of lizard that is poisonous.

And speaking about poisonous, Reptiland had its fair share of snakes! They had a King Cobra, Viper, Copper Heads, and Rattle Snakes, just to name a few!

Reptiland also had frogs. They had Golden Poison Frogs, Blue Poison Dart Frog, and some others. No need to worry, we did not lick any of them.

There was also a mammoth Anaconda! Thankfully it was behind glass, but I don't think I was its type because I did not have buns, hun!

Additionally, there was an alligator exhibit at 2:30pm, so Shannon and I decided to check that out...or maybe it was a crocodile exhibit? I am not sure, so let's go with it being an alligator exhibit.

Shannon and I got to meet the two adult alligators they had, Rocky and Adrian. I learned that alligators could go up to a year without eating. Also, after alligators mated and the babies were born, the mother had to protect her young from their father because the father would eat the babies. I learned more, but I do not want to spoil the entire show for you.

Reptiland also had a dinosaur exhibit which was fun and educational.

There was a Butterfly Conservatory that we toured and I enjoyed it. There were a lot of butterflies and moths. There was a small plaque that listed the differences between butterflies and moths, such as butterflies were active during the day and moths were active during the night. What the plaque failed to mention was that people like butterflies, not moths.

Reptiland was building a special home for Komodo Dragons, but the exhibit was not finished when we were visiting. That just meant that we needed to come back when the exhibit was finished!

For the record—in my book—Reptiland is the Second Happiest Place on Earth, the first place being Disneyland.

It was 3:30pm when Shannon and I left Reptiland.

Shannon and I continued south down 15 through Lewisburg, Sunbury, and Selinsgrove.

After we passed through Selinsgrove, we saw our first Amish people of the trip! They were in their black little horse drawn carriage. I noticed that this was a road frequently traveled by the Amish by the amount of horse shit that was piled up on the shoulder.

The Amish had put Shannon and me in the mood to listen to Weird Al's *Amish Paradise*. Shannon quickly found it on the IPod, so we rocked out to Weird Al for the rest of the trip.

As we drove south down Route 15, Shannon and I began to get hungry. I told Shannon that if she could make it to Harrisburg, then we could get Sonic!

I pulled off at the first sign for Sonic that I saw. Shannon ordered a Coney Dog with tots and a root beer. I ordered the Philly Steak and Cheese sub with tots and a root beer. Shannon devoured the dog in no time. I enjoyed the steak and cheese sub. It was a good Philly, not the best that I've encountered, but damn close to it!

We pulled into Hershey shortly after 5pm. We were staying at Simmons Motel and Suits right on the main drag of Chocolate Avenue. Simmons Motel was a nice little mom & pop's kind of place; I found it on Orbitz.com. The only down side to Simmons Motel was that our room smelled a little like old people, but I quickly fixed that problem. I ripped open the suit case and I found Shannon's hair spray bottle and I hosed down the room.

Now our hockey game wasn't until the following night. In the meantime, Shannon and I were going to go to Hershey Park *In The Dark*! Hershey Park was open on selected weekend nights during the month of October for Halloween. One of those nights happened to be October 19th! That night, the park was open from 5pm-10pm. Shannon and I quickly got out the door and walked the few blocks over to the main gate of Hershey Park.

As a kid, Shannon grew up in the next town over, Middletown. So she and her brother Kyle used to go to Hershey Park a lot as kids. Shannon remembered the park like it was yesterday.

I had been to Hershey Park before a few times. Mom told me the first time I was there that I was four or six years old, but I didn't remember. I think the last time I was in the park was probably close to 20 years ago.

As Shannon and I walked through the main gates of the park, Shannon was having flashbacks to when she was a kid. I, on the other hand, didn't remember a darn thing.

The first ride Shannon wanted to go on was the Comet. Years ago, Shannon's cool cousin Nicole (the same cousin we visited in Philly when we went to the Sabres/Flyers game) convinced the scaredy cat Shannon to ride her first roller coaster, the Comet at Hershey Park!

I liked the Comet because I enjoyed those old wooden roller coasters.

After the Comet, we hopped on the Sky View, which was pretty much a gondola ride around part of the park.

Once we were done with the gondola ride, we tried out the Reese's Xtreme Cup Challenge. The Cup Challenge was a ride where we were in a moving buggy and we had to shoot targets with a laser gun. There were some creepy looking animatronics on that ride, which scared the crap out of me.

Shannon and I were going to do the Monorail around the park, but we did not want to wait forever for it. Instead, we walked around the park a little more until we stumbled upon the Fahrenheit roller coaster. We waited in line for about 20 minutes. Shannon and I were next in line, when the roller coaster was shut down due to the lighting storm that was headed our way. It turned out that all rides were shut down as a precaution.

Shannon and I didn't want to get stuck out in the rain, so we found the Chevrolet Music Box Theater. We decided to watch a show and wait out the storm. That evening's show was Dr. Bunsen and the Burners. Dr. Bunsen and the Burners was a live rock show that was Halloween themed. The group covered such songs as Michael Jackson's *Thriller*, KC and the Sunshine Band's *I'm Your Boogie Man* and Bobby "Boris" Pickett's *Monster Mash*. It was mainly an interactive show for the kids.

By the time Dr. Bunsen's show was over, the rain storm had passed, but the rides were still in lock down.

In a different part of the park, there was another Halloween music show that was about to start. Shannon and I decided to check that show out.

By the time we got to the venue, the rides had started up again. Shannon and I ditched the music show and opted for more rides.

The next ride that we went on was another wooden roller coaster, the Wildcat. The Wildcat was fast and thrilling, but Shannon and I both liked the Comet more.

After the Wildcat, Shannon and I hopped on the Whip. The Whip was pretty cool. We sat inside a buggy and the buggy got dragged around a track. The buggies were connected by springs to a cable. When our buggy went around a corner of the track, it whipped us around. I thought it was interesting and nostalgic that they had pictures of the Whip from circa 1950 in the backdrop to the ride.

As the ride ended and Shannon and I exited the ride, I came to the realization that Sonic's Philly Steak and Cheese sub and amusement park do not go well together. I did not toss my cookies, but I did have a tummy ache.

The Music Express was next in line for us to try. The Music Express was another spiny ride, much like the Flying Bobs. The Music Express had ghoulish, Halloween music playing overhead, like Alvin and the Chipmunk's *Witch Doctor* and Blue Oyster Cult's *Don't Fear the Reaper.*

Once we got off the Music Express, we hopped onto the ride that was directly next in line, Lightning Racer; a dueling wooden roller coaster! By the time Shannon and I boarded Lightning Racer, only one coaster was going. It was after 9pm and at this point of the night all the coasters were being run in the dark, just to give us the extra spook factor! Lightning Racer was pretty quick and wild for being a wooden coaster.

Since it was past 9pm, Shannon and I knew our park time was limited, T minus 1 hour!

We quickly scurried back over to the other side of the park.

We came across another coaster called Side Winder, but it looked just like the Boomerang back home at Darien Lake Amusement Park, so we passed on it.

Instead, we boarded Storm Runner! Storm Runner reminded Shannon of Aerosmith's Rocking Roller Coaster at Disney's Hollywood Studios, in that the coaster shot us 0-60 mph in 4 seconds! Storm Runner was awesome! The ride shot us out so fast that as we flew through a cork screw turn it felt as if we were floating! It was a fun ride.

Shannon and I high tailed it on over to the Kissing Tower. The Kissing Tower was one of the very few things I remembered about Hershey Park from when I was a kid. Kissing Tower was a ride where we hopped into a spinning UFO that went up a 200+ foot tower. Since the UFO twisted up the tower, we got to see a 360 view of Hershey. When we went up it, it was already night time, so we got to see a whole lot of dark!

When the UFO finally landed, we had time for one last ride!

Shannon and I ran onto the Great Bear roller coaster. The Great Bear reminded us of the Mind Eraser back home at Darien Lake, but unlike Mind Eraser, the Great Bear did not throw us around or smash our heads into the restraints.

As we made our way out of the park, I was a little bummed out that I did not get my picture taken with a huge Reese Cup or Hershey Kiss! *Oh well, maybe next year.*

Shannon and I were exhausted, so we decided to walk back to the motel and call it a night because we had a big day ahead of us!

I woke up Saturday morning before the alarm went off. I had the alarm set for 9:30am. The goal was to be out the door by 10am so we could be in Pottsville, PA by 11am for the Yuengling Beer Tour!

Shannon and I stuck to our plan fairly well and we arrived at the Yuengling brewery ahead of schedule, but only by seven minutes!

The Yuengling brewery tour was a lot of fun and quite educational too!

I do not want to spoil the entire tour for you, but I will give you some of the highlights...

First of all, Yuengling is America's oldest brewery. It was founded back in 1829 by a German immigrant named Mr. Yuengling; go figure, another sauerkraut that came to this country to make beer! Mr. Yuengling, or David as some called him, started his brewery in Pottsville, a town in the middle of nowhere.

Our beer tour guide, Elaine, told us that the original brewery was on Center Street. The brewery was only there for a few short years before it burnt down. Mr. Yuengling then moved his brewery up the hill to W. Mahantongo Street and 5th Street. The location of the original brewery was now the site of the current town hall!

Elaine informed us that Mr. Yuengling chose the Mahantongo site because there was easy access to a natural spring. Also, the brewery was built on rocky terrain. That rocky terrain was mined out into caves to store the kegs of beer. The caves stayed at a nice 55^0 Fahrenheit year round. An and optimal temperature for storing beer.

Speaking about kegs, Elaine demonstrated to us on how kegs in the olden days used to be filled. In the basement of the brewery, there were keg filling levers for different sized kegs. A keg was filled with beer through a hole. When the keg was full of beer, a bung was hammered into the hole, hence bunghole....*I AM CORNHOLIO! I need T.P. for me Bunghole!! Are you threatening me?!--Beavis*

Once Elaine was done describing the bunghole process, she took our tour group into the caves!

The caves were really awesome and freaky at the same time. The caves reminded me of a scene from a Rob Zombie horror flick.

Elaine took us to a part of the cave where there was a broken brick wall. She informed us that there were three brick walls in the caves. All three brick walls were built by the US government during Prohibition in an attempt for the brewery to not have access to the beer storing caves, however their efforts were fruitless.

While in the caves, Elaine pointed out that the caves were wet and damp and some spots were leaking water. She informed us it was water from the natural spring that the brewery used to use. Elaine said the brewery used the natural spring up until about 40 years ago. The production grew too big, and the brewery switched over to town/city water.

And speaking of Prohibition, Elaine told us how the brewery survived during that dark period of American History. The Yuengling family had an ice cream factory across the street from the brewery which supplemented the income. Yuengling was in the ice cream business up until the 1980s. Elaine also informed that Yuengling was legally allowed to brew Porter beer during Prohibition. The US government deemed prescriptions of Porter beer to be healthy for pregnant and nursing women because the beer was packed with grains and nutrients!

Anyway, Elaine showed us a couple caldrons where the beer was brewed, and we got to walk around the bottling plant, and she told us how beer was made, and some other stuff too, but I didn't really remember because I wasn't paying attention.

Finally it was time to sample some beer!

Elaine told us that Yuengling only had seven beers on tap for us to try; Lager, Black and Tan, Light Lager, Premium, Lord Chesterfield, Porter, and Light. Elaine mentioned that Yuengling did make two seasonal brews, Bock and Oktoberfest. We were all shit out of luck with those two brews because they were out of them.

First of all, it was not Bock season. Second of all, the brewery was all tapped out of Oktoberfest. It turned out that Oktoberfest had been a huge seller and the brewery ran out of it!

Much to our dismay, we were limited to two samples. Shannon tried Lord Chesterfield and Porter. I sampled the Premium and a regular Yuengling. All four were tasty.

After beer sampling, our tour was over. Shannon and I then hit up the gift shop to buy crap for people.

After we left the brewery, we were both hungry.

On the way into town, we saw an old fashion diner right on the main drag in town. So Shannon and I decided to hit it up for some food.

As I yanked on the dead bolted doors to the Garfield Diner, Shannon said, "Um, Dude, I think the place is out of business..."

I turned around to look at Shannon and noticed a restaurant across the street. We decided to check that place out.

Once we turned the corner to look at the front of the restaurant, we noticed that it was a vacant store front.

We walked down W. Market Street some more. Shannon and I came to the intersection of S. 2nd Street and W. Market Street and noticed an establishment on S. 2nd Street that advertised that they had "Cold Beer and Burgers." Shannon and I figured, why not.

The door was wide open to the joint, so Shannon and I walked in. We quickly realized that it was a beer distributor and that they probably did not serve burgers any more. We didn't ask about the burgers, because we did not want to risk a stomach ache or food poisoning. Instead, I bought a 22 ouncer of Yuengling Premium and a 6 pack of Lord Chesterfield. I was going to pay with plastic, but the clerk informed us that they only accepted cash. I told him that that would not be a problem as I handed him a green back.

Shannon and I moseyed our way back to W. Market Street. We soon saw Roma Pizzeria and Restaurant. Not only were they open, but they had a huge neon Yuengling beer sign in the window.

I ordered two slices of cheese pizza which Shannon ordered a slice of tomato basil and a slice of cheese. The guy working the counter asked us what we wanted to drink. All I saw were pop fountains, so I asked the dude, "Do you have any beer?"

The pizza guy said, "Yea, sure. Bottles or draft?"

I inquired, "What kind of draft do you have?"

He answered, "Well, if you want to, there's a bar upstairs and we can have your slices delivered up to you if you would like."

I said, "That sounds like a wonderful idea!"

Shannon and I walked up a flight of wooden stairs to the second floor. The second floor had more restaurant seating, separate from the bar.

As we bellied up to the bar, I spotted that they had Yuengling Oktoberfest on draft! Naturally Shannon and I had to try it out, mainly because the brewery left some mystery about the beer. And now we were going to finally try it!

Oh it was worth the wait! Shannon and I understood why the brewery ran out of the Oktoberfest; because it was delicious! And you know what else was delicious? The slices of pizza!

After lunch, Shannon and I wandered back to the minivan to head back to Hershey.

Right outside Hershey was Casino Hollywood at Penn National Race Course. I was feeling the gambling itch, so we decided to stop.

Shannon and I hit up the roulette table. The table was a $5 minimum bet, so I threw down a $20 for starters.

I came into the game using my usual roulette strategy. Shannon and I played until the ball landed on 0/00. When it did, Shannon and I cashed in and we walked away up $35!

We walked around some and Shannon played a little video poker, but she did not win.

We tried our luck at the penny slots. There were so many slots that we didn't know where to begin. We finally settled on a couple machines, but before long, the one arm bandit took our dollars.

After that, Shannon and I walked outside to see the race track. That day, there was no racing going on.

Shannon and I decided to quit while we were ahead, so we cashed out, and hit the road again.

Once we got back to the motel, I needed to shower; I had to get the stank smell of stale cigarettes off of me.

Moments later, I was showered and dressed; it was time for some dinner. We agreed upon a nice local greasy spoon, The Hershey Pantry.

Shannon and I bellied up to the counter. Shannon had a chicken salad for dinner, while I opted on the Ultimate Grilled Cheese with a chocolate milk shake. Shannon ended up stealing most of my chocolate shake. I liked the Hershey Pantry. It was a nice little diner. The waitresses were nice too!

Now it was finally time for the main event! Hockey! The Rochester Americans vs. the Hershey Bears at Giant Center!

There were a few Sabres that were allowed to play that season for the Amerks; such as Luke Adam, Marcus Foligno, Mark Mancari, Cody Hodgson, Corey Tropp, Brayden McNabb, T.J. Brennan, and Joe Finley.

We all know by now that the Rochester Americans are the farm team for the Buffalo Sabres. Many of you might have been asking, "Who do the Hershey Bears feed?" Well the Hershey Bears were currently the farm team for the Washington Capitals. Oddly enough, from 1974-1979, the Hershey Bears used to be the farm club for the Buffalo Sabres…that and $1.50 would get you a cup of Tim Hortons coffee!

That night was Hershey's home opener. There was an elaborate pre-game ceremony, where all the coaching staff and players were introduced. The only person I recognized was Hershey's assistant coach, Adam Oates. I remembered Adam Oates from EA Sports NHL '94 for the Sega Genesis because Oates was on the starting line for the Boston Bruins.

After the singing of America's National Anthem, it was time for some American Hockey League action!

Hershey's Jeff Taffe opened the scoring at 7:57 by beating Rochester's goalie Dave Leggio by tucking the puck inside the right post (Leggio was in my 2002 graduating class from St. Joseph's Collegiate Institute).

Our first fight occurred midway through the 1st Period. Rochester's fighter Nick Tarnasky and Hershey's Matt Clackson did the tango and traded a few blows. The fight was good and it brought everyone in the Giant Center to their feet.

Rochester answered Hershey's goal a few minutes later; Rochester's Rick Schofield tied the game at 1-1. It was an ugly goal if I'd ever seen one. Schofield took a shot and the puck was deflected up into the air. No one knew where the puck had gone, including Hershey's goalie Dany Sabourin. The puck flipped over the back of Hershey's goalie and into the net. That goal was just what Rochester needed, some confidence. Up until that point in the game, Rochester had been struggling.

Toward the end of the 1st Period, Hershey's Garrett Mitchell and Tomas Kundratek both scored on Rochester's goalie Leggio. The Hershey Bears took a 3-1 lead into the locker room.

During the 1st Intermission, it was time for some beer. Shannon ordered a Raspberry Shock Top beer and I stuck with my old faithful and trustworthy Labatt Blue Light. I tried a sip of Shannon's Shock Top Raspberry and it tasted disgusting! The head from the Shock Top tasted like the bubbles of a fruity Herbal Essence Shampoo! Shannon was not a fan of her beer, but she felt bad wasting the beer, so she choked it down.

At the start of the 2nd Period, Rochester was on the penalty kill. Matters were made worse when Rochester's TJ Brennan took an Interference penalty. Needless to say, Hershey's Jon DiSalvatore was able to capitalize on the 5-on-3 power play advantage.

A couple minutes later Rochester's Marcus Foligno centered a pass to teammate Evan Rankin, who fired the puck past the Bears' net minder, cutting the Bears' lead in half; 4-2.

Not even four minutes later, Hershey was able to score another power play goal. The Bears' Ryan Stoa took a shot from the point. The puck was defected past the Amerks goalie and Hershey was now up 5-2.

Up until that point in the game, penalties were just killing the Amerks. The Amerks couldn't stay out of the box. They were playing great at even strength, but they just needed the right bounce to go their way. Plus they needed to get on the power play. I told Shannon, "If Rochester was on the power play, or had a two man advantage; we would be up by three goals too…"

At 12:27, Rochester found themselves on the power play due to a delay of game penalty called against Hershey's Jon DiSalvatore.

Rochester converted on the power play. Luke Adam was able to deflect a shot by teammate Marc Mancari to make it a 5-3 Hershey lead.

35 seconds later, Rochester's Marcus Foligno shortened Hershey's lead by 1, Rochester was now trailing 4-5.

With less than 3 minutes left in the 2nd Period, play was down in Rochester's zone. Rochester's Marcus Foligno got the puck and past it through center ice to teammate TJ Brennan. Brennan skated into the Hershey zone and snapped a wrist shot, placing the puck in the top left corner of the net! Rochester had battled back to make it a tied game, 5-5!

In the dying minutes of the 2nd, we had more fights on our hands! Rochester's Joe Finely skated into the Hershey zone and totally leveled a Bear from behind. The ref initially called boarding against Finley, but before the ref could blow the whistle, everyone grabbed a dance partner and started to tango! The Giant Center was on its feet again!

At the end of it all, the Amerks' Joe Finley and Matt MacKenzie and Hershey's Garrett Mitchell and Pat Wellar received 5 minutes for fighting. Mitchell and MacKenzie both got game misconducts.

At the end of the 2nd Period, both teams walked into the locker room with a tied 5-5 game.

Once the puck was dropped for the start of the 3rd Period, Hershey looked hungry. The Bears' Mattias Sjogren scored 1:19 into the period, giving Hershey the lead again.

Half way through the 3rd, Rochester was on the power play again. The Amerks' TJ Brennan was able to capitalize on the power play, tying the game up again, 6-6!

28 seconds later, Rochester's Marcus Foligno scored on the power play with a razzle dazzle, spinning back hander shot to make it a 7-6 Rochester lead!

A minute and a half later, Rochester's Marc Mancari scored another power play goal, bumping the Amerks' lead to 8-6!

With just minutes remaining in the 3rd period, the Bears pulled their goaltender for the extra attacker. The move paid off for Hershey when Ryan Stoa scored to make it an 8-7 Rochester lead.

Hershey could not get the equalizer in the dying minutes of the game, and Rochester skated away with an 8-7 victory!

After the game, Shannon and I were exhausted, so we decided to call it a night.

When we got back to Simmons Motel, we found *Hocus Pocus* on ABC Family. So that was what we fell asleep to.

We were awake by 9am on Sunday. We had a busy day planned for Sunday too!

We started the day off by visiting the Hershey Story, the Museum on Chocolate Avenue. The Hershey Story Museum was exactly what it sounds like, a museum on the history of Mr. Hershey.

Now I won't spoil the entire museum, but Shannon and I learned about how Milton Hershey came to his fortunes in the candy business.

However, I will tell you a couple things that I found extremely interesting. First, Mr. and Mrs. Hershey took a trip over to Europe in 1912. The museum had a copy of Mr. Hershey's canceled check for two tickets on the Titanic. Business matters back home ended the European trip early, so the Hersheys took a different boat back to the States!

Another thing I learned and found interesting was that Harry Burnett Reese used to work for Mr. Hershey. If you didn't know who Mr. Reese was, he was the dude that created the Reese Cup! It turned out that Milton was not upset with Harry, but rather he encouraged his new competitor!

During 1942 through 1947, Hershey stopped production of Hershey Kisses. The reason being was to save metal for the US during its effort in World War II.

And lastly, I learned that Hershey use to make bubble gum, but quickly dropped that line of candy.

Once we were done being educated, Shannon and I drove around the corner to Hershey's Chocolate World. I really wanted to ride the chocolate ride again and get my free piece of candy.

After we rode the chocolate ride and we got our free piece of Hershey's candy, it was time to hit the road.

We departed Hershey a few ticks before noon.

Shannon and I decided to have our breakfast meal at the same Sonic that we stopped at on the way into town.

Shannon ordered a Chicago Dog with sea salt, chili cheese tots, and a chocolate shake. I ordered the #4, the bacon cheeseburger TOASTER sandwich with tots and a root beer. It was wonderful! Being and eating fat never felt so good!

On our way back home, Shannon and I had one last road side attraction to visit. For years, I had seen billboards and TV commercials advertising our next stop. Additionally, Shannon and I had never been to it. We were finally going to visit the Corning Museum of Glass in Corning, New York.

Shannon and I arrived at the museum a little after 3pm, and we made it in time to catch the Hot Glass Show. During the Hot Glass Show, Shannon and I got to see a glass worker take a molten blob and turn it into a glass vase in 20 minutes. The glass worker made it look so easy.

The next live exhibit we watched was a Flame Working Demo. There we watched a different glass artisan make a glass swan out of two glass rods. The artisan heated up two glass rods under a flame, similar to a blow torch. The artisan talked to the audience and described to us what he was doing with the glass and how he was going to form the swan sculpture. It only took the glass maker about 20 minutes to create the beautiful glass swan piece.

The last and final live exhibit we saw was an Optical Fiber Demo. The Optical Fiber Demo was surprisingly fun and interesting.

Then the museum closed. Shannon and I wanted to go back and visit the Corning Museum of Glass again.

November 2012

'Twas November and the NHL lockout still continued.

As of November 2nd, the League had canceled the Winter Classic between Toronto Maple Leafs at Detroit Red Wings. The game was to be played at University of Michigan's football field.

Now it was that kind of stuff that was upsetting about the lockout. Of all 30 NHL cities, each and every community was losing out on revenue. The bars and restaurants and hotels and local tourism were losing out because of the money hungry players and owners. I strongly felt that every city should have teamed up and had a class action lawsuit against the owners and players for lost income. I felt that the cities should sue and show the owners and players that they were not going to put up with their crap. But it was not a perfect world, so there would never be a class action law suit.

Anyway, if there was a NHL season, that November Shannon and I would have traveled to Phoenix, Arizona to catch the Sabres play the Coyotes. But since there was no season, that did not happen.

I was looking forward to seeing Phoenix and I wanted to see the Coyotes play in Glendale before they moved. To date, the NHL owned the Phoenix Coyotes. The NHL and Coyotes were trying to find an owner who would keep them in town, but there were rumors that the team could possibly move to Quebec City in a few seasons.

In the meantime, Shannon and I were still following the Rochester Americans.

For the month of November, we followed the Amerks up north of the border, to the home town of Buffalo Sabre great Dave Andreychuk. That's right, we were headed to Hamilton, Ontario.

The Hamilton Bulldogs were playing host to the Rochester Americans!

But before I start on about the game, we had a couple extra-curricular activities to do beforehand. The main activity we had planned was tour the Labatt Blue Brewery in London, Ontario!

Shannon and I left the Greater Rochester Area at 8:30am on Saturday November 3, 2012. MapQuest told us that it would take 4 hours and change to make it from our house to the London.

Shannon and I left early so we would have enough buffer time for the US/Canada border.

When we got up to customs, the customs officer asked us where we were going.

I stated, "Hamilton for a hockey game."

The customs officer asked, "Who's playing?"

I informed him, "The Rochester Americans are playing against the Hamilton Bulldogs."

The customs officer said, "AHL."

I said, "Yea, we need to get our hockey fix somehow. I'm not a fan of what's going on with the NHL right now…"

The customs officer said, "Yea, I know. Tell me about it. They obviously don't care about the fans…I heard both sides are secretly meeting again and the NHL offered the players 50/50 on everything. Hopefully the players take it; otherwise we'll know who the real enemy is…"

I said, "If the players and owner want to screw us, we should screw them and each city should sue for lost revenue…"

After the quick chat with the customs officer, Shannon and I were back *on the road again.*

We arrived in London, Ontario ahead of schedule. We arrived at the brewery at 12:30 pm for our 2pm tour.

I was hungry and so was Shannon. Since we were in Canada, I needed my poutine fix!

We came across this place called Hey Daze on Richmond Street, a few blocks away from the Labatt Brewery.

Hey Daze had 13 different kinds of poutine from Pizza Poutine to Thanksgiving Poutine to Chili Poutine to Bacon Poutine!

There were so many choices that I did not know which one to order!

Shannon settled on Classic Poutine and I tried the Chili Poutine.

The Chili Poutine was good, but Shannon and I both preferred the Classic Poutine.

Before we knew it, it was almost 2 o'clock; time for our beer tour.

We arrived at the brewery at 1:45pm, 15 minutes ahead of schedule, just like the brewery had asked us to.

Our scheduled 2pm brewery tour did not start until closer to 2:30pm. Apparently we had to wait from some stragglers.

Before we could start the tour, all purses, cell phones, cameras, and jewelry needed to be locked up. Labatt did not want jewelry falling into the beer vats nor did they want people taking pictures of their "Top Secret" beer equipment...

Now when Shannon and I toured the Sam Adams, Budweiser, and Yuengling Breweries, and all three of them encouraged us to take pictures. Also, they didn't care if people were wearing jewelry or had purses or cell phones.

It was not like Labatt had any secret brewing process that they were trying to keep hidden. They told us the same thing the last three breweries told us; beer is made from hops, barley, yeast, and water (except Bud used rice as well).

The Labatt brewery looked like any other brewery we had been to.

Shannon and I agreed that the one thing we did not like about the beer tour was our tour guide. I don't remember her name, but she seemed like a Dumb Dora.

Our tour guide, Dumb Dora, talked about herself for most of the tour. I felt dumber for having listened to her; it was like listening to Billy Madison talk about his favorite book, *The Puppy Who Lost His Way*.

Dumb Dora did not mention that Canada had prohibition in the early 1900s. I had to look that information up myself on

Wikipedia. Parliament left prohibition decisions up to the provinces. Different provinces enacted prohibition during different years. In 1901, Prince Edward Island was the first province to make prohibition a law. In 1916, Alberta and Ontario followed suit. In 1919, Quebec voted in favor of prohibition, but it was quickly repealed...I don't blame them.

Dumb Dora did teach us a few facts about John Labatt and his brewery.

John Labatt was an Irish immigrant and had 14 children after immigrating to London...quite a busy man.

We learned that the brewery was still on its original 1847 Location.

Dumb Dora mentioned to us that the brewery was haunted! However Dumb Dora sucked at telling ghost stories, so the stories sucked too, much like most of the tour...I felt as if the Labatt tour would have been a hell of a lot better if we had a better tour guide.

Dumb Dora's ghost stories went like this, "Um yea, this place is haunted! Is it okay if I tell any ghost stories? No one is going to get scared or frightened?"

Now Shannon and I were thinking, "Lady, everyone here is on a beer tour and of legal age to drink beer. We're pretty sure we can handle one of your dumb ghost stories!"

Anyway, back to Dumb Dora's ghost stories. "Um yea, a lot of people think this place is haunted! People have seen things, doors slam shut, it's dark and creepy here in the buildings, and there're climate changes from really warm to really cold!"

Shannon tugged on my arm and said, "Maybe there's climate changes in the buildings because she told us that one beer kettle is at 90°C and in the adjacent room, they have frost brewed beer at 2°C! What a *pucking* whack job!"

Back to the rest of Dumb Dora's ghost stories... "And at night, the security guards go on rounds in pairs because they get creeped out and scared. This one security guard, he was doing rounds on the overnight, and he saw a black shadow and got so scared that he ran away and never came back to work! Yea, a lot of people here see dark shadows like apparitions. The one apparition is wearing overalls. Another security guard, who I know, saw a ghost. He was doing his rounds one night and he was walking down the hallway. And he like turned the corner and at the end of the hall, he saw a huge dark black shadow! My friend didn't know what to do and he was scared. As the shadow ran towards him, my friend was frozen still! The dark shadow ran right through my friend and he got chicken skin! Every time I see my friend now, I ask him if he's seen any ghosts! In fact, um, I saw him yesterday and I asked him again, and he told me he hasn't seen anything…"

I looked at Shannon and said, "You have got to be kidding me!? Those were the worst ghost stories! I have a ghost story for you. Last week I was dropping a duce on the can. When I finished pooping, I got up to look at my handy work. To my surprise, there was no turd in the bowl! I like to call it the 'ghost poop.'"

It was finally time to taste some beer!

We sampled five beers at the Labatt brewery. Out of those five samples, only one was a Labatt beer! I was so upset that there was only one Labatt product for us to sample. During the entire tour, Dumb Dora told us about many different brews that Labatt made, from Labatt Ice to Labatt Crystal to Labatt Lime. I was not expecting to sample Bud, Bud Light, Labatt Blue, Stella Artois (pronounced AR-**twat**), and Alexander Keith's. Shannon and I didn't need to travel up north to taste the same shitty Bud and Bud Light that we had back in the States. However, Shannon was excited to sample Alexander Keith's. Keith's is one of Shannon's favorite brews.

Speaking about Alexander Keith, our tour guide did give us some fun facts about Mr. Alexander himself.

Alexander the Great was a born in Scotland, but immigrated to Halifax, Nova Scotia back in 1817. Besides opening a brewery in Halifax, he was also their mayor for three consecutive terms.

After we finished sampling beer, we got Labatt brewery t shirts.

The tour ended with us seeing two retired Labatt delivery trucks. We got to see a 1919 beer delivery truck and a 1947 Streamliner.

Dumb Dora did tell us an interesting factoid about a Labatt Brewery policy and John Labatt, son of brewery founder John Labatt.

For a period of time, it was customary and company policy for the Labatt delivery trucks to help stranded motorists.

John Labatt's kid, John, was kidnapped back in 1934. The kidnappers requested money for John's return. Word leaked out to the media and there was a mass public frenzy. The kidnappers got scared and put John into their car and drove John to Toronto. The kidnappers then hailed a cab and sent John to the rendezvous spot at the Royal York in London, Ontario. John had been kidnapped for three days and was almost unrecognizable. Needless to say the kidnappers were caught.

Once we were done with the beer tour, Shannon and I ventured down the street to the Labatt Beer Store.

Shannon and I were quite unimpressed with the Labatt Beer Store. It was a Beer Store without variety! All they sold was Labatt Blue, Blue Light, Bud, and Bud Light. We could have picked up a couple single tall boys of Keith's or Blue or Bud or Busch. I felt gypped. I felt like Ralphy from *A Christmas Story* when he found out his Little Orphan Annie Decoder was just a cheap gimmick for Ovaltine. Dumb Dora had built up the Labatt product and we got to sample one Labatt beverage. Dumb Dora built up the Labatt Beer Store and there was nothing special.

Shannon and I ended up walking out of the beer store with two tall boys of Labatt Extra Dry and a can of Busch Ice. I had not sampled either on the beer tour and my curiosity was getting the best of me.

Once we loaded back into the van, we were bound for Hamilton! For hockey!

Well, actually, we headed towards the hotel first, then food, and then hockey!

Shannon and I checked into the Staybridge Suites at 5:30pm.

Once we were in our room, I popped open the can of Busch Ice.

Now I was a fan of Ice beers because it got me a buzz quicker. My four year old black lab Teppo Numminen liked Ice beer too! We both enjoyed Labatt Ice ('Batt Ice), Genny Ice, and Molson Ice. The Busch Ice tasted like any other quasi cold canned beer.

It was almost time for game time, but Shannon and I still had to eat before the game.

En route to Copps Coliseum was an A&W.

The last time I was at an A&W was probably back in 2003 in Syracuse, NY…Grandpa Ziggy, my buddy Mike, and I were on our way up to the 1000 Islands to go fishing. We stopped off in Syracuse to visit my sister Sarah. Sarah wanted to take us to Panera Bread; or as I called it, Pantera Bread. Mike and I didn't want to eat that healthy organic crap, so we defected and walked across the parking lot to A&W.

Anyway, enough with reminiscing; Shannon ordered a Mama burger with onion rings and a root beer.

I ordered a Mama Burger with Freedom Fries (I refuse to call them French Fries) and a root beer.

The food sucked. I remember A&W tasting a lot better back in Syracuse. Maybe the first time I had it I was naïve or maybe I wasn't drunk enough to enjoy it the second time around. Whatever the case may be, I did not enjoy my sophomore experience at A&W....Shannon did not enjoy her de-virgin-izing A&W experience either.

Shannon and I bushwhacked it through two parking lots before we reached our destination, Copps Coliseum (The last time I was at Copps Coliseum was back in September of 2005 to see Pearl Jam).

Once we walked through the turn styles, Shannon and I found the beer guy. We ordered up two tall Molsons and then looked for our seats.

At the time when I bought the tickets, I didn't really pay any attention to where we were sitting. But apparently $17 bought us seats in Section 105, 3 rows up from the ice! Our seats were right on the blue line of the goaltender!

Once we were nestled in our seats, we had a visitor. It turned out that Shannon's friend and high school classmate Laura was sitting just 5 rows behind us. Laura was there with one of her friends. We talked until it was time for the singing of both national anthems.

That evening's game was being televised nationally on TSN in Canada. Hopefully Team USA (Rochester) wasn't going to let Team Canada (Hamilton) beat them…

This was the second game of a Home and Home Series, with Rochester winning the night before at home 3-2.

The Hamilton Bulldogs were the minor league affiliate of the Montreal Canadiens.

The only exciting thing that happened during the 1st Period were the fights. Early in the 1st, the Amerks' Nick Tarnasky and the Bulldogs' Zach Stortini teed off on each other. This was a good old fashioned hockey fight with punches being thrown left and right. The fight ended when Tarnasky lost his footing and his legs gave out, spilling down to the ice.

Towards the end of the 1st, Rochester's Brayden McNabb and Hamilton's Darrel Boyce decided to drop the gloves by center ice. The two of them skated around a bit, but no one could get free to drop any major blows. By the time McNabb and Boyce got free from each other, the officials had skated in to break up the fight.

The 1st Period ended with a score of 0-0. Rochester's own, goalie Connor Knapp, blocked all 15 shots he faced. That night was Knapp's first professional AHL start.

Rochester opened the scoring in the 2nd Period with pair of goals by Brian Flynn.

By the end of the 2nd Period, Amerks goalie Knapp had blocked all 8 shots that he faced. Rochester took a 2-0 lead into the locker room, thanks to Brian Flynn.

During the 2nd Intermission, Shannon and I restocked on our Molsons.

As the 3rd Period started, I leaned over to Shannon and said, "The next goal is going to win the game. If Rochester scores, it will be too big of a deficit for Hamilton to come back from. If Hamilton scores, they will probably get the momentum to carry on and win the game…"

Rochester looked tired during the beginning of the 3rd Period, but Hamilton looked hungry for a goal.

Half way through the 3rd Period, Hamilton got on the board with a goal by Blake Geoffrion.

Though Rochester had a 2-1 lead, the tides were soon changing…

Hamilton's goal lit a fire under their butt. Less than 3 minutes later. Hamilton's Brendan Gallagher tied the game at 2-2.

A couple minutes later, the Bulldogs' Mike Blunden had scored to give Hamilton its first lead of the night.

With 5 minutes left in the 3rd, Hamilton's Geoffrion scored again to expand Hamilton's lead to 4-2.

Rochester answered quickly with a goal by Nick Tarnasky.

Rochester gave a good effort in the dying minutes of the 3rd, but Hamilton's goaltender Robert Mayer proved to be too much.

Rochester had lost 4-3 to Hamilton.

After the game, Shannon and I were exhausted. We talked to Laura and her friend for a few minutes. Then we parted ways and Shannon and I went back to the hotel.

Back at the hotel, Shannon made some popcorn and I fell asleep watching CBC.

That night was day light savings, so we gained an extra hour of sleep, and did I ever need it: I slept in until 10am. Shannon was cheery eyed and bushy tailed by 7am. She ran off to the gym and worked out. There was a pool, but she did not go in. She finished a book and started another.

It was close to check out time when I was ready to greet the world!

Before Shannon and I went up to Hamilton, I told my world traveler, Grandpa Ziggy, where we were going. Grandpa informed me that Hamilton had a huge Polish population. With that in mind, I had looked up some Polish eateries. I came across a restaurant called Taste of Poland. Sunday morning's adventure was to find Taste of Poland.

I had printed out MapQuest directions. The restaurant was only a few miles away from the hotel.

Once we found the restaurant, we noticed it was closed. I parked the van to check out the hours. It was just our luck; Taste of Poland was closed on Sundays.

The next item of business on our addenda was to find Dundurn Castle. I knew Dundurn Castle was on York Boulevard because I saw it on the map. However, the map did not tell me that York Boulevard was a one way street. I was on Bay Street, wanting to turn left, but I couldn't because of the one way. I looked at Shannon and asked her, "Do you want to waste time trying to find this castle or do you want to go wine tasting at Niagara On The Lake?"

Shannon lit up at the idea of wine tasting!

My next challenge was to try to find our way to the QEW.

There were no signs for the QEW or the 403. Instead, I followed Bay Street all the way to Bayfront Park. We drove past the entrance for the HMCS Haida, a WWII destroyer.

Shannon and I soon found ourselves on Burlington Street. We got the scenic tour of Hamilton's steel mills. The road reminded me of Route 5 in Lackawanna, NY, where all the Bethlehem Steel factories stood.

Burlington Street finally dumped us onto the QEW.

Within a half hours' time, Shannon and I were cruising down the main drag in Niagara On The Lake. We took the road through town, past all the quaint little shops, past the golf course, and parked the van at a scenic overlook of Toronto. The scenic overlook was where the Niagara River dumped into Lake Ontario.

I am not one for shopping, so I asked Shannon, "So do you want to go to any of these shops or do you just want to go drink some wine?"

Shannon responded, "Well I know you don't like shopping, so let's go to a couple wineries." And that was what we did.

The first winery we stopped at was Peller Estates. We both got a flight of samples. I had a red wine, which I did not care too much for. The bar maid asked me, "How did you like it, sir?"

I did not want to sound mean so I answered honestly, "Well, it's not for me. I'm more of a beer guy!"

The bar maid laughed and got us our second round. I tried an Ice-wine and I enjoyed it.

I don't remember what our bar maid's name was, but let us call her Brandy. Brandy asked me how the Ice-wine was.

I enjoyed it, so I answered her honestly again, "Oh it's good! It tastes just like Kool Aid, but not that bad Kool Aid at the religious cult meetings…"

Brandy laughed as Shannon gasped, "Oh God! I can't take you anywhere!"

I ended my flight of wine with a Sparkling Rose. I told Shannon, "Hey this tastes a little bit like mom's Thanksgiving Brunch! All it needs is a little orange juice and BAM! We got mimosas!"

Shannon just shook her head and rolled her eyes in disbelief.

Since we did some wine tasting at Peller's, they gave us a discount on wine. Shannon ended up walking out of there with a bottle of 2011 Riesling.

On our way to the next winery, we drove past Wayside Chapel. It was an extremely tiny little chapel on Niagara Parkway, though it was not the world's smallest chapel. I parked the car so we could take a closer look at it. As a kid, I remembered driving past it, so I figured that I would show Shannon. As we approached the chapel, there was an engaged couple with their photographer. We didn't want to intrude, so we congratulated them and continued on our merry way.

Our next stop was Reif Estate Winery. Shannon and I sampled some more wine there. Like I said earlier, I am a beer guy, not a wino. I couldn't tell you what we had, but I know Shannon enjoyed herself, and that was all that mattered.

The final winery stop was to the Ice House Winery. Shannon sampled by herself at that winery because I had to drive...I did steal a sip of her Ice Wine and her Ice Wine Slushy. I recommend the Ice Wine Slushy because it was a slushy for grown-ups!

Our last stop in Canada was to Duty Free. Shannon and I needed to stock up on some more Molson Brador because our rations had dried up eons ago!

After we breezed through customs, Shannon and I were off to Cheektowaga, NY to visit Grandpa Ziggy.

Before we got to Grandpa's, Shannon and I had to pick up pizza from Divas Pizzeria. In my opinion, Divas was the best pizza joint in town. There were a couple close seconds, but I always ordered from Divas. And I ordered my pie a certain kind of way too. My Uncle Michael turned me on to ordering my Divas Pizza like this: cheese and pepperoni, extra sauce, well done. Oh my God, the pizza was just magnificent! In my family, it's a delicacy!

Grandpa Ziggy was so excited that Shannon and I had showed up with Divas Pizza.

My 87 year old Grandpa Ziggy retired from drinking beer years ago, but every now and then, a nice cold Molson Brador brought him out of retirement.

Shannon, Grandpa, and I drank some Bradors, ate some Divas Pizza, and watched our Buffalo Bills lose to the Houston Texans, 21-9.

After the game, Grandpa loaded us up with some goodies.

Before Shannon and I made the trek from Buffalo to Rochester, we had a couple more stops to make.

I stopped at the local grocery store and bought a couple bouquets of flowers.

Next, Shannon and I stopped at the cemetery on Pine Ridge Road and visited Nana. It was coming up on the 3rd anniversary of her death. I got Nana red carnations. Nana's sister, Aunt Jane was buried a few plots down. I got Aunt Jane red carnations as well so they wouldn't fight.

Shannon and I stopped off to visit Nana and Aunt Jane's parents and other sister and gave them flowers too.

Then it was time to leave Buffalo and head back to Rochester.

December 2012

Surprise! The lockout continued into December!

During the first part of December, the Owners and Players decided to meet again to try to work out a deal.

Six owners met with 18 players to discuss each side's needs and desires. Talks seemed to go well considering the fact that they met for a couple days.

By the end of the week, the players had a new proposal and gave it to the owners. The owners reviewed the proposal and rejected it.

The lockout continued...

***

According to the Mayan Calendar, the World was going to end on Friday December 21, 2012. Thankfully enough for us, Shannon and I were able to fit one more hockey road trip into the mix before the World ended!

Shannon and I were making our way up north of the border again; this time, to the beautiful and lovely city of Toronto. I liked Toronto; it was a nice suburb of Buffalo. Beside the Sabres losing to the Leafs the last time we were in town, I never had a bad experience in Toronto.

Shannon, Teppo puppy, and I piled back in the Dodge Caravan; now with 204,000 miles. We left Rochester around 10:30am.

Before we headed up to Toronto, I had to run a couple errands.

First, the three of us stopped off at Grandpa Ziggy's in Cheekta-vegas (Cheektowaga). I had some scrap metal for him.

Also, I needed to pick up a mattress and an old desk from Grandpa's basement. Grandpa knew that we were going to Toronto and that we were pressed for time. We talked briefly before Shannon, Teppo, and I loaded back up in the van. I told Grandpa that I would see him tomorrow at mom's house for the Buffalo Bills game.

Our next stop was to my mom's house in South Central Grand Island.

My mom was having a Christmas party with about 10 girlfriends.

Mr. Teppo made his triumphal entrance into the party and all the ladies just loved him. Mr. Teppo was going to spend the night at my mom's house.

Shannon and I unloaded all the stuff from the van into the garage. Once the van was cleared out, it was time to go into the house to say hi to everyone. Some of mom's friend whipped out their cell phones to take pictures and such. They asked Shannon and me what we were up to. I informed then that since there was the NHL lockout, we decided to follow the Rochester Americans and that night, Rochester was traveling up to Toronto to play the Toronto Marlies. Also, I told them that we were going to try to make it to Casa Loma either that day or Sunday; since the last time we were in Toronto, we missed out on it. All the ladies loved my plan and said that Casa Loma should be beautifully decorated for Christmas.

Mom asked us if we were hungry and I told her we weren't. She asked us if we wanted any food or soup for the road. I reassured mom that we weren't hungry and that soup in the car was probably a bad idea. I told mom that there was still some more stuff that Shannon and I needed to bring into the garage. Shannon looked at me all puzzled because we had already brought everything into the garage. Shannon didn't say anything, but she followed my lead into the garage.

Before Shannon could close the garage door, I already had opened the door to the garage fridge and grabbed two Molson Canadian Lights. I gave one to Shannon and said, "It was estrogen over load in there and I needed something to take the edge off. I'm not used to that much estrogen…"

Shannon replied, "Me neither, which is odd since I shared a dorm room suit with three other females…"

Shannon and I quickly pounded our beers and said good bye to Teppo, mom, and the guests.

Shannon and I were back in the van by 2pm. We had one last quick pit stop to make. We stopped at a gas station because we needed some fuel and booze. As I pumped the gas, Shannon ran in to stock up on rations.

Shannon got herself some high octane girly, 8% alcohol, fruity drinks. Shannon got me a couple Molson and Labatt Ices. She knew I liked my ice beer, but wasn't sure which brand I liked...I liked them all.

Then it was time to invade Canada!

As Boomer from *Canadian Bacon* said, "To the Capital! Toronto!"

We took the Queenston-Lewiston Bridge to Canada. It was smooth sailing and there wasn't much of a wait.

As we approached the customs officer, Shannon gave me our enhanced licenses.

The customs officer wanted to know our citizenships, so I told him "US."

The customs officer wanted to know what we doing so I told him, "We are going to Toronto for the Rochester Amerks/Toronto Marlies game."

The customs officer asked me if I knew what my license plate number was he couldn't read it as we approached his booth. I knew he was full of shit for two reasons. The first reason why I knew he was full of shit was because I idled up to the customs officer's shack. The second reason why I knew he was full of shit was because as I approached the guard shack, there were several cameras taking pictures of us, the car, and license plates. I never knew what my license plate number was so I told him, "I don't know my license plate number."

The customs officer then walked to the rear of my 2003 Dodge Caravan to read the rear license plate. He noted that there were no seats in back, so he inquired what I did for a living, "What do you do for work? Are you a delivery person or a mover?"

Before I got to the border, I figured that question was going to come up, due to the lack of seats in the back of the van. So I was honest with the guy. I said, "No. I work for a research and development company. The reason I have the back seats out is because I stopped off at my Grandpa Ziggy's house in Cheektowaga to pick up a twin mattress and desk that I dropped off at my mom's in Grand Island."

The customs officer looked at Shannon and me as he handed our IDs back and said, "Have a good time in Canada."

Shannon and I made good time on the QEW because there wasn't much traffic.

Once we hit Toronto, we took the Lake Shore Boulevard exit. I knew that Ricoh Coliseum was somewhere off of Lake Shore Boulevard by Ontario Place, though I wasn't sure how far away Ricoh Coliseum was from our hotel. I booked our hotel, Westin Harbour Castle, through Orbitz. Westin was off of Lake Shore Boulevard, but I wasn't sure how far away it was. It turned out that they were two miles and change apart. It seemed to be too long to huff it out to the game…

It took some time to find the hotel because there was construction on Queens Quay.

As we searched for Westin Harbour Castle, I was looking for a hotel that looked like a castle, kind of like Excalibur in Las Vegas. I had never been to the Harbour Castle before, so I just figured that the hotel looked like a castle.

With her quick eyes, Shannon snared the Westin and directed me off Lake Shore Blvd to the Westin.

The Westin Harbour Castle looked nothing like a castle. It looked like your average sky scraper in your average downtown.

I pulled into the hotel, hoping there was parking. I was quickly greeted by valet. They told me that valet parking was $30 a night or I could drive down a few blocks and pay $20 a night. Normally I tried to be frugal and wise with my dollars, but I decided to pay the extra $10 to leave the van there. I felt that it was worth the $10 because I did not want to fight to find this supposed parking garage, find parking, and then lug our luggage a few blocks down to the hotel.

Shannon and I grabbed our bags and got a receipt from the valet. We walked through a huge rotating door that dumped us off into the lobby.

Shannon and I soon found the "check in" line. The line was at least 30 people deep. Shannon and I looked at each other and one of us said, "Ugh, it sucks that the line is so long…"

Shannon noticed that the people in front of us were enjoying cocktails. Shannon asked, "So do you want a drink?"

I said, "Hell yea! But I think it would be a little bit obvious if I grabbed the deuce deuce of Molson Ice from our bags..."

Shannon giggled and said, "Yea, I think that may be a bit obvious."

I said, "Ok, hang on a second. I'll be back and I won't make it that obvious..."

I walked through the lobby to the bar. I noticed that they had Shannon's favorite, Alexander Keith's India Pale Ale on tap. They also had Toronto's own Steam Whistle on draft. I ordered a tall boy of each. I paid and quickly closed my tab.

I found Shannon exactly where I had left her in line. I said, "Here you go, they had Alex Keith's for you. You better savor it because both of these were over $20!"

"Holy Shit?! 20 bucks?" Shannon exclaimed.

"Puckin' A right doggie!" I said.

"Good Lord! 20 bucks!" Shannon said.

"Yup...and for 20 bucks, we should keep the glasses. They are pretty nice glasses."

10 sips later, Shannon and I were checking into our hotel room. The receptionist asked us if we wanted to stay on a low or high level. I insisted that we stay on the highest level. The receptionist put us on the 35 floor. The receptionist asked for my ID, information, and a credit card for incidentals. After she took down all of my information, she asked Shannon, "May I have your information in case something happens to Mr. DeRose."

The first thing I thought was "What kind of hotel is this?!" The second thing I thought was, "Oh shit! What the hell is going to happen to me tonight that they need Shannon's contact info!? Am I going to get kidnapped or die tonight?!"

After the receptionist got all the information she wanted, she gave us our room keys.

On our walk over to the elevators, I saw some young lad that had a Rochester Americans embroidered fleece. I asked him if he was with the team and he said, "Yes. I am their strength and conditioning coach."

I said, "Good luck tonight! We'll see you at the game!"

Shannon and I found an elevator and boarded it. As the doors closed, I looked at all the buttons. Shannon found the 35th floor and hit the button for it. I noticed that the hotel was missing the 13th floor...it went 11th floor, 12th floor, 14th floor, 15th floor, etc. Translation: we knew that the 14th floor was actually the 13th floor. So technically we weren't staying on the 35th floor, but rather the 34th floor.

Once the elevator dumped us off on the 35th floor, I had to light up all the buttons for all the floors on the elevator...and yes, I am still mentally five years old!

Shannon and I found our hotel room and quickly settled in. I did just like John McClain did in *Die Hard*, and took my socks off to relax and walk around the room bare foot. It was so relaxing that I grabbed a Labatt Ice (For the record, Labatt was a Canadian beer, and my Labatt Ice was brewed at the Genesee Brewery in Rochester, NY; so we brought bastardized, flavorful, high octane "Canadian" beer into Canada).

By the time I was refreshed and dressed, it was only 4pm. Shannon and I were hungry; 'twas time to grab some grub.

When we were driving up to the hotel I noticed that there was a bar across the street from the Westin. Shannon and I decided to explore and check it out.

The bar turned out to be Harbour Sports Grill.

The place was empty but Shannon and I didn't mind. We grabbed a booth and ordered a pitcher of another local Toronto brew, Big Wheel. Big Wheel was tasty and helped to get our buzz on.

For dinner, I had potato and cheddar cheese pierogies!

Shannon had the Roast Beef Dipper, which was pretty much a beef on weck.

Dinner was delicious and we were full when we left.

We went back to the hotel to enjoy a couple more cocktails. Shannon had her Margaritaville Iced Tea and I enjoyed my Molson Ice.

Our hockey game started at 7:05pm. At the current point in time in our story, it was 6:05pm. I mentioned to Shannon that we needed to get going soon. She said, "Well we are not that far away from the arena. I can't imagine that it would take that long to get to the arena. Let me finish my drink, and then we can boogie..."

I thought about driving to Ricoh Coliseum, but there were a few deciding factors on why I did not…

1. I did not want to screw around with Toronto traffic.
2. I had a good idea on where Ricoh Coliseum was, but I did not want to screw around with Toronto traffic.
3. There were a couple Canadian Mounties in the valet area and I did not need any trouble with them.
4. I figured that a $20 cab ride to Ricoh Coliseum was cheaper than a DWI.
5. Driving drunk sucks enough as it is, let alone in downtown Toronto with all those speed bumps (pedestrians).
6. I like Canada and I would like to come back and if I get a DWI, I will probably be deported and not allowed back in the country for at least 10 years.

It was about 6:30pm when Shannon and I took the elevator down to the hotel lobby. The beers were finally kicking in and *everything was just fine, fine, fine 'cause I had one hand in my pocket and the other one was hailing a taxi cab* (that's my nod to Alanis Morissette…she's Canadian, you know, eh).

The cab driver, Apu Nahasapeemapetilon, asked us where we were going. We told him we needed to go to Ricoh Coliseum for the Toronto Marlies/Rochester Americans hockey game.

Apu told us he could get us there without a problem.

Lake Shore Boulevard was backed up, so he took a long cut which turned out to be a short cut.

Shannon and I made small talk with Apu for the duration of the car ride. Apu told us that Toronto's bar, hotel, and business industries had been suffering during the NHL lockout. We told him that we weren't surprised and that the fans should protest when the NHL season finally starts. We all agreed that the NHL owners and players were fighting over the fans' money, and if there were no fans, then there would be no NHL…

Apu dropped us off in front of Ricoh Coliseum minutes before puck drop. Apu told us that there would be plenty of cabs in front of the coliseum after the game. He also gave us his card so we could call him for a ride…well the only crummy thing about that was my phone had no reception or roaming coverage in Toronto.

As Shannon and I approached the coliseum, we were booed because we were wearing our Sabre jerseys, which was to be expected.

As we approached the turn styles, I gave the usher our tickets. As the usher scanned our tickets he said, "You can't wear those in here..."

I knew the usher was referring to our Sabre sweaters, so I ignored him.

The Toronto fan behind us said, "I don't think he heard you!"

I turned around and jokingly said, "You know I didn't hear what he said. You know there's a language barrier. I'm from Buffalo and we're in Toronto. The only language we speak is beer..." We all had a good chuckle.

Before we found our seats, Shannon and I needed to find the bathroom...wait, sorry. We needed to find a *washroom*.

Once we were relieved and washed our hands, we found a concession stand that sold beer; or as they say in Canada, a beer stand/stand de bière.

I asked the beer maid for two tall Molsons.

The beer maid looked puzzled and asked, "What kind of Molson do you want? All we have is Canadian."

I said, "Yes. Molson...Canadian. What other Molson products do you have?" I hope I didn't sound like a doofus, but the only two beers they were selling were Molson Canadian and Coors Light. I thought it was a no brainer, but what do I know?

The beer maid pulled the beer tap for Molson *Canadian*. The tap sputtered before blowing out a full cup of head. The beer maid said, "We are all out of Molson. Would you like to substitute Coors Light for it?"

Coors Light sucked. I told the beer maid, "Only if it is discounted."

The beer maid asked, "No. Why would the Coors Light be discounted?"

I said, "Because Coors Light sucks!"

Shannon chimed in and said, "We'll just find another beer stand."

We walked down the concourse and found another beer vendor.

This time I asked, "Do you have Molson *Canadian* on draft?"

This beer maid said, "Yes, what size Molson do you want?"

I said, "We would like two tall Molsons."

After the beer maid poured our beers she said, "That will be $26."

I thought "Holy puck! That's a pucking puck load for beer! I could have two 30 racks of Genny Cream Ale for that!" So I gave the beer maid my debit card.

The beer maid saw my debit card and said, "Oh I'm sorry, but we are not accepting credit cards tonight."

I whipped open my wallet and grabbed two $20 green backs for the beer maid. In return I got some funny money back...a $5 dollar bill with kids playing hockey on it and some Loonies.

Next, Shannon and I meandered our way on over to Section 114, Row N, Seat 2 and 3.

I didn't recall the name of the girl who sang both national anthems, but she sang them beautifully.

Next it was time for some hockey!

Tonight's game was going to be a battle of USA vs. Canada!

A battle of Good vs. Evil!

A battle of Garbage Plates vs. Poutine!

A battle of Genny vs. Molson!

A battle for Lake Ontario!

Toronto opened the scoring early in the game. Toronto's Nazem Kadri got the puck past Rochester's goalie Connor Knapp at 2:30 into the 1st Period.

At 5:37 of the 1st, Toronto's Ryan Hamilton made it a 2-0 Marlies lead. I looked over to one of the score boards to see the shots on goal. Toronto had two goals on only three shots. The first thing that I thought was that it was going to be a long game.

There were two Toronto Marlies fans sitting next to us, so I struck up a conversation with then. "Excuse me," I said. "I have a quick question for you."

The Toronto fan said, "Yes, eh?"

I asked, "What exactly is a Marlie?"

The Toronto fan said, "Marlie is short for Marlboro."

I was slightly confused, so I asked him, "So your team is named after a cigarette?"

The Toronto fan chuckled and said, "No, not a cigarette. A Marlie refers to royalty, kind of like a duke or a prince."

I said, "Oh, ok. I guess that makes sense."

Toronto dominated Rochester in the 1st Period. Somehow Rochester was able to muster up 10 shots on goal in the period, but Toronto's goalie Ben Scrivens wouldn't let anything in.

During the 1st Intermission, the Toronto fan and I talked sports. I never got his name, but we'll call him Horton.

I mentioned to Horton, "So the Buffalo Bills are playing up here next Sunday at the Roger Centre. Does anybody up here in Toronto care about the Bills?"

Horton said, "Yea, kinda. There is a knit core of fans that are Bills fans. And there are people up here who like NFL better than the CFL. But most Canadian Bills fans travel down to Buffalo for the games because it is a hell of a lot cheaper. Up here, a ticket to Rogers Centre is $200 or $300..."

I asked Horton what his thoughts were on the rumor that Toronto might get a second NHL team. Horton said, "Yea, there's talk about Markham getting a team. I think it would be great because I'm from there. It's almost impossible to get tickets to Leafs games in the first place, so there would be a lot of people who would enjoy a second team. Do I think it will happen? No. The Maple Leafs wouldn't let it happen. A new team on the block would take money away from the Leafs, and they would not put up with that..."

Toronto came out strong in the 2nd Period. Their hard work paid off 10:51 into the period when the Marlies Jake Gardiner scored to increase Toronto's to 3-0.

Not even 30 seconds later, Gardiner scored again to make it a 4-0 Marlies lead.

Then Rochester realized that they were supposed to be playing hockey. Rochester's Jonathan Parker put the Amerks on the board.

The 2nd Period ended with Toronto up 4-1.

During the 3rd Period, Rochester attempted a comeback.

Midway through the 3rd, Rochester's Parker scored again to cut Toronto's lead in half, 4-2.

Rochester's Luke Adam netted a goal with just over a minute left in regulation.

With last minute in the 3rd Period winding down, Rochester pulled their goalie, and was able to get the puck deep down in the Toronto zone. Rochester had a couple great scoring opportunities, but just couldn't seal the deal. With just seconds remaining, Rochester fired the puck a foot over the cross bar.

The Amerks had fallen short to the Marlies, 3-4.

Once the game ended, Shannon and I both needed to take a pit stop.

As we left the Coliseum, we received free samples of Kellogg's Frosted Flakes. Shannon was quite excited that she got free midnight munchies.

After we were outside the Coliseum, Shannon and I found ourselves one of many couples trying to find a cab.

We saw several couples being denied cab rides by cabbies because the cab fare was not the big ticket money maker that the cabbie wanted.

Shannon and I figured we would try to find a cab on the other side of the Coliseum, but there were no cabs there.

On the walk back to Ricoh Coliseum's main entrance, there was a homeless man with a sign for people's donations. I gave the man both of my Kellogg's Frosted Flakes. I felt that the food would have gone further than money would have. Also, I had been brain washed at Catholic school from K-12, and as Matthew 25:35 states, "For I was hungry and you gave me food, I was thirsty and you gave me a drink, a stranger and you welcomed me."

I'll tell you what, if that homeless man was thirsty for a drink, I would have given him one, but not a $13 beer from Ricoh Coliseum, otherwise I would have been sitting next to him with a sign.

Shannon and I saw a few more cabs in front of Ricoh Coliseum, but no one wanted to drive anyone because the cabbies were fishing for bigger game.

Shannon and I decided, "The heck with it, we'll walk back to the Westin…"

We started our venture down Lake Shore Boulevard. We saw a lot of cabs, but no one would stop.

Shannon was furious and stated that she was going to give the hotel hell for promoting a shitty ass taxi cab service. I told her not to worry about it and the walk would do us well.

Shannon and I eventually found ourselves at Queens Quay. I was hungry and Shannon was still cranky.

We walked past a Pizza Pizza and I told Shannon that some food would make her happy. I ordered a couple slices of cheese pizza and an order of poutine...I had to have my poutine fix in Canada!

We had our food to go since we were only a few blocks away from the Westin.

Needless to say, Shannon flipped off every cab that drove by...and there were a lot of cabs. I tried to reassure Shannon that those cabs weren't the cabs that c-blocked everyone at the game, but she didn't want to hear it.

By the time we reached the lobby to the Westin, Shannon was beyond ready to cause Bloody Hell! I told her I was going to wait by the elevators.

Shannon walked up to the Concierge desk because no one was at the Front Desk. Shannon expressed her great disgust with the taxi cab service that the hotel promoted. She told the Concierge that they should be disgusted and appalled with their cab's shitty service. Shannon stated, "I am not your normal foo-foo, high end hotel guest. I know you have a lot of high class people who stay here and they would not put up with this shit of being stiffed by the cab company you promote!"

The guy at Concierge said, "Yes ma'am, I understand."

That was when Shannon was taken aback and exclaimed, "No! I don't think you understand! Did you just walk back two and a half miles down Lake Shore Boulevard in the freezing cold when your taxi service wouldn't pick you up?! No! I don't think so!"

Needless to say, nothing got resolved, but Shannon got to bitch someone out and she felt better.

Shannon and I got back to the room where we could enjoy our Molson Ices, extremely crappy Pizza Pizza, and half way decent poutine.

After our midnight munchies, it was time for bed.

Check out time at Westin was noon, so I decided to utilize it. I didn't really get to sleep in much anymore, so I figured I would seize the opportunity.

The only thing Shannon and I had on our list of things to do were:

1. Visit Casa Loma because the last time we were in town, we missed out on it.
2. Stop at Duty Free to re-stock on Molson Brador
3. Take our time in Toronto because we did not want to get stuck in the Buffalo Bills traffic that was headed over the border to Orchard Park, NY.

I know some of you might be saying, "What?! You're in Toronto and you don't want to go to the Hockey Hall of Fame?!" My answer to that question was, "Hell no! Puck the NHL!" I was still upset at the NHL owners and players bickering about the fans' money. There was obviously no love shown for the fans. Owners and players were looking out for themselves. I told Shannon that I would go to the Hockey Hall of Fame only after the Sabres win the Cup…So in my lifetime, I probably will never go to the Hall of Fame…

Shannon and I left the hotel before noon.

We found Casa Loma by 11:30am.

In case you were wondering what Casa Loma is, I'll tell you.

According to the map they gave us, *"Casa Loma (was) the former estate of Sir Henry Mill Pellatt, a prominent Toronto financier, industrialist and military man. An unabashed romantic, Sir Henry engaged the noted architect E.J. Lennox to help him realize a lifelong dream- the creation of a 'medieval' castle on the brow of a hill overlooking Toronto. Begun in 1911, it took 300 men nearly three years to complete and cost $3,500,000 at that time. Sir Henry and his wife Lady Pellatt enjoyed Casa Loma for less than ten years before financial misfortune forced him to abandon his castle home. We hope you enjoy this intriguing legacy of an extraordinary Canadian."*

Casa Loma was fun and interesting. There were secret passages to the basement and second floor. We were even able to walk up spiral staircases to the top of a turret!

Speaking about secret passages, Shannon and I took the secret passage in Sir Pellatt's Study down to the Lower Level. The secret passage dumped us off into the Wine Cellar.

Once we left the Wine Cellar, we walked down the hall to where the swimming pool was supposed to be.

On the wall in the hallway were movie posters of movies that were filmed at Casa Loma. Such movies include *X-Men, Chicago,*

Cocktail, The Skulls, Extreme Measure, Maximum Risk, Darkman, The Caveman's Valentine, and *The Love Guru*; just to name a few.

Shannon enjoyed the Conservatory. The Conservatory had a bunch of plants and flowers in it. A portion of the ceiling was stained glass.

The Great Hall had a two story Christmas tree decorated in it.

I liked how Sir Pellatt's Suite over looked the Great Hall.

Down in the Billiard Room, little kiddies could visit Santa. When we were down there, we saw a five year old boy who was petrified of seeing Ole St. Nick. The boy tearfully told his mom, "I don't want so see Santa! I'll even go to the car!"

We left Casa Loma around 1:30pm. Our next destination was Duty Free at the Queens-Lewiston Bridge for some Molson Brador and Alexander Keith's IPA.

By the time we crossed the border it was 3:20pm and time for us to have our first meal of the day, breakfast.

I decided that we were going to have breakfast at the Mighty Taco on Grand Island. We would have had pizza with mom and Grandpa Ziggy at mom's house, but that plan was derailed...

Mom had left that Sunday morning to pick Grandpa Ziggy up so he could watch the Bills/Rams game at her house on Grand Island. We were going to order pizza and wings and enjoy the misery of the Bills. However, when mom went to pick Grandpa up, he wasn't feeling well. He asked mom to take him to ECMC (Erie County Medical Center) because he liked that hospital the best. Instead, mom took him to Sisters Hospital because that was where Grandpa's doctors were.

Mom ended up taking grandpa to the Emergency Room and waited there for hours.

Grandpa Ziggy was eventually admitted and it was found that he was dehydrated. Sisters Hospital decided to keep him for a few nights.

Anyway, mom and grandpa watched the Bills game from the "comfort" of the emergency room at Sisters Hospital as Shannon and I watched the same game from the comfort of the Grand Island Mighty Taco.

The Bills game turned into an exciting nail bitter...

By the time Shannon and I got to Might Taco, the Bills and Rams were already in the 4th Quarter.

Shannon and I had both ordered a #7 off the menu; the 3 cheese nacho burrito, nachos, and a drink. Shannon had a Cherry Coke and I had a Loganberry. By the time we were nestled in our booth, there was 6 minutes left in the 4ᵗʰ Quarter and the Bills were up 12-7.

It was business as usual; the Bills choked the game away and lost to the St. Louis Rams 15-12.

Once the game ended, Shannon and I left Might Taco.

We stopped at mom's house to pick up Mr. Teppo Puppy. Then we hopped back onto the 90, east bound towards Rochester.

***

Saturday December 22, 2012. According to the Mayan calendar, the World was supposed to end the day before, but it did not. To celebrate that the Mayans were wrong, our family decided to celebrate with another hockey road trip!

Shannon, Teppo, and I planned to travel down to the childhood home of Rod Serling; Binghamton, New York. It was the second game of the Home and Home Series and the Binghamton Senators were playing host to our Rochester Americans.

I had always enjoys my trips to Binghamton.

Back in the day, when I was a young whipper snapper at St. Joseph's Collegiate Institute, I was on the cross country team. At the time, the last race of every cross country season was always the Binghamton Invitational. The Invitational was always the last Saturday in October and it was held at Ely Park Golf Course on Mount Prospect. I still remember our coach Mr. Diggens driving the maroon colored Ford van from St. Joe's to Binghamton. We would leave that Friday before the race, right after school let out. Before the race (and almost every other race for that matter), Mr. Diggens would give us a pep talk. He would always tell us, "This isn't like the Bible here, boys. This is the real deal, this is cross country! Even though the Bible says, 'The first shall be last and the last shall be first (Matthew 19:30 and Matthew 20:16),' well that doesn't apply here in cross country! You need to apply yourselves!" As I recall, the varsity cross country team, that I was a part of, won the 2001 Binghamton Invitational.

Now the last time Shannon and I spent any significant time in Binghamton was back on February 22, 2008 because we saw the Foo Fighters at SUNY Binghamton. The Foos were awesome and put on an amazing show!

Anyway, enough reminiscing and back to the story...

Before we had left, Shannon and I looked up hotels on Orbitz. We found a couple hotels that were pet friendly. The few hotels Shannon called said they were only pet friendly if the animal was less than 25 pounds...well that ruled out the Black Lab named Teppo.

I called Days Inn because according to their web site, they were pet friendly.

When I called, I received the receptionist on the phone. I said, "Hi, my name is Adam and I saw on your web site that you guys are pet friendly."

The receptionist said, "Yes we are."

I asked, "I have a pet I would like to bring with me and I was wondering if there was a weight limit for a pet?"

The receptionist said, "No, there is no weight limit, but what kind of pet would you be traveling with?"

I said, "We would be traveling with a Black Lab."

The receptionist replied, "Oh! A Black Lab! That's not a problem! Just as long as you aren't traveling with a gorilla or something like that. You'd be amazed at what people try to bring in or think are pets..."

I inquired, "A gorilla?!"

The receptionist said, "Yea, there's some weird people out there but your Black Lab should be fine. There will be a $25 charge for incidentals."

I said, "Oh yea, that's fine."

I thought that it was a little entertaining that Days Inn charged $25 for incidentals. I knew full well that if Mr. Teppo destroyed something, that it was going to cost a hell of a lot more than $25!

Shannon, Teppo puppy, and I loaded back into the Dodge Caravan, now with 205,000 miles on it...People liked to bitch about how American cars sucked and how they were inferior to foreign cars. Well, I would beg to differ. Knock on wood, but the minivan had no problems. I did what my retired NFTA bus mechanic

Grandpa Ziggy said, "Always check the oil! Always change your oil! Always check your water level! You have to keep the engine happy. Besides the engine, everything else is an easy fix…" So, before we left for Binghamton, I checked the coolant level and it was fine. I checked the oil level, and she was down below the hash marks. I put about a quart of oil into my baby and she was ready to go on the road trip!

You may be wondering why Shannon and I were bringing our first born puppy, Teppo Numminen, with us. That is an easy question to answer…Every time Shannon went on these hockey road trips, we got that Catholic guilt trip feeling that we were leaving our puppy behind. On top of that, when we ask our friends and/or family to watch Teppo, they sometimes forgot about the furry little spud. Shannon and I did not want Teppo to feel neglected, so we brought him with us.

Our tiny little family of Wifey, Teppo puppy, and I left Rochester at 2pm, bound for Binghamton!

We hopped onto the 90 and traveled east bound towards Syracuse.

As we approached Syracuse, we took a short cut, 690 South.

We picked up 81 South in downtown Syracuse.

We were probably 20 minutes south of Syracuse when we hit a traffic jam. We sat in standstill for roughly 50 minutes. It turned out that the holdup was a car stranded in a ditch at the Lafayette exit. The roads were partially snow covered, which was why the car spun out.

We hit Binghamton around 5pm.

The first thing we needed to do was to grab some food. We grabbed dinner at Sonic. Shannon, Teppo, and I loved going to Sonic. Every time I saw a Sonic, I stopped so I could get my fix.

Every time I studied the Sonic's menu, I felt like a kid in a candy store. There were so many tasty options! Sonic was promoting their latest creation, Ultimate Grilled Cheese sandwiches. They had a Philly grilled cheese and steak, bacon ranch grilled cheese, and BLT grilled cheese. They also had a bacon grilled cheese burger! Oh my, my options were just endless!

I was in sensory overload and I went with the bacon ranch grilled cheese with chili cheese tots and a Dr. Pepper.

Shannon went with a Chicago dog, tots and a sweet tea. Shannon was trying to be on a healthy kick and wanted to eat less meat. Before we had left Rochester, she knew we were going to Sonic. She was proactive and asked how many times we would be stopping at Sonic. I told her, "Twice, once for dinner and once for breakfast." With that in mind, Shannon cooked herself two veggie dogs so she could substitute it for the hot dog on her Chicago dog.

Everything went well and dinner was amazing!

Mr. Teppo enjoyed Sonic too. He loved their tots. Teppo was a huge fan of their sweet potato tots, but those were a limited time offer only, and they did not have them anymore.

After dinner, we traveled down Route 11 for a few short miles. We were headed toward the pet friendly Days Inn.

Shannon and I found the Days Inn and we left Mr. Teppo in the locked van. Shannon asked me, "Do you think Mr. Teppo will be safe in the van?"

I said, "Oh yea, of course! Don't worry about him. We're just checking in and getting the hotel room key…"

Shannon and I entered the lobby and found our way to the main desk. A nice girl greeted us and checked us in. We told her about Teppo and she added the $25 incidental charge. I signed a paper and we got our hotel room keys.

Shannon and I walked back outside to the van to get our bags and Teppo.

As Shannon opened the sliding door to the minivan, she became pissed off because Teppo had eaten her veggie dogs and bag of healthy potato fries…I was mildly entertained.

Once the three of us found our room, I cracked open a Molson Ice. Then I proceeded to Teppo-proof the room…I put everything on higher ground or in a drawer: TV remote, Bible, phone, coffee maker, cups, garbage can, our luggage, etc. Anything that could be eaten or considered a chew toy was put in the bathroom or somewhere out of Teppo's reach. I did bring a couple of Teppo's toys so he wouldn't be bored.

Shannon and I left for Broome County Veterans Memorial Arena a little after 6pm though puck drop wasn't until 7:05pm. I left Sports Center on for Teppo so he wouldn't be bored.

Shannon and I left Days Inn and walked north up Front Street before hanging a right onto Main Street.

Now, before our little trip to Binghamton, I asked my boss Tess what there was to do in Binghamton because she grew up in the Binghamton area. She told me that she wasn't too sure what there was to do down there since she moved out of the area over 30 years ago. Tess did tell me that her daughter lived in the area. She said her daughter was living with her grandparents in the Binghamton area; she was attending SUNY Cortland. Tess asked her daughter what there was to do in Binghamton, and Tess's daughter said, "There's nothing much to do down here. Who would want to come here? There's nothing touristy here..." The one thing Tess's daughter recommended was Dillingers Celtic Pub & Eatery.

On the walk over to the arena, Shannon and I hunted down Dillingers.

Dillingers was located two blocks away from the arena.

It was only 6:30pm when we arrived at Dillingers; plenty of time to grab a quick round before the game. Shannon was thrilled because they had her other favorite beer, La Fin Du Monde. I was happy because they had Labatt Blue on draft. Shannon got happy whenever she found a bar that had La Fin Du Monde because not a lot of places stocked that beer. Out of the plethora of bars that we have encountered, Shannon said only two other places have had La Fin Du Monde, one being Montreal Poutine and the other being Canada at EPCOT in Disney World.

By the time all the beer evaporated from our glasses, it was almost 7pm! Shannon didn't want to leave Dillingers, but I reassured her that we could come back after the game.

Shannon and I walked the two blocks down to the arena.

We grabbed a round of tall Labatt Blues and then grabbed our seats in Section 16, Row A.

After the singing of the American National Anthem, it was time to drink some beer and watch some hockey. That night, the Amerks were facing the Binghamton Senators, minor league team of the Ottawa Senators.

Rochester gave the nod to Connor Knapp to start in net.

Binghamton got on the board first with a goal by Shane Prince.

About 2 minutes later, Binghamton's Andre Benoit scored a power play goal to make it a 2-0 Senators lead.

The 1st Period ended with the Senators leading 2-0.

Shannon and I noticed that most of the fans sitting around us we wearing Sabres paraphernalia, but cheering for Binghamton. Our neighbors told us that a lot of people in Binghamton were Sabre fans because they got Sabre coverage on TV. Even though the Amerks were the Sabres farm team, everyone in Binghamton wanted to cheer for their own local home team, which seemed to make sense.

The B-Sens came out in the 2nd Period and dominated play. Rochester struggled through the entire 2nd Period. Rochester couldn't get a puck to bounce their way. In the last minutes of the 2nd, Rochester's Jerome Gauthier-Leduc finally got the Americans on the board.

The Senator answered quickly with a goal by Mark Stone, to make it a 3-1 Binghamton lead.

Rochester couldn't get anything going in the 3rd Period either. It looked like they were a little tired from last night's game. However, Binghamton did not look tired at all. The Senators' Jakob Silfverberg scored on the power play midway through the 3rd to increase their lead, 4-1.

The B-Sens added a late goal by Mike Hoffman, to give the Sens a 5-1 victory over the Amerks.

After the feeble Amerks game, Shannon and I moseyed our way back on down to Dillingers. Shannon ordered up another La Fin Du Monte and I played it safe by ordering my trust worthy Labatt Blue.

After following the Amerks for a few months, I came to the conclusion that the Amerks seemed to play better at home than on the road. But I guess this could be true for any other team.

Shannon and I hung out at Dillingers for 3 or 4 rounds.

I began to get hungry, but I was not sure if the kitchen was still open at Dillingers. Plus, I did not want to wait 20 minutes for food. Shannon and I left Dillingers in search of food.

We walked into another bar, but they did not serve food. Instead, we grabbed a round of beer. Once the beer was gone, we left that bar.

Earlier in the night, on our walk to the game, we did see a couple restaurants on Main Street.

Shannon and I walked past a Chinese food joint, but I wasn't feeling Chinese.

I saw a pizza joint earlier in the night, but by the time we found it, it was closed.

I reconsidered and thought that Chinese food was fine. By the time we made our way back to the Chinese food joint, they too were closed.

Shannon and I then stumbled into a 24 hour CVS. Shannon did not want to look for food at CVS. Shannon wanted to find a bathroom at CVS. I could not find a bathroom at CVS so we left.

We eventually walked our way down Main Street and to our hotel.

To our surprise, Mr. Teppo had not destroyed anything.

I hooked Mr. Teppo's leash up and took him out to go pee.

Teppo and I walked down Front Street for a block or so. I was trying to see if there was a food joint or grocery store, but there was nothing.

Once Teppo peed, we walked back to the hotel room for nappy poo time.

Check out time was noon. I think the three of us finally woke up around 11am. Shannon and I showered and did the rest of that morning routine thing before we hit the road.

Days Inn had a continental breakfast, but we obviously did not wake up in time. It was ok that we missed the continental breakfast because Shannon, Teppo, and I were headed to Sonic again!

Since I had the Bacon Ranch Ultimate Grilled Cheese the night before, I decided to try the Philly Grilled Cheese and Steak. I opted on the jalapeno poppers as opposed to the tots. For my beverage, I chose a blue PowerAde.

Shannon was quite hungry. She ended up ordering a grilled cheese, a Chicago Dog, small tots, and a sweet tea.

Shannon's original plan was to take out the hot dog and substitute if for her veggie dog, but some other dog put a kibosh on that the night before. So Shannon just removed the dog and ate a bun full of condiments.

After we grabbed our Sonic meal, we hit the road again.

We finally got home around 3pm. Teppo and I vegged out and watch the Bills loss in Miami to the Dolphins 24-10.

January 2013

January 1, 2013! Happy New Year!

Yea, you guessed it, the NHL lockout still continued. However time was running short. The commish, Gary Bettman, gave a "drop dead" date of January 11, 2013. If both sides could not agree upon a deal, then the rest of the entire season would be canceled. If a deal could be hatched by the drop dead date, then there would be a 48 or 50 game season.

***

In the wee hours of the morning of Sunday January 6, 2013, the NHL owners and players finally ended the lockout. Both greedy sides agreed upon a way they could divvy up the fans' millions of dollars.

Well, I was wrong. I figured that the lockout would have been resolved by Christmas or there would be no season at all. Oh well, wasn't the first time I was wrong, nor was it the last time.

You know what? Puck the NHL! Shannon and I decided long before that we were going to boycott when and if there was a NHL season.

And another thing that really grinded my gears; with the NHL season reinstated, that meant that the Sabres could tap into Rochester and call up whoever they wanted. The potential of this looming over head stunk because I had become accustomed to watching the Amerks. I didn't want the Sabres calling up the Americans and screwing up the Amerks' feng shui.

At the current point in the Amerks' season, they were in 4th place in the North Division, 10th overall in the Western Conference.

Any who, Shannon and I had some more Rochester Americans and AHL games to watch! Our NHL Boycott started!

***

It was January 12, 2013 and Shannon and I were back on the road. We were headed about 87 miles east of Rochester. We were en route to the home of the Orangeman, to the birth place of Rod Serling, the home of hard core band Earth Crisis, and lastly, the home of Hofmann Hot Dogs! In case you were still clueless, I was referring to Syracuse, New York.

Shannon and I left Rochester early afternoon. We left Mr. Teppo at home because he needed to hold down the fort.

Shannon and I hopped onto the 90 and traveled east bound for about an hour, then we were in Syracuse.

Our first stop was Middle Ages Brewing Company, located in downtown Syracuse.

Shannon and I had never been to Middle Ages before, but Shannon had sampled some of their beer before. I wasn't sure what the place was going to be like. I had no idea what the building looked like, if there was a brewery tour, or what. All I knew was that there was going to be beer tastings!

Middle Ages Brewing looked like it was located inside an old school or warehouse.

As I opened the door to the brewery, there was a knight in shining armor. I wasn't sure if there was a person inside of it, so I knocked on it. It sounded hollow, so I thought it was just a statue. To make sure no one was in there, I tried to open the face mask, but that was welded shut. I was a little nervous about the statue because it had a huge sword. During the whole time there, I kept a watchful eye on him. I didn't want any funny business from the knight.

Once we were in the main room, we quickly bellied up to the tasting bar. Apparently there were no beer tours, just tastings, and I was perfectly content with that. Middle Ages offered free tastings, 6 samples of brew. We sampled ImPaled Ale, The Duke, Highlander Scotch Ale, Syracuse Pale Ale, Wit, and Double IPA. I am not a fan of "novelty beers" or IPAs. However, Shannon liked all sorts of malarkey beer, so she enjoyed herself, and at the end of the day, that's all that mattered. Middle Ages had other beers and ales that were not on the sampling list, so Shannon bought 24oz bottles of British Style Triple Crown, Wailing Wench, Druid Fluid, Kilt Tilter, Dragonslayer Imperial Stout, and Grail Ale.

Once we were done sampling beers, it was time to get some food.

Shannon and I intended on going to the original Dinosaur BBQ, right in downtown Syracuse.

The Dinosaur was a few blocks away from Middle Ages, so it wasn't too bad of a drive. As we passed by the Dino BBQ, there was a line of Orange out the door and around the corner. There must have been at least 50 Orangemen fans waiting in line to get a late lunch.

I knew that Syracuse University's Men's Basketball team was playing that day, but I didn't know the game was played at noon. It turned out the 'Cuse had beaten Villanova 72-61. After the game, a lot of the fans from the Carrier Dome ventured over to the Dinosaur.

Instead, Shannon and I went to Rosie's Sports Pub and Grille.

Shannon and I had never been to Rosie's or heard of it before, and I think everyone in the bar knew it. Shannon and I were the only ones in the joint not wearing Orange. We stuck out like sore thumbs with our Sabres gear on.

So there Shannon and I stood, at the lobby to the joint, waiting for a waitress. We waited about two awkward minutes before we squeezed our way up to the bar. Shannon ordered two Blues and asked the bartender how we get a table. The bartender told Shannon, "As soon as you see an empty booth, take it. Booths get taken fast!"

Shannon thanked the bartender and paid for our drinks.

As we scanned the pub, we could see that every booth was taken. Moments later, a group cleared out of the booth, and we snatched it before the bus boy could even clean up the table.

Once the bus boy cleaned off the table, he gave us a couple menus.

A few minutes later, Shannon and I had decided on what to get. Shannon was going to get a Buffalo Chicken Salad with fries. I opted for the Rosie burger with fries and a side of mozzarella sticks.

Shannon and I waited about five minutes for a server to show up. That's when I noticed the "Order Here" window at the end of one of the bars. I told Shannon, "Um, I think we go up to order our food."

Shannon said, "That's weird. Why would you say that?"

I pointed to the neon sign behind Shannon that said, "Order Here."

Shannon said, "Ok, I'll be back." Shannon went up to the window and ordered lunch, and paid for it there too. The cashier gave Shannon one of those vibrating, light up hockey pucks to let us know when our order was up.

In the meantime, we watched the first quarter of the AFC Divisional Playoffs. The Denver Broncos were hosting the Baltimore Ravens. I liked the atmosphere of the establishment. There were football helmets scattered throughout the place. There were NFL beer signs too, along with MLB and NHL paraphernalia.

Moments later, our hockey puck lit up and vibrated, it was finally time for lunch!

I chose the Rosie burger because it bore the name of the pub we were at. It consisted of burger, bacon, chili, and cheese. It sounded like a coronary waiting to happen. By the time I finished the motz stix, fries, and burger, I did not feel well. I attributed it to the greasy, not good for you food.

By the time we left Rosie's it was a little after 4pm and we had a lot of time to kill. Our hockey game didn't start until 7:30pm. We had initially banked extra time for the Dinosaur BBQ because we figured it would have been packed and the wait would have been at least an hour.

Since we had all this free time, we decided to find the Oncenter at the War Memorial.

On our way through downtown, we passed by Syracuse Suds Factory. Shannon expressed that she wanted to go. I said, "Ok, let's just find the venue, park, and then we can walk over." Shannon liked the plan.

A few blocks later, Shannon and I had arrived at the Oncenter. We parked the van behind Ale-n-Angus. Shannon needed to pee, so we stopped at Ale-n-Angus. While Shannon peed, I bought a Sam Adams Winter Lager and I got Shannon a Syracuse Pale Ale.

After we finished our singular round, we high tailed it on out of Ale-n-Angus. As we left, I told Shannon, "You know if you say Ale-n-Angus really fast, it kinda sounds like analingus."

Shannon shook her head and rolled her eyes while stating, "I married a thirteen year old."

On our way over to Syracuse Suds Factory, we walked past the Cathedral of the Immaculate Conception. As we walked past it, the great church bells began to ring, signifying that it was 5:30pm. Shannon enjoyed the architecture to the Cathedral because it reminded her of the great cathedrals that she saw in Europe.

A few blocks later and Shannon and I were walking up the steps to Syracuse Suds Factory. Shannon and I made our way up to the bar. I wasn't feeling like beer; I still felt full and had a stomach ache from lunch. Instead, I opted for a Syracuse Suds root beer. Shannon wanted to try something Suds made. She sampled their Black Cherry Weizen, but she didn't like it. She then sampled Suds' Pale Ale. She wasn't digging any of the brews so she played it safe and got a Molson Canadian.

Syracuse Suds was packed with Orangemen fans to the point where there were no open seats at the bar or pub tables.

We found a whiskey barrel that we leaned against as we continued to watch the Broncos/Ravens game.

Once we finished our drinks, we left Syracuse Suds and left the Amory Square area.

Next, Shannon and I headed for the big Christmas tree at Clinton Square.

The Christmas tree and ice skating rink were located on Erie Boulevard. Shannon and I were a little bummed out. If we had known that there was ice skating, then we would soytinly have brought our skates. At the time, it was 6:30pm. We thought about renting skates briefly, but we thought we were going to cut it a little too close with the game.

There was a plaque by the Christmas tree. The plaque informed Shannon and me about the ground we were standing on, Clinton Square. The plaque told us, *"Clinton Square first came into being in the early 1800s where roadways from the north and south joined in what is now downtown Syracuse. By the mid-1800s, the construction of the Erie Canal, known then as "Clinton's Ditch" after New York's Governor Clinton, further transformed this busy intersection into a bustling hub of trading and commerce. Surrounded by shops, stores and exchanges, Clinton Square became the economic and social center of downtown Syracuse. In the early 1900s, the Soldiers and Sailors' monument was constructed on the square to honor Syracuse and Onondaga County Civil War veterans. The monument was dedicated in 1910. In 1925 the Erie Canal was filled in and Clinton Square became a major transportation route. Since then, Clinton Square has had several redesigns. In the fall of 2001, the Soldiers and Sailors' Monument was renovated and rededicated. In 2001 renovations transformed Clinton Square into a spectacular public gathering space. The latest project involved closing a section of Erie Boulevard and creating a large reflecting pool and outdoor performance area on the site of the old Erie Canal. Once again as in the early 1900s, ice skaters glide across the ice every winter in Clinton Square and summers are filled with festivals and events of every kind drawing thousands of people into downtown for live music, food, and entertainment."*

It was 6:45pm when we left Clinton Square. Shannon and I decided to head back to the Oncenter.

It was 7pm by the time we got to the Oncenter. We thought about just heading into the arena, but we wanted to grab another beer. We figured that beer at the Oncenter would have been pricey, so Shannon and I decided to go back to Ale-n-Angus.

When we entered Ale-n-Angus, it was standing room only. We couldn't even make our way to the bar because it was four people deep!

Instead, Shannon and I walked down Harrison Street to Panini's Restaurant. They had a little mini wine and beer bar. They also had the Broncos/Ravens football game on. Shannon and I grabbed two Coronas and sat down at a pub table. We enjoyed our Coronas as Shannon talked about work. By the time we finished our singular round of Coronas, it was 7:30; time for hockey!

That night's game between the Rochester Americans and the Syracuse Crunch was the first time Shannon and I had ever been to the Oncenter at the War Memorial. I liked the outside architecture of the War Memorial because it had that old circa late 1940s feel to it. I loved how that night's game was billed on the outside of the building in bright red changeable letters in front of transparent Plexiglas rails; similar to that of the classic art deco movie theaters. I enjoyed how the outside of the arena was unchanged and still looked classic.

The inside of the War Memorial was another blast from the past. The floors were those marble confetti floors. The walls were those green glazed ceramic tile blocks. The metal work of the hand railings was stainless steel; it reminded me of an old Catholic school...better yet, it reminded me of the Enchantment Under the Sea dance that took place at Hill Valley High School in *Back to the Future*!

The only thing I disliked about the War Memorial were the mannequins! Yes, that was right, I said mannequins! There were mannequins in glass cases throughout the arena. Each mannequin was dressed up as a different American soldier, spanning from the American Revolution through contemporary times. Well, I am not sure of the actual soldiers depicted because I was petrified and blocked the mannequins out of my vision. I placed my hand up to my face to block my peripheral vision, so the creepy mannequins wouldn't scare me.

We finally made our way to the concession stand and bought two Molson Canadians. Next we made our way down to seats 1 and 2 in row A, Section 24. As Shannon and I nestled into our seats, we took in the ambiance of the arena. The arena reminded me even more of the gymnasium at Hill Valley High School. There was a stage built into the arena, but during the hockey game, moveable seats were put in to the stage to accommodate fans. I liked how the War Memorial was an all-purpose municipal building (When I got home from the game, I looked up the Oncenter War Memorial Arena on Wikipedia. The War Memorial was built back in 1949-1951. An interesting fact was that the War Memorial was in the 1977 hockey movie *Slap Shot*. According to Wikipedia, the War Memorial was "used as 'Hyannisport' where the Hanson Brothers charged into the stands to accost a fan and are subsequently arrested").

Shannon and I ended up sitting next to an older couple and they were cheering for the other team, the Crunch! I ended up striking up a conversation with them. I did a little research about the Crunch before coming to the game. I knew that the Crunch used to be Anaheim Mighty Ducks' farm team, but that season, they had a new affiliate, Tampa Bay Lightning. Knowing that tid bit of information, I asked my neighbors what their thoughts on the new affiliation were...

The old lady told me, "We are thrilled to have Tampa as a new parent club. The last two years of being affiliated with the Ducks were miserable. Nobody came to the games; we even gave up our season tickets because they were so miserable. Fans here would 'boo' the Crunch and cheer for the other team."

I asked the old lady, "Who was your major league affiliate before Anaheim?"

The old lady said, "Columbus Blue Jackets and the before that, the Vancouver Canucks."

I asked, "Well how was Columbus?"

The old lady said, "Good at first, but like everything else, it went downhill. That was a long 10 years we had with Columbus."

I asked the old lady, "Well how are the Crunch this year?"

The old lady told me, "Oh the Crunch are really good this year. You know, we're able to keep a lot of good players because of the NHL lockout. Since the lockout ended, Tampa called up six players from the Crunch, including our top line!"

I said, "That stinks...Buffalo called up six Amerks, but only three made the team."

I was a little bummed out that the Sabres had called up Marcus Foligno and Cody Hodgson because those two had a presence on the ice for Rochester. Oh well, life went on, and it gave another opportunity for other players to blossom.

Like any other hockey game, the opening minutes were always exciting!

Syracuse took two early penalties in the first five minutes of play but Rochester could not produce on the power plays.

Play during the 1st Period went both ways, fans were on edge!

There was a little less than 5 minutes left in the 1st when an errant pass by Syracuse eluded Rochester and made its way across the Amerks' blue line! As the puck coasted into the Rochester zone, two sets of eyes grew large; the pressing Syracuse forward and the Amerks goaltender Leggio!

Leggio decided to skate out from the net. He was at his right faceoff circle when he dropped down to the ground and slid, trying to block the Crunch player and the puck. In the process, Leggio tripped the Crunch player and the Crunch player missed the wide open net!

'Cuse went on to the power play but Leggio blocked them.

The 1st Period ended in a 0-0 tie.

Shannon and I gripped our clear plastic cups full of Molson as the 2nd Period commenced!

Moments into the 2nd Period, there was more action than anyone had bargained for. In less than a minute into the period, Syracuse dumped the puck into the Rochester zone. Rochester intercepted the pass. The Rochester defenseman passed to puck to fellow teammate Zemgus Girgensons. Girgensons dumped the puck over the Amerks blue line and into the Neutral Zone. The Crunch's

Richard Panik skated up to an unsuspecting Girgensons and dropped him like lumber. Girgensons was laid out and fell backwards towards the glass. As Girgensons fell back, his head rattled right off the glass like a rag doll. Rochester's T.J. Brennan was in the vicinity and instantly bum rushed the unsuspecting offender. Rochester's Brennan wanted to wallop Syracuse's Panik! Though neither player, Brennan or Panik, threw any punches, they grappled momentarily before falling to the ice. Officials came in to break up the fight as Girgensons lay life less on the ice, next to the Crunch bench.

As two linesmen grappled to break the fighters apart, the Amerks trainer scurried on the ice past both benches to check on the motionless Girgensons!

While Brennan was skated to the box, Panik was escorted to the locker room. Brennan received two minutes for roughing and five minutes for fighting and Panik received a five minute major for interference, five minutes for fighting, and a ten minute game misconduct for interference, all while the entire War Memorial stared at a motion less Zemgus Girgensons!

The entire War Memorial was silent! You could hear a pin drop!

Moments later, one of the Zamboni door opened and paramedics scurried out onto the ice with a stretcher.

Girgensons still laid there, not moving.

Being in the medical field, Shannon said, "What the hell are they waiting for!? They are not doing anything by staring at him! They need to put a neck brace around him and get him off the ice!"

A few minutes later, Girgensons got up under his own power and stumbled. He was right in front to the Crunch's bench, so he exited that way. He did not return to the game and Shannon was extremely upset at the medical staff!

Rochester started the action early during the 2nd Period with 4-on-4 play. Rochester's Rick Schofield scored a rebound goal to give the Amerks a 1-0 lead! The Crunch goaltender Riku Helenius didn't even have a chance. There were enough Amerks fans to cheer and make some noise for Schofield's goal.

Half way through the 2nd Period, we had our second fight!

Rochester's Joe Finley decided to drop the gloves with Syracuse's enforcer Eric Neilson at center ice! The two skated around and do-si-do-ed at center ice before trading punches! As the refs and linesmen looked on, flailing punches were thrown back and forth, but I have to say, I felt that Neilson got the better of the fight. The two fighters each got five minutes apiece.

A few minutes later Rochester's Tarnasky scored on the power play to give Rochester the 2-0 edge!

The 2nd Period was plagued with penalties, 12 to be precise, but neither side could capitalize after the lone Rochester PP goal.

The 2nd Period ended with the 2-0 Rochester lead.

The 3rd Period was exciting!

Syracuse came within one goal of Rochester with a power play goal off the stick of the Crunch's Brett Connelly. Connelly slapped home the rebound past Rochester Goalie Dave Leggio. Boys and girls, we had a 2-1 Amerks game on our hands!

A few minutes later, Rochester was on the power play and then quickly found themselves up 3-1 on a power play goal by Kevin Porter!

With about 5 minutes left in the game, the faceoff was deep in the Syracuse zone. Luke Adam won the draw for Rochester. The puck dribbled back to the point to Marc Mancari who passed it to T.J. Brennan. Brennan blasted a rocket from the middle of the faceoff circle and scored to up Rochester's lead to 4-1!

The score would remain the same as the Amerks would top the Crunch on the road 4-1!

Shannon and I were relieved that we did not have to walk the "Walk of Shame."

Once we left the Oncenter, there was just one last place in 'Cuse that we needed to visit.

A month or two ago, I had asked my coworkers Jeff and Josh (both native Syracusians) what I needed to do or see while in their home town. Jeff and Josh unanimously said, "Mother's Cupboard. You need to go to Mother's Cupboard. It's a great greasy spoon!"

Minutes later, Shannon and I were on 690 westbound, bound for Mother's Cupboard for some midnight munchies! We took the Thompson Road exit and headed north to James Street. We took a left onto James and drove for a bit and didn't see Mother's Cupboard.

We drove up and down James Street a couple times before I finally spotted it. The reason why we couldn't find Mother's Cupboard was because it was closed and all the lights we off! I was bummed out that we missed it. I thought a greasy spoon diner would be open for the late night crowd, not the early bird. Mother's Cupboard's hours were 6am-1:30pm. That just meant that we had another reason to go back to Syracuse.

Shannon and I were kind of hungry and thankfully there was a Wegmans grocery store kitty corner to Mother's Cupboard.

At Wegmans, Shannon and I both made pit stops to the lavatory. We ended up grabbing a loaf of Cheese Bread…Danny Wegmans made mad good Cheese Bread. We also picked up some salt and vinegar kettle cooked potato chips. We walked past the toy isle and I picked up a couple monster trucks for my niece Hannah and nephew Jonah. I grabbed a Dr. Pepper so I wouldn't fall asleep on the ride back to Rachacha.

Shannon and I arrived back home on the farm around midnight. Mr. Teppo was quite excited to see us. He had to pee and wanted to know about the game. So Teppo and I both went outside to pee and I told him all about it!

February 2013

I was still pissed off and bitter at the NHL. I wanted to continue my protest and strike against the NHL. Shannon had already crumbled and forgave the NHL and Sabres. She said, "Even though I liked our hockey trips with the Amerks, they just aren't the same as the Sabres. The trips are fun because I get to hang out with you and do fun stuff, but the Amerks just can't keep me interested like the Sabres do…"

I said, "I don't mind watching the Amerks. See! I admit it. I like the Amerks and you are slowly converting me to be a Rochersterian! The Sabre sucked during that abbreviated season. I bet the Amerks could beat the Sabres. If the Sabres were going to suck so much, they should have stayed locked out!"

Wednesday February 20, 2013 was a day that brought huge changes to the Buffalo Sabres organization.

That morning, Cody McCormick was put on waivers.

Later that afternoon, Buffalo Sabres general manager Darcy Regier relieved head coach Lindy Ruff of his head coaching duties!

Ruff had had coached the Sabres for 16 seasons.

The decision came after the 6-10-1 Sabres lost 2-1 at home the night before to the Winnipeg Jets.

The news was bitter sweet.

I enjoyed Ruff as a coach, but the dull, boring, and lack luster hockey was stressful and tough to watch.

Ruff had great success with the Sabres. Ruff had brought them to the Eastern Conference Finals 4 times; 1997-1998, 1998-1999, 2005-2006, and 2006-2007. In 2007 the Sabres had the most points in the NHL, which won them the President's Trophy. Ruff did bring Buffalo to the Stanley Cup Finals in the 1998-1999 season, which the Sabres lost when the infamous "No Goal" happened. In 2006, Ruff won the Jack Adams Award for Coach of the Year.

In regards to "No Goal" I remember when and where I was for that game. I was a freshman at St. Joes. June 19th was a school night [probably during NYS Regents week] and the game was running late. I had fallen asleep in front of the TV after the second overtime period. Buffalo Sabres play-by-play announcer Rick Jeanneret had woken me up during the wee hours of June 20th. (by the way, RJ is the best play-by-play announcer ever, **Period!**). Brett Hull cheated when he scored the goal and that weasel faced douchebag Bettman & Co. brought out Lord Stanley's Cup and gave it to those cheaters! Ruff whistled and yelled at Bettman to get his attention to tell him about the illegal goal, but Bettman didn't care. He had achieved his goal in spreading hockey in the South. It takes a real man to admit this, but at the age of 15, I cried.

While I am on a rant about hockey, hockey (professional or armature) only belongs in places where people actually know what ice is. People in the South think it's something that you put in your drinks. People in the Rust Belt and Canada know ice 9 months out of the year!

I felt as if Ruff was a part of the Sabres problem, but also a scape goat. I thought the Sabres needed a player personnel change as well. The Sabres should have shipped out bums like Jason Pominville, Drew Stafford, Ville "Lame-O" Leino and Jochen Hecht. I felt that if management shipped out or traded a few players, then that would have shaken up the team a lot; but I'm just a fan, so what do I know...

Sabre management called up Rochester Amerks head coach Ron Rolston to be the Sabres interim head coach.

Rolston had been in Rochester for a few seasons and I enjoyed his coaching. I noted last season when Shannon, Grandpa Ziggy, and I went to an Amerks game that the Amerks play was much better than the Sabres effort.

I noticed that the Amerk players showed up to play, they finished their checks, and they did this weird thing on the power play...they scored power play goals!

On February 21, the Bums and new head coach Rolston traveled up to Toronto. The Sabres welcomed their new coach with a 3-1 loss...it was going to be an even longer, shortened season.

Two nights later, the Bums were at home, hosting the New York Islanders. Buffalo's stellar performance earned them a 4-0 loss vs. the feeble Islanders. Rightfully so, the Bums were booed off the ice.

By that point in time, the Bums were 6-12-1, second to dead last place in the League. The playoffs weren't even an optimistic dream. The zeitgeist was to hope for a better next season and to trade some players.

It was difficult to trade crappy players because no one wanted a crap player on their team. Normally good players are traded for good players, just like shit players are traded for another team's shit players.

In the Bums' defense, shit makes a good fertilizer for things to grow. And it takes a while for things to grow and blossom. Maybe the Bums' shitty play would blossom into something next season...

By now, Terry Pegula was already into year two of ownership of the Bums. When he purchased the team two years ago, he promised the Stanley Cup would be in Buffalo. As for myself, the only logical way that I thought the Stanley Cup would ever get to Buffalo would be on one of those Stanley Cup traveling tour gigs. Buffalo fans would probably end up seeing the Cup at the Boulevard Mall or something like that.

March 2013

I had originally planned for Shannon and me to have a weekend getaway down in Cleveland to see the Lake Erie Monsters host the Rochester Americans during the first weekend in March.

Well, that didn't work out quite as planned...you see Matchbox 20 was playing at Turning Stone Casino in Verona, New York. Shannon and her friend Teri liked Matchbox 20. Me, on the other hand, I liked hockey. It turned out there was a simple fix to the situation. Shannon and I were going to switch dates with our friends Brian and Teri. Shannon and Teri were going to go and see Matchbox 20 while Brian and I traveled down to Cleveland to see the Amerks.

Brian and Teri drove up Saturday night from Pennsylvania and spent the night with us.

The next morning, Sunday March 3rd, Brian and I were packed up by 9am in my Dodge Caravan; now with 210,000 miles on it!

Later that morning, the girls drove out to Turning Stone.

Brian and I hopped on the 90 and headed west for a few hours until we hit Cleveland.

On the way down, Brian asked me what I wanted to do or see in Cleveland. I told him that I wanted to see the house from *A Christmas Story*. I also mentioned that my sister Sarah recommended Melt Bar and Grilled. Sarah said she saw it on Man vs. Food and that it was a grilled cheese bar! Brian and I were pretty stoked about it.

Brian plugged the address to the *Christmas Story* house into his phone, and the phone gave us directions to the house.

We arrived at 3159 W. 11th Street, Cleveland, Ohio shortly after 1pm.

As Brian and I walked up to the house, we noticed that the place looked deserted. The house and museum normally opened at noon on Sundays, but there was not a soul in sight.

Brian and I found a sign in the museum window that read, "We will be CLOSED February 25th to March 13th for yearly maintenance and repairs."

Well that's a bummer! Everything was closed; the house, the museum, and the gift shop. Brian and I ended up taking a couple pictures of the house before we hopped back into the van. That just meant that we had to come back to Cleveland!

Onward to Melt!

Brian plugged the closest Melt into this phone's GPS and a few minutes later, we arrived.

Brian and I chose to sit at the bar. We ordered a round of beers before ordering food. Brian and I split an appetizer of Melt Pierogies. For dinner, Brian ordered the Monte Cristo Melt and I chose the Lake Erie Monster Melt.

Brian and I saw the Melt Challenge, but we gratefully declined. The Melt Challenge entailed wolfing down a 13 cheese grilled cheese sandwich, fries, and slaw! The menu said there was over three and a half pounds of cheese in the meal! And if you finished, you received a t-shirt, a $10 voucher, and you get put into the Hall of Fame…three and a half pounds of cheese is a shit ton of cheese!

Brian was able to house his Monte Cristo. I ended up getting a doggie bag for my meal. I was able to put away one half of the melt, some fries, and slaw. Anyway, my left overs were going to make a good midnight munchies snack.

After lunch, 'twas time for some hockey.

On the way from Melts to Quicken Loans Arena, we passed by the Cleveland Clinic, where back in 1992, Grandpa Ziggy had open heart surgery. I think the Buffalo Bills losing Super Bowl XXVI 37-24 to the Washington Redskins gave Grandpa Ziggy his heart attack.

Before long, Brian and I found parking and we were walking into the Q.

As we walked up to the Q, we learned that it was puppy night. The Lake Erie Monsters were sponsoring a night where you could take your dog! Brian and I were a little bummed out. Brian could have taken his dog Mokey (named after a Fraggle) and I could have brought Teppo.

Anyway, once we were inside the Q, Brian wanted to check out the Cavaliers gift shop. I wanted to check out the beer line. So we did both.

Minutes later, Brian and I found our seats and got ready for some hockey! The Amerks were taking on the Lake Erie Monsters. The Monsters were the Colorado Avalanche's farm team.

The 1st Period was uneventful in that there was no scoring. On the other hand, we did have a fight break out. We had to wait until the last minute of the period, but Rochester's Nick Tarnasky and Lake Erie's Daniel Maggio dropped the gloves deep in the Rochester zone.

The fight turned out to be a good match with bombs dropped back and forth. Tarnasky snuck in an upper cut or two. The fight ended with Maggio getting tired and falling backwards, down to the ice.

As the 2nd Period started, Rochester had Luke Adam out on the ice. I mentioned to Brian, "I have no idea why the Amerks have scrub work Luke Adam out there on the ice! He sucked when he was in Buffalo, which is why they sent him down to Rochester…Look at that, he just turned the puck over in his own zone! Horrible turn over!" Seconds later, Rochester recovered the puck and skated into Lake Erie's zone. I commented again, "Oh boy, look out! 'Stone Hands' Luke Adam has the puck and he has all that glass to shoot at!" Brian laughed and then Luke Adam fired the puck past the Monsters' goaltender Sami Aittokallio and scored, giving Rochester the 1-0 lead! "No way!" I shouted! "Well, I guess every now and then a blind squirrel finds a nut…"

Rochester's scoring didn't end there. Midway through the 2nd, Mark Mancari made it 2-0 Rochester and in the dying minute of the 2nd Period, Maxime Legault made it 3-0 Rochester.

About five minutes into the 3rd Period, Legault scored on the power play to add to Rochester's lead, 4-0.

A few minutes later, Lake Erie finally got on the board when Andrew Agozzino beat Amerks goalie Dave Leggio. Leggio was pissed that his shutout had been blown and fired the puck down the ice.

With five minutes left in the 3rd Period, we had our 2nd fight of the night! Rochester's Frederick Roy (son of goaltender and four time Stanley Cup winner Patrick Roy) teed off with Lake Erie's Tyler McNeely. The fight broke out around center ice and was boring at first because the two pussy-farted around in a circle, waiting for the other to make the first move. The two finally grabbed each other's jerseys and tossed a couple jabs, while still skating aimlessly in a circle. Roy finally came over the top, landing a couple head shots. McNeely came back with a couple punches. Roy dropped a punch which caught McNeely right in the schnoz. The linesmen came in to break up the fight, but Roy and McNeely weren't done. The two tangoed some more. The fight was going McNeely's way because McNeely was able to grab Roy's jersey in a way that Roy couldn't throw any punches. McNeely got in a few face shots before Roy was able to get free. Roy came back with a couple wind up, over the top punches that he landed on McNeely's dome. The two traded hay makers. Roy hit McNeely with a punch as McNeely fell. McNeely was still hanging onto Roy's jersey, so the two tumbled to the ice. It was a good fight! Everyone was on their feet and cheering!

As the final minutes of the 3rd Period neared, Lake Erie's Luke Walker was able to cut the Monster's deficit in half, 4-2.

Rochester proved to be the better team and won 4-2.

After the game, Brian and I had to get gas for the minivan. We pulled off at some gas station for some petrol. I went inside the gas mart because I was looking for some post cards for Grandpa Ziggy. I did not find any, but I found the next best thing, the Cleveland Sunday paper. Grandpa enjoyed reading the paper. He liked to know what was going on in the world and in different communities.

Once we were gassed up, Brian and I were back on the 90 again, east bound to Rochester.

On the ride back, we listened to the Buffalo Sabres choke away another game. This time it was in the Big Apple to the Rangers. The Sabres had a 5-on-3 power play advantage during overtime, but couldn't do squat. Instead, the Sabres choked in the shootout.

Brian and I finally got back to my house a little after 11pm.

***

Sunday March 10th was Teppo's big day! No, it wasn't his birthday, but rather he had a hot date with his humans in the Flour/Flower City (depends which Rochester century you are from). Teppo was going to his first hockey game! The Rochester Americans were having their first ever Pucks and Paws hockey game. I thought it was awesome that I could finally take my furry four legged drinking buddy to a hockey game! Unfortunately for Teppo, the War Memorial did not sell ice beer. Teppo would have to suffer with Molson Canadian.

Well, I will let Teppo tell his experience on going to his first ever hockey game...

Thanks Boss! One day my humans put my walking harness on me! I got super excited! I knew we were going to do something awesome like go for a walk at the park! Instead we got to go for a car ride! I love car rides! Before we hopped into the van, Boss-Man told me to pee and poop, but I was too excited to do either! We drove down the road and I got to stick my head out the window! I love sticking my head out the window! It's a lotta fun! Boss-Man drove me and Boss-Woman to a building that had a lot of cars in it. I didn't know where we were going but I was excited! When we hopped out of the car, there were other humans with their dogs. We walked outside and there was a patch of grass. Boss-Man told me to poop or pee, but I was still too excited to do either. We crossed a road and as we approached the doors to another building, I got really nervous. I got so nervous that I pooped on the sidewalk. Boss-Man had come prepared with baggies and picked up my warm, hot, steamy pile of poop, hehe. We soon entered another building. This building was filled with other doggies! For some reason we had to stand in a line with the other humans and dogs. There were a lot of dogs to say "hello" to, but Boss-Man wouldn't let me sniff their butts. He kept on telling me, "Cut that out" or "Stop sniffing that dog's butt!" We walked around this building some more before we entered a dark room. This was when I got frightened and scared. Boss-Man and Boss-Woman wanted me to sit down on a broken chair, but I was too overwhelmed! Instead, I just laid down on the cold, sticky floor. There was a lot of noise and flashing lights, so I was even more scared. I shivered and hid from the noise. For some reason the noise did not scare the humans. Eventually my humans picked me up and plopped me on the broken seat. It seemed that when I sat on the seat, it was not broken. The seat only broke when I got up. Once I was in my seat, Boss-Man and Boss-Woman gave me some Molson Canadian beer. I felt good and a bit more relaxed when I got some beer into my system. I then realized we were at this hockey thing and I really enjoyed the beer. As I looked around, there were a lot of dogs sitting on their humans' lap or the broken chairs. We sat in these broken chairs for a bit. I was content to be hanging out with my humans. At one point, there was a parade of dogs on the white thing the humans called "Ice." It was interesting, but also weird at the same time. Eventually Boss-Woman got up and left! I was scared because I had no idea where Boss-Woman was going! As

I whimpered and cried for Boss-Woman to return, Boss-Man told me that she would be okay and that she would be back soon. Moments later, Boss-Woman returned! I was happy and I gave her kisses! Boss-Woman also found more beer, so I gave her even more kisses! Boss-Woman poured me some beer in my travel water bowl! A few minutes later, Boss-Man told me that the hockey game was going to Overtime just for me because I missed the entire 1st Period because I was hiding. During this overtime thing, all the humans were yelling and I got scared, so I hopped off my broken seat and hid on the ground again. Finally all the noise died down and Boss-Man and Boss-Woman were happy and petting me and flopped my ears all around. It was dark out when we left the building. We got to go on another car ride, so that made me happy! Boss-Man and Boss-Woman stopped for food, but they didn't give me any, and they sucked for that! Finally we were all safe at home! I was quite tired and exhausted for all that day's excitement, so I quickly ran upstairs and went to bed.

Thank you for your report on your big day and the hockey game Teppo.

No problem! Thank you Boss-Man!

Now I will tell you what happened through the eyes of the humans, Boss-Man and Boss-Woman…

The afternoon game between the Abbotsford Heat (Calgary Flames farm team) and the Rochester Americans was a 5pm start.

When the three of us got to the War Memorial, we had to wait in the puppy line to enter the arena.

While we waited, Mr. Teppo had to sniff everything: human or puppy.

Teppo sniffed some dude's butt and the guy turned around. The guy looked at Teppo, pet him, and said, "Hey buddy, how are you doing?"

I said, "This is Teppo Numminen!"

The guy said, "Hi Teppo! Where's your stick?"

I said, "Awe, he had to leave it in the van, otherwise he would be chewing it all game!"

As a part of Pucks and Paws, the first 300 puppies through the gate received a Rochester Amerks Pucks and Paws bandana. We would have put it on Teppo, but knowing him, he would have eaten it.

There were two sections at the arena dedicated for the puppies and their humans.

Teppo was petrified and didn't know what to think. During the singing of the Canadian and American National Anthems Teppo howled along and hit the high notes with the singer.

For the entire 1st Period, Teppo hid under the seats.

Rochester's Matt Ellis beat Abbotsford goaltender Danny Taylor early in the 1st Period to give Rochester the 1-0 lead. When Ellis scored, the celebratory horn went off, but it was a short and quick horn; most likely to not frighten any of the furry creatures. The lights, people cheering, and loud music frightened Teppo. Teppo was okay with loud noises only when he was making them.

As the 1st Period was coming to an end, Rochester's Phil Varone put Rochester ahead, 2-0.

For the 2nd Period, Shannon and I picked Teppo up and plopped him on his seat. He seemed to be fairly comfortable. He was quite happy when we gave him some beer in his portable water bowl. Teppo enjoyed watching the 2nd Period, but he didn't like it when midway through the period, the Heat's Akim Aliu beat Amerks goalie Dave Leggio. The Heat trailed 1-2.

During the 2nd Intermission, there was a small parade of puppies on the ice. Shannon and I thought briefly about taking Teppo down there to be a part of the parade, but he seemed fairly content in his seat.

I enjoyed the parade of the puppies and their humans. One dog decided to mark his territory on the ice with a nice messy dump!

Once the poop was cleared up and the parade ended, the Zambonis came onto the ice and prepped the ice for the 3rd Period of play.

Rochester hung onto their one goal lead for most of the 3rd Period. It looked like Rochester was going to win until Abbotsford's Drew MacKenzie tied the game with six minutes left.

After that, both teams played for the win, right down to the last seconds of regulation.

Since both teams were tied 2-2 after regulation, the game went to a five minute 4-on-4 Overtime Period. I told Teppo that they were going to Overtime because he hid and missed the 1st Period. Overtime was quite exciting with back and forth play. With about two minutes left in Overtime, Abbotsford's Brett Olson took a

322

hooking penalty. Though Rochester had the man advantage, Abbotsford's goalie Taylor proved to be too strong.

We were now going to the Shootout!

Teppo was not a fan of the Shootout. All the fans were hooting and hollering and Teppo became frightened again. Teppo hopped off his seat and hid underneath it.

Abbotsford shot first in the Shootout.

In the 1st Round, Akim Aliu shot first for the Heat. Aliu was able to beat Leggio and gave the Heat a 1-0 lead.

Phil Varone shot next for Rochester and was able to beat Taylor to tie it 1-1.

For the 2nd Round, Roman Horak skated for the Heat, but he was unable to beat Leggio.

Brayden McNabb skated next for Rochester, and he was unable to beat Taylor.

So after 2 Rounds, it was still tied 1-1.

Steve Baertschi skated next for the Heat. The entire War Memorial was on their feet and paws, booing Baertschi, hoping that he would miss. There were cheers throughout the arena when Baertschi missed.

Nick Crawford shot next for Rochester, but he was unable to score.

The 3rd Round was still tied 1-1.

Abbotsford's Ben Walter shot next. I was not sure if the booing got to him, but he was unable to score on Leggio.

Mark Mancari skated next for Rochester and scored to give Rochester the 2-1 lead after 4 Rounds.

It was the 5th Round of the shootout. All Amerks' goaltender Leggio needed to do was block the shot and Rochester would have won. Unfortunately, Blair Jones of Abbotsford beat Leggio and tied the game at two apiece.

It was now up to Rochester's Nick Tarnasky! If Tarnasky could score, then Rochester would win! Tarnasky picked up the puck at center ice, skated down, took his shot, but was unable to beat Taylor.

Round 6!

Tyler Ruegsegger was on deck for Abbotsford. Amidst boos, Ruegsegger picked up the puck at center, skated down to Leggio, and scored to give the Heat a 3-2 lead.

It came down to this, do or die for Rochester's Patrick Rissmiller. Rissmiller could keep the Amerks alive in the Shootout or be the most disliked player in Rochester for a day. Rissmiller chose to keep the Amerks alive in the Shootout! The War Memorial cheered like wild when Rissmiller tied it up at 3.

It was now Round 7 of the Shootout!

Abbotsford's Greg Nemisz was now facing Leggio. Leggio proved to be the better player because he did not let Nemisz's shot in.

It was now up to Rochester's Rick Schofield. Schofield could have been the hero and won the game, but he didn't.

The Shootout, tied at 3-3, was now going to the 8th Round.

Anticipation grew as the Heat's Carter Bancks picked up the puck from center ice. Thankfully Bancks did not score.

It was now up to Rochester's Luke Adam. Luke could have been the most popular guy in Rochester for the afternoon if he scored, but he didn't.

Going into Round 9, it was still tied 3-3!

Ben Street was the next shooter for the Heat. He was booed the entire time, from when he picked up the puck at center ice and all the way down to the Rochester net. Street got cheers when he missed and Leggio made the save.

It was now up to Rochester's Shawn Szydlowski. Sadly, Szydlowski did not score.

We were now going to the 10th Round of the Shootout! Shannon, Teppo, and I were absolutely getting our $15 worth out of the tickets.

Brett Olson skated next for the Heat. Though Olson was able to beat Leggio during regulation, he was unable to beat Leggio during the Shootout!

Next up was Rochester's Alex Biega. With all the humans and puppies in the War Memorial supporting Biega, Biega skated down the ice, took his shot, and beat Taylor to win the game for Rochester! The War Memorial went crazy!

I think Teppo was quite excited when the game ended. He was quite content with a car ride back home.

Shannon and I were a little hungry, so we stopped off at Empire Hots and got a grilled cheese trash plate to go.

Once at home Shannon and I wolfed down the trash plate as we watched the Sabres lose in Philly, 3-2.

April 2013

The NHL trade deadline was April 3 at 3pm Eastern Standard Time.

As the day approached for the dealing, many Buffalo fans were calling for anyone and everybody on the team to be pedaled away. The talks ranged from goaltender Ryan Miller, to dud forwards as Jason Pominville and Drew Stafford. Even that bum Thomas Vanek was a potential on the auction block.

As time dwindled closer and closer to 3pm on April 3rd, it looked like Buffalo's general manager Darcy Regier wasn't going to do anything drastic…and then he pulled the trigger! Twice!

On April 2nd, defenseman Robyn Regehr was sent packing to LA LA Land in exchange for a 2nd round pick in 2014 and 2015.

Then! On April 3rd, a few ticks before the 3pm deadline, it happened!

The Sabres team captain, Jason Pominville, was sent packing to Minnesota!

Buffalo had dealt Pominville and a 4th round draft pick in the 2014 draft in exchange for forward Johan Larsson, goalie Matt Hackett, a 1st round draft pick in 2013, and a 2nd round draft pick in 2014. Not that I am a hockey expert, but I think that was a great trade for Buffalo.

Moving on…

***

Captain's log, stardate 04.06.2014. Our destination: the Adirondack Region.

'Twas Saturday April 6, and Shannon and I were back *on the road again!*

Shannon and I had the last leg of the Amerks' regular season road trip games to wrap up! Shannon and I piled back into the Dodge Caravan, now with 212,000 miles on it. We were headed east bound down the 90 for two games in two nights!

While Shannon and I were en route to Glens Falls to see the Amerks take on the Adirondack Phantom, we had a planned pit stop in Utica, New York.

Shannon and I had a hot date at the Utica Club Brewery! Actually, it was not called the Utica Club Brewery, but rather FX Matt Brewing Company.

We got to FX Matt Brewing Company shortly before our 1pm beer tour.

The brewery conveniently made all tour goers wait in the gift shop as they waited for their tour to begin. There were hats, t shirts, glassware, beer paraphernalia, and beer for purchase.

Our tour started at 1:15pm. Our tour guide Dave told us to follow him up the stairs and into the Visitors' Center. The Visitors' Center reminded me a lot of the lobby to Disney's Haunted Mansion attraction.

There was a desk that had a guest book that all patrons signed. As we waited in the center, I looked around some more and noticed a lot of antiques. There was a glass case that housed early bottles of the brewing company, plus almost all the lines of beer and pop they had sold throughout their 120+ year history.

Once the last person signed the guest book, Dave began our tour. He told us the room we currently stood in was a part of the original brewery but in the 1960s, it was converted over into the Visitors' Center. The center was designed with a Victorian feel and furnished with antiques.

Dave told us that the desk that had the guest book on it was an antique and originally owned by P.T. Barnum, the circus guy.

Dave mentioned that there were two Tiffany lamps the brewery owned. One of which was sitting on P.T. Barnum's desk.

Also, Dave pointed out a fancy grandfather clock. The grandfather clock was a beautiful German made piece. The center cabinet was made of stained glass circles. He opened the glass door and noted that the piece was a very big music box. Dave pointed out that there were only four remaining grandfather clocks of that kind. Furthermore, the grandfather clock was appraised years ago, for insurance purposes, at well over $1 Million.

Next, Dave brought us to the glass case that housed all the bottles of beer and pop Matt Brewing Company had and currently made throughout the years.

Dave pointed out to us a bottle of Utica Club and said, "You movie buffs might recognize this bottle of Utica Club! Patrick Swayze drank from a bottle similar to this one in the 1980s movie *Dirty Dancing*.

Dave showed us a couple beer steins that were a part of Utica Club's TV commercials back in the 1950s and 1960s. The commercials revolved around two beer steins, a tall German (Schultz) and a short Irishman (Dooly). They had a couple other beer stein friends. Dave informed us that we could watch the old commercials upstairs in the tasting room at the end of the tour.

Lastly with the beer display case, Dave showed us a camouflaged green can of Utica Club. Dave said, "As they story goes, back during World War II, to save on metal for the war effort, the US government put a ban on canned products such as beer. This ban lasted until the Korean War. However, there was a few times where the US government would let breweries, under contract, make canned beer. FX Brewery received one of those contracts and made special green camo beer cans of Utica Club. These cans were then shipped overseas to the GIs. One GI serving in the South Pacific was from the Utica area. He was surprised to get a treat that reminded him of home. As opposed to cracking open the can and chugging down his beer, he decided to keep it with him as a keepsake. The can followed that soldier with him for the remainder of his tour. When he got back home to New York, he gave his dad the can of Utica Club, stating that it reminded him of home. The dad then met with the owner of the brewery, Francis Xavier Matt I, and gave him the can of beer and said, 'Your beer brought my son back home alive from the war, so I am giving you back your beer!'"

After we left the main room, Dave led us down a hallway.

He pointed out a portrait of the founder, F.X. Matt. The hallway had other paintings of family members; Walter Matt (F.X.'s son and successor) and F.X. Matt II (Walter's son and successor).

Next, Dave gave us the history of the brewery. Founder F.X. Matt I was born in Germany. He worked at Duke of Baden Brewery which was located in the Black Forest region of Baden, Germany.

After F.X. learned to make beer he decided to leave Germany. In 1880 he immigrated to the States. F.X. eventually found his way to Utica, NY. Once in Utica, he worked at Charles Bierbauer Brewery. By 1888, he took control of the brewery and reorganized it as the West End Brewing Company. At this point in time, there were already roughly 12 breweries in Utica!

Dave told us an interesting story about F.X. When F.X. was 69, he suffered a heart attack. Word spread around town like wild fire and like an old fashion game of telephone, word eventually made it to the newspapers.

By the next morning, F.X. had recovered from the heart attack. While reading the morning paper, he came across his obituary! Thankfully F.X. was able to live to the ripe old age of 99!

During the 1950s, F.X.'s son Walter purchased the company.

One of Walter's greatest contributions to the beer community happened in the late 1970s. Though I have never experienced one, I have heard many great things about them...ladies and germs, West End Brewing Company was the first to introduce the Beer Ball! The Beer Ball was also known as the Party Ball.

By the time my career of drinking had begun, the Beer Ball was just a legend; like Atlantis!

I remember hearing stories around the camp fire from my elders who talked about this great invention and innovation of beer drinking! I would ask my elders what happened to such a wonderful thing, but they never knew. They just said one day it disappeared!

Was it Aliens? Area 51? The government?

All the blame can be put on the money hungry, greedy, selfish, piggish New York State. Dave enlightened us. He said New York State saw how much money they were losing out by not taxing Beer Balls high enough.

The standard Beer Ball held about 55 twelve (12) ounce beers. For you Canadian folk, that's about 55 three hundred fifty five (355) milliliter beers.

New York State viewed the Beer Ball as a keg and started to put a keg deposit on it. For those of you who don't know, the deposit on a keg was and is significantly greater than a bottle of beer. Tragically, New York State's deposit on Beer Balls was too much money. That drove Beer Ball sales down into the ground. Breweries were forced to cease production of the Beer Ball...Thank you stupid New York State!

However, Dave did tell us a funny story about the Beer Ball. According to New York folk lore, back in the day, a whole bunch of students at SUNY Oswego drank enough Beer Balls that **ALL** the street lamps on campus were converted to Beer Balls!

In 1980, F.X. Matt II acquired the company.

Dave gave us all another little history lesson. By the early 1980s, fizzy tonic piss water beers were all the new rage. Bud and Coors were big on the block and were forcing mom and pop breweries out of business.

New owner F.X. II decided to rename the brewery. He renamed the brewery in honor of his grandfather; F.X. Matt Brewing Company.

In the process of tapping into his roots, F.X. II decided to venture back to the Old Country and learn about beer; its heritage.

When F.X. II came back from Germany, he was a new man who saw the light. While in Germany, he was impregnated by the Beer Gods. When he got back to Utica, he gave birth to the Saranac product line!

Dave also threw in a quick fast fact, F.X. Brewing was the second oldest family run brewery in America; Yuengling being first.

The next room we ventured into had a German feel to it. This is where Dave told us about the beer making process with hops and barley and all that other stuff.

Dave talked about the product line and the different Saranac ales that were out along with some seasonal brews. Dave added that the brewery had recently purchased Lake Placid Brewery and Flying Bison Brewery.

Dave took the tour group into another room and closed the door behind us. He said that the room we were in was made up to look like a Speak Easy during Prohibition. He pointed out that the door he had just closed came off of a Speak Easy. Dave said, "This is how a Speak Easy would work...Someone would knock on the door, and I would open up this little window, like so. I would see who was there and then ask them for the secret password. Once I got the secret password, I would open the door, and let the patron in."

Dave noted that the brewery's other Tiffany lamp was in the Speak Easy room.

Since the topic of Prohibition was brought up, he informed us on how FX Brewery survived Prohibition; by making soft drinks. Also, the brewery would make "near beers." The brewery would boil the ingredients to make the mash and bottle it. They would then sell the canned near beer at grocery stores with a label on it, stating that the product was for cooking purposes only. There was a warning label on the cans that said not to mix with brewer's yeast and water...a nice middle finger to the US government and Prohibition.

As we were about to leave the Speak Easy, Dave asked if there were any questions.

I raised my hand and asked him, "How did the brewery get the first license to brew beer after Prohibition?"

Dave answered, "Simply you have to be at the right place at the right time..." Dave went on to educate us and said back in 1933, there was talk down in Washington D.C. to repeal Prohibition. The word on the street was that it could come in as little as a couple days, weeks, or months. Owner FX had a hunch that it was going to be sooner rather than later. FX "fell ill" and missed his train back to New York. A couple days later, the brewery received a telegram from FX, telling them to start brewing again. It only took the brewery 90 minutes to have its first case of legal beer to roll off the bottling line. Beer delivery trucks were lined up around the brewery to start delivering to the Northeast!

Dave said that before Prohibition, there were about 22 breweries in New York State. When Prohibition was repealed 13 years later, there were only two breweries that survived the storm. One being FX Matt Brewery and the other being Genesee Brewery in Rochester.

Speaking about beer again, Dave told us a few different lines of beer the FX Matt Brewery was licensed to brew, such as Sam Adams, Brooklyn Ale, McSorley's, and the infamous Billy Beer! Billy Beer was "crafted" by former US President Jimmy Carter's younger brother, Billy.

Next, we all boarded an elevator, like in Willy Wonka, only that this wasn't a great glass elevator.

The elevator brought us up to the brewhaus. We got to see the copper kettles where the first step of the beer making process started. The next room we went into housed huge silos for the fermenting part of the process. We walked onward into a building that housed more silos for aging the beer. For the last part of the tour, we got to see the bottling plant. Since it was the weekend, we did not get to see the canning or bottling lines run.

While on the 2nd level of the packaging plant, Dave told us about a fire the brewery had back in 2008. Dave said the fire happened in the packing plant and fire fighters were able to quickly put it out. However, there was enough fire and smoke damage that beer making was halted. The brewery had a problem because they still had beer in the fermenting and aging silos. Fortunately, the High Falls Brewery (makers of Genesee beer) in Rochester came in to help. They allowed FX Brewing to bottle and can their beer in Rochester at the High Falls Brewery, thus saving the day and the beer!

From the packaging plant, we walked back through the entire brewery to the beginning of the tour, the first room of the Visitors' Center. There was a stair case that went up to the tasting room. Each beer tour guest received two coupons for beer samples. I sampled a pint of Utica Club and Utica Club light. Shannon selected a sample of Saranac IPA and Saranac Black Forest. We enjoyed our samples while we watched old TV commercials of "Schultz and Dooly."

By the time we finished our brews and toured the gift shop again, it was after 3pm and we needed to get back on the road. Shannon and I were still about two hours away from Glens Falls.

Before leaving town, we stopped off at Hess so we could stock up on beer. I grabbed two 6 packs of Utica Club. They also had a few cases of Genny Bock, so I picked up one of those too.

Shannon and I hopped back on the 90 and drove down a few exits and got off at Exit 28 because MapQuest told us to. We took Route 29 east, up through the foothills of the Adirondacks, and through Saratoga. Then we picked up I-87 north and before we knew it, we had arrived at our destination!

It was shortly after 5:30pm when we reached Glens Falls and we were hungry. We didn't feel like going to some crappy chain like Pizza Slut or Subway. Shannon and I saw this place, Carl R's Café that advertised $4 margaritas, so we decided to dine there.

Shannon instantly liked the place. The place looked like it used to be a Mexican restaurant with the yellows and oranges painted on the walls. In the center of the restaurant was a bar with hot pink neon lights that read "Carl R's Café." There were a lot of green leafy plants everywhere, so it looked as if my mom had decorated the place.

Shannon had her margarita and I had a Molson Export.

For an appetizer, we had Mexi-tots, which were chili loaded potato skins, and they were dynamite!

Shannon ordered seared tuna while I had a Caesar salad with shrimp.

There was also a live musician, Bobby Kendall, who played during the dinner hours. Bobby played covers of Eagle Eye Cherry, Darius Rucker, Dave Mathews Band, and Green Day. Shannon liked Bobby so much that she bought his CD. I told her to get it autographed because he might be famous one day.

Once we were done with dinner, we had to book it because it was almost 7pm and the game started at 7. Shannon wasn't really interested in the AHL game, but rather the live music.

Minutes later, Shannon and I checked into our hotel at The Queensbury Inn. I asked the receptionist for walking directions to the Glens Falls Civic Center. Receptionist Kim told us to walk down the main drag and to stop when we get to the traffic circle. She said the civic center was right behind the Burger King.

Shannon and I ran up to the room and changed. I put my Blue and Gold Sabres jersey on. Since it was nice out, Shannon opted for a Sabres t shirt. I had already cracked open a can of Utica Club when we got to the room and by the time we were finished getting dressed, the can was still half full. I wasn't sure what the open container policy was in Glens Falls, so I put the Utica Club in a coffee cup.

Shannon and I scooted out of the room, down the hallway, down the elevator, and out the door onto Ridge Street.

As we walked down Ridge Street, I finished my beer right in front of the police station.

Seconds later, Shannon and I were at Will Call at the Glens Falls Civic Center.

Now the last time Shannon and I were at the Glens Falls Civic Center was back in the Fall of 2007. Shannon was still on her medical rotation up in the Adirondacks. I had driven up from Buffalo to Newcomb to take Shannon to Glens Falls to see the Foo Fighters!

That evening, the Adirondack Phantom were hosting our Rochester Americans. The Phantom were the farm team for the Philly Flyers.

As we entered the civic center, I had forgotten how tiny and cozy the civic center was. As we searched for the closest beer line, I noticed we had missed about seven minutes of the game and we had also missed Rochester's first goal! It turned out that Patrick Rissmiller scored first for Rochester.

Shannon and I found a beer line that served Labatt Blue. As we were in line, Adirondack scored to tie the game at 1-1. Adirondack's Jon Sim beat the Amerks' net minder Leggio to tie the game.

Once we had our Labatt Blues at hand, Shannon and I made our way to our seats.

As we sat and watched the game, Shannon and I got whiffs of someone's rotten stank breath! That shit was so potent that it could take lead paint off of a nuclear fallout shelter! The 1st Period wasn't even over before Shannon and I got up to find asylum elsewhere.

During the 1st Intermission, Shannon and I walked around the tiny civic center. We found a couple empty seats at the top of the section behind the net where the Amerks would be shooting at for the start of the 2nd Period.

While we waited for the 2nd Period to start, Shannon and I sipped our beers. A couple moments later, two dudes wearing Amerks track suits sat down next to us. A couple minutes later, a grandmother came up to the two Amerks and asked them if they could autograph two Buffalo Sabre t-shirts for her grandkids, and they respectfully did so. I asked the two dudes why they weren't playing that night and they told me that they had the night off.

The 2nd Period did not stay tied 1-1 for long. Rochester's Frederick Roy beat the Phantom's goalie Brian Boucher to give Rochester a 2-1 lead.

Minutes later, Rochester's Drew Schiestel added to the Amerks' lead, 3-1. Drew's goal caused a goaltender change for the Phantom. Brian Boucher was yanked and Cal Heeter was tossed in!

Within a minute of Schiestel's goal, the Phantom struck back with a goal from Marcel Noebels. The Phantom trailed the Amerks 2-3.

Rochester took a 3-2 lead into the locker room for the 2nd Intermission.

During the 2nd Intermission, Shannon and I refilled our beers because they had evaporated so quickly.

While we were awaiting the start of the 3rd Period, Shannon and I noticed a couple guys behind us wearing very nice Amerks polo shirts. I mentioned to Shannon that those dudes were either really big Amerks fans or they must have known somebody on the team. I decided to engage them in conversation, "Hey guys, Go Amerks!"

They joyfully replied back, "Yea! Go Amerks!"

We chit chatted for a few minutes and it turned out that one of the guys was brother to the Amerks' interim head coach Chadd Cassidy, and that was how he got a fancy Amerks polo shirt.

Once the 3rd Period started, the Amerks did not waste any time adding to their lead. It took Marc Mancari 34 seconds to give Rochester a 4-2 lead.

To Adirondack's credit, they did not roll over. Instead they fought back and a minute later, Jon Sim put one past Leggio and put the Phantom within one of the Amerks; 4-3 Rochester lead.

It was a little after the halfway point of the 3rd Period when the Phantom's Garrett Roe tied the game at 4 all.

Regulation ended in a tie, so the contest went to Overtime.

Overtime was exciting. There was some quick back and forth hockey, but that too ended in a tie.

'Twas time for the Shootout!

Rochester was nominated to shoot first in the Shootout. AHL hockey rules had 5 Rounds of the Shootout!

Rochester's Patrick Rissmiller skated first for the Amerks, but was unsuccessful against Heeter.

Adirondacks' Jason Akeson skated first for the Phantom, but he was unsuccessful against Leggio.

Tied 0-0, Rochester's newly acquired Johan Larsson skated next, but he couldn't slip the puck past Heeter.

Kyle Flanagan shot next for the Phantom, but Leggio proved to be the better player.

Headed into Round 3, the contest was still tied 0-0.

Rochester's Marc Mancari skated next and scored!

Jon Sim skated next for Adirondack and matched Mancari's effort by scoring against Leggio.

The Shootout was now tied 1-1 going into the 4th Round.

Rochester's Colin Jacobs was able to score and regain Rochester's lead.

Adirondack's Marcel Noebels skated next. Though Noebels got a goal during regulation, he was unable to score in the Shootout.

Rochester had a 2-1 lead going into the 5th Round of the Shootout. All Alex Biega needed to do was to score to officially put the game away. Unfortunately Biega was unable to get the puck past Heeter.

It was now up to the Phantom's Danny Syvret to keep his team afloat. Too bad for him because Leggio stopped his shot!

The Amerks had defeated the Phantom 5-4 in the Shootout! As my mom would have said, "Shannon and I got our money's worth out of the tickets!"

After the game ended, Shannon wanted to hit up the microbrewery that we saw on the way into town; so we moseyed on up Glen Street to Davidson Brothers Brewing Company.

Davidson Brothers was a microbrewery, bar, and restaurant. Shannon and I stopped in just for drinks. Shannon opted for beer sampler platter, which included Davidson Brothers' Wheat Ale, Brown Ale, Red Ale, Dacker, Smoked Porter, and Scotch Ale. I was feeling conservative and went with a Blue Light.

Davidson Brothers had a few TVs, all of which were showing the NCAA Final Four Men's basketball game. Everyone in there was cheering for the Syracuse Orange to beat Michigan. Syracuse looked like they didn't show up for the game because they displayed a lack of effort, drive, and heart. Sadly, Michigan beat Syracuse.

Once we left Davidson Brothers, I was feeling slightly hungry. I noted on the walk in that there was a pizzeria around the corner.

It was around 11pm when we got to the pizza joint, but it was already closed.

We did notice that back across the street from where we had come was a jazz bar. Shannon liked jazz, Adam did not like jazz. I tried to make Shannon happy, so we went to the jazz bar.

When we got into the jazz bar, the band had just taken a break. The bartender made Shannon some sort of chocolate martini. I decided to play it safe again and had a Blue Light. We stayed there until the band came back out again. Shannon quickly realized that the band was not a jazz band when their first song was a cover of The Kink's *Come Dancing*.

After *Come Dancing* it was time for bed.

By the time we got back to the hotel room, I glanced at the clock and it was only midnight! Man, were we old farts or what!?

I still had the midnight munchies, so I finished off my leftovers from Carl R's.

I woke the next morning around 9am. There was a rumble in my tummy, and I didn't think it was gas. I quickly hopped out of bed and duck walked over to the commode. I duck walked because I didn't want anything to squeak out.

Once I plopped my ham down on the seat, I gave it all I had and let 'er rip. I had to say that my own brew was too much for me and I almost passed out due to the mass abundance of methane gas.

When I was finished, I got up to check out my handy work...

"Wow!" I exclaimed! I did not realize how much poop I had in me! I was so full of shit, that I made my own Hershey Kiss Island! It was like a Hawaiian island: there was so much pooh that a tiny poop island formed. I named my little poop island *Aloha!*

Then it was time for a shower.

Yesterday when we checked in, the receptionist Kim told us the hotel offered a free continental breakfast. Normally I never partook in the continental breakfasts because I was not a breakfast person. However, that morning, I was feeling hungry, so I woke Shannon up and we went down to the lobby for breakfast.

Breakfast was nice. I had a bowl of fruit, a chocolate Belgian Waffle, and some OJ.

While we were having breakfast, we notice a few older people come in who were wearing Rochester Americans sweatshirts.

Shannon and I struck up a conversation with them. "Hey, did you guys go to the game?" I asked.

The one lady said, "Yes we were there! Were you?"

I said, "Yes, we were there. It was a good game. Are you going to Albany this afternoon?"

The lady said, "Yes, we're going. We are a part of the Rochester Americans Booster Club..."

I didn't know that the Amerks had a booster club or that the Amerks Booster Club followed the team on the road once a month. We talked for a few minutes before Shannon and I finished our breakfast.

Shannon and I then went back up to our room and gathered our stuff.

When we checked out, I asked Kim the receptionist where the actual Glens Falls was located.

Kim informed me that the "falls" were located just behind the civic center. I thanked Kim and then Shannon and I left.

As we exited the Queensbury Hotel, Shannon noticed the pool and hot tub! She was upset that we didn't get to utilize either. Shannon said that we needed to come back and stay at the Queensbury again and check out the rest of Glens Falls, Saratoga, Lake George, and the rest of the Adirondacks. I did not object, but I told her that we should do it next hockey season since the current AHL season was almost over and that next season would be the last season that the Phantoms would be in Glens Falls. The Phantom were slated to move to Allentown, Pennsylvania for the start of the 2014-15 AHL season.

Once Shannon and I were packed up in the van, I drove across the street to the Rite Aid. I was looking for some post cards that I could send to mom, Grandpa Ziggy, and a few other people. Rite Aid did not stock post cards, so I got Grandpa Ziggy the next best thing, the newspaper. Rite Aid had two different papers, so I got him both; the Post Star and the Times Union.

After Rite Aid, Shannon and I drove down Ridge Street, through the traffic circle and onto Glen Street towards the falls.

We found a parking spot right next to the falls.

Well, I won't lie. Because I grew up in South Central Grand Island, Niagara Falls was always in my back yard, and I became accustomed to and a little spoiled with that. Now whenever I saw a water fall, I would yawn and say, "You call that a waterfall?"

Needless to say, Glens Falls was tiny. To put it in prospective, it was smaller than the High Falls in Rochester.

Though, I am glad to say that I saw the Glens Falls!

Shortly thereafter, Shannon and I were en route to Albany, New York...

It was about an hour ride from Glens Falls down to Albany. We were en route to the New York State Museum in downtown Albany. However, our first mission was to find downtown Albany.

From Glens Falls, we took I-78 south to the 90. From the 90, we picked up I-787. 787 dumped us off in downtown and right in front of the USS Slater. The USS Slater was a restored World War II Destroyer Escort, and made its home right on the Hudson River.

I was tempted to see the USS Slater, but Shannon and I were strapped for time. It was noon when we hit downtown and the game was at 4pm. Shannon and I had a greater interest seeing the NYS Museum.

It was a challenge to find parking downtown, but we finally found a spot.

As we walked up to the NYS Museum, the wind almost swept us away! It was quite a windy day in the capital city region.

The bulk of the NYS Museum is located on the first floor, so that is where we started.

I enjoyed that the museum was free, but I instantly was not thrilled with the museum because there were mannequins and taxidermy wildlife scenes almost everywhere...it creeped me out.

A section of the museum was Minerals of New York and featured a whole bunch of rocks and minerals that were mined in New York. Thanks to that exhibit, I now had a new favorite rock, Cummingtonite $(Mg,Fe)_7Si_8O_{22}(OH)_2$. I giggled uncontrollably like Beavis and Butt-Head for about five minutes when I read the name of the rock.

Another part of the museum was about Adirondack Recreation back in the early 1900s. A part of the exhibit featured a car that was manufactured in Syracuse, NY! The car on display was a 1921 Franklin 9-B Runabout. According to the plaque, the Franklin on hand had a wood frame, an aluminum body, and an air cooled engine.

The museum had displays about New York's native people, the Indians. There were some Indian artifacts and a replica Longhouse.

The museum had a Mastodon skeleton, which was very interesting to look at. The Mastodon's tusks were too heavy to be displayed with the skeleton, so casts were made of the original tucks. The Mastodon's left tusk was on display in a case and the right one was in a vault or library within the museum.

Shannon and I made our way to the New York Metropolis part of the museum. This area was about the development of the Big Apple, the birth of its skyscrapers, Fifth Avenue, South Street Seaport, and Harlem in the 1920s.

There was also a Sesame Street exhibit, which brought me back years. The museum had an original set from the show. Even Oscar the Grouch was there, garbage can and all!

Next, Shannon and I toured the World Trade Center exhibit. The exhibit featured artifacts that were removed from the debris of the Twin Towers. A fire truck from Engine 6 was the main focal point of the exhibit. Engine 6's fire truck had been partially destroyed during the events of 9/11. Engine 6 not only lost a fire engine, but it also lost four fire fighters. The exhibit paid homage to the four fallen heroes of Engine 6; Paul Beyer, Billy Johnston, Tom Holohan, and Tom O'Hagan. The exhibit was quite moving. There was also a piece on the history of the World Trade Center, from its conception and building process to the first attack in 1993, and the horrible day in 2001.

Next to the World Trade Center exhibit was the Fire Engine Hall. I enjoyed the Fire Engine Hall. There were roughly 15 fire engines on display and I liked how a few of them were built locally in New York; Elmira and Seneca Falls.

Shannon and I stopped off in the gift shop where they had post cards. I bought a few post cards for mom and Grandpa Ziggy. I always tried to think about grandpa when I went on the hockey trips. I tried to get him a post card or the paper from where I had been because I knew he appreciated it.

Grandpa Ziggy especially enjoyed getting post cards because he would send them off to his family in Poland and show him how beautiful America was.

When Shannon and I were finished with the 1st Floor, it was around 2:30pm. I told Shannon that I wanted to check out the carousel on the 4th Floor. Shannon thought it was a little weird that I wanted to see a carousel, but I wanted to see if it was a carousel that was built in North Tonawanda, NY.

Shannon and I hopped onto the elevator and went up to the 4th Floor.

When we arrived on the 4th Floor, I was so excited to see that the New York State Museum had a Pierce-Arrow! Pierce-Arrow was a Buffalo made luxury car from 1901-1938. Just like Syracuse's Franklin, Buffalo's Pierce-Arrow fell victim to the Great Depression.

The Pierce-Arrow on display was 1931 Pierce-Arrow Type 43. According to the plaque, it was a seven passenger sedan. It was one of 160 Type 43 and cost $2,995 back in the day ($42,900 in 2010).

Along with the Pierce-Arrow, the museum displayed a 1932 Packard. Though Packard was originally a Detroit built car, the 1932 Packard Phaeton had a little New York State and American history to it...It was once used by New York State Governor Franklin D. Roosevelt. That's right, before FDR became President of the US of America, he was New York State's Governor.

According to the plaque in front of the automobile, the model 905 1932 Packard Phaeton on display was purchased by FDR in 1932 for his use in Albany. "When he was elected to the Presidency, it became part of the State Fleet. Though kept in running condition, it was rarely used after 1942 when Governor Thomas Dewey acquired a Cadillac. However, Governor Hugh Carey transported Queen Beatrix and Prince Claus of the Netherlands in the Packard when they arrived in 1982."

Who knew that cars had a big part in American history!? There should be classes in schools about American Automotive! American Cars had such great art and beauty from their curves, lines, and designs along with great technological history and advancement.

After seeing the Packard, I rushed over to the carousel. The Herschell-Spillman Carousel was made in North Tonawanda, New York! Accompanying the New York State made carousel was a music box. The music that was provided by a Wurlitzer Band Organ, also made in North Tonawanda! According to the plaque, "The Model 125 Wurlitzer Band Organ was constructed around 1925 by the Rudolph Wurlitzer Company of North Tonawanda, New York, which was located near the Herschell-Spillman Company...In 1956 the organ was removed for repairs while at Olivercrest Park and never returned. With the death of the owner J. Fenton "Bog" Olive, memory of the music machine passed away. Forty-four years later, news reached Bruce Plano of Cuba, New York of the State Museum's plans to restore the carousel. Plano had bought the forgotten Wurlitzer and kept it in his garage. He called the State Museum and reunited the carousel with the band organ, and it has remained here ever since...The Wurlitzer Band Organ was designed to play outdoors to attract large crowds at fairs and carnivals. The band organ is so loud that it causes some of the State Museum's windows to vibrate!"

Around the corner, there was a Salamanca Back Bar that was built in Buffalo.

I liked how the New York State Museum was a New York State pride museum. Though I felt as if they could have had more New York made artifacts and history.

After we toured the 4th Floor, it was time for food!

For lunch, we decided to hunt out Wolff's Biergarten und wurt haus. Our buddy Karl recommended Wolff's to us, so we needed to find it.

Wolff's was located on 895 Broadway, just outside of downtown.

As we drove down Broadway, we figured that we were getting close to Wolff's because we saw a building with a huge German flag flying on top of it.

Wolff's looked like it was inside an old fire engine house. The building had a huge red garage door too. It reminded me of the Ghostbusters HQ in NYC.

Shannon and I made our way to the order counter. Shannon ordered the Vegetarian Currywurst. I ordered Wolff's mac and cheese with sides of sauerkraut and red cabbage.

Next we ordered beer. For our first round, Shannon had Weihenstephaner Vitus and I had a Weihenstephaner Korbinian. As we waited for our food, the NY Yankees game was on one TV while rugby or soccer was on the other tube. Wolff's had a taxidermy deer bust, which creeped me out, so I sat with my back facing it. There were also four real dart boards up against the back wall with metal tipped darts.

Our food finally came and it was awesome! The red cabbage tasted just like Nana used to make it. The sauerkraut was wonderful as well. The kraut had caraway seeds mixed in with it and it tasted like eating sauerkraut on a rye bread sandwich! Wolff's mac and cheese was exquisite. There were big kid sized macaroni that were doused in a creamy cheese. I would drive back there again just for the food.

I knew Shannon and I would be hungry after the game. I looked at the menu and it said that Wolff's closed at 4pm on Sundays. So Shannon and I ordered the Loaded Pig to go. The Load

Pig was a grilled stuffed sausage with sauerkraut and a spicy onion relish, smothered with cheese sauce and topped with bacon! It also came with fries and a single bypass.

While we waited for our Loaded Pig, I revisited the bar and ordered an Oktoberfest for Shannon and me to split. Once our to-go meal came, we polished off the Oktoberfest and split for the Time Union Center.

Shannon and I drove back down Broadway towards downtown and found parking next to the Times Union Center.

It was a quiet afternoon at the Times Union Center; there were not a whole heck of a lot of people at the game. If anything, fans may have been split 50/50; half for the Albany Devils and half for the Rochester Amerks.

In case you couldn't figure it out by their name, the Albany Devils were the farm team for the New Jersey Devils.

Though there was no scoring in the 1st Period didn't mean that nothing happened! Amerks forward Cody McCormick got dinged half way through the 1st Period with two minutes for roughing and a ten minute misconduct penalty.

On a brighter note, recently acquired goaltender Matt Hackett turned away all 13 shots that he faced in the opening period. The 1st Period ended in a 0-0 stalemate.

It wasn't until the last minutes of the 2nd Period that we got our first goal of the game. The goal was unfavorable for Hackett and Amerks fans. Reid Boucher blasted a one timer past Hackett for a 1-0 Devils lead.

During the 2nd Intermission, Shannon went to get some beers. Shannon got me a Corona in a can. Normally I do not complain about beer or mind canned beer, but Corona did not taste as well in a can; I prefer it in a bottle. On Shannon's behalf, it was the thought that counted!

Albany kicked off the 3rd Period by netting their second goal from the hands of Jean-Sebastien Berube; 2-0 Devils lead.

Less than a minute later, we had our first fight of the afternoon! Albany's Jay Leach and Rochester's Corey Tropp dropped the gloves right in front of the Albany bench. Tropp landed a couple sucker punches to Leach's kisser, but Leach came back hard. Leach then gave a few good right handed blows to Tropp's dome. The two grappled as they tried to get their throwing arms freed. The two threw a couple more punches that landed, but you could tell they were getting tired. Towards the end of the tango, the two were throwing "air bombs" that were nowhere near close to hitting anything. The officials soon skated in to break up the paddy cake session.

A few minutes later, Rochester was on the power play. Moments later, they found themselves down by one goal. The Amerks had come through on the power play with a goal by Nick Crawford that clanked off the pipe. Rochester trailed, 1-2 with more than 12 minutes left to go in the 3rd Period!

As the seconds ticked by in the 3rd, the clock was an enemy to the Amerks. It didn't help either when Drew Schiestel took a delay of game penalty with under 8 minutes left in the 3rd. And matters only seemed worse when Amerks' Maxime Legault took a 4 minute double minor high sticking penalty with under 5 minutes left in regulation.

During that double minor, thankfully the Amerks penalty kill showed up and put on some offense! The Amerks were able to gain control of the puck in the neutral zone and Rochester's Zemgus Girgensons skated into the Albany zone, and was able to snap a wrister past the Devils goaltender Keith Kinkaid! Girgensons' shorthanded goal had tied the game!

Regulation ended in a 2-2 tie.

During Overtime, the Amerks just smothered the Devils with shots. Rochester tallied 9 shots to Albany's 1. However, none of the shots reached the back of the net!

Ladies and Germs, we were going to our 2nd Shootout in as many nights!

Once again, Rochester had the honors of shooting first in the Shootout!

New boy Johan Larsson skated first for Rochester. Larsson put Rochester on the board with a quick wrist shot that made it past Albany's Kinkaid.

Mike Sislo shot next for Albany but new Amerk Hackett made the save.

Cory Tropp went 2nd for Rochester and was able to get the puck past the Albany net minder Kinkand.

The Devil's Reid Boucher tried his luck, but Hackett snatched the puck out of the air.

At the beginning of Round 3, Rochester led 2-0.

Colin Jacobs skated next for the Amerks. Jacobs skated in on the far side and quadruple deked twice before sending the puck into the back of the net via the 5 hole!

Rochester was up 3-0 half way through the shootout! All Rochester needed was for Hackett to stop the next shooter and they would have won their second shootout in a row!

Albany's Matt Anderson grabbed the puck at center ice and skated into the Amerks' zone. Anderson rushed into the zone and tried to be all razzle dazzle, but Hackett came up with the right pad save to win the game for Rochester!

It was a weird feeling leaving the game. First of all, it was 6:30pm and the sun was still out! Secondly, the Amerks had won both weekend games; both in the shootout!

Once we hopped in the van, we were bound for Rochester. We took I-787 to the 90 and the 90 took us all the way back to ROC City. It was a scenic drive back down the 90 because we were parallel with the Erie Canal and we could see the foothills of the Adirondacks off in the distance. It was around 10:15pm when we got home.

2013 Playoffs

There were hockey playoffs in Western New York! I was still boycotting the NHL. The Sabres stank and did not make the playoffs, but the Rochester Americans did! The Amerks squeaked into the 7th playoff seed of the Western Conference of the AHL.

Rochester was to face one of their arch nemeses, the Toronto Marlies, in a best of 5 game series.

Rochester was swept in 3 games. The first round of the AHL playoffs were a best of 5 game series.

2013 Offseason

On May 7, 2013 (My Nana's birthday, may God rest her dear soul) Sabres General Manager Darcy Regier announced that interim head coach Ron Rolston had now become the official head coach of the Buffalo Sabres.

I liked the move. As I mentioned earlier, I felt as if Rolston did a good job in Rochester. I think he did a good job when he took over as interim coach in Buffalo, considering the hand that he had been dealt.

Other than that move, not much else was done as in personnel. Once Free Agency came, Darcy did what he had always done best, nothing. There were no big name Hollywood players to bring to Buffalo.

The Sabres also parted way with Nathan "Rudy Ruettiger" Gerbe. I liked Gerbe, but he was just too tiny. And that butt monkey Zdeno Chara loved to pick on Gerbe. I liked how Gerbe wouldn't shy away or back down from that fartknocker.

There was a lot of talk about Thomas Vanek and Ryan Miller being traded during the Offseason, but that never happened. Both players were on the last year of their contract, so there were high hopes that both would show up to play for the upcoming season. Only time would tell.

President Ted Black of the Buffalo Sabres announced during the summer that the team would have a new 3rd jersey for the upcoming season. There were hopes that the new 3rd jersey would make the Sabres not suck and play better. I reiterate, *there were hopes*. The 3rd jersey looked like crap in my opinion. It was a yellow jersey on the front and a blue jersey on the back...it looked like boxes of mac and cheese were skating around on the ice. People dubbed the 3rd jersey the "turd burger."

The Sabres named Thomas Vanek and Steve Ott as team co-captains...*woo-hoo, who cares.*

On another note, former head coach Lindy Ruff found work in Dallas as the Stars' new head coach.

After being fired by new head coach Rolston, assistant coach James Patrick found a job down in Dallas as Lindy's new assistant coach. Buffalo management should have made a package deal, a trifecta, and shipped Darcy Regier out along with them.

Well, Sabres owner Terry Pegula had owned the team for three seasons. When he first bought the team, he said Buffalo would have a Stanley Cup within three years. I suppose if one wanted to be optimistic or see some truth in Pegula's promise, then there was some merit to his promise. Though the Sabres did not make the playoffs last season, let alone win the Stanley Cup, it did make an appearance in Buffalo in August 2013. South Buffalo's own and Chicago Blackhawk's forward Pat Kane, who won the Cup in 2013 with the Blackhawks, brought it home to Buffalo for all to see. Collectively as a community, we were all happy for Pat, a local boy winning the Cup. It seemed for now; it would be the closest thing for Buffalo to winning the Stanley Cup...

Another thing that happened was the reorganizations of the conferences and divisions.

Lastly, my boycott of the NHL had come to an end. I had a started a journey four years ago and I needed to finish my mission: watching the Buffalo Sabres play in every NHL arena! It was time for the home stretch!

October 2013

Shannon and I didn't have any hockey road trips slated for October. All of the Sabres away games for the month of October were cities that we already visited, and we couldn't repeat cities.

But to give a brief update on the Sabres during the month of October, nothing much was happening, quite literally. By the end of October, the Sabres were 2-12-1. The Sabres went 0-7 before finally getting their first victory against the New York Islanders.

And funny I should mention the New York Islanders. On Sunday October 27, Sabres GM Darcy Regier traded the Bums' captain Thomas Vanek to the New York Islanders for Matt Moulson and a couple drafts (*"Mmm...beer"*—Homer Simpson).

Moulson scored two goals in his Sabres debut.

November 2013

The month of November brought the first road trip of the new hockey season!

It was the wee hours of Thursday morning November 7, 2013. My alarm woke me up at 3:40am. I had a 5:41am flight from Rochester to Philly and then from Philly to Los Angeles.

Surprisingly I had my bag packed the night before. The only thing I needed to do was to brush my teeth, feed Teppo, and let Teppo go to the bathroom.

I was in my van and on the road by 4am.

Moments later I drove around the corner and picked up my father-in-law Jimbo. The plan was for me to drive to the airport and Jimbo would take my van so he could get to work at Kodak (Yes, Kodak was still around in 2013. A few months earlier, Kodak had emerged from bankruptcy. I bet George Eastman was spinning in his grave, seeing what had been done to his company over the years).

I was flying alone from Rochester to LA. Shannon was in Houston at a work conference. The plan was for Shannon and me to meet up with her cousins in LA and go to the Buffalo Sabres @ LA Kings game. Then after the game we were to drive out to Las Vegas for Shannon's family reunion; that was the plan, sounded simple enough…

I was at the Rochester airport by 4:30am.

Shannon had booked my flight through US Airways. I went to the US Air kiosk to check my bag and get my boarding pass.

My bag that I was checking contained two 30 packs of Genesee Cream Ale for Shannon's Uncle Bill. The two 30 packs in my suit case were overweight. Check in bags could only weight up to 50 pounds; my bag was 63 pounds.

The US Air lady working the desk asked if I could put anything from my suitcase in my bag.

I told the lady, "I don't think so…it's beer."

The US Air rep looked at me with a puzzled look, "Beer?"

I said, "Yea, I'm bringing some beer out to Vegas for my Uncle Bill. It's a family reunion and they can't get our beer out there."

The US Air rep looked at me and said, "Well, if we can get your first bag underweight, it will be free. The second bag will be a $30 charge. I think we have a box in back that we can put your beer in."

A few moments later, the rep was back with a box, one big enough to fit the 30 pack of Genny Scream Ale.

I paid the extra $30 and got my boarding pass.

Soon I was waiting in line for security. After some time, I passed through security and found my way to my gate. A few minutes later, I was aboard my plane to Philly.

Now the plan was for me to land in Philly at 6:55am and for me to catch my connecting flight that departed Philly at 7:35am. I was to land in LAX by 10:42am, pick up the rental car, putz around

LA for a bit, pick Jen and Chad up at Union Station at 2:40pm, pick up Shannon at LAX at 4:30pm, and drive to the Staples Center for the hockey game...the plan was like communism, in theory it worked.

My flight landed in Philly on time, at 6:55am. Then we had to taxi off the run way and down the tarmac to the terminal. We arrived at Terminal F, but apparently the airport wasn't ready for us; so we just sat there for a few minutes. It was well after 7:10am when the airport put the accordion thing on the airplane's door. Then we were allowed to exit the aircraft.

By the time I exited the plane, it was 7:15am. I needed to get from Terminal F to Terminal A before 7:35am, otherwise I would miss my flight.

I had to wait for a metro bus to pick me up at Terminal F to bring me to Terminal A.

Once at Terminal A, I had to take an escalator to the main floor. Once I reached the top of the escalator, I encountered two "traffic cones." There were two old ladies that parked their butts right at the top of the escalator, who were obviously lost. They were lucky that I didn't topple over them and break both their hips.

As I ran down the concourse to my gate, I glanced at the time, 7:30am! "Good!" I thought, "I still have time to make the flight!"

As I approached the desk at my gate, the two US Air reps told me that I missed my flight.

I looked at them and said, "No I didn't. The plane is right there. My flight doesn't leave for another 5 minutes!"

They informed me that they close the door to the airplane 10 minutes before takeoff, hence I was late. They told me to go to US Air customer service in Terminal B to iron everything out...Pucking US Air!

I angrily walked over to Terminal B. At the very end of Terminal B was where US Air Customer Service was located. Yet again, I stood in another line.

A few minutes passed and I was soon talking to the customer service rep. I told her what had happened. The customer service rep gave me a stand by voucher for a 10am flight and an official voucher for a 4pm flight, which would get me into LA at 7:15pm at the earliest!

As I walked away from customer service, I called Shannon up to tell her what had happened. Shannon was quite upset with US Air. It wasn't my fault I missed my flight, it's not like I took a half hour long dump between connecting flights. Shannon told me I needed to go back to customer service and complain, so that's what I did.

I went back to customer service and got the nice lady again. I told the customer service lady my story; that I needed to be in LA by 3pm to pick Jen and Chad up at the train station and Shannon up at LAX by 4:30pm because all four of us were going to the Sabres/Kings game at 7:30pm that night.

The lady was nice and was able to reroute me to LA, via Cleveland.

My new itinerary had me leaving on US Air to Cleveland at 9:30am. Once in Cleveland, I was switching carriers. I was to take a United flight at 12:30pm that would get me to LAX with plenty of time. I thanked the customer service lady.

It was now 7:45am and I had some time to kill before my next flight, so I decided to do one of the things that I was best at; I found the closest bar and bellied right up to it!

I found myself at Jet Rock Bar and Grill; it was located kitty corner to gate B1, my gate for Cleveland.

I noticed that the bar had Southern Tier Pumpking Ale, so I ordered one of those. The bartender grabbed a glass, poured the brew, and put it on the bar for me.

"Wow!" I said in shock. "That's one tiny ass cup!"

I didn't know what the bartender's name was, but let's call her Brandy. Brandy said, "Yes, I know. It's a specialty beer and we can only serve it in 12 ounce glasses."

Brandy came back through with the bill. I hope my eyes didn't shoot out of my head like Roger Rabbit, but I was shocked that the 12 ounce beer was $7.80. Back home, I could go to Wegmans or Beers of the World where it was cheaper and I get more fluid ounces, but oh well, I was on vacation.

The Pumpking Ale was very delicious. It tasted just like pumpkin pie!

Once I finished my Pumpking Ale, I still had time for another beer. Brandy asked me if I wanted another Pumpking.

I said, "No, but what kind of beer can I get that's more than 12 ounces?"

I ended up getting a pint of Goose Island. Shannon had Goose Island a few years back when we went to Chicago to watch the Sabres lose to the Blackhawks.

There was nothing like beer for breakfast; rockin' a buzz at 8:45 in the morning.

Once I finished my second beer, it was time to close out my tab and pee before I hopped on the airplane.

The flight to Cleveland was a cold one. It felt like someone had left a window or two open in the airplane.

I landed in Cleveland at 11am. Once in the airport, I walked to find my terminal and gate. Once I established my bearings, I decided to grab a bite to eat. I had some shitty Villa pizza.

To wash the taste of shit pizza out of my mouth, I had a tall boy of Edmund Fitzgerald Porter at the Great Lake Brew Pub. I figured the Edmund Fitzgerald was a wise choice for a beer before a hockey game because Gordon Lightfoot sang about the Edmund Fitzgerald in the song *The Wreck of the Edmund Fitzgerald*. Also, Gordon Lightfoot was Canadian, and hockey was a Canadian thing.

It was noon and I pounded the rest of my Edmund before cashing out at the bar; the last thing I wanted to do was to miss another flight!

I made it to my gate on time and was in my seat well before the airplane's doors were closed.

My flight from Cleveland had landed at LAX at 2:15pm Western Standard Time. Though I was a few hours behind schedule, I thought I still had enough time to get the rental car, pick up Jen and Chad from Union Station, get Shannon from LAX, and make it to the game on time; with the possibility of grabbing some beers before the game.

I made my way through the airport and down to the luggage carousel and waited for my bag...and waited...and waited. My bags never showed up.

It was around 3pm when I was talking to Candice at United Baggage Claim. I told her what had happened with my flights; how I missed my US Air connection in Philly and how I got bumped to United in Cleveland. After almost an hour, Candice was able to locate my bags; they were still in Cleveland. Candice told me that I would be able to pick up my bags at LAX at 7:30 that night.

I told Candice that I was unable to pick up my bags at 7:30 that night. I informed her how I still had to pick up the rental car, pick up Jen and Chad from Union Station, and then come back to pick up Shannon at LAX before we left for the Sabres game at Staples Center. I added that after the game, all four of us were driving right out to Vegas for a family reunion.

In the meantime, I had called Jen and told her that I probably wouldn't be able to pick her and Chad up. I informed her that Staples Center wasn't too far away from Union Station. Jen said that she and Chad would take a cab over to Staples Center and find a watering hole. I told her that that sounded like a great plan and that I would call her when I got the car situation ironed out...

Candice told me that US Air didn't have any flights going to Vegas that night, but United did. I told Candice that that sounded good and that I could pick up my bags at the Las Vegas airport the following day.

Candice wanted to know what my two bags looked like. I told her that one was a cardboard box and the other was a blue plastic clamshell suitcase with wheels and a handle.

Candice asked, "What's in the box you checked in?"

I said, "Uh...beer."

Candice looked up from her computer monitor with a shocked look. "Beer?" she asked.

I said, "Yeah, beer."

Candice sounded concerned, "Well how did you pack it? Did you pack it properly?"

I answered, "Oh yes. It's fine. It's a 30 pack of cans, not glass. US Air helped me pack it this morning at the airport in Rochester."

Relief came from Candice's voice, "Oh okay! What's in the blue suitcase?"

With a little hesitation, I said, "Uh...more beer."

"Wow! Good Lord, you guys know how to party! You brought two 30 packs of beer with you, you're going to the hockey game tonight, and then to Vegas! Wow! You guys know how to party! That must be some special kind of beer?!"

I told Candice, "Yes, well it's for my Uncle Bill out in Vegas. We have a family reunion and he can't get this kind of beer out there."

Candice asked, "What kind of beer is it?"

I said, "Genesee."

"Genesee?" Candice said with a puzzled look. "Isn't that the dark beer?"

I said, "No, that's Guinness that you are thinking of."

Candice inquired, "Well then what's Genesee?"

I said, "Genesee Brewery is located on the Genesee River in Rochester. The Genesee River flows north bound through the City of Rochester before it dumps into Lake Ontario of the Great Lakes."

"Oh, ok. Must be some kind of beer?"

Genesee Cream Ale is definitely some kind of beer; it's **EPIC!**

After Candice and I ironed everything out at Baggage Claim, it was close to 4pm. Candice gave me directions to the bus stop for the car rental shuttles.

Minutes later, I was on the bus for Dollar Rent A Car.

It was about a 10 minute bus ride from LAX to Dollar rental.

The bus took its sweet ass time pulling into the Dollar facility. As soon as the doors to the bus opened, I flew off the bus like a bat out of hell and into the Dollar rental facility. That's when I was greeted by a huge line of people waiting for cars. No lie, the line was at least 75 people deep! "Oh *puck*!" was what I uttered when I saw the line. Yet again, I was to wait and stand in another line!

Seconds later, Shannon texted me that she landed in LAX from Houston. I gave Shannon a call and said, "Hi Shannon, my phone is chirping at me and it's about to die. I just got to Dollar car rental. Can you take the shuttle from LAX and meet me here?" Shannon agreed and said she would try to get there as fast as she could, but I told her to take her time because I was going to be at Dollar Rental for a while.

It took Shannon almost an hour to meet up with me at Dollar rental. She had to wait for the plane to dock at the gate, get off the plane, get her bag at the carousel, and hop on the Dollar shuttle so it was around 5pm when Shannon met up with me! In the meantime, Shannon and I were giving Jen updates on our status in line.

It was 6pm when Shannon and I were finally in our rental car! We selected a Dodge Avenger over a Toyota Corolla. I was not going to willingly drive a Toyota, nor would I ever own a Toyota. I could not support any country that bombed the USA. It's like what Grandpa Ziggy said, "Toyota?! Who would buy a Jap car? They make the world's poorest tools! Why would you want to buy a car from them?!"

Dr. Emmitt Brown shared the same thoughts and ideas as Grandpa Ziggy. In the beginning of *Back to the Future Part III*, Doc blamed the DeLorean on not working due to faulty Japanese electronic components. However, Marty McFly tried to tell Doc that the best stuff was made in Japan.

As Americans, we were dumb. We had sold out, sold our sovereignty. Japan bombed Pearl Harbor, and now we buy cars from them. Tell you what, in about 30 years from now when Al Qaeda makes their own production car, Americans will buy them up like hot cakes. Just like Toyota had a gas pedal problem, the Al Qaeda car would have an exploding problem. The dumb Americans would be driving their Al Qaeda made cars and wonder why they were exploding down the highway.

Anyway, enough with politics and back to hockey and beer drinking!

The Sabres game that night was slated to start at 7:30pm. Shannon and I had an hour and a half to drive the 10 or so miles from LAX to Staples Center. I figured we had enough time to meet up with Jen and Chad before the game and grab a beer or two.

Shannon and I weren't even on I-105 and we hit grid lock traffic. We were on the entrance ramp to I-105 and it was a parking lot. It took us an hour to drive I-105 to I-110 to Staples Center.

About an hour later, Shannon and I found parking two blocks away from Staples Center. Shannon phoned Jen to find out where Jen and Chad were.

Jen said she and Chad needed to close out their tab and then they would try to find us.

Minutes later, both parties were lost. Shannon and Jen were both on the phone, trying to find out where we were. Since we could see Hooters, we decided to convene in front of it. Moments later we bumped into each other in front of the Hooters on Figueroa Street.

The four of us walked back to the car to put Jen and Chad's luggage in the Avenger. Then, with Sabres jerseys on, we walked into the Staples Center for the game!

Headed into that night's game, the Sabres were DFL (dead *pucking* last) in the league.

Our tickets were in the 400 level of the Staple Center. Once we found where our seats were, it was time to find beer.

I knew that since we weren't in Western New York, the beer selection was going to suck. I sucked it up and I ordered a Butt Light at the concession stand. Shannon ordered a girly drink, Shock Top with an orange.

We plopped down in our seats just in time for play.

As I took a look around, I noticed that half of Staples Center was full. I was extremely surprised! I was amazed that a city with over 10 million people had trouble filling a 20,000 seat hockey arena. Thankfully there was a good Buffalo presence at the game. Of the half-filled Staples Center, at least a quarter of the fans were Sabre fans.

The Sabres came out strong in the beginning of the 1st Period. The Sabres peppered LA's goaltender Jonathan Quick with a ton of shots, but Quick was too quick to the Sabres.

Late in the 1st Period, Buffalo first found themselves on the penalty kill. Moments later, the Sabres found themselves down a goal. LA's Michael Richards scored on the power play with under 30 seconds left in the period.

During the 1st Intermission, Shannon and her cousin Jen talked and caught up.

The 2nd Period was not a good period for the Sabres.

The Sabres had two power plays early in the 2nd Period, but couldn't do squat with either of them, hence the "power-less play."

Midway through the 2nd Period, the Sabres found themselves shorthanded, again. The Sabres were on a 3-on-4 penalty kill. One could see the upcoming play happen before it unfolded, the Kings' Anze Kopitar scored a power play goal against Buffalo's goalie Jhonas Enroth to give the Kings a 2-0 lead.

Toward the end of the 2nd Period, a King took a run at a defenseless Sabre. Buffalo Sabre Tyler Myers did not take too kindly to the Kings' aggression. For once, Myers threw his Prada purse down, threw off his fancy elbow length dress gloves and attacked the opponent! Myers started a fight with Kings Matt Frattin. Myers threw three hay makers, all of which were whiffs that hit the numbers on Frattin's back. The linesmen came rushing in to break up the cat fight. The two players both got five minute majors for fighting, but Myers got whacked with another two minutes for holding; a chicken poop penalty if you ask me.

Throughout the game, Chad was feeling the side effects from the happy hour that he and Jen experienced before the game. Unfortunately for Chad, during the 2nd Intermission, he was cock blocked at the concession stand from getting a round of beer. The beer wench told Chad, "I'm not serving you. Your eyes look bloodshot."

To that, Chad said, "I'm not feeling well. I'm sick. I have the flu..."

Chad was still c-blocked. Instead, Chad walked to another concession stand where he was able to get another beer!

The 3rd Period started and the Sabres couldn't get anything done. LA's goalie Quick was too much for the weak, young, talentless Sabres.

With time ticking away at the end of the 3rd Period, the Sabres pulled their goalie. I thought it was quite dumb that the Sabres were pulling their goaltender for the extra attacker. Obviously, for the entire game, the Sabres could not get their act together. Even when they were on the power play and had the extra attacker, they still couldn't do anything. I wanted to know what made Coach Rolston and the rest of the bums on the Sabres bench think they had a shot at breaking Quick's shutout.

Needless to say, Jonathan Quick got his shutout as the Kings defeated the Buffalo Bums 2-0.

After the game, Jen, Shannon, Chad, and I piled back into the Avenger. We hopped onto I-10 east and snaked our way to I-15 north to Las Vegas!

As we left LA, we saw the exit for San Dimas, the home of Bill S. Preston ESQ. and Ted Theodore Logan!

It took a little longer than anticipated to get to Vegas.

The four of us finally pulled into the party house at 3am Pacific Time Zone (6am Eastern Time Zone). I had been up for well over 27 hours! It was bedtime. By the time I hit the hay, I was wide awake! It took me probably 20 minutes to unwind and pass out.

I was wide awake by 9:30 Friday morning; I had barely gotten 6 hours of sleep. There were about 20 Parker family members at the party house in North Las Vegas. It took a while to coordinate 20 people to agree upon something and then to do it. It was around noon when everyone went out for lunch.

After lunch, everyone returned back to the party house to hang out. I however needed to run out to McCarran International Airport and pick up my luggage of beer for Uncle Bill!

My mom in law Joan, brother in law Kyle, wife Shannon, and I hopped into the Avenger to go to the airport.

What should have been a quick 15 minute trip turned into an hour long ride to the airport because I-15 was a parking lot.

I eventually got my luggage from United.

After the four of us left the airport, we made our way to valet parking at Harrah's Casino. I had been to Vegas a few times before and I liked to park at valet at Harrah's because Harrah's was a centralized location on the Strip. Plus it is right next to my favorite casino in Las Vegas, Casino Royal.

Joan, Kyle, Shannon, and I walked through Harrah's to Casino Royal. I wanted some $1 Michelob beers and to do some gambling; roulette to be specific.

For the record, the last time Shannon and I were in Las Vegas was two years previous. Casino Royal used to have $1 strawberry or lime daiquiris. However, they had discontinued the daiquiris.

Once I got a round of Mic Lights for everyone, I was going to play some roulette. As soon as I approached the roulette table, I noticed the group of numbers I always played (0/00 and 26) had come up one right after each other. I decided to not play.

Instead we all walked over to the Venetian. Kyle had not been to the Venetian before and Shannon and I liked to walk through the shopping area. I was not a shopper, but the inside of the Venetian reminded me of Italy at EPCOT in Disney World.

While at the Venetian, Shannon had some cantaloupe and green apple gelato. It tasted good, but it wasn't my thing.

We left the Venetian and went back to the Strip. We were going to show Kyle the inside of Caesars Palace when the volcano show at the Mirage started, so the four of us rerouted to the Mirage to watch the volcano show. The volcano show reminded me of

Disney's Fantasmic at Hollywood Studios (formerly MGM Studios) in Disney World, except that there was no Mickey Mouse or other characters; just fire and brimstone.

After the four minute volcano show, we walked next door to Caesars Palace.

I told Kyle that Caesars has two animatronic shows at the Forum Shops. I informed him that they were pretty old and crappy animatronics, possibly Disney rejects.

Then Kyle said, "Oh you mean like the ones in the Carousel of Progress at the Magic Kingdom?"

I said, "Yes, just as creepy and scary, but they don't sing *There's A Great Big Beautiful Tomorrow.* They talk about being Roman gods and there's water and fire. One of the 'stages' even doubles as an aquarium."

Fortunately for me, I did not have to deal with any creepy animatronics because they were down for maintenance and restoration.

We did not stay too long at Caesars because we needed to meet up with the rest of the family for dinner at 6pm at Big Dog's Draft House on Ranchero Drive.

I was still full by the time we got to Big Dog's Draft House, so I just ordered a Leg Lifter Light beer. I enjoyed the Leg Lifter Light beer; it went down easy.

After dinner, the entire Parker clan went back to the party house compound. I gave Uncle Bill his two 30 packs of Genny Cream Ale and he was very grateful.

A quick aside: Back in the day when Uncle Bill still lived on the east coast, he loved to pound Genny Cream Ale (AKA Genny Scream Ale, Screamers, and Green Monsters) but Uncle Bill's wife, Aunt Teresa, did not like them. Aunt T said that the next day, Uncle Bill's beer farts would smell so rotten and nasty. Eventually Aunt T banned the Cream Ale from the house. Needless to say, Aunt T was not thrilled about my gift to Uncle Bill.

After the family got settled in, everyone but me was content with going in the hot tub and/or having a camp fire. I still wanted to get in the sights of Vegas because my flight back home was a little more than 24 hours away. The entire Parker clan was staying in Vegas until Tuesday. I was staying until Saturday night because I was taking a red eye back to WNY. I didn't have any vacation time from work, only unpaid time off. I wanted to conserve my "unpaid days off" because Shannon and I had more hockey trips planned for the upcoming hockey season.

So long story short, Shannon and I left the Parker family reunion for an hour or two to visit Old Town; Freemont Street!

Shannon and I wandered all up and down Freemont Street. I was looking for a roulette table that was a $5 minimum and that had room at the table. I was finally able to find a table at Freemont Casino. I put $20 down on the table and got 20 blue roulette chips in return. I played my 0/00 strategy (as I had mentioned earlier in the book). It took 15 or so rounds, but my 00s came up and I walked away from the table $15 up! I knew I was not going to get rich playing pennies on the roulette table, but at least the casino didn't get any of my money!

Shannon played some penny slots at Four Queens and was in the black, $3 worth!

We stopped into Mermaids Casino for a few minutes. Shannon and I played some nickel slots. I liked the machines at Mermaids because when we cashed out, it dispensed nickels. The machines had that classic pay out sound with the bells ringing and the nickels hitting the metal tray. I also like hearing the scooping noise of coins and the way the nickels clanked when we dumped them into our winnings bucket. I was not a fan of the new slot machines that just printed out a winnings coupon; it took away the fun and experience of winning at a slot machine.

After we had our fix of the Freemont Experience, Shannon and I high tailed it on back to the party house.

Most of the Parkers were gathered around a camp fire. That's when I broke out the Genny Cream Ale and Boone's Farm Strawberry Hill!

It was around 2am WST (5am EST) when I turned in.

I slept in until noon on Saturday.

The one big thing I wanted to do on my last day in Vegas was to go to the Pinball Hall of Fame; yes I am a huge dork.

Jen, Chad, Shannon, and I piled into the Dodge Avenger and drove out to the Pinball Hall of Fame on Tropicana Avenue.

I watched a pinball documentary late one night on Netflix. I liked pinball and it reminded me of my youth. I only liked the old pinball machines; the electro mechanical ones with bells, not that new solid state crap with computer boards and LEDs.

The four of us arrived at the hall of fame early in the afternoon. Shannon seemed a little disappointed; she thought it was a glorified arcade. She seemed to warm up to it once she saw the old pinball machines.

I enjoyed the Pinball Hall of Fame. There was a Canadian Club themed pinball machine that I played. I tried to play every baseball themed pinball machine because those ones were my favorite. They had Quick Draw, the same pinball machine that my Great Uncle Marty had in his house!

Chad and Jen seemed to have fun at the hall of fame. I think Shannon and I spent close to $10 in quarters and stayed nearly an hour.

Once we got pinball out of our systems, it was time to hit the Strip and gamble!

I ended up driving everyone to Harrah's and used Harrah's valet service again.

From Harrah's, we walked next door to Casino Royal. Everyone was a little hungry, so we walked to the rear of the casino. Shannon and Jen had Subway and Chad had a foot long hot dog.

However, I had the world's best nachos! I loved going to Casino Royal because the food court in back had the greatest nachos I had ever experienced. What set those nachos apart from any other nachos I've had before was the cheese. First of all, the cheese was nice and hot, not that solidified crap. Secondly, the cheese had a little spice to it. Thirdly, there was a correct cheese to nacho ratio; the perfect amount of cheese for chips. When I finished the nachos, there would be no left over wasted cheese. Plus there would be enough cheese for all the nachos. Lastly, the cheese would penetrate the nachos just enough that the chip would not be too hard, nor would the chip be soggy and floppy...I'm having flashbacks and getting hungry just thinking about them right now!

After food, it was time to grab some $1 Michelobs and gamble!

Shannon played some slots with Jen and Chad.

I played some roulette, and yes, I used my 0/00 strategy. After a few rounds of beer and rounds of the roulette table, 00s came in, I won, and I cashed out. I originally put $20 on the table and walked away with $64.

I met up with Shannon, Jen, and Chad. It was about 4pm and we needed to bounce. We were supposed to meet the rest of the troops at the Heart Attack Grill on Freemont Street for dinner at 5pm.

As we left Casino Royal, we walked a part of the Strip. I needed to replenish my collection of Hooker Trading Cards. If you don't know about the Hooker Trading Cards, then just sit right there and I will tell you all about them...

On the Strip, migrant workers would stand in front of the casinos and hand out trading cards with call girls on them. Along with a provocative picture of a female (sometimes dressed, sometimes nude, depends who you get), there was a phone number, and the "business card" stated that most major credit cards were accepted.

Now I was not looking for a nice time with Amber, Chelsea, Veronica, or whoever the broad may be. I liked to collect the cards because when I got back home to WNY, I would hand out the trading cards to my buddies. My buddies and myself will leave the cards in public places around town. For example, my buddy Dave and I have been known to place a Hooker Trading Card or two inside a menu at Denny's...it makes for great humor!

Anywho, back to Vegas.

Once Jen, Chad, Shannon, and I got the Avenger from Harrah's, we cruised down Las Vegas Boulevard. We passed by Trump Tower, Riviera, Circus Circus, Stratosphere, and the former sight of the Sahara.

Soon we came upon the Gold and Silver Pawn Shop from History Channel's Pawn Stars. We had some time to kill, so the four of us decided to check it out. I was hoping that Chumlee (one of the stars) was working because he was my favorite one of the bunch. I liked how Chumlee was a doofus.

None of us bought anything from the pawn shop. They did have a replica proton pack from Ghostbusters for sale, only $200!

Jen, Chad, Shannon, and I made it to the Heart Attack Grill at 5pm sharp. Needless to say, the rest of the troops weren't there. It was about 5:40pm when the rest of the family stumbled in.

Personally, I thought the Heart Attack Grill was disgusting. I did not mind that the waitresses wore tight skimpy nurse outfits, but everything else was gross. All the patrons were given a wrist band and hospital gowns to wear.

If a patron weighed more than 350 pounds, the meal would be comp.

Speaking about the meals, they did not look appetizing. The fries were deep fried in lard and the butter milk shakes were made with butter. Additionally, the buttermilk shakes were garnished with a slice of butter on top!

The burgers did not look tasty either. A single patty burger was creatively named the "single by-pass" burger. Patty increments went up to a four patty burger, referred to as the "quadruple by-pass" burger.

If one did not finish his or her burger, one would have been subject to a paddling in the middle of the restaurant.

Lastly, for desert, one had the option of ordering a pack of Lucky Strike non filtered cigarettes!

I opted for the healthier alternative, Old English "800". My O.E. was served to me in a brown paper bag that read, *"Feeling Ghetto?"*

In the bathroom, there were two urinals. One urinal had a picture of Barack Obama and the other had George W. Bush so you could pick on which president to piss on.

My father in law, Jimbo, was a quasi-vegan. He had dreamed aloud for the last few years on visiting the Heart Attack Grill. Jimbo opted for one of the by-pass burgers. For an additional $5, he got 20 pieces of bacon on his burger! My mother in law was not thrilled with her husband. Jimbo got the cold shoulder from Joan the rest of the evening.

Once the family was done with dinner at the Heart Attack Grill, it was time to gamble! We were just two blocks away from El Cortez Casino. I wanted to go to El Cortez because former mobster Bugsy Siegel used to own it.

Once at the El Cortez, my father in law Jimbo and I plopped our butts at a $2 minimum roulette table.

While Jimbo and I were playing, Cousin Tracy came up to us and told us that her mom, Aunt Kathy, had lost her wallet. Aunt

Kathy wasn't sure if she lost it at the Heart Attack Grill or at the El Cortez. Aunt Kathy and a few other family members went to the security desk at El Cortez to report the missing wallet. Security told Aunt Kathy that she was pretty much S.O.L. but they would check their security cameras just to verify. Aunt Kathy told security that she had credit cards and about $400 in cash in her wallet. Aunt Kathy wasn't sure if she dropped her wallet or if she had been pick pocketed.

Security went back and looked at their tapes. They were able to see Aunt Kathy walk into El Cortez. From the film, they were able to see Aunt Kathy take her wallet out of her purse to get something. Security was also able to see Aunt Kathy attempt to put her wallet back into her purse, but apparently the wallet fell out of the purse. Security could see Aunt Kathy's wallet lying on the gaming floor, right next to some heifer playing a slot machine. The heifer noticed the abandoned wallet, picked it up, and went to the bathroom. Moments later, the heifer came back to the same slot machine that her fat ass was originally at, and continued to gamble.

Upon further investigation, security found Aunt Kathy's wallet in the bathroom. Aunt Kathy's ID was still in the wallet, but missing were the cash and credit cards.

With the evidence at hand, security went in for the kill and pinched the heifer, who was still playing the slots. It turned out that the heifer had about $350 cash and Aunt Kathy's credit cards on her.

Aunt Kathy decided to not press charges on the perp because Aunt Kathy did not want to fly back from New Jersey to Las Vegas for court.

After that was resolved, Jimbo and I played some more roulette.

I eventually had to piddle, but I did not want to leave the table until 0/00s came up. A few rounds later, 0 came up and I won! The cocktail waitress was taking her sweet ass time getting to our table, so after I cashed out, I asked Jimbo and Cousin Tracy if they wanted any beer. They unanimously said, "Yes!"

After I piddled and washed my paws, I found the closest bar, Parlour Bar. Elvis was performing on stage for about 25 people. I ordered and over paid for the three Miller Lites that I bought; $14 for a round of shit beer!

Jimbo and Cousin Tracy were grateful for their brews.

About a half hour later, the troops decided to disembark. People wanted to go their separate ways and check out different parts of the Freemont Experience.

It was around 9pm when my mother in law Joanie, Jimbo, Shannon, and I left El Cortez to check out the rest of the Freemont Experience. We walked up and down Freemont for a bit.

Time was closing in on 10pm when we decided to head back to the car. My flight back home was leaving in a few hours. The game plan was for me to drop Joanie, Jimbo, and Shannon off at the car rental agency at the airport so they could pick a car up. I was to return the Avenger back to Dollar Rental and catch my 12:50am flight to Chicago. The plan went smoothly.

The flight from Vegas to Chicago was painful. I was tired and I could not fall asleep. I had the last seat in the airplane, so my seat couldn't recline. Additionally, I had an aisle seat, so there was not real place for me to put my head.

I landed in Chicago at 6am. My flight out of Chicago to Rochester left at 9am.

My flight landed in Rachacha at 11am. My buddy Karl picked me up from the airport. Karl was hungry so we had breakfast at Charlie Riedel's Restaurant.

Once at home, Teppo puppy greeted me and showered me with kisses.

After I showered and brushed my teeth, it was time to lie down and watch the Buffalo Bills play the Arm-Pittsburgh Steelers. I fell asleep minutes into the 1st Quarter.

***

Wednesday November 13, 2013 brought big changes to the Buffalo Sabres. Apparently Sabres owner Terry Pegula finally saw what was happening to his hockey team and listened to the fans.

A press conference was held at 10:30am in the lobby of First Niagara Center. The public was informed that general manager Darcy Regier and head coach Ron Rolston were relieved of their duties.

Former Sabre and NHL Hall of Famer Pat LaFontaine would be in charge of hockey operations for the Sabres. LaFontaine did not want to be general manager because he did not think he was qualified for the job.

Former Sabres head coach Ted Nolan was named interim head coach.

Whoa! It was like a blast from the past! It was 1997 all over again!

As it was, the team was already teetering on the edge of Niagara Falls. Hopefully LaFontaine and Nolan could right the ship and do a 180. Only time would tell.

December 2013

On Monday December 30th I went to work early so I could get out early.

Shannon and I had a 6pm flight to catch at the Rochester Airport.

We were *supposed to* fly from Rochester, to Chicago. In Chicago, we were *supposed to* catch our connecting flight to Winnipeg. We were *supposed to* land in Winnipeg around 10:30pm. Tuesday morning in Winnipeg, we were *supposed to* take a tour of the Royal Canadian Mint…emphasis on *supposed to*…

While I was still at work, I got an email from Orbitz; who we booked the trip through. Orbitz told me at 3:36pm that both my flights were on time.

Life rarely goes according to plan…

Shannon and I were dropped off at the Rochester Airport at 4:30pm. We had plenty of time to check our bag and go through security.

We made it through security without a problem. With over an hour and a half to kill, Shannon and I decided to kill some time at a bar.

We were on our second Genesee draft when I learned that our flight from Rochester to Chicago was delayed.

Our flight was supposed to leave Rochester at 6:30pm. We did not leave Rochester until after 7pm. It turned out that our plane was late due to mechanical issues.

By the time we landed in Chicago, our connecting flight to Winnipeg was canceled.

Shannon and I spent the next hour and a half waiting in line at United Airlines Customer Service kiosk.

It turned out that there were no other direct flights scheduled to go to Winnipeg; not until after the New Year!

We told the United Customer Service agent that we needed to be in Winnipeg by tomorrow night because we were trying to make the Buffalo Sabres @ Winnipeg Jets hockey game.

The agent processed what we said and worked his magic on his computer. After a few minutes, he said, "Ok, I can have you guys on a flight tomorrow morning going to Cleveland. From Cleveland you would fly to Montreal. From Montreal, you would have a direct flight to Winnipeg, getting you there at 7pm!

Shannon said, "Thank you, but we can't do that! Our hockey game starts at 6pm!" After some more searching, Shannon and I ended up getting a Tuesday morning flight out of Chicago to Fargo, North Dakota.

Then became the issue on where we were going to sleep.

The United agent gave us a paper with a list of different hotels on them. The Untied agent said hotels ranged from $70-90 a night.

Shannon asked why we had to pay for a hotel that night.

The United agent told us because our flight was a weather related cancelation.

Shannon told the United agent that our original flight was delayed due to a mechanical issue and that no matter what, we were going to miss our connecting flight to Winnipeg.

The United agent was nice and worked his magic again and got us a hotel night stay at the Intercontinental Hotel, right by O'Hare Airport.

Next, Shannon and I made our way through the airport and found our way onto the shuttle for the Intercontinental.

The Intercontinental was a nice and new hotel; very contemporary.

Once in our room, I noted that they had a very nice bathroom. The bathroom was new aged and different; the shower did not have a door and the shower faucet came down from the ceiling. The room was a little too classy for me.

Anyway, once we got settled in our room, I had to sort out the rest of the trip. I had to try to cancel hotel and car rental reservations and make new reservations.

I was unable to get ahold of the Best Western in Winnipeg because my phone couldn't make international phone calls. Instead, I called Orbitz and waited on hold with them for a half hour before I talked to a person. I ended up getting stuck with the hotel charges for the Best Western in Winnipeg for that Monday night. Best Western told Orbitz that since it was after 4pm, then I could not cancel my reservations. I told Orbitz that I got an email at 3:36pm from Orbitz telling me everything was fine and on time. I tried to ask the Orbitz rep if they would reimburse me my money for the lost hotel night and they said "no."

The next phone call was to Alamo car rental.

The original plan was to fly into Winnipeg Monday night. On Tuesday Shannon and I were going to take a tour of the Royal Canadian Mint and then go to the Sabres and Jets game that New Year's Eve. After the game, we were going to try to find some New Year's Eve festivities. New Year's Day, we were going to pick up a rental car from Alamo and drive from Winnipeg to St. Paul/Minneapolis, Minnesota.

I got a hold of Alamo without a problem. I was able to get a rental car for the next day, with a 10am pick up in Fargo, North Dakota. Alamo did not have a problem with me taking the car over the border into Canada, nor did they have a problem with me dropping the car off at the St. Paul/Minneapolis Airport on New Year's Day. Once I had that settled, I canceled my other car rental reservation; the one where I would pick the car up at the Winnipeg airport on New Year's Day and drop it off at the St. Paul/Minneapolis Airport the same day.

Once I got that order of business straightened out, the next matter Shannon and I had to deal with was where to find food; we were so hungry!

While I was on hold with Orbitz, Shannon and I looked at the menu for the hotel's restaurant, Fresco 21. Not only did the food not look appetizing, but it was pricey.

I told Shannon that I would just go out and find a 7-11 or a gas station and buy some beer and Pringles. Shannon was nervous with me walking the streets of a strange city by myself…she thought I might get mugged or shanked.

I told Shannon, "It's almost zero degrees outside. It's way too cold, windy, and snowy for any thug to mess with me."

Shannon gave me that look of concern, the same look of concern when a girl found out the rubber broke.

I said, "If it bugs you that much, just call the front desk and see how far away the closest gas station is."

Shannon called down to the front desk and asked. Apparently the closest gas station was a 5 minute car ride, which I found hard to believe.

Though I didn't want to, we went down to Fresco 21 to pay for some overpriced food.

Shannon and I grabbed an open table at Fresco 21. We ordered waters because we didn't want to pay $6 a person for drinks.

After we ordered food, I excused myself from the table so that I could call the Royal Canadian Mint and leave them a message to inform them that I was canceling my reservations.

As I called the mint, I wandered around the hotel's main floor. While wandering, I found myself in an art gallery, looking at crappy art work. None of the art work had price tags on them. Instead they had tags to inquire at the front desk for purchase of the pieces. As the old saying went, "If you have to ask how much it is, you can't afford it." Tell you what, they couldn't pay me money to take that crap artwork home with me!

Eventually our food came.

I had a Margarita Pizza.

Shannon had a BLT, minus the B. Last summer, while Shannon was at work, she assisted in a surgery where the doctor scraped plaque out of someone's carotid artery. That experience scared Shannon straight and she tried even harder to have a healthier diet.

After dinner, we went back up to the room. By the time we tried to turn in, it was after midnight.

Shannon and I had the alarm set for 5am. The plan was to wake up before 5am. Shower, get ready, and be out the door before 5:30am.

We wanted to try to catch 5:30am shuttle to the airport.

All that went according to plan.

Shannon and I had no problem back at O'Hare Airport. We checked our bag, got our boarding passes, and had no problem with security.

Shannon and I thought everything was going to be a cluster *puck* at the airport, but surprisingly, everything went smoothly.

As we were waiting at the terminal for our flight, the morning news was being played on the overhead TVs. The massive winter storm and flight cancelations were the big news story. There was another news story that got some press. Apparently there was a train that derailed somewhere in North Dakota! Details were not available at the moment. Instantly Shannon got on the phone with her dad and asked him to research the story.

Jimbo got back to us and said that it appeared that a train somewhere between Bismarck and Fargo, North Dakota derailed and a couple tanker cars caught fire. Jimbo added that it looked like Shannon and I would be of harm's way.

Before we knew it, we were boarding our 8am flight to Fargo!

Shannon and I landed in Fargo at 10am on Tuesday December 31, 2013. Our flight attendant informed us that the current temperature was -17^0F!

Throughout my 29 years of existence of life on this planet, I had only experienced temperatures colder than that once; and I remember when and where I was!

A week or two before our vacation, I was at work. I was assisting my coworker Dan on a test. We had to test the integrity and performance of a product at -30^0C (-22^0F) in a cold environment laboratory. Though Dan and I were prepared to enter the lab by wearing winter coats, it was still freaking cold in there.

The moment I walked into the lab, my nose hairs instantly froze. I literally had icicles in my nose, it was that cold!

Anyway, back to Fargo's warm airport…

Fargo had a nice, cute, and tiny airport. It reminded me of my Fisher Price airport play set that I had as a kid!

As Shannon waited for our bags, I got the rental car from Alamo.

Once we had our bags and keys to the rental, it was time to brave the cold!

As we walked outside the airport and into the -17^{0}F (-27^{0}C) cold, we instantly had icicles in our noses!

It took us a while, but we finally found our Hyundai shit box. I threw our crap in the back seat and fired that bitch up!

The car didn't want to start at first, but once I MF-ed the car a couple time, she fired right up.

The next order of business was to find the ice scraper; it was in the back seat.

Alamo had supplied me with the world's worst ice scraper, it scraped absolutely nothing. I think the heat generated from my up and down motion began to melt some of the ice.

Once I had sufficiently scraped the ice on the outsides of the windows, it was then time to scrape the insides of the windows. Insult to injury, the windshield wipers were frozen to the windshield.

It was 10:45am when Shannon and I were finally on the road; north bound on I-29.

Winnipeg was only three and a half hours away from Fargo.

Pembina, ND was the last stop before the border. I decided to pull off and fill up that shit box we were driving.

Gas in North Dakota was a hell of a lot cheaper than in Western New York. I paid $3.09 for a gallon of gas in ND vs. $3.69 in Henrietta, NY.

As we approached the customs booth at the border, the driver side window in the rental car was still frozen shut! There were about six cars in front of us, so I had some time to monkey around with trying to free up the window. A good portion of the inside of the driver's window still had ice around it, especially by the weather stripping. The entire ride up to the border, I had the heat cranked and I kept scratching away at the ice on my window. While I was idling in line for customs, I worked on scraping the window some more. As I worked the power windows motor, I also pushed up and down on the glass. We were on deck to talk to customs when I finally freed up the window!

Getting into Canada wasn't too bad. The conversation with the Canadian Customs guy went like this:

Customs guy: Citizenship?

Me: US.

Customs guy: Where are you going?

Me: Winnipeg

Customs guy: For how long?

Me: The night, returning tomorrow.

Customs guy: What are you doing in Winnipeg?

Me: We are going be watching our Buffalo Sabres lose to the Winnipeg Jets tonight.

Customs guy: Ok, you can go.

Just to keep you up to date, the Buffalo Sabres still sucked; they were still dead last in the League. I think that had to show how great of fans Shannon and I were; we were traveling to freezing Winnipeg to see the shittiest team in the NHL play the Jets!

As we drove up Route 75 towards Winnipeg, we came across the town of St. Jean Baptiste, Canada's Soup Pea Capital!

Shannon and I decided to pull off there to find some beer before we hit downtown Winnipeg.

We saw a mini mart on the main drag. I figured there was beer there, so we parked the car and wandered in.

Shannon and I walked up and down the aisles, trying to find beer.

The only thing we found were Pringles, which were located next to the Non-Alcoholic Beer.

I grabbed two cans of Pringles and walked to the counter to check out.

As I was being cashed out, I asked the clerk, "Is there anywhere I can get beer here?"

The clerk said, "Certainly, eh."

"Great!" I said. "Where's that?"

The clerk said, "At the lumber yard, of course, eh!"

I shook my head in disbelief. "Of course, the lumber yard!"

The clerk said, "Yeah, who'da thunk it? Eh."

As I chuckled, I said, "Yeah, the lumber yard...Hey I have another question for you. Where's the lumber yard?"

As the clerk pointed, he said, "Across the street."

I thanked him.

Shannon and I hopped in the car and drove across the street to the lumber yard.

The beer selection at the lumber yard wasn't what I thought it was going to be. I had dreams that there was going to be Molson Brador, XXX, Stock Ale, and other delicious Molson products.

Shannon was salivating for some Alexander Keith's...There was none of that.

Shannon and I settled on a 6 pack of Labatt Blue and a 6 pack of Labatt Light. I also bought an 8 pack of Bud Light for my coworker Mark.

The afternoon I left work for our trip, I wished Mark a Happy New Year and shook his hand.

Mark told me, "You know, it's supposed to be -30^0C up there in the North Country?!"

I said, "Yeah, I know...Don't worry Mark. I know you don't like Canadian beer, but I hear the Bud Light tastes better up there. Don't worry, I'll bring you back a 6 pack so you can taste test..." Mark was a huge Bud Light fan.

To that, Mark let out a huge chuckle.

Once we had our beer at hand, Shannon and I walked up to the counter to check out.

The cashier chick had a hard time trying to find our age on our New York State Driver Licenses. She said she never saw a New York Driver License, just North Dakotans' licenses.

I asked her what the current temperature was and the last she heard, it was -35^0C (-32^0F).

Once we had our beer loaded up in the car, it was time to finish our last leg up to Winnipeg!

It was a little before 3pm when Shannon and I found the Best Western in downtown Winnipeg.

When we checked in, I tried to ask the front desk if they would waive my missed night from the night before and they declined.

As I wore my Sabres winter hat, I asked the receptionist what there was to do in Winnipeg.

The receptionist said, "Well there's a Jets game tonight!"

Shannon said, "Yeah, we know. We came all the way from New York for the Sabres game!"

The receptionist said, "Oh, that's awesome. Yeah, I can't think of anything else to do. Just don't go outside because it's cold out!"

Shannon and I said, "Yes! We know!"

I asked, "Are there any New Year's Eve festivities tonight?"

The receptionist said, "Um, I think there might be fireworks at the Forks."

I asked, "Do you guys do a Ball Drop downtown?"

The receptionist said, "Ball Drop? No we don't do a Ball Drop."

I said, "Oh, ok. I wasn't sure. I know in Buffalo we do a Ball Drop, but I wasn't sure if that was a Buffalo thing or if every city does that."

"No we don't do that," said the receptionist. "It's too cold here to do that."

The receptionist was nice. He gave us a map of the town and highlighted where we were and where the MTS Centre was and a nice sports bar; Tavern United. The receptionist told us how parts of downtown Winnipeg were connected by tunnels or skywalks.

Once Shannon and I made it to our room, I took off my sneakers and socks. I took a deep breath and proceeded to walk around the hotel room, just like John McClane in *Die Hard*. Suddenly I heard a rumble! At first I thought it was the gun fire of German terrorists, but I quickly realized it was my stomach! It was telling me that the turtle was poking its head out of its shell! I quickly snatched a Labatt Blue and duck walked over to the can.

After the poop and shower, it was time to find food.

As soon as Shannon and I left the Best Western, our noses had icicles in them again. Shannon was an ice cube by the time we made it a block up to Cityplace.

Shannon and I walked around Cityplace until we found Tavern United.

We looked over their menu at the door and I was instantly sold, they had Pierogie Poutine!

As we walked in, we were greeted by a room full of slot machines and a bouncer. The bouncer looked our NYS IDs and let us in.

Shannon and I ended up taking a pub table that over looked the first floor.

I did not mind the Tavern United because all the waitresses were dressed in black knee high stockings; though not the ones with lines up the back like in Van Halen's *Everybody Wants Some*.

The rest of the uniform outfits consisted of a short red and black plaid skirt and tight black shirt...it reminded me of the

Catholic school girl outfit that I had fantasied about back in my youth!

Shannon ordered a Farmery beer, local to Winnipeg.

I went for ole faithful, Labatt Blue.

For our late lunch, Shannon ordered a salad and Freedom Fries.

I tried to order the Pierogie Poutine, but that was on their "non-game night" menu. Instead, I opted for regular poutine.

Midway through dinner, our waitress asked us if we wanted more drinks. I wanted to switch to Molson.

I asked out waitress, "What kind of Molson products do you have?"

Our waitress said, "Molson Light, Molson Lager, Coors, Coors Light…"

I said, "Really? Do you have any Molson Canadian?"

She said, "No. What kind of Molson are you looking for?"

I asked, "Do you have any Molson XXX?"

She asked, "What's Molson XXX?"

To that, I asked, "So you probably don't have Molson Brador?"

She said, "No. I have never heard of those."

"Ok, I'll do a Molson Regular or whatever you called it…not the light Molson."

Our waitress said, "Molson Standard Lager, ok."

After our waitress walked away, I looked at Shannon and said, "I don't think we're in Kansas anymore Toto!"

Shannon shook her head "no" as she looked at me.

Minutes later, our waitress came around and dropped my Molson Standard Lager off at the table.

At first glance, Shannon and I thought she had given me a Bud Red Heavy.

The label on the bottle looked like a spitting image of a Budweiser label, but after further investigation, we came to realize that it was a bottle of Molson Standard Lager. According to the label, it was a, "Manitoba Original. Standard Lager is brewed especially for Manitoba to an original process dating back to 1877."

Anyway, I didn't have a problem with the beer because it was 5% alcohol.

By the time we finished dinner, the place was packed.

Shannon and I were still "casino-ed out" from our trip to Vegas the month before. Instead, we decided to walk around Cityplace for a bit.

Everybody recommended Shark Club because it was the newest bar and gaming centre.

Shannon and I made our way over to Shark Club and went in. The place was packed! It was another new age, darkly lit place for yuppies to hang out. There were a couple peoples wearing hockey jerseys in there, but most of the peeps were chicks dressed to the 9s and dudes in suits. I waited at the bar for a bit for service, but I was ignored.

I decided to leave. Shannon wasn't thirsty and I didn't want to have a shit ton of beer because I didn't want to be peeing all game long.

The time was 5:15pm. The game did not start until 6pm. Shannon and I were just a skywalk away from the MTS Centre.

I told Shannon, "I'm not sure what to do. If you want to, we can just walk in and grab our seats and watch the Sabres warm up?"

Shannon said, "OK that sounds fine to me. I don't want to go outside."

Shannon and I walked from the Shark Club over to MTS Centre and over to the stairs for the 300 Level. I got patted down and had the metal detector wand waived over me. Shannon had her purse search and a pat down.

We then walked up the stairs to the 300s.

We gave the usher our tickets to scan.

The usher scanned both our tickets and they registered "invalid."

The usher scanned them again and they came up again as "invalid."

The usher told us to go to the box office to sort out the order.

Shannon and I were devastated as we walked down the stairs to the box office. We were just in a haze, a fog, a total whirl wind! I had over paid for those tickets on Stub Hub. I had been looking for Sabre @ Jets tickets for the past few seasons and I finally found "cheap" enough seats, only to find out that we got boned, the tickets were frauds! As we walked down those stairs to the box office, I wasn't sure if we were able to get tickets for that night's game!

You see, Winnipeg finally got their team back in the fall of 2011. Everyone in Winnipeg was thrilled to have their team back. Tickets were hard to come by. The tickets I found were astronomical! Originally, I cheapest tickets I saw were $250 on StubHub!

The current season was Winnipeg's third year in the league. Ticket prices were still high.

I tried to buy tickets through Winnipeg's official website, but I couldn't find any. From what I had found, Winnipeg had sold almost all of their tickets to season ticket holders. The team withheld a few individual tickets for each game. These individual tickets would come up in a lottery for fans a few weeks before the game. I was not about to plan a very expensive vacation around a lottery, in the hopes that I might be able to land tickets.

I checked out the NHL ticket exchange, but even those tickets were sky high, over $200 a seat!

I had always had great luck with StubHub before; no issues. That was why I bought my tickets through StubHub.

By the time Shannon and I reached the Winnipeg Jets box office, Shannon was on the verge of tears.

Stub Hub had a policy that if there was an issue with their tickets, to call them. Shannon and I could not call them because our phones did not work in Canada.

We told the guy at the box office what happened.

The guy called his manager over.

The manager looked at the tickets and recognized the name of the season ticket holder. The manager said that the Jets have had a problem with that guy over selling, double selling, and triple selling tickets. The manager informed us that the Jets have suspended that season ticket holder's contract and they have contacted various second party ticket agency outlets. The manager advised us to only buy tickets through an "authorized" source like the NHL Ticket Exchange...the same *pucking* ticket exchange that sold tickets for double or triple the face value!

Thankfully the box office had extra tickets for that night's game.

The cheapest tickets for the game were $70! *Pucking* highway robbery if you ask me! But what could we do.

Shannon and I traveled all that way to watch our horrible last place Sabres play, of course we vomited up the $140 to watch the Sabre lose!

Winnipeg got on the board first with a goal by Keaton Ellerby at the half way point of the 1st Period. Ellerby's shot from the point eluded the Sabres goaltender Jhonas Enroth.

Buffalo had some signs of life, but for the most part, they looked like they were just going through the motions. Buffalo did have a goal, but the ref instantly disallowed it.

MTS Centre was a full house. Besides Shannon and me, I think we saw only two other Sabre fans.

The Winnipeg Jets added to their lead in the 2nd Period with a goal by Jacob Trouba.

With about 90 seconds left in the 3rd Period, Winnipeg capped off their victory with and empty net goal by Anthony Peluso.

The Sabres dull and boring performance made it an easy night for Winnipeg's goaltender Al Montoya to get a shutout victory.

Other than Shannon and me, Jhonas Enroth was the only one from Buffalo who showed up for the game. Despite letting in two goals, Enroth was amazing! He stopped Winnipeg's 7 or 8 break away chances. It was very frustrating to watch our beloved Sabres get shut out again, 3-0.

After the game, I was brain fried and exhausted. All I wanted to do was to go to bed. The last thing I wanted to do was to party, get drunk, watch the Ball Drop, wake up hung over the next morning, and drive 7.5 hours to St. Paul as Shannon slept off her hang over. It may sound like a selfish, butthole thing, but I didn't care.

Shannon was exhausted and slightly tired after the game.

Though the game ended around 9pm, Shannon did not want to walk down to the Forks and wait around for fireworks in -36 degree weather.

We ended up walking back to the hotel. We popped into our left over fries and cracked open a couple Labatts.

I passed out before the Ball dropped.

January 2014

After the Ball dropped, Shannon woke me up and said, "Kiss me before I kiss someone else!"

I think I woke up enough to give her a kiss with some tongue...there may have been some extra circular activities that followed. (*From wife: no tongue...barely woke up enough for a peck on the cheek*)

New Year's Day, I was wide awake by 8am, but I did not want to get out of bed! I was on vacation, and I was going to stay in bed for as long as I could!

Shannon woke up and she wanted to go down to the gym. I vegged out and watched TV instead.

After Shannon's gym stuff, we packed our bags and got ready for checkout.

A lot of people recommended the Forks, so Shannon and I decided to check it out.

Since it was New Year's Day, we weren't sure how much of the Forks was going to be open.

We ended up checking out the Forks Market.

About a quarter of the shops were open at the market. Shannon and I walked around on both the first and second floors. I bought some post cards for friends and family.

Eventually we worked up an appetite.

Shannon got a veggie wrap from some vender.

I went to Skinner's and ordered poutine and a real Pepsi in a glass bottle! The Pepsi tasted different because it was in a glass bottle and it was made with real sugar, not that corn syrup crap they used back in the States.

Corn is weird. My thing with corn is whenever I eat it, it comes out looking the same way it went in, undigested! That made me wonder if corn syrup did the same thing. They were both corn products.

I have to say that I thought beer was healthier than pop. For instance, 12 ounce cans of Genny Light contained 100 calories, Bud Light contained 110 calories, and Bud Light Platinum contained 137 calories, and all contained no sodium.

A 12 ounce can of Coca Cola contained 140 calories and 40mg of sodium.

The argument could be made that Diet Coke had no calories, regardless of how much was consumed. A 12 ounce can of Diet Coke still contained 40mg of sodium. People may think that Diet Coke is a "healthier" option, but the beverage contains aspartame, a sweetening agent that some believe to cause cancer. The FDA said aspartame was safe, but would you really want to listen to another government agency that lied to its people?

Anyway, when was the last time that pop helped people have fun at a sporting event or lose their inhibitions and score at the end of the night? Yes, thank you beer!

Continuing on, I drank the Pepsi, made with real sugar, because it was 11am. The last thing I wanted to do was to crack open a beer before a seven and a half hour car ride. With me, beer is like Lays Salt and Vinegar potato chips, I just can't have one! Beer is also like Pringles, once I pop, I can't stop.

Anyway, back to the story, again!

After we left the Forks Market, Shannon and I began our seven and a half hour drive from Winnipeg to the Twin Cities of Minnesota!

On our way back to the States, Shannon and I stopped at Duty Free. I was hoping that we could replenish our depleted stock of Molson Brador.

Once we entered Duty Free, I saw liquor everywhere, floor to ceiling! At first I did not see the beer. I walked around a little and finally found a wood pallet with canned beer.

I found a Duty Free employee and asked her if the pallet was the only beer selection they had. She told me that the pallet was it!

The beer selections were twenty four 12 ounce cans of Labatt Blue, Labatt Light, Molson Canadian, Molson Dry, Kokanee, Bud Light, and Coors Light.

There was no Molson Brador, Stock Ale, Ice, or XXX. Shannon was bummed out because there was no Alexander Keith's.

We bought a flat of Molson Dry, 5.5% beer.

At customs, Shannon and I got grilled by the customs officer. The conversation went a little like this:

Customs officer: Citizenships?

Me: US.

Customs officer: Where do you live?

Me: Rochester, NY.

Customs officer: Where did you go in Canada?

Me: To Winnipeg to watch the Buffalo Sabres lose.

Customs officer: Whose car is this?

Me: Alamo Car Rental's.

Customs officer: Why do you have a rental car? Did you not want people to know where you were from?

Me: No, because it's a long way to drive from Rochester, NY to Winnipeg, Manitoba.

Customs officer: How did you get here?

Me: We flew from Rochester to Chicago. We were supposed to fly from Chicago to Winnipeg, but our flight got canceled. Instead, we were rerouted to Fargo, North Dakota, where I picked up the rental car.

Custom officer: Where are you going now?

Me: We're driving to St. Paul, Minnesota so we can watch our Buffalo Sabres lose again.

Customs officer: Did you buy anything in Canada?

Me: Beer.

With that, we were granted access back into the States.

Every time I came back over the border into the US, I always got the 5th degree; it was like talking to my mom!

I didn't understand why a white boy from Buffalo who wore a Sabres hat needed to be interrogated.

Customs should not be worried about me, but rather the turban wearing Durka Durka who can barely speak English.

Oh well, what do I know. At least I didn't get a full body and cavity search.

The rest of the ride to St. Paul/Minneapolis was boring and uneventful.

We got to the St. Paul/Minneapolis Airport by 7:30pm.

Shannon and I had to drop off Alamo's Hyundai shit box. Then we picked up a different rental from Ace Rental. We did this because it was cheaper. The Alamo rental for two days was $200. The cost to rent from Ace Rental per day was $24. It seemed like a no brainer.

Ace Rental was nice. By the time the shuttle had dropped us off at Ace Rental, our car was already warmed up in the parking lot! Ace gave us a Killed In Action (KIA) Soul, another Korean shit box.

It was a quick drive from Ace Rental to Crowne Plaza St. Paul Riverfront.

We had no problem checking in.

Shannon and I were staying on the 9th floor.

As we entered the elevator to go up to the 9th floor, I noticed that the hotel had 22 floors. I made sure to look for the 13th floor!

I said, "Hey Shannon, look! They actually have a 13th floor!"

Shannon replied, "Do you know what that means?! The 13th floor is *actually* the 13th floor!"

After we got into our room, we unloaded our bags and I unloaded a huge dump into the toilet, I Jackson Pollock-ed the bowl!

After I showered and got dressed, we went back down to the lobby to grab a bite to eat.

We dined at the Port of Call Lounge in the Crowne Plaza's lobby.

I attempted to be healthy and had a Salmon Caesar Salad. Shannon had something else that had leafy greens in it.

Last call was 10pm, so Shannon and I closed out our tab and went back up to the room.

Back at the room, we turned on the boob tube and vegged out.

Shannon and I would have gone exploring, but it was 0^0F outside. Not to mention that it was New Year's night, and we didn't think much would be open.

The next morning, January 2, 2013, Shannon and I woke up and decided to go to the Mall of America for the afternoon.

When we left the parking garage at the hotel, we had to pay for that night's parking.

I asked the parking attendant what we needed to do or see in the Twin Cities. I never got her name, but we will call her Miss Cleo because she looked like that big black fortune teller that used to have infomercials on TV in the late 1990s. The conversation went a little like this:

Me: Hi, how are you doing?

Miss Cleo: OK, how are you?

Me: I'm good. Is it cold outside?

Miss Cleo: Of course! It's like one degree outside!

Me: Oh, OK. I was just wondering. So what's there to do here in the Twin City?

Miss Cleo: You're not from here?

Me: Nope. We were wondering what things we needed to do here.

Miss Cleo: Where are you from?

Me: Buffalo.

Miss Cleo: Buffalo, Minnesota?! They should have the same weather back there as we do here!

Me: No, Buffalo, New York!

Miss Cleo: Oh! You guys are from New York! Well…you sure don't sound like you're from New York.

Me: Oh, no. We're not from "the City." We're from Buffalo, New York. Completely different!

Miss Cleo: Where is Buffalo then?

Me: On the complete opposite side of the state. We're considered "Upstate."

Miss Cleo: How far are you guys away from New York City?

Me: About 7 hours or so.

Miss Cleo: Where's Buffalo by?

Me: Niagara Falls.

Miss Cleo: Yea, I heard of Niagara Falls. Where's that by?

Me: Besides Buffalo? Um…we're close to Toronto. We're a part of the Great Lakes.

Miss Cleo: Oh, OK. Yeah, I would recommend that you go to the Mall.

Me: Ok, great! That's where we are going now. Anywhere else?

Miss Cleo: Yes! Mickey's Diner! It's a few blocks down on the corner of 7th and St. Peter. It's really great for breakfast!

Me: Thank you!

After Shannon and I paid for our parking, we headed to the Mall of America.

At the Mall, I parked in the first parking garage I saw. Once the car was parked, we left our coats in the Soul because we didn't want to lug them around the Mall. We entered the Mall on the 2nd level of Sears.

Inside, the Mall looked like any other mall; just like the Walden Gonorrhea (Galleria) in Cheektowaga, NY or Carousel Mall in Syracuse, NY.

Shannon and I walked around the 2nd floor of the mall for a bit until we saw Nickelodeon Universe, which was located in the center of the Mall.

I told Shannon that if there was a Teenage Mutant Ninja Turtles ride, then I wanted to ride it!

It turned out there was a TMNT ride! The ride seated 12 passengers, one human per turtle pod. Each turtle pod had a weapon on the back of the shell, designating which turtle it was. Each pod had wings. The ride rotated in a diagonal circle, kind of like the ring around the planet Saturn. As the turtle pod flew around the air, one could swing and tilt the wings of the pod and spin around. The ride looked like a lot of fun.

Shannon and I walked around Nickelodeon Universe and checked out all the rides.

When we were done looking at Nickelodeon Universe, we continued on and explored the 1st floor of the Mall.

It was around noon and Shannon and I were getting hungry.

We stopped into the Twin City Grill to have lunch. Shannon had a salad and a flat bread sandwich. I had grown up mac and cheese with Moose Drool Ale. The food was good at Twin City Grill.

After lunch, Shannon saw that Bath and Body Works had an after holiday sale, so we went in.

Tell you what, no matter how much I farted in that place, I could not smell my own scent! It was drowned out by sweet pea and other girly scents…I quickly vacated the premises because I knew I was getting nowhere with trying to mark my territory.

While I waited for Shannon, I saw a kiosk that advertised Minnesota Sea Life Aquarium at the Mall of America. The kiosk had $3 off coupons for adults. There was also a map of the aquarium and it showed that there was a hands on exhibit and tunnels through the tanks!

I grabbed two coupons and ran back into Bath and Body Works. Thankfully I found Shannon in the checkout line. I was doubly thankful that she was only buying three bottles of smelly crap.

Like a little kid, I bounced around until she finally checked out. Then I grabbed her hand and rushed her over to the aquarium kiosk to show her.

Shannon said, "Oh, that looks cool, and it gives us something else to do."

After we walked half of the Mall, we were finally at the check in desk at the Sea Life Aquarium.

Sea Life was running a special that if you bought a fully priced admission ticket to the aquarium and threw in an additional $10, Sea Life would give us an unlimited ride access pass to Nickelodeon Universe! Shannon was unsure about it until she looked over at me. I was bouncing around and shaking my head yes, as if I was a 10 year old on a sugar high, trying to behave!

Needless to say, we went with the Sea Life/Nickelodeon Universe ticket combo.

Shannon had always found enjoyment out of learning centers, especially places that had signs to read! Sea Life was filled with fun fact plaques and signs.

The first part of the aquarium had an interactive touch tank where we could touch a star fish or tentacle coral.

The star fish that I touched didn't feel like other star fish that I have touched. These star fish were not soft and spongy, but hard and had texture to them.

The tentacle coral felt like nothing. I touched it and the tentacles moved back. Shannon was watching me as I was trying to touch the tentacle coral and I told her, "I can't touch it. Every time I think I'm touching it, it sways away. It feels like I'm touching nothing."

Shannon said, "Really?"

I said, "Yea, try."

I took a step back so that Shannon could walk up and stick her hand into the water.

As Shannon's hand touched the coral tentacles, I grabbed her and shouted, "Ahhhh!!!"

Shannon shrieked and jumped about a foot into the air. The employee working the touch tank tried not to giggle out loud, however, she laughed out loud when Shannon elbowed me in the ribs.

There was a tank with Sand Eels. The Sand Eels reminded me of the little tiny worm puppets on Sesame Street. The Sand Eels were little critters that burrowed into the sand and ate plankton; you know that bad guy from Sponge Bob, the owner of the Chum Bucket.

There was also a tank filled with Lionfish. That was the same fish that Detective Frank Drebin killed in *The Naked Gun*.

Then we walked into the Shoreline room. There was a tank with mini sharks swimming around. I liked the sharks, Shannon did not because she was fearful of sharks.

The next room we encountered was about jellyfish, which I learned, were not actually fish, but were the deadliest creature in the waters.

Sea Life had a blacked out room with about eight cylindrical tanks that contained moon jellyfish. Each tank had lights on the bottom that illuminated the water and the tank. Colors changed vary gradually from green to red to blue to orange and so on. I was mesmerized by the moon jellyfish; it looked like a whole bunch of breast implants floating around.

After the moon jellyfish exhibit, there was another tank with a different species of jellyfish. These three jellyfish looked like the ones from Sponge Bob; umbrella shaped with long, string tentacles.

Shannon and I continued on into the octopus room. There was a sign that said octopuses are as smart as a dog! I showed Shannon the sign and asked her, "Does that mean octopuses lick their own butts like Teppo?"

The octopus exhibit had two baby cuttlefish.

My coworker Scott was petrified of the cuttlefish. As evolution continued, Scott's theory was that the cuttlefish will be the demise of the human race.

Seahorses were the next exhibit after the octopuses. There were a few tanks of various sea horses. I learned that one group of sea horses mate for life.

Finally Shannon and I approached the part of the aquarium that contained the walk through tunnels, like in *Jaws 3-D*. Unlike the movie, these tunnels were not destroyed by a killer shark.

The first tunnel tank we walked through had some sea turtles and sharks. Thankfully there were no Great White sharks. There were Nurse, Saw, and Sand Tiger Sharks.

When we were in the tunnel, it was feeding time for the Saw Sharks. A dead fish was attached to a long pole. The pole was put into the water and placed in front of the Saw Shark and the decapitated fish was released. The shark would then eat.

From the salt water tank, we walked into the fresh water tank. There were Muskie, Lake Sturgeon, and turtles; just to name a few fresh water creatures.

The aquarium wrapped up with a Rainforest themed exhibit. It featured a couple tortoises, Poison Dart Frogs (good for licking), piranha, a huge ass snapping turtle, and a pair of crocodiles.

After that, our adventure at Sea Life Aquarium was finished.

Next it was time to ride rides!

The first ride we rode was the Log Chute. I liked the Log Chute and it had two big drops.

Next, Shannon and I ran over to the Ninja Turtle ride, Shell Shock. Shell Shock was a lot of fun, I recommend it.

Then Shannon and I ran over to Sponge Bob's Rock Bottom Plunge roller coaster. For this roller coaster, we were strapped in via shoulder harness because we went upside down! The first part of the ride dragged us up to the top of the Mall at a perfect 90 degree angle. Once at the top of the Mall, we went over the first hump and it was another 90 degree plunge back to the 1st level of the Mall. There were some cork screws and loop de loops. When the ride ended, both of our equilibriums were a little off.

Sponge Bob had a pineapple shaped bounce house that we did not go in. I liked bounce houses only when beer and large breasted women were in them.

When Shannon and I originally got to the Mall, Nickelodeon Universe was quiet. Now that it was midafternoon, the place was busy and long lines began to form at every ride.

Shannon and I wanted to try Pepsi Orange Streak roller coaster because the coaster ran around the entire theme park. We did not go on it because the line was way too long.

Instead, Shannon and I found a ride with a short line, Danny Phantom Ghost Zone. This ride moved in a circle, like a clock on the wall. It moved really fast clockwise and counter clockwise.

The Fairly Odd Parents had a roller coaster, the Fairly Odd Coaster. Shannon and I got dizzy just looking at it. We decided we did not want to get sick. The ride moved around like a normal roller coaster on a track. However, the coaster pod itself rotated 360 for the entire ride; I did not want to toss my cookies.

There was another instant sickness spinny ride that we steered clear of, Brain Surge.

Though I was not a fan of the Jimmy Neutron cartoon series, we went on Jimmy Neutron's Atomic Collider ride. In Atomic Collider, we sat in a pod. The ride went up in the air and spun around in a circle. Our pod then spun in a circle as the ride spun in a circle. Confused? Yes, I was, especially when the ride finished.

The bad guy from Sponge Bob, the Flying Dutchman, even had his own attractions!

One ride was called Anchor Drop, which was a three story slide! Unfortunately our admission to Nickelodeon Universe did not cover that ride; it was an additional $5 or something.

The second attraction was called Gangplank and that too was an additional fee! The attraction looked like a lot of fun. It was a three story rope course maze.

Moose Mountain Adventure Golf was a miniature golf course up on the 3rd floor, and that too was an additional cost. Shannon and I did not mini golf.

We capped off our rides with Ghost Blasters. Ghost Blasters was a ride where we sat in a car and we shot ghosts in a haunted house. A lot of the scenes in that ride looked eerily similar to the ones found at Disney's Haunted Mansion, but we didn't care.

Once we were done theme parking it, Shannon wanted to window shop in the American Girl Store. We walked around the store and looked at a whole bunch of overpriced made in China junk. I took a brochure of the store for my niece Hannah because she was into that stuff.

Shannon and I then made our way up to the 3rd floor. I was told that there was a mail box next to Best Buy and I needed to drop off my post cards.

After I dropped off my post cards, we wandered around the 3rd floor for a bit.

It was close to 5pm when we decided to bust a move back to the hotel.

We got back to the hotel by 5:30pm. I cracked open a Labatt Blue and got ready for the Sabres game.

It was 5:45pm when we were walking up Kellogg Boulevard, towards Xcel Energy Center for the game.

Shannon was freezing as we walked up the four long blocks to Xcel Energy Center. Once we got inside the Center, I asked the guy selling programs if there were any bars close by. He said that there were some bars inside Xcel Energy and there were a string of bars directly across from the arena.

Shannon and I chose to go to the bars across the street; we did not want to pay for overpriced arena beer.

We braved the cold and went back out into the 0 degree temperature.

We soon found ourselves walking into a pizza bar called Zamboni's. Shannon ordered a veggie pizza, minus cheese and local beer, Surly Furious. I played it safe with a cheese pizza and a PBR.

While we waited for our dinner, Shannon and I grabbed our drinks and sat down at a table.

We were sitting at our table when a guy at the bar turned around and looked at us. He was wearing a Minnesota North Stars shirt and when he saw our Sabres gear, he started to shake his head no. He said, "How can you wear that here?!"

I said, "Uh...because I came all the way from Buffalo to watch our Sabres lose...Buffalo, New York that is!"

The guy seemed impressed and said, "Ah, gotcha. Well welcome to Minnesota!"

I said, "Thank you."

Shannon told him that we were on a mission to watch the Sabres play in every hockey arena and that we were in the home stretch of our trips.

To that, they guy said, "Oh that's so awesome! I'm Greg and this is Amy!"

We shook hands and exchanged hellos.

We talked with Greg and Amy for a bit and they were both very nice. Greg noticed my PBR and said, "I really like that you are drinking PBR, but have you tried Hamm's yet? It's a good local beer."

I said, "No I haven't."

Greg said, "Let me buy you a beer then!" And like that, Greg bought me a very tasty Hamm's beer. I thanked him for the beer.

Greg asked us how our visit to the Twin City was going and we told him it was going well.

He told us that if we had time on Friday, we should visit the Grain Belt Brewery in New Ulm. He did mention that it was a good half hour outside of town.

I wanted to reciprocate and buy Greg a beer, but it was already 6:50pm and the game was to start at 7pm.

Instead, Amy, Greg, Shannon, and I walked from Zamboni's to Xcel Energy Center together.

Greg asked where our seats were. I told him that we were sitting in Section 119. Greg said him and Amy were sitting in Section 118.

Once we got into the arena, I thanked Greg again before parting ways.

Shannon and I found a beer vendor at the top of our section. I bought some sort of local brew, though I forgot the name of it. After we got our beer, we went down and found our seats.

We got to our seats in time for the American National Anthem.

During the 1st Period, in between play, the arena announcer came on the PA and asked the crowd to salute Buffalo Sabres goaltender Ryan Miller and Minnesota Wild defenseman Ryan Suter for making Team USA Men's Olympic Hockey Team. Naturally everyone cheered for both players (Minneapolis native and Wild forward Zach Parise also made the roster for Team USA but was scratched for tonight's game due to a foot injury so his name was not mentioned in the salute).

Buffalo looked strong and full of energy during the 1st Period. Buffalo had their chances on the power play, but couldn't do squat with them.

The 1st Period ended in a 0-0 tie.

We talked to the Wild fans in front of us. They were amazed and thought it was awesome that Shannon and I flew from Western New York to watch the Sabres.

The one guy, Marty, invited us to the bar with him and his friends. Shannon and I thanked him for the offer, but we stayed in our seats.

Soon the 2nd Period started.

Minnesota didn't waste any time getting on the board.

Almost five minutes into the 2nd Period, the Wild's Marco Scandella shot the puck past Buffalo's goalie Ryan Miller to give the Wild a 1-0 lead.

During a stoppage in play, I asked Marty how Jason Pominville was working out for the Wild.

Marty said that originally, Pominville came in as a huge ball of fire and lit the ice up. He added that at the beginning of that season, Pominville was playing well and scoring, but has since fizzled out. About two minutes later, wouldn't you know it, Jason Pominville scored. It was very aggravating to see Jason Pominville score against Ryan Miller. How come Pominville couldn't score like that when he was on the Sabres?! To add insult to injury, it was also Jason Pominville Bobble Head night; tell me that wasn't a coincidence!

In the final four minutes of the 2nd Period, Minnesota's Jason Zucker added to the Wild's lead.

By the time the 2nd Period ended, the Sabres were down 3-0!

During the 2nd Intermission, Marty again invited us up to the bar with he and his friends.

Shannon and I decided to join this time.

Marty introduced us to all his friends and he bought Shannon and me a beer. Marty and his friends were very nice and friendly. They too thought it was cool that Shannon and I traveled from WNY to watch the Sabres lose.

The Minnesota Wild's mascot, Nordy, was a wild animal that had a mullet! I thought that was awesome. Back in the day when I used to go up to Canada to drink, my buddies and I would drink to mullets. On any given night, we could get extremely wasted playing that game. The tradition continued that night, and every time we saw Nordy, we drank!

Soon the 3rd Period was to begin, so we all migrated back to our seats.

Buffalo had an early power play in the start of the 3rd Period, but wasted it.

Buffalo didn't get on the score board until the last couple minutes of the 3rd Period. On a delayed penalty, Buffalo's Tyler Myers finally broke the shutout and gave Shannon and me something to cheer about! The Sabres crashed the net and the puck deflected off Myers and went past the Wild net minder Niklas Backstrom.

Since Buffalo only trailed 3-1, Head Coach Ted Nolan pulled goalie Ryan Miller for the extra attacker.

Buffalo had the puck deep in the Wild zone and then lost control of the puck. The Wild got the puck out to their player Kyle Brodziak. Brodziak brought the puck in over the Buffalo line. Two Sabres tripped up and took down Brodziak. Since Brodziak was attempting to take a shot at the empty net and got tripped up, the ref gave Brodziak credit for the goal any way.

Buffalo ended up losing 4-1.

When the game was over, we thanked Marty again for the beer and his hospitality.

Since we didn't get to go bar hopping in Winnipeg, Shannon and I decided to go bar hopping in St. Paul.

Our first stop was Eagle Street Grille. Eagle Street was a happening place with a live band, tons of people, and fireplaces.

As Shannon and I hung out, we met some fellow Sabres fans. It turned out that the family of the Sabre fans used to live in Angola, NY. The family had obviously since moved out of WNY. The one son lived in Minnesota and his dad lived in Omaha, Nebraska. The son drove about two hours for the Sabres game. The dad drove ten hours up from Omaha to watch our favorite hockey team. The four of us commiserated and reminisced about Buffalo over a round of beers.

Shannon and I got bored with standing, so we sat down in front of the warm fire place.

Moments later, a Wild fan and his girlfriend came up to ask Shannon and me why we were wearing Sabre jerseys in Minnesota.

I told the dude that Shannon and I came all the way from Buffalo, NY to watch our Sabres lose. I also added that we were in Winnipeg a few nights before to watch the Sabres get shutout 3-0.

I think the guy took pity on Shannon and me. At that moment, the shots lady came by and asked if anyone wanted shots.

I said, "No thank you."

The Wild fan said, "Awe, come on, you have to!"

Shannon said, "Thanks, but no thanks. I don't want to be drinking hard liquor."

The Wild fan said, "Awe, come on!"

The shots lady told Shannon, "Oh you don't have to worry, there's almost no alcohol in these…"

The Wild fan said, "Awe, come on! You guys have to do shots! I'll buy you guys this round!"

Shannon and I looked at each other, shrugged our shoulders, and said, "Okay!"

The shots we had were mini slushes in plastic shot cups.

As we raised our shots, I said, "To good hockey!"

Shannon, the Wild fan, and his girlfriend all said, "To good hockey!"

We threw back the shots and the shot lady was right, those slushy shots tasted like virgins.

I would have bought the Wild fan a drink, but he and his girlfriend stumbled away.

Shannon and I were thirsty again, so I went up to the bar to fetch another round. After waiting five minutes at the bar with cash at hand and no service, I decided it was time to find the next establishment on our bar hopping adventure.

Shannon and I walked down a block and found ourselves walking into Patrick McGovern's Pub.

We bellied up to the bar and ordered a round of drinks.

I asked a couple of the bartenders that were working, "Hey, I have a question for you guys. What is there to do in Buffalo, Minnesota and Rochester, Minnesota?"

They looked at me and the one bartender said, "Um, nothing really. No one really goes to Rochester or Buffalo. There's not much to do there. Why do you ask?"

I answered, "Well Shannon is from Rochester, New York and I'm from Buffalo, New York. I wasn't sure if there was anything in the Minnesotan cities."

The bartenders unanimously agreed that there wasn't anything to do in either Minnesotan city.

I noticed the one bartender was wearing a Minnesota Twins baseball hat. I told him that the Rochester (New York) Red Wings were the farm team for the Twins. I said, "As it says in the outfield at Frontier Field, 'Twins of Tomorrow.'"

We talked with the bartenders and some of the patrons a little more. I asked them where Shannon and I should go for a Juicy Lucy. Everyone said to go to Matt's Bar or 5-8 Club; though most people leaned towards 5-8 Club.

Eventually I asked them, "Hey, wasn't a part of Disney's *The Mighty Ducks* filmed here? I thought I remembered the Ducks meeting Minnesota North Star Mike Madano."

Everyone said, "Yeah!"

The one bartender said, "I can't believe you remember that movie. Yes, a lot of the movie was filmed here. Actually, Mickey's Diner up the road here was in the movie too."

Shannon said, "Mickey's Diner! Miss Cleo told us to go there for breakfast."

The bartender said, "Yeah, it's just up the street here on 7th. It's two blocks past Xcel Energy Center."

It was closing in on midnight and I was getting hungry again. I asked the bartender, "Would Mickey's still be opened?"

"Of course!" The bartender said, "It's a 24 hour diner."

Shannon and I closed out our tab and thanked our bartender.

Our next stop was to walk up the four blocks to Mickey's Diner to get some midnight munchies.

I did not mind walking in the 0 degree weather, though Shannon was a different story. She was frozen and not a happy camper.

Once we got inside Mickey's Diner, Shannon's attitude changed because she was in a warm place, out of the cold.

Shannon ordered pancakes and I had the O'Brian Special; two scrambled eggs, toast, and potatoes O'Brian (hash browns). Shannon and I shared each other's dishes. The food was great. Mickey's Diner was a great greasy spoon.

After our meal, we walked the few blocks back to the hotel.

Friday morning, January 3rd, we had nothing planned. I tried to find the Grain Belt Brewery, but I could not find New Ulm, Minnesota on the map we had in our room.

Shannon and I did see that Summit Brewing Company, another local brewery, gave beer tours and had samplings. I called Summit Brewing to see if we could squeeze into a beer tour, but beer tours were completely filled for the day.

Instead, Shannon and I decided to go to the Minnesota History Center and learn about Prohibition!

The History Center was just up the street from where we were staying, which made it easy to find.

The Prohibition exhibit was called "American Spirits, The Rise and Fall of Prohibition."

Shannon and I enjoyed the exhibit.

One of the things I learned was that mixed drinks were a result of Prohibition. All the bathtub brews and moonshine tasted so awful, that the alcohol needed to be cut with something. During Prohibition, sales of Coca-Cola and Kool Aid soared.

The museum had a couple other good exhibits that we walked through.

Minnesota's Greatest Generation exhibit was about the people that grew up during the Great Depression, World War II, and Baby Boomer Era. This exhibit was fun because we could walk inside a 1950s soda fountain. There was a Douglas C-47 Skytrain airplane that we walked in and watch a short film about WWII. We got to assemble bomb shells on an assembly line to support the war effort. There were some other interesting things in there too.

Shannon and I went into Then Now Wow exhibit which contained hands on and interactive exhibits about early life in Minnesota. There was a tepee like the ones the Dakota people lived in and mud houses like the early settlers lived in. There was also a real train box car that we walked into.

Within the Then Now Wow exhibit, there was a special section to commemorate when the I-35W Mississippi River Bridge collapsed on August 1, 2007. The exhibit highlighted the bravery of 20 year old Jeremy Hernandez. Hernandez was a staff member for a day camp. Hernandez was on a school bus with 63 children that became stranded on the collapsed bridge. Hernandez kicked out the back door to the bus and carried the kids to safety.

Then Now Wow also had an exhibit on what life was like as a miner. This exhibit was hands on and pretty awesome. Shannon and I walked through the tunnels of a mine. We loaded sticks of dynamite into holes of the cave and then blew up the walls.

From the museum, we could see the State Capitol building and the Cathedral of St. Paul.

The last exhibit we went into was Open House: If these Walls Could Talk. This was another hands on exhibit where we could touch things. I liked museums where I do not get yelled at for touching the exhibits.

In Open House, Shannon and I walked through a "house" through the course of 100+ years. We got to see what kind of families lived in the house and listened to their stories.

It was after 2pm when Shannon and I decided to high tail it on out of the Minnesota History Center.

Shannon and I were hungry and we needed to try a Juicy Lucy before we left town.

Most sources advised us to go to 5-8 Club, so we went there.

Shannon plugged 5-8 Club into her phone and GPS told us how to get there.

Once at the 5-8 Club, we seated ourselves at a pub table in the bar area.

Shannon ordered a Summit Pale Ale and I had a Nordeast Grain Belt Beer.

Shannon and I split a Juicy Lucy and an order of Pizza Jo's.

While we waited for our lunch, I bought $5 worth of pull tabs, though we did not win.

When our lunch came, I really enjoyed the Pizza Jo's. Pizza Jo's were potato wedges with sauce and cheese, baked like a pizza.

The Juicy Lucy was also very good.

It was 3:30pm when Shannon and I left the 5-8 Club.

Shannon and I returned our rental car to Ace Rental at 4pm. We then took the Ace Rental shuttle to the airport.

It was minutes after 4pm when we got to the check in line for Southwest Airlines. That's when we found out our flight to Chicago had been canceled.

Shannon and I waited in line for over an hour before we got to talk to a Southwest rep.

The Southwest rep asked us where we were flying to.

Shannon said, "Rochester, New York."

The rep said, "I can't do Rochester. Everything is canceled to there. The soonest I can get you home would be a Monday flight."

Shannon said, "No, we cannot do Monday. We have to be back at work on Monday and we took enough time off from work already."

The rep said, "Ok, hang on...Is there anywhere else I could fly you guys to?"

I said, "I have family in Charlotte."

The rep said, "Nope, can't do Charlotte."

I said, "What about Raleigh?"

The rep said, "Nope, can't do Raleigh."

I said, "Buffalo?"

The rep said, "Nope, I can't do Buffalo."

I said, "What about Baltimore or Philly?"

The rep said, "Nope, neither."

Shannon chimed in and said, "What about Vegas?"

The rep said, "Nope, can't do Vegas."

Shannon was a little agitated by this point and tried to nicely ask, "Well where can you fly us to, then?"

The rep said, "Austin, Texas."

Shannon blurted out, "Austin, Texas?! That's in the complete opposite direction of Rochester."

The rep said, "I know, just hang with me."

It took the rep about 20 minutes of clicking on a keyboard and calling people before she had our flights straightened out.

At first, the rep did not tell us where we were flying to other than Austin, TX. She said, "I have you guys getting home tomorrow afternoon. Right now I have you on a flight to Austin. When you land in Austin, you will have to go to the luggage carousel and pick up your checked in bags. Then you have to check them back in again."

Shannon asked, "Why do we have to pick up our bag? Why won't it just fly with us to Rochester?"

The rep said, "Well, you will be flying Southwest to Austin. From Austin, you will be on AirTran. Since the merger of the two companies, our computers are not synced up yet. That's why...Next!"

As Shannon and I walked away towards security, Shannon looked at our flight vouchers. She said, "Well, if we are flying to Austin, my cousin Hailey lives there. Depending on what time we land there and need to depart from there, maybe she could pick us up. Maybe we could spend the night with her?"

Upon further investigation of our tickets, Shannon realized that our flight to Austin wouldn't land there until 10pm and that our next flight out of there was 6:30am! Shannon didn't want to bug her cousin like that.

After Shannon and I cleared through security, we went to our gate to make sure everything was still on time, which it was.

Shannon and I had over two hours to kill before we needed to board. She asked me if I wanted a beer. I told her that I did not want to pay for an overpriced airport beer. Shannon opted for an overpriced beer.

In the meantime, our flight to Austin was delayed.

Eventually it came time to board our plane to Austin. We took off late from the airport and landed very late at Austin; quarter after midnight.

Shannon and I exited the plane and went down to the luggage carousel to wait for our bag. It was almost 12:45am by the time we got our bag.

Shannon and I ended up sleeping overnight right next to the luggage carousel because we had nowhere to go!

Shannon and I slept like crap. It didn't help that the cleaning crew was running the floor Zamboni buffer right next to our heads.

I woke up at 4:40am and decided to take a stroll. I went upstairs to find the Southwest/AirTran check in counter. I quickly found it and noticed a line of about 50 people in it! The line was not moving because the check in counter did not open until 5am.

I rushed back downstairs and woke Shannon up. I told her that there was already a line for Southwest. We grabbed our bags and ran back upstairs.

It was around 5:30am when Shannon and I checked ourselves and our bags in.

Then we stood in another line; the security check point.

It was close to 5:45am by the time we passed through security and into Terminal H.

Shannon and I were starving, so we had a quick breakfast because our flight to Atlanta was departing at 6:30am! Shannon and I wolfed down our breakfasts and ran to our gate.

We stood in another line at our gate, as we waited to board our plane; naturally we were the last group to board.

The AirTran rep scanned our tickets and they were not registering, we couldn't board the plane! The AirTran rep told us to talk to the other AirTran rep at the gate.

By the time we go to the gate desk Shannon was on the verge of tears again. Shannon told the AirTran rep that our tickets didn't work and that we needed to be on that flight to get home! The AirTran rep looked at the tickets and scanned them. The rep looked at the tickets and told us that we never checked in. Shannon told her that that was impossible since we checked us and our bag in and got issued tickets just an hour earlier! The lady thankfully printed us out new tickets. Shannon and I ran back to our gate and hopped onto the airplane just before the gate and airplane doors were closed.

Our flight from Austin took off late, which was not good, because when we landed in Atlanta, we only had 10 minutes to catch our connecting flight to Baltimore!

Once we landed in Atlanta, the flight attendant got on the PA and said, "If Atlanta is your last destination, please be courteous and hang tight because there are people trying to make their connecting flights." I was in the very back of the plane and naturally, no one gave a puck what the flight attendant said; the whole entire airplane got up before me. I was sweating bullets, thinking that we were going to miss our connecting flight!

15 minutes later I finally exited the airplane and I found Shannon. Shannon and I were not seated together on that flight. Thankfully, our connecting flight to Baltimore was delayed by half an hour. That meant that Shannon and I were able to make our connecting flight.

Once we landed in Baltimore, we had a couple hour layover.

In Baltimore, we landed in Terminal B. Our flight to Rochester was to take off from Gate A11.

During our layover, Shannon and I had lunch. After lunch, we went over to A11 where we found out our flight home to Rochester was delayed by a half hour. Our flight was supposed to take off at 2:30pm, but was rescheduled for 3pm. At 3pm, we were told that our flight had been moved to Gate B2! There was a huge group of people that made a mass exodus to Gate B2!

Our flight did not take off from B2 until 4pm; an hour and a half after the regular scheduled time.

Shannon and I finally landed in Rochester a little after 5pm.

Shannon waited at the luggage carousel for our bag. In the meantime, I ran out to the Long Term parking garage to get the car. The morning before, Friday January 3, 2014, Shannon's parents took a flight out of the Rochester airport. They left us their Ford Taurus so we would have a ride home.

At the luggage carousel, Shannon gave me the keys to the Taurus. I ran outside into the 36^{0}F weather and it felt like a heat wave compared to the -35^{0}F weather we experienced in Winnipeg.

I found the Taurus in parking spot #7 of 2E. I tossed the two back packs into the trunk. I unlocked the doors to the Taurus and hopped into the driver's seat. I put the key into the ignition and turned the car over...*Tick! Tick! Tick! Tick!* The battery was dead. Shannon and I were so close to home, but still so far away!

I went back into the airport and found Shannon and broke the bad news to her.

With our bags at hand, we walked over to the information booth.

I told the granny that was working there, "Hi, my battery is dead. Do you guys have a jump pack or anyone that can help me?"

The granny said, "Oh sonny, you're the 3rd person this week with the same question. Yes I can help."

I was thinking that she had a jump pack behind the desk. Instead she gave me two phone numbers to call.

I called the first phone number. It rang for about 20 times before I hung up.

I called the second number and got a reordering, "*Hi, You've reached the Greater Rochester International Airport. If you know your party's extension...*"

I hung up the phone and called our friend Karl for help. The past week, Karl was watching our 5 year old black lab Teppo Numminen.

Karl said he would drive out and give us a hand.

A half hour later, Karl was at the airport and picked us up. The three of use drove around the airport and into the Long Term parking garage.

Karl popped the hood of his Honda Civic and I popped the hood of the Ford Taurus. With a set of jumper cables, we were able to fire up the Taurus.

It took Shannon and me over 26 hours to get back home to Western New York!

***

On Thursday January 9, 2014, the Buffalo Sabres hired a new General Manager, Tim Murray. Tim Murray looked like a younger version of Perry Mason.

Hopefully this guy could right the ship...

***

Wednesday January 29, 2014.

Brigid, Shannon, and I were ready to board our early morning flight at the Rochester Airport. Brigid was Shannon's coworker, friend, and international travel buddy.

From Rochester, we had a two hour layover in Charlotte, North Carolina.

During our layover, I saw there was a Bojangles' in the airport terminal! I was starving, so I decided to make Bojangles' my breakfast destination! I had an egg and cheese biscuit with fries and a black coffee. I was still hungry, so I went back and ordered a sweet potato pie, which was out of this world!

It was about noon when we took off for Phoenix, Arizona.

The first two hours of our flight were extremely turbulent. For a while there, I didn't think we were going to make it to Phoenix. The turbulence was so bad, that the flight attendants waited the two hours until we hit smooth air to bring out the refreshment cart.

We landed in Phoenix a little after 3pm.

Once we grabbed our bag from the carousel, we hopped on a shuttle to the rental car agency.

While I waited to get the car, I struck up a conversation with the rental car agent. I asked him what there was to do in Phoenix. He couldn't really give me a good answer. He asked what we were interested in. I told him that Brigid wanted to go to a winery. The rental car guy told us there weren't wineries in Phoenix, but in Sedona. I told him that I wanted to see a ghost town and he recommended Jerome. Nothing he recommended was in Phoenix.

I did tell the rental car guy that we were in for the Sabres @ Coyotes game the following evening.

The rental car guy informed us that since the Phoenix Coyotes were purchased from the NHL, season ticket holders now had to pay for parking. He said when the NHL owned the team, there was free parking for season ticket holders. He went on to advise us to park at the AMC Movie Theater or mall for free parking, otherwise we would be gouged $15-$20 for parking. I thought that was good, sound advice.

The last piece of advice that the rental car guy gave me was to not drink any alcohol. He noticed the strange look on my face and he told me that the Sheriff Joe Arpaio of Maricopa County wanted to abolish drunk driving, a vendetta. I was told that there are random DWI stops and if I got pinched, I would be thrown in the clink for at least a month and I would have to wear a pink jump suit. I was also told there were pink jump suit chain gangs.

In the rental car parking corral a red Chevy Impala caught Shannon's eye.

Once we were settled into the red Impala, we were ready to explore Phoenix.

Shannon's parents were in Phoenix the week before and recommended the Desert Botanical Garden. My in laws enjoyed the garden and the Dal Chihuly glass art exhibit that was there. So our first stop was to the Desert Botanical Garden.

We got to the Desert Botanical Gardens in time for their 4-8pm exhibit.

Once we paid our admission we walked into the botanical gardens. Right away we saw our first Chihuly piece. It was a very large blue orb with white icicles protruding out of it; it reminded me of the end of *Star Wars, The Empire Strikes Back* when the Death Star exploded.

Brigid, Shannon, and I found an adult beverage kiosk. The ladies got wine but I ordered a local brew, 8th Street Ale; brewed by 4 Peaks Brewing Company. I didn't really like pale ales, but it was good enough that I had two of them.

The Chihuly's glass artwork was placed throughout the cacti in the botanical gardens.

After the sun went down, Chihuly's artwork was illuminated, which added a different element to his work.

As we walked through the gardens, we overheard a couple talking about sweet potato and caramelized onion tacos. Shannon and Brigid started to water at the mouth just hearing about them.

I decide to ask the guy about these tacos. The guy, Patrick, told me they were at Sol Cocina in Scottsdale.

I asked Patrick what there was to do in Phoenix. Though Patrick had grown up in Phoenix, he couldn't really tell us where to go or what to do. The only advice Patrick had for me was to not drink and drive, otherwise I would be thrown in jail and wear a pink jumpsuit. I took note of everything.

Eventually Brigid, Shannon, and I saw everything we wanted to, so we left.

The next stop on our trip was to Ted's Hot Dogs in Tempe, Arizona!

Ted's Hot Dogs was a Buffalo delicatessen and staple of the community. Besides their eight Buffalo locations, there was a satellite location in Tempe. I wanted and needed to go to Ted's in Tempe and do a comparison taste test!

From the Desert Botanical Gardens, we were only about 10 minutes away from Ted's.

We found Ted's without a problem.

As soon as I walked into Ted's Hot Dogs, I felt like we had just flown back to Buffalo!

There were Buffalo News paper kiosks with the past week's paper in them. There was Weber's Mustard for sale along with Sahlen's hot dogs.

A sign on the wall in the kitchen read, "Sahlen's hot dogs, Imported daily from Buffalo, NY."

There was a line of at least 15 people deep, so it took us a while to order.

I ended up having a Loganberry Milkshake, fries, and a foot long hotdog with the works...everything tasted just like home!

Ted's was decorated as if it was still in Buffalo. On the wall were posters of the Taste of Buffalo, Buffalo News articles, and awards Ted's has won. Additionally, the walls had pennants of almost all the WNY area colleges; Syracuse University, Rochester Institute of Technology, Niagara University, University at Buffalo, Buffalo State, Daemen, Hobart, Geneseo, Canisius College, D'Youville, St Bonaventure University, and others.

I told Shannon that if there was a Mighty Taco built next door, that I would seriously consider moving to Phoenix.

After dinner, we hopped on the highway and drove out to our hotel, the Ramada in Peoria.

Thursday, January 30, 2014, game day!

Our game wasn't until 7pm, so we still had a whole day of exploring to do.

That morning, we decided to go hiking at Lost Dutchman State Park.

We got out to the park around 10am. We hiked around through the desert for at least an hour and a half. At one point, we reached the summit of our trail. From our vantage point, we could see downtown Phoenix, which was 40 miles away.

After our hike, I wanted to go to an authentic ghost town, but we couldn't find one.

However, across the street from Lost Dutchman State Park was a cheesy tourist attraction, Goldfield Ghost Town. I thought that was the closest we were going to get to finding a ghost town, so we went.

Within the ghost town were little artisan shops. There was a saloon that we stopped into for appetizers. There was a church at the end of the ghost town. Every Sunday at 11am, the church held Mass.

Shannon and Brigid wanted to go horseback riding, so the three of us went for a half hour session.

After we got done horseback riding, it was time to find food. Shannon and Brigid wanted to try the sweet potato and caramelized onion tacos at Sol Cocina in Scottsdale.

I drove the ladies the 35 minute car ride up to Sol Cocina.

We sat at the outside bar at Sol. We saw our buddy Patrick from the night before; he was waiting tables.

The ladies had some wine and I had a Corona. We all ordered a sweet potato with caramelized onion taco and it was good. I was full from the appetizers at the ghost town, otherwise I would have ordered another taco.

As we sat at the bar, they had the Golf Channel on. I disliked golf, but the TV was showing the live Waste Management PGA tour that was happening down the street in Scottsdale. I thought that was interesting.

When we were done with lunch and cashed out, it was around 5pm.

We drove up Scottsdale Road to Loop 101.

We took Loop 101 eastbound to Glendale.

By the time we parked the red Impala at the shopping center, it was almost 6pm.

The three of us then changed into our Sabres garb. Brigid wore a Buffalo Sabres t-shirt. Shannon's Christmas present came in late, but in time for our Phoenix hockey trip. I had taken her new Blue and Gold jersey to a pro shop and had Teppo Numminen's name and number stitched on it! I had my black "Goat/Beauty and the Beast" Sabres jersey done up with Teppo's name and number too, just so we would match and not fight.

After we were dressed, we headed on over to Jobing.com Arena.

Westgate was located right next to Jobing.com Arena.

Westgate was a built up area that had many bars, restaurants, a mini Bellagio water show, and pregame festivities.

Brigid, Shannon, and I stopped into McFadden's Saloon. Brigid had a wine and Shannon and I each had a pint of beer.

After getting our drinks, the three of us made our way to the outside bar area. Brigid commented on how many Sabres fans there were, and there were a ton! I think Buffalo fans out numbered the Phoenix fans!

Soon it was 6:45pm, almost game time.

The three of us finished up our drinks and made our way into Jobing.com Arena.

We made our way up to Section 226 where our seats were. Brigid grabbed another wine while Shannon got another beer.

We had about 15 minutes to kill before the game started, so we decided to wander.

I had heard that the Phoenix Coyotes had retired Teppo Numminen's number, so we walked around the upper concourse until we saw Teppo's number. We took a picture of Teppo's retired number so we could show our Teppo puppy back home.

Soon the lights went down and the music cranked. The fans started to yell and cheer. The PA announcer guy informed us that Ryan Miller's career against the Phoenix Coyotes was 5-0. Shannon and I looked at each other with a grimace. I said, "Oh boy, we'll probably witness his first career loss against the Coyotes since we have a black cloud over us!"

Headed into tonight's game, Buffalo was still in dead last place in the league!

There was some opera singer dude who sang the American National Anthem.

Soon it was time to start the game and drop the puck!

Instantly a *"Let's Go Buffalo!"* chant started!

With the first stoppage of play, the Coyotes jumbotron zoomed in on Buffalo Sabres defense coach Teppo Numminen, with caption, "Welcome back Teppo Numminen." Teppo acknowledged it and waved. Personally, I think Teppo saw Shannon and me wearing Buffalo Sabre Teppo jerseys and waved to us!

Buffalo broke the shutout when Tyler Ennis' snap shot beating Phoenix's goalie Thomas Greiss. The whole place went crazy! There were a lot of cheers and it felt like a Buffalo home game!

For being Buffalo, they played a strong 1st Period. However, late in the 1st Period, Buffalo took a penalty and the Yotes took advantage of the power play and scored. The Coyotes' Antoine Vermette scored on Buffalo goalie Ryan Miller to tie the game 1-1.

18 seconds later, Phoenix's Dave Moss put the Coyotes up by 1; 2-1 Coyotes lead.

After the Coyote's second goal, I looked at Shannon and said, "And it begins, business as usual!"

Moments later, the horn went to signal the end of the 1st Period. I was not surprised, but rather upset that Buffalo was outshot 12-20 at the end of the 1st Period! You can't win games when you don't shoot the puck!

I commented to Shannon that I was a little surprised that half of the arena was full. I added that I was not surprised that there were more Sabres fans than Coyote fans.

During intermission, I looked through the game program and the roster. I was surprised and glad to see Buffalo native and former Buffalo Sabre Tim Kennedy had found work with the Coyotes.

Soon enough, the 2nd Period started. Early in the 2nd Period, Buffalo found themselves on the power play.

I have to say that the Sabres surprised me when they scored on the power play! Alexander Sulzer blasted a shot from the point which got to the goalie. The goalie couldn't get the rebound. Buffalo crashed the next. The Sabres Villie Leino had a whack at the puck before Sabres Captain Steve Ott put it in the net! The Sabres tied it 2-2!

During the 2nd Period, one of the linesmen got hit in the side of the head with the puck. He fell to the ice and eventually the whistle was blown. The linesman turned out to be ok.

With less than 5 minutes left in the 2nd Period, the Yotes were pressing in the Sabres zone. A shot was taken at the net, but the puck got deflected and hit the referee right in the face! Blood started pouring out! The play was whistled dead and the ref skated from the right corner of Ryan Miller to the Coyotes bench and down the hall to the locker room. There was a blood trail across the ice.

Before the 2nd Period ended, the injured ref was back out on the ice.

The 2nd Period ended with both clubs going to the locker room with a 2-2 tie.

During the 2nd Intermission, the ice crew was out to try to scrape up the blood from the ref.

At some point during the game, it was advertised that there was a Tim Hortons coffee kiosk at Gate 2 on the 1st Floor! During the 2nd Intermission, I was on a mission to get some Timmy Hos and perform a taste test! I wanted to see how it compared to the stuff back home.

I fought through a lot of people, but I finally made my way to the Tim Hortons kiosk. There were already 20+ people in the line, all wearing Buffalo gear.

I ended up ordering a black coffee and a hot chocolate.

I brought the drinks back up to the ladies. Shannon loved her hot chocolate. The medium black tasted just like it did back home. The coffee cup even said, "Roasted in Rochester, NY." I told Shannon again, "If they build a Mighty Taco out here, I think I will move here!"

The 3rd Period started and Buffalo quickly found themselves in the penalty box. Buffalo's Zemgus Girgensons came to the rescue for Buffalo by scoring a shorthanded goal on Thomas Greiss! Buffalo went ahead 3-2!

Buffalo held their lead all period.

With about a minute and a half left, Phoenix pulled their goalie, but it wasn't enough! Buffalo had won 3-2 in the desert!

After the game, the ladies wanted to go to Margaritaville in Westgate.

At Margaritaville, Shannon ordered the Perfect Margarita, Brigid got some mixed drink that tasted like Pine-Sol, and I got water on the rocks.

After drinks we left Margaritaville.

On the way back to the hotel, the ladies were hungry. They eventually settled on EZ Mac from a gas station.

We got back to the hotel closer to midnight.

The alarm went off at 6am on Friday January 31, 2014.

Shannon, Brigid, and I needed to pack up our belongings and head out to the airport because we had a 9am flight to Denver, Colorado.

We had no issues with checking out of the hotel, returning the car, or getting through the airport.

Our flight took off on time and we landed on time in Denver at 11:30am.

As we waited forever at the luggage carousel for our bag, the three of us leafed through brochures. Eventually our bag came and then we hopped on the shuttle to the rental car agency.

For some reason, I used Dollar Rental again. I should have learned my lesson from when we rented with them in LA. Needless to say, we waited at least an hour in line at Dollar Rental before we got our car. The line at Dollar Rental was so deep that the line went outside the building and people were waiting in the snow and freezing cold! We ended up getting some Nissan Versa shit box. That car was a far cry from the Chevy Impala we had the day before. That Nissan shit box struggled to get out of its own way. Accelerating onto I-70, the shit box was red lining at 5,000 rpm to get us up to speed on the highway.

Shannon had asked me what I wanted to do or see while we were in Denver. I told her that I wanted to go to the Coors Brewery tour in Golden, Colorado.

Shannon didn't want to. She asked me why I wanted to.

I said, "When in Rome, do as the Romans. When we were in St. Louis, we went to the Bud brewery. When we were in PA, we went to the Yuengling brewery. When we were in Boston, we went to the Sam Adams brewery."

Shannon said, "Ok, I get it! I get your point."

So we drove out to Golden, CO for the Coors beer tour.

It was about a 45 minute drive from the Denver Airport to the Coors Brewery.

We arrived at the visitor parking lot at the brewery and then parked the Nissan shit box. Then we boarded a bus which drove us around the block to the main visitors' entrance.

Our bus drive would have dropped us off in front of the doors to the visitors' entrance, but there were two big white tour buses parked in the drop off spot. Our bus driver was complaining up a storm and radioed the lobby to bitch about the two buses in her way. Anyway, our bus driver dropped us off and we had to walk a little further to get into the brewery, no big deal.

After Brigid, Shannon, and I got into the lobby, I noticed the guy in front of me was wearing a Sabres jacket. Since I was wearing my Sabres hoodie and hat, I said, "Go Sabres!" The guy wearing the Sabres coat pretended to not hear me. I looked around and saw some dude with a Buffalo Bills hat on and I thought that was cool.

Brigid noticed the guy wearing the Bills winter hat and said, "Woot-woot! Go Bills! Represent!"

As I looked around the lobby, I realized that the group in in front of us was a mainly a sausage fest, almost no chicks to be seen. As I looked at the group of guys around us, I started to notice some familiar faces. I finally elbowed Shannon and said, "Hey, there's your boyfriend over there, the tall one in the black hat."

Shannon looked around the room and finally located the tall glass of water wearing a black hat and thought nothing of it.

That's when I told her, "That's Ryan Miller…"

Then Shannon's eyes lit up!

We were standing in the lobby of Coors Brewery with the Buffalo Sabres! Brigid, Shannon, and I thought it was pretty awesome.

I thought about walking up to them and striking up a conversation, but I didn't want to bug them. I have heard stories of people who have met their favorite celebrity and the celebrity was put off or upset. All the players were talking to each other so I felt awkward butting in and running my yap.

I was hoping that we would be on the same beer tour with the Sabres but that didn't work out. The Sabres ended up having their own special tour. I overheard that when their tour ended they would be invited up to the employee lounge on the 6th floor and they would meet owner Peter Coors.

We had to wait for the Sabres tour to start before our tour could start.

During parts of our tour, we did run into the Sabres group.

On our beer tour, we got to learn how beer was made, again.

Our tour guide Jade took us through the brewery and showed us different parts of the beer making process.

At one point in the tour Jade asked us if anyone had any questions. One college kid piped up and asked, "What's the deal with Keystone? I hear that it's made at the bottom of the barrel of when they clean out the beer vats." Naturally everyone laughed because that was the folk lore about the 'Stones.

Jade laughed too and said that Keystone wasn't made when the beer vats were cleaned. She said that Keystone had a wider tolerance for when the beer was made. She said Keystone was still made with the same quality ingredients as all the other Coors products were.

Jade brought us to the quality control room. At the quality control room, beer was sampled every hour of every day, 365 days a year. Jade told us that if the beer didn't live up to their quality standards, then the beer went to another on site facility and the bad beer was converted into an ethanol fuel for cars.

In the next room, we sampled a small Dixie cup of either Coors Banquet or Coors Light. Jade told us how Coors Banquet got its name. During the gold rush era, miners would come down from the mountains each day and celebrate with a party or banquet with their gold findings; hence the Banquet Beer.

Also, Jade told us how Coors Light, *the Silver Bullet*, got its nickname. As the story went, when one of the Coors kids was in college the student body beer of choice was Coors Light. However they did not refer to it as Coors Light. Due to its silver and narrow bullet shaped can, the students started calling the beer the Silver Bullet. The Coors college student told this to her family and thanks to drunk college students, the marketing idea of *the Silver Bullet* was born!

As the tour progressed, we got to see other parts of the brewery and the beer making process including the hops aging room and packaging room.

We learned that during Prohibition, no employee was laid off. Instead, the brewery produced near-beer and malted milk.

During our tour of the brewery, Shannon and I could see the tour group ahead of us, which was the Buffalo Sabres. However, we never fully caught up to them.

Jade showed us a list of different beers that Coors brewed and other products that they were in partnership with. Jade told us that even though Coors was in partnership with Miller, the Coors facility in Golden did not brew Miller. Jade also touched on Coors' partnership with Molson. Originally Coors wanted to open up a brewery in the Great North. Canadian law stated that new breweries to Canada needed to put a brewery in every Providence. Coors didn't want to because that was not financially feasible. Instead, Coors partnered with Molson to be able to see Coors products up in Canada. Jade told us that no Molson product was produced at the Coors facility in Golden or anywhere else in the State. Molson was strictly brewed in Canada.

Jade told us that Coors brewed a beer called Colorado Native, which was made only from Colorado grown ingredients and was sold only exclusively in Colorado. Unfortunately the tasting room was tapped out of it. Jade mentioned that area bars or beer distributors may have some left over.

Next we all went to the tasting room!

The rule was three tastings per person. Brigid didn't like beer, only wine, so she deferred her beers to Shannon and me.

Naturally Shannon and I had to try fresh Coors and Coors Light; you know, when in Rome...

There were about six different beers on tap and we sampled them all.

I asked our tour guide Jade if there was a correct way to order the Coors Banquet beer. I told her that I didn't want to sound like a doofus or a tourist while ordering a Coors.

Jade informed me that "Coors," "Banquet," or "Coors Banquet" were all acceptable terms for correctly ordering an original Coors.

Once we left the brewery, we were in search of a microbrewery that also served food. We were told to go to Mountain Toad Brewery because it was a microbrewery and had a food truck next to it.

At the Mountain Toad Brewery, Shannon ordered a huge flight of beers. Shannon loved them but I wasn't a fan. They were mainly dark and heavy beers; a sipping beer. I liked beers that went down quick, something that I can pound two or three of before walking into a Bills or Sabres game. I think I drank about half of one of the eight ounce beers before I felt full.

For dinner, Brigid had chicken. Shannon had some fried tofu crap. I attempted the brisket, which was good enough to rival Dinosaur BBQ or Sticky Lips BBQ in New York State.

After we finished dinner, we drove around downtown Golden for a few minutes.

On our way out of town, we stopped at a liquor store to pick up beer. Brigid picked up a four pack of wine. I picked up a 12 pack of Bach 19 Bock, a 12 pack of Colorado Native, and a big bottle of Coors.

After we stocked up on supplies, we headed back to our hotel, La Quinta, which was right by the Denver Airport.

It was around 8:30pm when we checked into the hotel.

Once we unpacked, we walked across the street to Ruby Tuesdays. Shannon and Brigid wanted to get something small to eat and some drinks. I was full, so I just had water and mozzarella sticks.

Soon it was bedtime.

February 2014

We woke up around 9am on Saturday February 1, 2014. Originally I wanted to go to the Denver Mint, but it was closed to tours due to remodeling; that was the third mint tour that I missed out on.

The girls really wanted to check out the Molly Brown House Museum.

I had no idea who Molly Brown was but I didn't have a problem taking the girls there. Heck, I was dragging them to a God awful Sabres game, the least I could do was to humor them and take them to a girly museum.

The Molly Brown House was located in downtown Denver.

We had an 11am tour. The tour mainly revolved around the history of Molly Brown's house, as opposed to her life; though we did learn about Molly's life. During the tour we learned about how she grew up in Hannibal, Missouri and moved to Colorado and married James Brown (not the Godfather of Soul). Molly Brown always wanted to marry rich, but at the time she married James, he was not wealthy. Eventually James struck it rich with the mining industry. The couple had two kids. One of Molly Brown's claims to fame was that she was on the Titanic and survived! We learned about Molly being a philanthropist and an activist for workers' rights. In her later years, she tried her hand at acting.

Our tour ended at noon.

Brigid, Shannon, and I hopped into the car and drove over to the Pepsi Center. We paid for parking and then tailgated. Brigid had some of her wine while Shannon and I sucked down a few Colorado Natives. While we pregamed, we noticed quite a few Sabres fans! I was pleasantly shocked to see Sabres fans because I did not think there would be many Buffalonians out there in Denver.

It was 12:40pm when the three of us decided to venture into the Pepsi Center.

Our seats were in Section 322.

Before the National Anthem, there was an honor ceremony for the players and coaches going to the 2014 Sochi Olympics. Honors for the visiting Buffalo Sabres were given first. Ryan Miller was honored for Team USA. Henrik Tallinder and Jhonas Enroth were honored for Sweden. Sabres interim head coach Ted Nolan and forward Zemgus Girgensons were honored for Latvia.

For the Colorado Avalanche, Paul Stastny was honored for Team USA. Matt Duchene was honored for Team Canada. Semyon Varlamov was playing for Team Russia. Gabe Landeskog was playing for Team Sweden.

As each Olympian was named, a pair of pee wee hockey players skated out from the Zamboni entrance with a flag of the country for each Olympian.

Then the National Anthem was sung.

I was amazed at how empty the Pepsi Center was for a Saturday afternoon game. I'd say that probably half the arena was full and that a quarter of the fans were Sabre fans. I think most Denver people we more excited about tomorrow's Super Bowl 48 because their Denver Broncos were playing in it.

The couple in front of us was from Dunkirk, New York and they moved out there years ago because the husband was in the Service. The wife, Jeanette, told us that there were a lot of WNY transplants in Denver due to being in the Service.

Jeanette told us that there was a Buffalo backer bar in downtown called Lodo's Bar and Grill. She told us that Lodo's had Canadian beer and really good chicken wings. They added that they were going there after the game.

The 1st Period was dreadful and pitiful for the Sabres. I wasn't sure if the Sabres were hung over from hanging out at the Coors Brewery the night before or if they were skating slowly because they were stoned (As of January 1, 2014, recreational use of pot was legal in the state of Colorado).

Buffalo dug themselves a pretty big hole!

By the end of the 1st Period, Colorado had a 3-0 lead with goals from Tyson Barrie, a power play goal from Jamie McGinn, and an even strength goal by Gabriel Landeskog.

In the 2nd Period, Colorado added to their lead. Marc-Andre Cliché made it a 4-0 Avalanche lead.

Midway through the 2nd Period, Buffalo finally broke the shutout. Matt D'Agostini scored on Semyon Varlamov to make it a 4-1 Colorado lead.

Colorado answered with a power play goal from Nathan MacKinnon.

All the while, fans were taunting the Buffalo goalie Ryan Miller. I thought that was a little dumb. Just an hour earlier during pregame ceremonies, they were cheering him on for being one of Team USA's goalies. Now the same fans were taunting one of their own...oh well, people are dip shits.

At the start of the 3rd Period, we had a goaltender change. Buffalo's head coach Ted Nolan pulled Ryan Miller and put Jhonas Enroth in net.

Colorado's Landeskog and McGinn both scored again on Enroth.

The Colorado Avalanche destroyed the Sabres 7-1, what a horrible game for Sabre fans.

After the game, we decided to let traffic die down.

Brigid, Shannon, and I found a bar across the street from the Pepsi Center called Tailgate Roadhouse. We ordered pizza and had a round of drinks. The place was pretty cool. There were tailgates of cars from the 1950s, hence the name and theme of the place.

We were there for about an hour before we decided to check out the Buffalo backer bar, Lodo's.

Brigid put Lodo's into her phone's GPS and we were there within minutes.

Lodo's was pretty awesome. There were Sabre fans everywhere; it felt like being back home.

We ended up getting a booth. The pizza from Tailgate Roadhouse held me over for only so long. I was ready to try out Lodo's chicken wings. The also served Molson XXX! I finally found an establishment (besides the Joe in Detroit) that served XXX, so I needed to get a bottle of that too. Unfortunately they did not have any Molson Brador, but the XXX still tied me over. Shannon and Bridget were still full, so they didn't have anything.

While we dined, some guy came over the PA and announced that former Buffalo Bill great Andre Reed was finally being inducted into the Football Hall of Fame! The whole bar cheered in celebration. Seconds later, the Bills Shout song was played and everyone sang and yelled along! I was happy for Andre Reed to finally get into the Hall of Fame. It was Andre's 5th time on the ballot to get in.

The three of us still wanted to explore downtown, so after Lodo's we walked down Larimer Street.

Along the way, we saw a Starbucks. Brigid liked Starbucks, so we went in so she could get some sort of coffee concoction. I didn't like Starbucks and I refused to go there. I am brand loyal when it comes to my hot beverage of choice. If I was doing hot chocolate or a black coffee, then I was only going to Tim Hortons. If I was doing a black French Vanilla, then it was Dunkin Donuts.

While wandering, we stumbled upon a Polish pierogie bar called Polished Tavern. By now, Brigid and Shannon were hungry, so we stopped in. Shannon and I shared the pierogie sampler platter; hearty potato and cheese, feta and spinach, and succulent sauerkraut and mushroom. Shannon had some foo foo girly mixed drinks. I had a Warka beer. Brigid ordered some food and wine. The place was nice. All the bartenders and staff were straight off the boat, which added to the ambiance.

After late night munchies, we started to head back to Lodo's.

On our walk back, we saw Coors Field, home to the Colorado Rockies.

Across the street from Lodo's was the Cowboy Lounge, a line dancing country bar. Shannon and Brigid had the biggest woodies and wanted to go in there.

I don't like Country Music.

I don't like Western Music.

I don't like dancing.

I can't stand line dancing.

I don't like cowboy boots.

I don't like country music because it's not my style. If country songs were played backwards, it was a great story! The dog was not dead. The pickup truck worked. You were not hung over. Your old lady came back.

I don't like Western Music because it is not Rock-n-Roll.

I don't like dancing because I am white and my body doesn't move that way. The only dancing I do is sideways dancing, *giggity*. Occasionally I will slow dance with the wife.

I couldn't stand Line Dancing because I was forced to do that crap when I was just a wee young lad at St. Stephens. In music class, Mrs. Orlowski made us do line dancing to Billy Ray Cyrus' *Achy Breaky Heart* and Marcia Griffith's *The Electric*, better known as *The Electric Slide*. I was scarred for life.

I don't like cowboy boots. Cowboy boots only look good on hot girls. Period.

I have two rules for boots.

    1. Must be water proof. It helps for shoveling snow.

    2. Must be steel toe for work.

When we first got to the Cowboy Lounge, it was dead. Shannon and Brigid did some line dancing by themselves. As the minutes passed and it got later in the night, more and more people showed up.

Our original game plan was to leave downtown at 10pm. We had a 1am flight out of Denver. We gave ourselves three hours so we could fill up the rental car, drop the rental car off, take the shuttle over to the airport, check in, make it through security, and make our flight.

Shannon and Brigid lost track of time, but I did not.

I was a party pooper and a wall flower. I sat at the bar and constantly checked the time.

It was 10:30pm when Shannon and Brigid came back to our booth to sip some more drink. I told the ladies that it was 10:30pm.

They said, "OK" and began to walk back out onto the dance floor.

I called them back and told them that we had to leave, but they did not want to.

I said, "We were supposed to leave at 10pm. It's now 10:30pm. I have no idea where I am or where I have to drop off the rental car. We need to go now so we can catch our flight back home."

The ladies weren't thrilled with me. They finished their drinks and we left.

I found a gas station to fill up the rental car.

Then we dropped of the rental car. Originally the rental agency didn't want to drive us back to the airport because their shuttle guy was on a 15 minute break. I was a little upset about that. It was already 11:15pm. The shuttle driver's entire work shift is a break! Besides driving a bus and moving bags for tips, there was no actual work. I think the shuttle driver was more pissed off that I was interrupting his smoke break.

Eventually we made it back to the airport.

We made it through security and found our terminal.

It was 12:30am and it was time to board.

The plane was full and Shannon and I weren't allowed to board.

The airlines wanted to put us on a flight Monday morning, but we told them that would not work because we both had to work on Monday.

The airlines then put us on a noon flight on Sunday.

Yet again, Shannon and I had to sleep overnight at another airport. Thankfully it wasn't in the luggage carousel this time.

Shannon and I boarded our noon flight from Denver to Boston.

We had a couple hour layover in Boston. We grabbed a bit to eat and watched a part of Super Bowl 48, Denver Broncos vs. Seattle Seahawks.

We had a short connecting flight to JFK Airport in NYC.

We had an hour long layover at JFK before we boarded our flight to Rochester.

It was midnight by the time Shannon's dad Jimbo picked us up from the Rochester Airport.

Our puppy dog Teppo was thrilled to see us when we finally arrived home.

***

On the eve of our next road trip, the Buffalo Sabres made a big trade. On Friday February 28, 2014, General Manager Tim Murray traded goalie Ryan Miller and Captain Steve Ott to the St. Louis Blues for goalie Jaroslav Halak and forwards Chris Stewart and William Carrier and draft picks. Shannon was absolutely devastated when she heard the news. Ryan Miller was her favorite player of the team. When I made her watch hockey back in 2004, Ryan Miller and Teppo Numminen were the two players that she latched onto. She was upset that her childhood hero had been peddled away. I tried to explain to Shannon that Miller was going to be a free agent at the end of the season. Most likely, Miller would not resign and return to the Sabres at the end of the season. As opposed to letting Miller walk at the end of the season, Murray traded Miller to at least get something for him, which I thought was a good idea.

Anyway, Miller would be joined by with his former Sabre teammate Derek Roy. Additionally, Miller would be playing with former Team USA teammates Kevin Shattenkirk, David Backes, and T.J. Oshie.

Once I told that information to Shannon, she quickly got a new 2nd favorite team. She hoped that Miller would go all the way and win the Stanley Cup with the St. Louis Blues. I told Shannon that it was quite possible for that to happen. I told her that after Buffalo lost in the 1999 Stanley Cup Finals, goalie Dominik Hasek was eventually traded to the Detroit Red Wings where he won two Stanley Cups...Buffalo was the farm team for the NHL.

March 2014

Saturday March 1, 2014; Shannon, Brigid, and I had a 1pm flight from the Rochester Airport.

Our first layover was in the city of Atlanta, former NHL home to the Atlanta Flames (1972-80) and Atlanta Thrashers (1999-2011).

Shannon, Brigid, and I finally landed at the Dallas Fort Worth airport at 6pm, local time.

Once we got our luggage, we hopped on the shuttle to Dollar Rental Car.

Dollar Rental advised me to use their insurance on the car. I informed them that I already got insurance on the car through Orbitz. Dollar Rental informed me that that was a 3rd party insurance company and they only covered a limited amount. The 3rd party insurance didn't cover for days lost. For example, if the car was in an accident, I would still have to pay for the car for however long it was in the repair shop; highway robbery if you ask me. Also, I had insurance on my cars and house to begin with. That stupid car that I was about to rent had three insurances covering it! By using Dollar Rental's insurance, they told me if I was in an accident, I could "walk away" with no fault or money out of my pocket.

There I had my choice between a Fiat 500 or some Mazda shit box; I went with the Fix It Again Tony.

Next, we checked into our hotel, Days Inn Irving.

After we dropped our luggage off, we grabbed a bite to eat at Subway.

While we ate our dinner at Subway, my mom texted me and informed me that Buffalo Sabres hockey operations president Pat LaFontaine had quit and no details were given. That was aggravating to hear because Patty gave the Sabres some much needed street cred.

After dinner, Brigid, Shannon, and I hopped back into the car and we headed westward towards Fort Worth because we were going to a rodeo at the Stockyards.

The parking lot at the rodeo was awesome! Nothing but American pickup trucks! Most of the pickup trucks were diesel duallies, Texas Edition.

I had never been to a rodeo in person. My only exposure to a rodeo was what I had seen on ESPN.

The rodeo was a lot more fun in person than on TV.

We got to the rodeo late, so we missed the opening ceremonies; however we got there in time to see the calf roping. I was cheering for the calves to get away unscathed; nothing like cheering for the underdog!

After calf roping, we enjoyed some bronco riding. The bucking broncos were fun and interesting to watch. Most riders stayed on until the buzzer rang.

Once bronco riding finished, the rodeo clowns invited all the children into the arena. The rodeo clowns did some calisthenics with the kids, and then a calf was released into the arena. The 5-13 year olds had to chase down the calf. Whoever wrangled the calf won a prize. I thought that was so weird! I had never experienced anything like that. My first thought was of a five year old getting trampled by a calf. My second thought was that must be the norm in Texas.

After the kids wrangled the calf, it was time for some barrel racing. The women riders had a timed event. They had to circle around three 55 gallon drums and cross the start/finish line. The barrel races were entertaining.

After barrel racing, the ladies tried their hand at calf roping. Almost all the calves escaped untied!

Once the ladies' calf roping finished, the rodeo clowns invited the kids down to the arena again. They did some more calisthenics and then chased down a sheep. It was still weird for me. I couldn't believe in this sue happy country that we live in, that parents and the rodeo were fine with that. However, posted all around the metal fence to the arena were signs that read something along the lines of, "Enter at your own risk. Rodeo not responsible for injuries."

It did not take long for the 50+ kids to corner and wrangle the sheep.

Next on the bill was the famed bull riding!

Brigid, Shannon, and I were sitting right next to the cages that held the bulls. It was interesting to watch how the cowboys loaded up the bulls into their cages. Quite a few bull riders wore protective vests, similar to ones catchers wear in baseball. Some bull riders opted for a Dominik Hasek styled goalie helmet for head protection.

Most bull riders did not stay on the bull very long, under 10 seconds.

After the rodeo ended, Shannon and Brigid wanted to grab a drink at a bar that had live music. We soon found ourselves at the Love Shack. Shannon had a Butt Light Margarita, Brigid had white wine, and I had a root beer. We listened to two dudes on acoustic guitars sing country in an open air bar in 70 degree weather. It was a little after 11pm local time when we called it a night and headed back to the hotel.

When we woke up on Sunday March 2nd, it was 30^{0}F. Back in Rochester, it was warmer, 34^{0}F.

The first thing on the docket for Sunday was breakfast at a Waffle House!

Once we got to a Waffle House, we had to wait about 20 minutes for a seat because they were slammed. As we waited, I loaded up on all the free coffee I wanted. Once we were seated, I looked over the menu. I ordered a single Waffle House waffle, a grilled cheese, and hash browns that were smothered (onions), covered (cheese), diced (tomatoes), and peppered (jalapenos). Breakfast was delicious!

After we finished breakfast I asked Shannon for a dollar so I could play a couple songs in the juke box. I advised Shannon and Brigid to wait for me in the car. The first song I selected was a Johnny Cash song…the second song I selected was the *Waffle House Theme Song*. I made sure that it would be playing well after we left the Waffle House!

Moments later we were on Highway 114 towards Dallas. While we were on the highway, we encountered a traffic jam and came to a crawl. Suddenly we saw lightning and heard a loud thunderous boom. Seconds later, it began to hail. I had never experienced thunder, lightning, and hail at the same time, I thought it was very strange.

We finally arrived in downtown Dallas a few ticks after 1pm, just in time to miss the downtown guided tour trolley bus ride. The next bus tour was for 3pm.

To kill two hours, the three of us decided to visit the Old Red Museum.

Old Red was built in 1892 and was originally the courthouse, but now it was a museum dedicated to the history of Dallas.

In the lobby, we saw an old neon Pegasus sign, the former symbol of the Magnolia Oil Company. The sign on display was originally built for the 1939 World's Fair in New York.

On the 2nd Floor of Old Red was the main exhibit of the museum.

We learned how John Neely Bryan started up Dallas by the Trinity River. He advertised plots of land to settlers moving west.

The museum documented the history of Dallas from its establishment by Bryan to present day.

When 3pm rolled around, it was time to hop on our trolley for our tour of downtown Dallas.

The trolley tour was about a 75 minute bus ride through downtown. Our tour guide showed us Pioneer Plaza, John Neely Bryan's log cabin, the historical West End, Dallas Arts District, El Fenix restaurant, 6th Floor Museum/Texas School Book Depository, the spot where JFK was shot, Margaret Hunt Hill Bridge, a few different old and new Jesus churches, Thanksgiving Square, an art museum, the Neiman Marcus flag ship store (all the old fart ladies on the tour went crazy, but they were upset that it was closed on Sunday), the Bank of America building (which was lit up green at night), Reunion Tower, Dallas World Aquarium, Dallas Federal Reserve, American Airline Center, Pioneer Plaza (where Brigid, Shannon, and I got out to get our pictures taken with the 70 bronze steers and three cowboys), the Adolphus Hotel (opened by Mr. Budweiser himself, Mr. Adolphus Busch), the police station where Jack Ruby shot and killed Lee Harvey Oswald, and a couple other notable structures in downtown.

Once our tour ended, we hopped back into the Fix It Again Tony and drove up to Medieval Times, the ladies wanted to do that for dinner. Thankfully Medieval Times was running a promotion; otherwise it would have been expensive. Tickets were normally $60 a person, but if one brought a non-perishable food item, the ticket would have been half price. Needless to say, the three of us brought a non-perishable item.

Brigid, Shannon, and I ended up cheering for the Red and Yellow Knight.

Before we were allowed to enter the main event area, we stood around in the gift shop/bar area. Shannon and I both got a beer. Our round of beer was almost $20! We had to buy a stupid novelty cup to get beer, which was why they cost so much.

Dinner and the show were alright. Our Red and Yellow Knight was almost the winner of the tournament. Our knight made it to the final battle round, but lost to the Black and White Knight.

After our dinner and show ended, the three of us wanted to check out Reunion Tower in downtown Dallas.

We parked the car and walked into Hyatt Regency hotel and then took the escalator down to the lobby of Reunion Tower. The three of us had to go to the bathroom, so we did that before walking over to the ticket counter.

As I was whizzing at the urinal, I thought I had a little gas. As I was about to fart, I thought it was a gamble and I did not want to risk shitting my pants. I quickly finished my whiz and duck walked over to the shitter. I quickly grabbed an ass gasket, placed it on the seat, dropped trow, sat down, and unleased.

My crap was so violent and painful and it burned! It felt like I was passing pins and needles. I put all the blame on the Waffle House. It must have been all the coffee and the peppered hash browns that did me in.

After I finished pooping, I didn't think that I needed a colonoscopy for another few years. I was fairly confident that the jalapenos would have burned off any polyps that were down in that region.

I washed my hands with soap, warm water, and friction for a minute.

When I joined back up with Brigid and Shannon, I told them all about my burning poop.

Shannon told me that Reunion Tower closed early due to the inclement weather.

I asked Shannon, "Did they close the tower down when I was pooping because I would have felt bad."

Shannon said, "No. They closed the tower at 5pm."

At the time, it was about 7:30pm.

The three of us rode the escalator back up to the hotel lobby. We asked the lady at the front desk what there was to do in downtown Dallas.

The lady at front desk told us that there wasn't much to do in Dallas on a Sunday night. She said that the city was normally quiet on Sunday and Monday nights. She also added that many things would be closed due to the weather. However, she did direct us to Market Street in the West End. She said some bars and restaurants might still be open.

Brigid, Shannon, and I soon found ourselves at Gators in the West End. Gators was a bar and restaurant. It had a Jimmy Buffets theme to it and had about five fake gators hanging from the ceiling. Shannon had a local IPA while Brigid had a girly mixed drink and I enjoyed a local Texas beer, Firemans #4.

After a round of drinks, we decided to go back to the hotel.

On our way back, we stopped off at 7-11 to stock up on some booze. Brigid bought a four pack of white wine. I grabbed a 6 pack of Modelo and Texas brew Shiner Bock.

We went back to the hotel and watched the rest of the Oscars with host Ellen DeGeneres.

We woke up Monday March 3, 2014 at 8am.

I turned the news on and the main story was the horrible weather that was plaguing the Dallas-Fort Worth area; it was 18^0F and icy. Shannon looked up the weather in Rochester and it was warmer.

The news was reporting that most area schools were canceled. Many of the highways had car accidents that were causing major backups.

Brigid, Shannon, and I were out the door by 9:30am and ready to head back to downtown Dallas and do some more exploring.

We arrived at the 6th Floor Museum (formerly known as the Texas School Book Depository) at Dealey Plaza at 10am.

We parked the car and walked up to the museum to find out that it did not open until noon. That was a little upsetting. I thought that museums opened early because they were always filled with students on field trips.

The three of us walked back to the car to figure out a new game plan.

We thought about going back to Reunion Tower. Brigid looked up Reunion Tower on her I-phone and found out that Reunion Tower was still closed. It would reopen later in the day at 3pm.

I did see on Trip Advisor that there was an 8 Track Museum in the arts section of Dallas. Shannon called the phone number and got ahold of the owner/curator. He said that he wasn't at the museum yet because of the bad weather. He said the museum was open by appointment only and that we could schedule an appointment for later in the day. We decided to pencil him in for a mid-afternoon tour.

Since everything in Dallas closed due to the weather, we weren't sure what to do.

Brigid, Shannon, and I decided to check out the "Grassy Knoll" from the JFK assassination since we were parked just behind it.

It was a little eerie walking around the area and seeing two "X"s painted on Elm Street to signify where JFK was shot.

There were a couple plaques in the area that we read.

Once we were done with the grassy knoll, we walked up Elm Street, back to Market Street and the West End.

We eventually found a retail cowboy outfitter shop that was open, so the girls wanted to go into it.

In the meantime, I couldn't get over how Reunion Tower was still closed; I was flabbergasted. How does one close a tower and why? If the tower was closed, did that mean the adjoining hotel was closed? Did that mean the tallest building in downtown Dallas, the Bank of America Building, was closed too? Did Bank of America tell their workers, "Hey, it's cold and windy today. Don't come to work…"

The girls ended up buying some jewelry at the cowboy outfitter store.

I tried going to the bar next door, but they were closed. Hoffbrau Steaks said they opened at 11am, but the sign on the door lied. It was a few minutes after 11am when I tried it again and the doors were still locked. Eventually the doors were unlocked. Brigid, Shannon, and I had an early lunch there.

Brigid had a steak with an Irish Coffee.

Shannon had some veggies and fried okra with local beer Rahr Ugly Pug.

I had steak fries, mac and chees, and another local beer, Rahr Blonde.

Hoffbrau Steaks was good. I enjoyed that they played the Oldies, it was a well-deserved reprieve from all the country music that I was tortured with on the trip.

One of the Oldies that played overhead was Dusty Springfield's *I Only Want to be With You*. I was a fan of Dusty and really enjoyed that song, but I needed some clarification on the lyrics to the song. So I asked Shannon and Brigid, "What is Dusty Springfield singing? Is she singing '*Ever since we met, you've had a hard on me?*'"

Shannon shook her head no and Brigid giggled.

The girls told me that Dusty was singing, *"Ever since we met, you've had a **HOLD** on me."*

I preferred my own Weird Al version better.

Once we were finished with lunch, it was noon. We then walked the few blocks back to the 6th Floor Museum.

At the museum, we bought our tickets and took an elevator up to the 6th floor. There we learned about the 35th President of the United States of America, John F. Kennedy.

The museum touched on what was happening in the early 1960s and about JFK's presidential race. The exhibit showcased major conflicts that JFK dealt with while in office; such as the Cuban Missile Crisis, racial equality, and the space race just to name a few. It then transitioned into JFK's visit to Texas.

JFK was to visit five cities in Texas as he prepared for his 2nd presidential term campaign; San Antonio, Houston, Ft. Worth, Dallas, and Austin.

The exhibit showed opposition and protest groups to JFK's Dallas visit.

There was a day by day, hour by hour, minute by minute, and second by second documentation on the assassination of JFK.

The museum had the section where Lee Harvey Oswald shot Kennedy walled off by glass. The area was reconstructed to make it look like the way it did on November 22, 1963.

The exhibit told the story of JFK being driven to the hospital, Oswald killing Dallas police officer J.D. Tippit, and how the Dallas Police apprehended Lee Harvey Oswald later that day at a theater. There was a piece on Jack Ruby killing Oswald at police headquarters.

The 6th Floor Museum was educational and interesting. I thought it gave a great description of a piece of American History.

After the 6th Floor Museum, we decided to explore more of Dallas. We ended up canceling our 8 Track Museum tour. However the 8 Track Museum guy recommended Dolly Pythons, a second hand store.

Since we had nothing to do, Brigid, Shannon, and I decided to check out Dolly Python. The store was like an antique co-op store with many venders. A lot of the stuff was overpriced junk that I could find in my grandparents' house. There were also a lot of cool things, but they too were way overpriced.

Since it was after 3pm, Reunion Tower was supposed to be open.

When we arrived at the lobby of Reunion Tower, we learned that the tower was open, however the bar Cloud Nine was still closed. Also, we were told that we were under dressed for Wolfgang Puck's restaurant, which I was fine with. I didn't want to pay for an overpriced beer anyway!

Brigid, Shannon, and I took the 60 second elevator ride up to the observation deck of Reunion Tower. There we got a 360 view of Dallas. Off in the distance we could see Ft. Worth. There were interactive touch screens that pointed out local interests on downtown and the surrounding areas. There wasn't much to do on the observation deck level. Since Cloud Nine was closed and we weren't allowed into Wolfgang Pucks, we decided to leave.

The ladies were hungry, so we decided to go to El Fenix. Our trolley bus guide said that El Fenix was the oldest Tex-Mex restaurant in Dallas. So Brigid, Shannon, and I had a late lunch there.

After lunch, we hopped back in the car and drove over to the American Airlines Center.

We found a place to park the car and started to tailgate.

It was 6:30pm when we decided to walk the few blocks up to the AAC. It was a very cold and brisk walk; it was 30^{0}F and windy!

That game was Buffalo's first and only game in Dallas for the season. Earlier in the season, former Sabres head coach Lindy Ruff and his Dallas Stars came into Buffalo and beat the Sabres 4-3.

Shannon and I each grabbed a beer, then found our seats.

I was amazed at how empty the AAC was! By puck drop, the arena was probably a quarter filled. Out of those fans, at least a quarter of them were Sabre fans!

Buffalo Sabre Tyler Ennis opened the scoring and broke the shutout barely three minutes left in the 1st Period. Ennis was able to send the puck past Stars goalie Kari Lehtonen. For being an empty arena, there were a lot of cheers!

During the 1st Period, Buffalo found themselves in the penalty box three times, but goalie Jhonas Enroth played great and kept it a 1-0 Buffalo lead after one period of play.

The entire 1st Period was a boring and dull affair. The Sabres looked as if they were going through the motions, and their shots on goal proved it. Dallas had 16 shots on goal compared to Buffalo's five shots.

Just 90 seconds into the 2nd Period, Dallas' Jordie Benn found the back of the net and tied the game 1-1.

Buffalo did show some signs of life during the 2nd Period. While on the penalty kill, Buffalo got the puck and skated into the Dallas zone and rang the puck right off the post. Unfortunately the puck did not go in. Dallas picked up the loose puck and skated into the Buffalo zone and hit the post as well, but did not score.

With less than 30 seconds left in the 2nd Period, Buffalo decided that they would stop playing, however Dallas didn't stop playing, and it paid off for them.

Dallas' Alex Goligoski scored with five seconds left in the 2nd Period, giving Dallas a 2-1 lead.

Minutes into the 3rd Period, Tyler Ennis scored again for Buffalo to tie the game 2-2. A minute or two later Buffalo finally got a power play, but naturally they didn't do anything with it; go figure.

Halfway through the 3rd Period, the refs called another chicken shit penalty against Buffalo. Dallas went on the power play and Alex Chiasson scored a power play goal to give Dallas a 3-2 lead. As soon as Enroth was scored on, he skated right over to the refs to complain. Of course the refs didn't give a *puck* about what Enroth had to say. The refs and linesmen met, but never reviewed the goal; typical crap.

The Sabres tried to battle back, but the refs wouldn't let them.

With 2:20 left in the 3rd Period, the refs slapped Buffalo with a Too Many Men on the Ice penalty. While on the penalty kill, the Sabres had some offensive chances, but they were all for naught.

With 20 seconds left, the Sabres were at full strength and pulled Enroth for the extra attacker. The effort was a day late and a buck short.

Buffalo had lost 3-2 in Big D.

Lindy Ruff achieved his 600th career coaching win, 99.5% of those coaching wins were in Buffalo.

After the game, we decided to let all the traffic die down. We found a bar next to AAC and stopped in there. Brigid got a water, Shannon got some novelty IPA beer, and I got a Molson. I was surprised to find Molson in Texas!

Once we finished our round, we left for the hotel.

The ladies were hungry for McDonalds fries, so we stopped to pick some up.

Next I stopped to fill up the car before we returned it to Dollar Rental. I filled up the car, but the gas gauge never moved. I put over $30 bucks into the car and figured we were good to go.

Once back at the hotel, we got our bags ready for the morning and we set our alarms for 6:30am for our 9:45am flight.

The three of us checked out of the hotel and were in the car by 7:15am.

When I returned the car to Dollar Rental, the attendant checked out the car to make sure there weren't any scratches or dents in the car. Then he checked the gas gauge and told me that I never filled up the car. I told him that last night I filled up the car at 7-11 on Beltline Road by John Carpenter Freeway. The kid asked if I had a receipt and I told him that it never printed one out. The kid said that the gas tank a 7/8 full. I told the kid that the gas gage never moved when I was pumping the car and that when the gas pump clicked off, I figured the car was full. I didn't want to try to top off the tank because I didn't want to be wearing any gas. I told the kid, "Why would I put gas in the car if I'm not going to fill it up all the way?!" The kid dinged me for not having a full tank! I was so infuriated that I wanted to go ape shit on the car! I felt like kicking in a door panel and smashing the windshield! I didn't give a puck. I already got *pucked* on car insurance for the damn thing. I was so close to destroying that car and I wouldn't have cared because as Dollar Rental told me in the insurance policy, I could "walk away." The voice of reason in the back of my head told me not to destroy the car. Instead I asked the kid, "Well can I take the car and put the 1/8 of gas in it?"

The kid told me, "Once the car is in here, it cannot be taken out."

I said, "Fine, do you have a hose so I can syphon the $30 of gas that I put in there last night?"

The kid told me, "No." The kid printed out the receipt and told me if I wanted to dispute the charges to talk to the front desk.

I let Shannon look at the receipt and she said Dollar Rental charged me $82 for gas! I was furious with that bullshit and I marched right down to Dollar Rental's front desk to dispute the charges.

I tried my best to not yell at the lady because I knew it wasn't her fault.

I told her what happened and how I filled up last night and how the gas gauge needle never moved. I told her how the kid said the car was 7/8 full.

I asked the lady how much Dollar Rental charged for gas. She told me that Dollar Rental charged $9 a gallon.

I asked, "How can you charge me $82 for gas?! The kid said the gas gauge was only 7/8 full. I don't understand why; if you charge $9 a gallon for gas, that I am off 10 gallons when the needle says I am off 1/8th of a tank. That math doesn't add up for me."

The lady was nice and it turned out that Dollar Rental put a $50 charge on for not having a gas receipt! The lady was able to waive the $50 charge, but I still ended up paying $32 in gas, in addition to the $30 I put in the night before.

Long story short, puck Dollar Rental! I advise everyone to never use those scum bags!

Shannon told the lady that we needed to catch our flight and we couldn't wait around any longer because we needed to catch the shuttle back to DFW. Shannon asked if they could top off the car and see how much gas we were off by. Shannon left her name and number.

Brigid, Shannon, and I hopped onto the shuttle and made it to DFW airport. We check our bag and cleared security.

We had a layover again in Atlanta.

Shannon's dad Jimbo picked us up from the Rochester airport a little after 5pm

I do have to say that Texas was what I thought it was going to be like. The best way to describe my thoughts on Texas was that it was like the Quebec of America, and that was not a bad thing. Texas was its own little world within the United States.

On Wednesday, I was back to work.

My coworker Alex came up to me to bust my balls. Alex said, "What the hell dude?! You're not allowed to go to any more Sabres games. You must have a black cloud around you! The Sabres were on a three game winning streak heading into the game in Dallas. You go to that game and the Sabres lose!"

I said, "Hey Al! I was just looking out for the Sabres best interest! They are still in last place in the league and I didn't want them to crawl out of last place and screw up their 1st over pick in the upcoming draft! It all makes sense."

Needless to say, Shannon never got a call back from Dollar Rental in Dallas.

***

That Wednesday back was March 5, 2014, AKA, the trade deadline.

I had been used to boring General Manager Darcy Regier for the last 17 seasons, so I wasn't expecting any trades to happen.

Apparently I was wrong. New General Manager Tim Murray was nothing like Darcy. Buffalo traded Brayden McNabb, Jonathan Parker, and a couple draft picks to LA Kings for Nicolas Deslauriers and Hudson Fasching.

In another deal, Buffalo traded Matt Moulson and Cody McCormick to Minnesota Wild for Torrey Mitchell and two draft picks. Moulson and McCormick would be joining former Sabre Jason Pominville.

Additionally, Buffalo traded newly acquired goalie Jaroslav Halak and a draft pick to Washington Capitals for goalie Mike Neuvirth and defenseman Rostislav Klesla.

Lastly, the Sabres picked up Cory Conacher off waivers.

That was quite a busy day a 1 Seymour H. Knox Plaza! Now it would be a matter of time to see how these new boys pan out…

***

The Grand Finale!

I think now would be a great time for a Weird Al reference! Honestly, I would not mind being a *Canadian Idiot*. I have no problem being a beer-swillin' hockey nut. And yes, even though they use stupid Monopoly money, at least their funny $5 bill has kids playing hockey on it! Growing up so close to Canada (I saw it every day on the school bus on my way to St. Stephen's School) made me very fond of curling. I think curling is more of a sport than

NASCAR. At least you can have a beer while playing curling…and the beer will stay cold too!

March 17, 2014 was St. Patrick's Day and the day Shannon and I had a mid-morning flight out of the Rochester Airport.

We had a two hour layover at Chicago's O'Hare airport.

It was about 6pm when our plane landed in the hometown of Canadian rock sensation Loverboy; Calgary, Alberta, Canada!

While I'm on the topic of Canadian rock bands, here's my list of (in no particular order) Canada's best bands:

- Loverboy
- The Guess Who
- The Tragically Hip
- Three Days Grace

Honorable mentions are:

- Billy Talent
- Steppenwolf

While I'm on the topic of Canadian music, here's a list Canadian exports that the world could have done without:

1. Rush
2. Nickelback
3. Barenaked Ladies
4. Rush (Rush sucks so much that they made the list twice)
5. (Two way tie) Justin Bieber/Celine Dion

After exiting the plane, Shannon and I had to go through Canadian Customs before we could get our bag.

The customs officer looked at our passports and asked us what our purpose in Canada was. I said, "To watch the Buffalo Sabres lose!"

The customs officer laughed and said, "Well you just missed them by an hour. They already came through." Seconds later, Shannon and I both got stamps in our passports.

Our bag came out quickly and we were soon out the door to get our rental car.

Avis ended up giving us a Killed In Action Soul and a map of Calgary.

Shannon and I put our luggage in the automobile. I wasn't sure whether to call the Soul a car, a crossover, or a SUV. Come to think of it, it was more like a glorified go kart...

Shannon and I put our luggage in the go kart and took a look at the map to try to find where our hotel was.

I was pretty busy the past few nights, so I never printed out directions from the airport to the motel, but I knew the motel was in Calgary proper.

As I drove, Shannon tried to find Banff Trail on the map, but she couldn't.

We ended up driving past a strip plaza, so I pulled in there. There was a mini mart store with a post office in it. I needed post card stamps, so I figured that I would go to the post office, get stamps, and ask for directions. I thought, who better to ask for directions than the post office, they knew where every place was; didn't they?

I waited in line and got my post card stamps. I asked the post office girl if she knew where Banff Trail was. She told me that she was unfamiliar with that road and that she took public transportation to work, so she really didn't know the roads too well. She mentioned that the cashier of the mini mart might know.

Shannon had a rule that it wasn't officially vacation until we bought cans of Pringles, especially the salt and vinegar kind!

Shannon and I stocked up on three cans of salt and vinegar Pringles and headed towards the cashier.

While we were being cashed out, I asked the cashier chick if she knew where Banff Trail was. She had no clue and told us that she had just moved there from Prince Edward Island.

Once we left the mini mart, I decided to go into Tim Hortons to get a coffee and ask for directions. It was Roll Up the Rim season for Tim Hortons, and the previous week, I had won a free coffee. I wanted to redeem my free coffee and ask for directions to Banff Trail.

At Tim Hortons, I never asked for directions. There was a big enough language barrier talking to the Tim Hortons kid because he had a thick foreign accent, and it wasn't a French accent either. Also, I think my Roll Up the Rim coupon confused the kid because my American winning coupon was written in only English (the Canadian winners were written in English and French).

Once Shannon and I got our hot beverages, we went back to the go kart. I took a quick look at the map. Shannon was quite upset with me when I was able to find Banff Trail on the map. Now we were in business; we were back on the road and we knew where we were going.

Shannon and I took the scenic way around town. I was surprised to find that Calgary was so hilly. I really didn't know what to expect of Calgary. I thought Calgary was going to be flat and boring like Winnipeg.

On our drive to the motel, we passed a mall that had a liquor store in it, so we stopped in. Shannon grabbed a six pack of Alexander Keith's Hallertaur Hop Ale. I played it safe and went with a 12 pack of Molson Canadian.

I asked the sales clerk kid if there were any other places we could buy beer or if the liquor store was it. The kid looked at me puzzled, so I asked him, "Can you buy beer at the grocery store or at a gas station?"

The kid said, "Whoa! No man! Where are you from?"

I said, "Buffalo."

The kid had a confused look on his face.

Shannon added, "New York. Buffalo, New York."

The kid said, "Whoa, that's far away! No, you can only buy beer at the liquor store. Man, if you could buy beer at the gas station or grocery store that would be a lot more convenient!"

Our grand total for a six and 12 pack was $40! Goddamn! I had no idea how Canadians could afford to get drunk! I was used to paying $12 for a 12 pack of Molson, not $25!

Minutes later, Shannon and I found our motel, the Ramada Limited on Banff Trail.

After we checked in and got settled in our room, we decided that we should get some food in us besides Pringles and beer.

We found a microbrew in one of the advertisement books, so we decided to go there for food.

Well, we got lost trying to find the microbrew. In the meantime, we passed by Olympic Park a couple times.

Shannon and I ended up settling on boring old Boston Pizza. Shannon got an overpriced veggie pizza and I got a very overpriced pierogie pizza. Since it was St. Patrick's Day, Shannon got her draft beer dyed green. After our overpriced blah dinner, we went back to the motel and crashed.

Shannon and I woke up around 8am on Tuesday March 18th. Let me rephrase that, we woke up at 8am Mountain Standard Time, 10am Eastern Standard Time. Shannon felt like a bum for sleeping in so late, however I did not.

Originally Shannon had a lot planned for us to do, until she found out that everything we wanted to do was canceled. Apparently the week we were in Calgary was the week that all the Winter tourist activities closed.

Shannon had wanted to go skating at the Olympic Speed Skating track, but that closed the week before.

Shannon wanted to do a bobsled ride at Olympic Park, but that too closed the week before.

That morning Shannon and I decided to check out Olympic Park.

Once there, we saw the Canadian Sports Hall of Fame was there. We didn't have anything else to do, so we decided to check it out. In the lobby of the Canadian Sports Hall of Fame, they had Heidi and Howdy, the two mascot bears from the Calgary 1988 Olympic Winter Games. I'm not going to lie, Heidi and Howdy were creepy. The entire time I had my back to them, I could feel their eyes watching me! I was scared. I thought they were going to come to life and try to kill me, just like the Pittsburgh Penguins' mascot Icey tried to kill Jean-Claude Van Damme in *Sudden Death*.

The sports hall of fame was fun and interesting. Every exhibit had a hands on interactive kiosk.

Shannon really enjoyed the figure skating exhibit. I lost her in there for at least a half hour.

I made my way to the hockey section.

The part that I liked about the hockey section was the exhibit that was dedicated to the World Hockey Association. The exhibit had banners, pennants, programs, photos and other novelties from the WHA teams. The exhibit documented the short lived life of the WHA. When the WHA folded, four teams were absorbed into the National Hockey League. On display was a letter from the NHL to the Edmonton Oilers, Winnipeg Jets, Quebec Nordiques, and New England Whalers congratulating them for being the newest franchises in the NHL for the 1979-80 season.

For their inaugural NHL season, the New England Whalers changed their name to the Hartford Whalers.

Sadly, in the late 1990s, the Whalers swam south for warmer waters and became the Carolina Hurricanes.

Like the Whalers in the 1990s, the Jets and Nordiques eventually relocated. The Winnipeg Jets became the Phoenix Coyotes and Quebec Nordiques became the Colorado Avalanche.

The Edmonton Oilers were the only WHA team, turn NHL team, to still be in its original city.

The WHA exhibit had a list of former players that made it into the hockey hall of fame. Bobby Hull, Wayne Gretzky, Mark Messier, Gordie Howe, Jacques Plante, Frank Mahovlich, Dave Keon were a few of the names I recognized.

The Canadian Sports Hall of Fame was fun. Shannon and I spent at least two hours in there; I would recommend it.

When we were done with the hall of fame exhibits, we decided to wander around Olympic Park.

The building across the way from the hall of fame was a training facility. Located at the training facility was Team Canada's Hockey program headquarters. The facility also had four ice hockey rinks. While we were there, there were about six people practicing figure skating in one rink, and two rinks had hockey going on. Lastly, the facility had an indoor starting track for bobsled, luge, and skeleton. There was also a snack bar for the athletes.

After wandering around the facility, Shannon and I hopped back in the go kart and explored more of Olympic Park. We drove up a steep winding road to the start of the bobsled track. We parked the car and walked around the starting line. Bobsled rides had ended the week before, so the track was deserted. It was very interesting to see the track and course up close. Next to the bobsled building was a cutaway to show how the track was made; rebar and a lot of concrete.

We hopped back in the go cart and drove back down the windy road.

We stopped off and checked out the start of the luge track.

Bobsled shared the same track as luge and skeleton, however the luge and skeleton starting line was a bit further down the track than the bobsled start line. We walked up to one of the big turns on the course and took some pictures, like tourists would do.

Our last stop at Olympic Park was to the Welcome Centre at the ski hill.

Right in front of the Welcome Centre was the bobsled from Disney's *Cool Runnings*, a movie about the 1988 Jamaican Bobsled Olympic Team. *Cool Runnings* was one of my favorite childhood movies and one of my favorite John Candy movies. I do have to say that John Candy was my favorite Canadian actor; Jim Carey was a close second...Let me rephrase that; John Candy is my favorite dead Canadian actor and Jim Carey is my favorite current living Canadian actor! Mike Myers, Eugene Levi, and Howie Mandel are both up there in my book.

Of course Shannon and I had to get our pictures taken in the bobsled.

A plaque next to the bobsled said that some scenes from the movie were actually filmed on location at the bobsled track there at Olympic Park.

Shannon and I went into the Welcome Centre, but it turned out to be a building for ski rentals with a restaurant on the second floor. We walked out to the foot of the skiing hill to look around. There were quite a few people skiing and snowboarding. Off to the left of the ski hill were a couple ski jumps, but they were not in use.

After we exited the Welcome Centre, we saw the Olympic Torch from the 1988 Olympics. Shannon and I were shocked at how small the torch was. The torch was probably 20 feet tall, and the dish part was probably 10 feet in diameter. We thought that the torch was going to be really big because the torches always looked so massive on TV. We took some more pictures like tourists and then left.

When we left Olympic Park, it was early afternoon, and Shannon was getting hungry. The salt and vinegar Pringles could only hold her over for so long.

In one of the travel brochures, Shannon came across a local microbrewery and restaurant, Wild Rose Brewery.

At the Wild Rose Brewery, there were too many beer choices for Shannon to choose from, so she selected an eight glass sampler platter. For food, she got some tofu salad and I got the pierogie soup.

Wild Rose offered brewery tours, but we were there on a non-tour day.

After lunch, we went back to the hotel and changed into our Sabres jerseys and shot gunned a few beers.

I noticed that there was a metro rail station a block away from our hotel, with service to the Scotiabank Saddledome. I figured that taking public transportation to the Saddledome was cheaper and safer than me driving in a new foreign city.

We waited about three minutes for our rail car to come. Then we had a 20 minute or so ride to the Saddledome.

The rail took us through the city limits and downtown before dropping us off in front of BMO Centre. We walked through BMO and then over a catwalk to get to the Saddledome.

Shannon and I were two hours early to the game, but that was ok. I would rather be super early than late to a game.

There were no bars next to the Saddledome that we could see, so we went in search of one. As we walked, we saw the downtown Calgary skyline. Calgary looked like a mini Toronto with all the new tall glass buildings and Calgary Tower. The tower reminded me of Alfa from the original Power Rangers TV series; the one that had Amy Jo Johnson as the hot Pink Ranger!

We walked a few blocks before we came across another microbrewery, Vagabond.

Shannon and I bellied up to the bar. The bartender asked Shannon what kind of beer she wanted. She couldn't make her mind up so the bartender poured her three different samples; she eventually settled on a hoppy beer.

The bartender asked me what I wanted.

I asked him, "What kind of Molson products do you have?"

He said, "We have them all."

I asked, "Does that mean you have Molson Brador?!"

The bartender said, "No."

I asked, "Do you have Molson XXX?"

The bartender said, "No."

There was another bartender there, who had his back to us, and he said to our bartender, "They must not be locals."

Our bartender said to him, "Did you notice their jerseys?"

The bartender with his back to us turned around and saw Shannon and my Sabres jerseys and said, "Ah, yeah, that explains it."

I figured that bar didn't have any Molson Ice, so I went with a Molson Canadian instead.

While Shannon and I sat at the bar, two Flames fans came in and sat next to us at the bar. The two Flames fans, Jeff and Don, were very nice. We got to talking and Shannon and I told them about how this trip was our grand finale of our hockey trips. They thought our hockey trips were a very cool idea. Shannon and I asked Jeff and Don what there was to do in Calgary. They asked us what we have already done. I told them we did Olympic Park, Canada Sports Hall of Fame, and Wild Rose Brewery. Don chimed in and said that he installed all the glass at the hall of fame. Both Don and Jeff recommended that if Shannon and I had the time, to go to Banff. A lot of people recommended Banff, including my coworker Lynn. Shannon and I made a mental note to go to Banff for the following day.

Jeff and I continued to talk about hockey, football, work, Canada, and beer.

It was 6:15pm and Shannon and I were ready to cash out. After our experience with tickets in Winnipeg, we liked to get to the arenas early, in case there was a problem with the tickets.

We told Jeff and Don that Shannon and I were going to bounce. We shook hands and Jeff said that he would take care of Shannon and my beers. Shannon and I thought that was very nice and we thanked Jeff for our beers.

Shannon and I walked the couple blocks back down to the Saddledome; the only arena that I'd been to that looked like a stack of Pringles.

Thankfully our tickets worked and we were allowed into the Saddledome!

We walked one lap around the arena trying to find our seats, but I didn't see a sign for them anywhere. I finally asked an usher where PL15 was. The usher instructed us to climb up to the top of the section that we were in. Once we at the top, we would take another set of stairs to the Press Level, our section. By the time Shannon and I climbed to our seats, both of us were out of breath!

Our seats in the Press Level were in the upper portion of the Pringle.

As we found our seats, we found other fellow Sabre fans, Mike and Tara. Since we had about 15 minutes before the game started, we talked with them for a bit. Mike was originally from Buffalo but moved out to Montana. While in Montana, he met Tara and converted her to a Sabres fan. Mike and Tara drove up from Montana for that night's game in Calgary and the following day, they were driving up to Edmonton for Thursday night's Sabres/Oilers game. It was nearing game time, so we parted ways, but said we would meet up later.

When the Calgary Flames were announced to the ice, all the local fans cheered, but the really cool thing were the huge flames and fire balls that burst out of the Jumbotron!

After the National Anthems were sung, it was time for some hockey!

Of course Shannon couldn't see because there were tall people sitting in front of her. Since the section next to us was completely empty, Shannon and I moved over to where we could see much better.

Making his first NHL start was the Sabres goalie Nathan Lieuwen...there's a little more to the story here. The previous Thursday, newly acquired goalie Michal Neuvirth started in net for Buffalo, as they lost in Carolina. On Saturday the Sabres had a game out on Long Island, and Neuvirth did not play due to soreness. Sabres #1 goalie Jhonas Enroth got the start and loss against the Islanders. The next day, Sunday, Buffalo hosted Montreal. With Neuvirth sidelined, Buffalo called up Nathan Lieuwen from the Rochester Americans. Enroth got the start for that game, but during the game, he got injured. Under that circumstance, Nathan Lieuwen got to play in his first NHL game. He did well during the 3rd Period, blocking all 10 shots he faced.

For the Canadian west coast swing, the Sabres left Enroth at home. The Sabres brought Neuvirth and Lieuwen and also called up Matt Hackett from Rochester, just to be on the safe side.

With the amount of young and inexperienced guys playing, you could say that Shannon and I were watching the Buffalo Amerks or the Rochester Sabres.

Buffalo's Drew Stafford opened up the scoring. With less than 7 minutes left in the 1st Period. Buffalo was pressing deep in the Flames zone. The Flames defenseman skated behind his net with the puck and left it there for his teammate. The Flame player did not expect Stafford to pick the puck up and score a wraparound goal on the Flames goalie Joni Ortio.

Minutes later, Buffalo scored again, but the ref called no goal. Moments before Buffalo scored their second goal; a Sabres player was shoved into the Flames goalie, Ortio. Seconds later, with Ortio out of position, Buffalo scored. Though the ref disallowed the goal due to goaltender interference, the ref did not give out any interference penalties…just another example of the NHL being just like the WWF; rigged.

The boring 1st Period ended with the Sabres leading 1-0. Buffalo managed to muster only 4 shots on goal, while Calgary got 6 shots on goal.

During the 1st Intermission, Mike and Tara moved over and sat in the row in front of us. Mike said the fans were too rowdy and giving him crap for cheering for the Sabres. During intermission, the four of us talked about hockey and life back home in Buffalo.

The Sabres continued their boring and dull play into the 2nd Period. They struggled to get shots on net, only netting 5 shots on goal during the 2nd Period.

As per usual, the Sabres went to sleep in their own zone towards the end of the period. Buffalo wasn't even chasing Calgary around, but instead the Sabres were watching the Flames skate around them in the Buffalo zone. Calgary's hard work paid off when with 62 seconds left in the 2nd Period, Calgary's Joe Colborne beat the Sabre goalie Lieuwen.

Seconds later, the 2nd Period came to an end and the two clubs went to the locker rooms with a 1-1 tie.

During the 2nd Intermission, Shannon and I went to the Saddleroom Restaurant to split a beer. While we shared our beer, I told her my thoughts on the game. I said, "I think we will lose 3-1. Calgary will score a quick goal. With under 2 minutes left, Nolan will pull the goalie and Calgary will score an empty netter."

Shannon yelled at me for jinxing the Sabres.

Soon it was time for 3rd Period of play.

It was almost the half-way point when Calgary took the lead. The faceoff was deep in the Buffalo zone. Calgary won the draw, the puck came back to the point, the defenseman blasted the puck towards the net, and Calgary's Mike Cammalleri deflected the puck in. The Flames now lead 2-1.

A few minutes later, Buffalo found themselves on the power play, but there was nothing powerful about it.

While on the power play, Buffalo coughed up the puck. Calgary's Paul Byron picked the puck up, skated into the Buffalo zone, and scored easily on Lieuwen to give the Flames a 3-1 lead.

Buffalo never rebounded. For the 3rd Period, the Sabres totaled 5 shots on net. If you were keeping score and did your math correctly, the Sabres only had 14 shots on goal, compared to Calgary's 26! It's tough to win a game when you don't shoot or can't get the puck on net.

Sadly, Buffalo lost 3-1.

Shannon and I said bye to Mike and Tara. We said that we hoped to see each other in Edmonton...

After the game, Shannon and I hopped back on the rail and went back to the motel for the night.

On Wednesday morning, Shannon and I packed up our gear, checked out of the Ramada, and made our way to Banff.

We drove west bound on Route 1. As we passed Olympic Park, the road began to climb. Once we reached the crest of the road, we could see the Canadian Rockies in the far distance, and they looked beautiful.

The drive from Calgary to Banff was about an hour and a half. The scenery was just spectacular, especially once we got into the Rockies.

During the drive along Route 1, I saw these overpasses with foliage on them every few miles. At first, I thought the overpasses were for snowmobilers for during the winter so they wouldn't have to cross the highway. Shannon quickly pointed out that I was wrong. She told me they were land bridges for the wildlife. The moose, deer and other critters could use the overpass so they would not become road kill.

Once in Banff, we didn't really know where to go, so we drove around for a bit. We ended up stopping at Bow Falls. We got out of the go kart so we could explore. Since a part of the river was frozen, Shannon and I walked out on the ice. Shannon took pictures of the mountains. We saw a couple other shutter bugs and some guys trying to fish. As we walked around Bow Falls and Bow River, we saw a plaque that informed us Marilyn Monroe stood where we were standing while filming scenes from the 1954 movie *River of No Return.*

Shannon was getting hungry. When Shannon got hungry, she got cranky. When she got cranky, she was not fun to be around. To prevent her from turning into a monster, I found a place to eat, the Banff Street Brewery.

At the Banff Street Brewery, Shannon ordered a flight of beers and sweet potato fries. I went with the poutine, which was always a safe bet.

After lunch, we walked around and went to some of the tourist gift shops.

We had heard that there was a natural spring in Banff, which was how the area was discovered.

Shannon and I decided to check out this natural spring.

I was so excited about this natural spring. I hadn't seen any pictures of it, so I used my imagination! I thought we would have to huff it a few hundred meters into the snowy woods, and in the middles of nowhere would have been a huge hole with hot water in it!

What I was not expecting was that the natural spring had what looked like a swimming pool built above it. Also, I was not anticipating seeing fat old blubbery people in it. Shannon and I decided to pass on the natural spring.

There was still more exploring to do. Shannon and I hopped back in the go kart and continued westward some more to Lake Louise.

Once we got to Lake Louise, the storm clouds began to move it, so we could not see the huge, mammoth mountain that fed Lake Louise its water. The lake was still frozen, so Shannon and I walked out on it.

The one resort on Lake Louise had some of the snow plowed so people could go ice skating on the lake. There was also an ice sculpture that looked like the façade of a castle.

After our short time at Lake Louise, Shannon and I decided to make our way to Edmonton. So we drove back to Banff, then back to Calgary, and then we headed north to Edmonton.

When we left Lake Louise, it was about 4:30pm. By the time we arrived in Edmonton, it was almost 9pm.

We were staying at a Travelodge on the west side of town. Shannon and I had a map with us, but we were lost.

We ended up driving past a different Travelodge, so I decided to ask them for directions to the Travelodge we were staying at. They were quite helpful and steered us in the right direction. Minutes later, Shannon and I were at our correct Travelodge.

Our Travelodge not only had a pool and hot tube, but it also had a two story water slide!

After we checked in and got into our room, I convinced Shannon that we should go down to the pool. I told her that the slide was only open from 2pm-10pm.

Seconds later, I was in my swim trunks and at the top of the slide! I dipped my tootsies in the water to test out the temperature; the water was freezing! I had gone too far to turn away and not do the water slide!

I plopped down on the slide and realized the water was freezing! Yes, there was some shrinkage.

At first, I had a lot of speed and momentum going, but the further down the slide I went, the slower I went. Eventually I plunged into the cold pool at the bottom of the slide. I hopped out and ran back up to the top of the slide again!

Shannon didn't go down the slide. I could tell that she was cranky, which meant that she was probably hungry.

Once I got the slide and pool out of my system, I went back to the room to shower and wash out the chlorine.

Built into the Travelodge was a restaurant called Smitty's, so that was where Shannon and I went for dinner.

Shannon had a red wine with her salad. I had water with my poutine and pierogies.

Dinner was good.

After dinner, we went to bed.

March 20, 2014, game day!

Our game of the Buffalo Sabres at Edmonton Oilers did not start until 7:30pm, local time. That meant that Shannon and I had a whole day to explore Edmonton. Unfortunately during the night, there was a surprise snow storm. There was about two inches of snow on the ground with more still coming down.

I went to the front desk to drop off some post cards and ask what there was to do in Edmonton. The ladies at the front desk recommended the art museum, the science center, and the West Edmonton Mall.

I reported my findings back to Shannon. Shannon wanted to check out the Old Strathmore section of Edmonton, so that was what we did.

Old Strathmore reminded me of all the shops on Delaware Ave in Buffalo. Shannon found a couple used book stores that we went into. As we walked up and down the shops, we were constantly being pelted in the face with snow and wind.

We eventually found ourselves at Good Food Beer Market. Shannon ordered some local beer and I had an Old Style Pilsner, which turned out to be a Molson product. We also got an order of pretzels to share.

After our bite to eat, we decided to try to find the Farmers' Market that we heard about. The market was only a few blocks away. The only problem we had was that the market was only open on Saturdays.

Next we drove through downtown Edmonton and checked out some of the scenery there.

We drove past a casino, but I wasn't feeling lucky…in the gambling kind of way.

Since most people we asked raved about the West Edmonton Mall, we decided to go there next.

My thing with malls was if you've been to one mall, you've been to them all.

After we parked, to help relieve my mall anxiety, I grabbed one of the Molson Canadians from the car and poured it into my old Tim Hortons cup.

There was a bingo parlor at the mall. I thought about going in, but the joint reeked of cigarette smoke from outside!

The West Edmonton Mall was alright; quite similar to the Mall of America in Minnesota.

The West Edmonton Mall had a mini golf course, amusement park, water park, aquarium, and an ice rink; where 2014 Canadian Olympic figure skater Kaetlyn Osmond practiced. While we were there, she was practicing on the ice, along with other figure skaters.

Once we had our fill of the mall, it was time to get food again. Shannon wanted to get subs at Subway.

We got our subs to go and ate them back at the hotel room.

It was 6pm when we put on our Sabre jerseys for the game and headed out the door.

By the time we got to Rexall Place and found parking, it was almost 6:45pm. Shannon and I hung out in the go kart and tailgated.

It was weird because no one else was tailgating. I wasn't sure if tailgating was not permitted in Edmonton, so we kept it on the down low.

7pm rolled around and we decided that was a good time to start our march across the parking lot and into Rexall Place.

Once inside Rexall Place, Shannon and I needed help again to find our seats because we didn't see a sign for our section. We asked an usher how to get to our seats in Section 303. Just like in Calgary, we had to walk to the top of one section, and our seats were behind that section. The seats that Shannon and I had for the game were the last row up in the rafters. We were so high up and close to the ceiling that we could look down into the press box; which was a horse shoe shaped catwalk that went around the perimeter of the ice.

Right before the game started, a huge oil tower was lowered from the rafters and placed on the ice, right in front of the Oilers bench. The PA guy announced and welcomed the Edmonton Oilers to the ice and the players walked from the locker room, through the bench, underneath the oil tower, and onto the ice.

Both American and Canadian National Anthems were sung. Then, it was hockey time!

That night's game had the last place Sabres facing off against the second to last place Oilers…we were in for a real treat; a battle of the worst of the worst!

Making his Buffalo Sabres debut was goalie Matt Hackett.

For two teams that rarely play each other, they started off playing as if there was a deep rooted rivalry. Both teams skated hard and hit anything that moved. The Sabres were throwing body checks, something that we hadn't seen all season.

Within the opening five minutes we had our first fight. Edmonton's Luke Gazdic got the best of Buffalo Zenon Konopka.

Minutes later, Buffalo's Cory Conacher got two minutes for roughing up Edmonton's goalie Ben Scrivens. However Scrivens got two for unsportsmanlike conduct. What had happened was Buffalo skated into the Edmonton zone, but the play was whistled dead. Conacher skated behind the net and past Edmonton's goalie Scrivens. Scrivens threw a punch at Conacher. Without missing a beat, Conacher roughed up Scrivens. That little commotion drew the attention of players and refs. Both teams skated 4 aside, but no goals came of it.

Late in the 1st Period, Buffalo found themselves shorthanded. Yet again, they fell asleep deep in their own zone. Edmonton's Taylor Hall scored a power play goal to give the Oilers a 1-0 lead. The Oilers would take that lead with them into the 1st Intermission.

During the 1st Intermission, we saw our new friends Mike and Tara! It turned out that Mike and Tara were sitting 2 rows and 2 seats over from Shannon and me! The four of us talked for the duration of the intermission.

Throughout the 2nd Period, players from both sides still hit each other and penalties were given out like free candy.

Midway through the 2nd Period, Buffalo found themselves on the power play. Shannon and I were nervous and we wanted the Sabres to defer their powerless play. We were fearful that Edmonton might score a shorthanded goal, just like Calgary did the game before.

To our surprise and delight, newly acquired and Canisius College grad, Cory Conacher scored on the power play for Buffalo! Conacher had tied the game 1-1! We broke the shutout!

For a change, Buffalo showed up to play. By the end of the 2nd Period, Buffalo had 16 shots on goal for the period, 24 total. That was a hell of a lot more shots than that feeble effort they put up the previous game in Calgary.

During the 2nd Intermission, I leafed through the program that I got. I learned that the Oilers were slated to get a new hockey arena for the 2016-17 hockey season. The Oilers' future new home, Rogers Place, was to be in downtown and have public transportation.

Just 69 seconds into the 3rd Period, Conacher added to Buffalo's lead again. He tipped another puck past Edmonton's goalie Scrivens. Buffalo now had a 2-1 lead.

Conacher was all over the ice. Later in the period, he assisted on a Drew Stafford goal, to up Buffalo's lead 3-1.

As time ticked by in the game, more and more Oilers fans filed out of Rexall Place. I was so confused why they would leave with time still on the clock. There was plenty of time left for the Sabres to screw up the game.

Thankfully the Sabres didn't blow the game. They ended up skating away with a well-deserved 3-1 victory.

After the game, Shannon and I got our picture taken with the rink in the background; it was a thing that we did at every game we went to.

I stopped at the Oilers team store to pick up my boss's husband some Oilers gear because he was an Oilers fan. After that, Shannon and I hopped in the car and drove back to the Travelodge.

Friday morning, Shannon and I packed up our bags again and checked out of the hotel. We tossed our bags in the go kart and made our way to the Edmonton Airport.

At the airport, we dropped off the rental car at Avis. We had no problems with Avis, unlike stupid dysfunctional Dollar Rental in Los Angeles, Denver, and Dallas.

Shannon and I checked in and made it through security with no problem.

Our 11:30am flight to Vancouver boarded on time.

An hour and half later, our flight landed in Vancouver.

Shannon and I grabbed our bag at the luggage carousel and a couple brochures at the information desk. Then we boarded the subway. The subway took us all the way from the airport to downtown Vancouver.

Once downtown, we walked a few blocks down to Sandman Hotel.

After we checked in and dropped our bags off in our room, Shannon wanted to explore the town. We rifled through the brochures we had and Shannon soon came up with a game plan. She wanted to go to the Farmers' Market and pick up some food so that the next day when we rented bikes, we could already have food with us.

With a game plan at hand, Shannon and I started our walk from the Sandman Hotel to the Farmers' Market.

The Farmers' Market was a nice little area of town. When we first got to the market, it was a zoo; just like Wegmans on a Sunday after church! We couldn't even walk through the market because there were so many people.

We left the Farmers' Market because it was too busy.

We wound up at Granville Island Brewing. Shannon and I each got a flight of beers. The one beer we both enjoyed was Lions Winter Ale. I thought it tasted like chocolate pudding but Shannon thought it tasted like a Tootsie Roll. We bought a 6 pack of cans of the winter ale for later consumption.

We walked around Granville Island a little more before heading back to the Farmers' Market.

It was a lot quieter the second time around the market. Shannon tried to find some food that we could toss in our backpack for our bike journey the following day. We ended up getting two loafs of sour dough bread; buy one get one free. We also found a couple food vendors, so we had a late lunch there too.

After food, we decided to explore some more.

Shannon and I walked along the water to Vanier Park. I was amazed at the amount of cargo ships hanging out in the English Bay area, as I counted at least a dozen. I was not used to seeing that many cargo ships in one area. I was only used to seeing a one or two at the grain mills on the water in Buffalo, along with the two war ships at the Naval Park. It was a bit of a shock to see a city where the sea ports were still used.

During our walk, we came across a dog park on the beach. It was cool. There were about two dozen dogs there with their humans. The dogs were swimming and catching balls and Frisbees. Teppo Numminen would have enjoyed it.

On our walk back to the hotel, we swung through Yaletown to check it out. All the bars we walked past looked out of our price range.

It was about 8pm when we got back to the hotel and we were exhausted.

The following day was Saturday March 22. The weather was on again off again showers for the entire day. Shannon and I postponed our bike adventure until Sunday. Sunday was supposed to be a warmer and sunnier day.

Shannon and I did not have a set game plan for Saturday, so we decided to wander around town.

We decided to check out Olympic Village because we weren't too far away from it. We walked out of our hotel and walked down Cambie Street, where we took the Cambie Street Bridge over to Olympic Village.

We soon came across a liquor store, so I picked up an 8 pack of Old Style Pilsner.

Shannon and I wandered around the Olympic Village area, trying to find the 2010 Olympic Cauldron, but we couldn't find it anywhere. We walked around the False Creek area before deciding to wander over to Chinatown.

The Chinatown in Vancouver reminded me of the Chinatown in San Francisco because it was built into a hill.

Shannon wanted to check out one of the market shops in Chinatown, so we walked into on. There were salt dried fish and shrimp and who knows what else, but they smelled horrible. The stench of dead dried fish and other awful aromas were so bad that I had to leave the market or risk tossing my cookies.

After our brief stint in Chinatown, Shannon wanted to check out Gastown, Vancouver's birthplace.

We got lost in our search for Gastown. We walked around Hastings Street and then crossed over onto Cordova Street. Cordova Street eventually dumped us into Gastown.

Shannon was hungry, so we went in search of a place to eat.

During our search to find food, we saw the famous Steam Clock of Gastown.

Shannon decided that we should have lunch at the Steamworks Brewery.

Shannon had a Smokey Porter with her salad. I had an Imperial Red with my Caesar Salad and poutine…they had really good poutine.

We asked our waitress where the cauldron to the 2010 Winter Games was because we couldn't find it at Olympic Village. Our waitress told us that Olympic Village was where all the athletes stayed. She informed us that we were just a few blocks away from the cauldron. She said that the cauldron would not be lit, but it was occasionally lit for special occasions. She also added that she was a part of the Olympic Opening Ceremonies, she was a flag twirler.

After Shannon and I paid our bill, we walked up the few blocks to see the 2010 Winter Olympics Cauldron.

The cauldron was a lot bigger and fancier than the one in Calgary. The one in Vancouver was more artistic.

From the cauldron, we hopped on the Skyline.

Apparently Shannon and I looked lost because some guy with a squeeze box came up to us and asked us if we needed help or directions. Shannon said that we were looking for any brewery to visit. The guy with the squeeze box thought long and hard and said, "Well I don't drink so I can't help you." He did recommend some restaurant.

Shannon and I thanked the guy and left.

Moments later a guy in a suit came up to Shannon and me. He said, "Excuse me, but I overheard your conversation with that hippie. First of all, don't trust a man who doesn't drink beer. Second of all, if you want to go to a great place with a wide variety of beer, then go to the Craft Beer Market..." The nice guy gave us directions on how to get to Craft Beer Market. We thanked him and we quickly hopped on the Skyline to the Main Street/Science World exit. We were en route back to Olympic Village to check out Craft Beer Market.

Shannon and I stayed there for three rounds of novelty beers. It was an interesting place. It was located inside the old Salt Building. The Market had over 100 beers on tap, though they did not have Molson XXX or Brador.

On our walk back to the hotel, we walked past BC Place, which hosted the Olympic ceremonies.

Once back at the hotel, we relaxed a little. Eventually we got hungry, so we went back out and grabbed a pizza.

While we waited for our pizza, Shannon wanted to go into a Chinese grocery store, I reluctantly went in.

As soon as we entered the grocery store, we were dumped off into the seafood section, and it was quite gross. Thankfully I had a nice shine going on, otherwise I didn't know if I could have lasted in there.

For instance, I asked Shannon, "Why would someone buy a fish's head?"

Shannon's answer was, "To make soup. Why?"

I pointed and said, "Well there's a whole bunch of chopped carp heads right there...and they are staring at me!"

There was a tank of live lobster, which reminded me of a story.

As a kid, I always got dragged to Tops Friendly Markets after church on Sundays. Of course we would go through the meat and seafood section. I was always curious why the lobsters had rubber bands around their pinchers. Mom told me that they were there so they didn't pinch people. I told mom that I wanted to buy a lobster and keep it as a pet. Mom told me, "No!" I told mom that I saved enough money to buy one. I told her that the sign for lobsters was only $7.99. I told mom that I had $8. Mom told me that lobsters were only $7.99 a pound. I told her that I was fine with buying one lobster. Mom informed me that the lobsters weighed about 2-4 pounds each, so I was looking at $16-32 a lobster, not including tax. The point of the story was that I was not good with math and I never had a pet lobster.

The rest of the Chinese grocery store was creepy and disgusting. There were live bull frogs, king prawns (like Pepe from the Muppets), and other dead stuff that was looking at me…creepy!

We eventually got our pizza and took it back to the hotel.

Sunday March 23, game day! Our hockey game that day did not start until 5pm, so Shannon and I had time to do more exploring of Vancouver.

The weather was nice to us on that Sunday. Shannon and I walked from our hotel back down to the cauldron. Around the corner from the cauldron was a bike rental shop. Shannon wanted to rent a tandem bike, but I refused. Instead, we each got our own bike.

We followed the bike trails along the perimeter of Stanley Park. The bike ride around Stanley Park was nice and scenic. There were a lot of walkers, runner, and bikers. We spent about two and a half hours biking around Stanley Park.

After we returned the bikes, we were hungry again.

Shannon wanted to try to find another place to eat in Gastown.

We came across the Black Frog. Shannon like their healthy menu options, so we had lunch there.

Shannon had a veggie sandwich and a beer. I had a grilled cheese on multigrain, poutine, and a Kokanee. The poutine there was good.

I asked our bartender why there was so much Edmonton Oilers paraphernalia in a restaurant that was in the heart of downtown Vancouver. The bartender told us that the owners were originally from Edmonton. When they moved to Vancouver, there was no place for them to watch Oilers games on a regular basis. When they opened the restaurant, they made it an Oilers bar, and it had done quite well for them.

When we were finished with lunch, we went back to the hotel.

Shannon and I relaxed for an hour or so at the hotel before getting ready for our game.

It was 4:15pm when Shannon and I put our Sabres jerseys on and walked out the door for the game at Rogers Arena.

Tonight's matchup would be a battle of the only two 1970 expansion franchise teams, the Buffalo Sabres vs. the Vancouver Canucks!

After we passed through the turn styles at Rogers Arena, someone asked Shannon and me if we wanted a free sample of beer! I wasn't about to turn down free beer, even if it was Budweiser Black Crown. Shannon and I both got a tiny three ounce sample of the beer. I asked if I could get seconds, but I was denied.

Yet again, Shannon and I had difficulty finding our Standing Room Only seats in Section 417. We asked an usher how to get to our seats and we were informed that we needed to take an elevator or staircase up to our seats.

Prior to the start of the game, the Vancouver Canucks had an honor ceremony for their Captain Henrik Sedin. Sedin recently played his 1000th NHL game in a Canucks uniform. The ceremony consisted of Sedin's wife and kids coming out onto the ice with him. The Vancouver Canucks organization honored Sedin with an oil painting of him and a vacation trip to some horse race thing. Apparently Sedin enjoyed horse racing.

Before the game started, we weren't sure which Sabres team was going to show up...the team that didn't show up to Calgary or the team that played a good, hard 60 minute battle against Edmonton.

Just 71 seconds into the 1st Period, Sabre forward Tyler Ennis scored, beating Vancouver's goalie Eddie Lack.

A little over two minutes later, Buffalo had the puck and was working with a delayed penalty. Buffalo was able to work the puck into Vancouver's zone and Buffalo's Jamie McBain was able to beat the Canucks goalie Lack to give Buffalo a 2-0 lead.

Things never went well for Buffalo when they scored quick and early, let alone two quick goals. Shannon and I both thought that the Sabres caught the Canucks off guard. We figured with enough time, the Canucks would be right back in the game.

Right around the halfway point of the 1st Period, Vancouver's Brad Richardson beat Buffalo's goalie Nathan Lieuwen, to cut Buffalo's lead in half.

Under two minutes later, Vancouver's Shawn Matthias tied the game, 2-2.

Former Sabre Zack Kassian assisted on both goals.

Like the "broken record" for the season, Buffalo struggled again with shots on goal, just 6 to Vancouver's 15 at the end of one period of play.

Buffalo continued to struggle during the 2nd Period. Vancouver constantly sent two guys deep in the Buffalo zone to press. As soon as Vancouver pressed, Buffalo would turn the puck over, deep in their own zone.

The press obviously worked towards Vancouver's advantage since Buffalo only got 4 shots on net during the 2nd Period.

Yet again, with time winding down in the 2nd Period, Buffalo got sloppy and went to bed. With 100 seconds left in the 2nd, Vancouver's Yannick Weber gave the Canucks a 3-2 lead. Yannick's goal was assisted by former Sabre Kassian.

During the 2nd Intermission, Shannon and I grabbed an overpriced Alexander Keith's to share.

Buffalo showed signs of life in brief stints during the 3rd Period, but it was too bad they couldn't put the puck in the net.

You know who could put the puck in the net?

Vancouver's David Booth at 2:23 into the 3rd Period.

Do you know who assisted on Booth's goal?

I'll give you a hint…Kassian had his fourth assist of the night!

As time dwindled down in the 3rd Period, Sabres interim-coach Ted Nolan called a time out. With the Sabres being down 4-2, Nolan pulled Lieuwen for the extra attacker, though it was too little too late.

Vancouver blocked any scoring attempt from Buffalo.

In the dying seconds of the game, one of Buffalo's defensemen (I won't name names) didn't even bother to make an attempt for one last rush. He just stood with the puck, deep in his own zone by the net and waited for the last 10-15 seconds to expire.

Ted Nolan was a coach who constantly expressed to never give up and to always try, yet there was a defeated lazy player who stood with the puck by his own net. Man, I wish I could get paid millions of dollars to be lazy and play like crap.

I made peanuts compared to what the Sabre players made. It aggravated me so much to see these guys not give a crap and play a halfhearted, boring ass game. I didn't make a lot of money at work, but I spent it traveling to watch a team that represented my community and myself. My community was not a group of lazy people who gave up at the end. My community worked and fought hard until the end. Apparently some over privileged millionaire hockey bums didn't know that, didn't see that, or just didn't care.

Buffalo lost 4-2, and that's all I've gots to say about that.

After the game, we went right back to the hotel. I didn't feel like buying any more overpriced beer. Plus we still had beer back at the room.

Once back at the hotel room, we got our bags packed and ready for our flight in the morning.

It was around 9pm when Shannon got a text from Air Canada telling us that our flight was going to be one hour delayed tomorrow.

On Monday morning, our alarm woke us up at 6:30am.

Shannon and I gathered our gear and we headed down to the lobby so we could check out.

We walked up Georgia Street to the subway bound for the airport.

Eventually we boarded a Boeing 777. I had never been on a plane that big before. There were two 1st Class sections. In coach, there were three rows of seating, each with three seats. There were TVs built into the head rests, so I was content. I watched a few episodes of Just For Laughs.

When we landed in Toronto, we had to hustle. We had to run from our terminal to Terminal F. At Terminal F, we had to go through customs. Shannon and I only had about 40 minutes to scan our passports, be accepted into the USA, go through security, and make it to our terminal. Naturally, our gate was Gate F93, one of the furthest gate in Terminal F.

Thankfully Shannon and I made our flight.

We walked out onto the tarmac to get to our plane. Our plane was a tiny little twin prop puddle jumper. There were no overhead bins, so we had to check our backpacks with the co-pilot.

Shannon and I climbed up the stairs into the plane. We were sitting in row 9, the last row of the airplane! There was one row of seats, isle, and another row of singular seats.

There were about 10 of us passengers on this puddle jumper.

As the pilot prepared the plane for takeoff, our co-pilot acted as the flight attendant. He told us how to buckle our seat belts. He told us about cabin pressure loss and masks falling down. He told the people on the wing seats how to open the emergency doors. He concluded his speech with, "If there's anything else you guys need, just tap the pilot or myself on the shoulder, but not while we are taking off..." With that, our flight attendant/co-pilot hopped into the cockpit, and we taxied down the runway.

I felt like we were in a plane from Indiana Jones, so as the plane hopped off the runway and into the sky, I started humming the Indian Jones theme song, *dun dun dah! Dun dun done! Dun dun dah! Dun dun done! Dun dah dah, dun dah dah! Dun dun done!*

Once in the air, I could see downtown Toronto.

We flew over Lake Ontario and swooped down into New York State and quickly landed in Rochester. The entire flight took about half an hour.

Shannon's dad, Jimbo, was waiting for us at the airport.

I would say that the Canadian trip was a success. We got to see the Sabres win one of the three games. And the two games the Sabres lost, they did not get shut out. Also, we did not get arrested, detained, or deported!

And like that, our mission was over. Shannon and I had seen the Buffalo Sabres play in every current NHL arena!

April 2014

The Sabres finished off the season with 52 points, dead last, worst team in the -League. However, they were far from being the absolute worst team in NHL history.

Now the only thing one could do was to hope and be optimistic about the future.

Headed into the draft lottery, the Sabres mathematically had the best shot at getting the 1st overall pick. Well, as fate or karma would have it, the worst place Sabres couldn't even win the 1st overall draft pick.

The Florida Panthers won the 1st overall draft pick. Buffalo wound up with the 2nd pick.

Hopefully Buffalo's scouts and management could pick someone with talent, as opposed to a meat head flop. Hopefully the Sabres new management and regime could make something happen and turn this team around.

Tampa Bay Lightning were dead last and turned things around and a few years later won the Cup in 1998-99.

Carolina Hurricanes were dead last and turned things around and a few years later won the Cup in 2002-03.

Pittsburgh Penguins were dead last and turned things around and a few years later won the Cup in 2003-04.

Los Angeles Kings were tied for dead last and turned things around and a few years later won the Cup in 2007-08.

Epilogue

Former Sabre Head Coach Punch Imlach had an epilogue at the end of his book, *Hockey is a Battle*, and so I figured that I would have one too.

During our journey, Shannon and I watched the Buffalo Sabres win 10 games (I'm counting the Sabre playoff win against Boston in the "win" column, not the home loss on New Year's Eve to Ottawa, just in case you are counting), and lose 20 games.

During our journey, we watched the Rochester Americans win 5 games and lose 3 on the road.

The journeys were fun and adventurous and at times, a lot of work.

Shannon and I absolutely went to places that we had never been and probably saw things that we will never see again. I got to watch the Sabres with my best friend. *We were always insisting that world be turning our way...On the Road Again!*

Well...Maybe next year!

www.ingramcontent.com/pod-product-compliance
Lightning Source LLC
Chambersburg PA
CBHW070326090426
42733CB00012B/2383